LT. Cdr. Allan Koss

MW01043438

NAVAIR 01-60FGB-1

North American T-28 Trojan Pilot's Flight Operating Instructions

by United States Navy

This manual is sold for historic research purposes only, as an entertainment.
It is not intended to be used as part of an actual flight training program. No
book can substitute for flight training by an authorized instructor. The licensing
of pilots is overseen by organizations and authorities such as the FAA and CAA.
Operating an aircraft without the proper license is a federal crime.

I	THE AIRCRAFT
II	INDOCTRINATION AND TRAINING
III	NORMAL OPERATING PROCEDURES
IV	FLIGHT PROCEDURES AND CHARACTERISTICS
V	EMERGENCY PROCEDURES
VI	ALL-WEATHER OPERATION
VII	COMMUNICATIONS EQUIPMENT AND PROCEDURES
VIII	WEAPONS SYSTEMS
IX	FLIGHT CREW COORDINATION
X	NATOPS EVALUATION
XI	PERFORMANCL DATA
	ALPHABETICAL INDEX

NAVAIR 01-60FGB-1

NATOPS FLIGHT MANUAL

NAVY MODEL

T-28B/C

AIRCRAFT

This document is subject to special export controls and each transmittal to foreign governments, foreign nationals or agents thereof may be made only with the prior approval of NAVAIRSYSCOMHQ, Washington, D.C.

BASIC AND ALL CHANGES HAVE BEEN COLLATED
TO MAKE THIS A COMPLETE PUBLICATION.

I	THE AIRCRAFT
II	INDOCTRINATION AND TRAINING
III	NORMAL OPERATING PROCEDURES
IV	FLIGHT PROCEDURES AND CHARACTERISTICS
V	EMERGENCY PROCEDURES
VI	ALL-WEATHER OPERATION
VII	COMMUNICATIONS EQUIPMENT AND PROCEDURES
VIII	WEAPONS SYSTEMS
IX	FLIGHT CREW COORDINATION
X	NATOPS EVALUATION
XI	PERFORMANCE DATA
	ALPHABETICAL INDEX

ISSUED BY AUTHORITY OF THE CHIEF OF NAVAL OPERATIONS
AND UNDER THE DIRECTION OF THE COMMANDER,
NAVAL AIR SYSTEMS COMMAND

15 MAY 1966
Changed 15 June 1970

── LIST OF EFFECTIVE PAGES ──

TOTAL NUMBER OF PAGES IN THIS PUBLICATION IS 306 CONSISTING OF THE FOLLOWING:

Page No.	Issue
*Title	15 June 1970
*A	15 June 1970
*Flyleaf 1	15 June 1970
*Flyleaf 2 Blank	15 June 1970
*Letter of Promulgation	15 June 1970
*Reverse Blank	15 June 1970
i	Original
*ii thru iv	15 June 1970
v	15 June 1970
vi	15 June 1970
1-1 thru 1-2	Original
1-3	15 September 1967
1-4 thru 1-6	Original
1-6A	15 September 1967
1-6B Blank	15 September 1967
1-7 thru 1-8	Original
1-9	15 September 1967
1-10 thru 1-13	Original
1-14 thru 1-15	15 September 1967
1-16	Original
*1-17	15 June 1970
1-18 thru 1-19	15 September 1967
1-20	Original
*1-21	15 June 1970
1-22 thru 1-23	Original
*1-24	15 June 1970
1-25	15 September 1967
*1-26 thru 1-27	15 June 1970
1-28 thru 1-31	Original
1-32	15 September 1967
1-33 thru 1-34	Original
1-35	15 September 1967
*1-36	1 June 1967
1-37	Original
1-38	15 September 1967
1-38A	1 June 1967
1-38B	1 June 1967
1-39	Original
*1-40	15 June 1970
1-41 thru 1-42	Original
*1-43	15 June 1970
1-44	1 October 1968
1-45 thru 1-46	Original
1-47	15 September 1967
1-48 Blank	15 September 1967
1-49 thru 1-52	Original
*1-53 thru 1-54	15 June 1970
1-55 thru 1-59	Original
1-60 Blank	Original
*2-1	15 June 1970
2-2	Original
3-1	Original
3-2 Blank	Original
3-3	Original
3-4 Blank	Original
3-5	Original
*3-6	15 June 1970
3-7 thru 3-10	Original
*3-11	15 June 1970
3-12	1 October 1968
3-13	Original
3-14	1 October 1968
3-15	Original
*3-16	15 June 1970
3-17 thru 3-18	Original
3-19	Original
*3-20 thru 3-22	15 June 1970
3-23	15 June 1970
3-24 (Blank)	15 June 1970
4-1	Original
*4-2 thru 4-4A	15 June 1970
*4-4B Blank	15 June 1970
4-5 thru 4-10	Original
5-1 thru 5-2	Original
*5-3 thru 5-5	15 June 1970
5-6 thru 5-8	Original
*5-9 thru 5-12	15 June 1970
6-1 thru 6-4	Original
7-1	Original
7-2 Blank	Original
8-1 thru 8-11	Original
8-12 Blank	Original
9-1	Original
9-2 Blank	Original
10-1 thru 10-7	Original
10-8 Blank	Original
10-9 thru 10-13	Original
10-14 Blank	Original
10-15 thru 10-22	Original
11-1 thru 11-19	Original
11-20 Blank	Original
11-21 thru 11-71	Original
11-72 Blank	Original
11-73 thru 11-123	Original
11-124 Blank	Original
*Index 1	15 June 1970
Index 2	15 September 1967
*Index 3 thru Index 4	15 June 1970
Index 5	15 September 1967
Index 6 thru Index 7	15 June 1970
Index 8	Original
*Index 9 thru Index 13	15 June 1970
Index 14	15 September 1967
*Index 15 thru Index 16	15 June 1970

*The asterisk indicates pages changed, added, or deleted by the current change.

TABLE OF CONTENTS

FOREWORD

SCOPE

The NATOPS Flight Manual is issued by the authority of the Chief of Naval Operations and under the direction of Commander, Naval Air Systems Command in conjunction with the Naval Air Training and Operating Procedures Standardization (NATOPS) Program. This manual contains information on all aircraft systems, performance data, and operating procedures required for safe and effective operations. However, it is not a substitute for sound judgement. Compound emergencies, available facilities, adverse weather or terrain, or considerations affecting the lives and property of others may require modification of the procedures contained herein. Read this manual from cover to cover. It's your responsibility to have a complete knowledge of its contents.

APPLICABLE PUBLICATIONS

The following applicable publication complements this manual:

NAVAIR 01-60FGB-1B (checklist)

HOW TO GET COPIES

AUTOMATIC DISTRIBUTION

To receive future changes and revisions to this manual automatically, a unit must be established on the automatic distribution list maintained by the Naval Air Technical Services Facility (NATSF). To become established on the list or to change distribution requirements, a unit must submit NAVWEPS Form 5605/2 to NATSF, 700 Robbins Ave., Philadelphia, Pa. 19111, listing this manual and all other NAVAIR publications required. For additional instructions refer to BUWEPSINST 5605.4 series and NAVSUP Publication 2002.

ADDITIONAL COPIES

Additional copies of this manual and changes thereto may be procured by submitting Form DD 1348 to NPFC Philadelphia in accordance with NAVSUP Publication 2002, Section VIII. Part C.

UPDATING THE MANUAL

To ensure that the manual contains the latest procedures and information, NATOPS review conferences are held in accordance with OPNAVINST 3510.11 series.

CHANGE RECOMMENDATIONS

Recommended changes to this manual or other NATOPS publications may be submitted by anyone in accordance with OPNAVINST 3510.9 series.

Routine change recommendations are submitted directly to the Model Manager on OPNAV Form 3500-22 shown on the next page. The address of the Model Manager of this aircraft is:

Chief of Naval Air Basic Training
Attn: T-28 NATOPS Evaluator
NAS Pensacola, Florida — 32508

Change recommendations of an URGENT nature (safety of flight, etc.,) should be submitted directly to the NATOPS Advisory Group Member in the chain of command by priority message.

YOUR RESPONSIBILITY

NATOPS Flight Manuals are kept current through an active manual change program. Any corrections, additions, or constructive suggestions for improvement of its content should be submitted by routine or urgent change recommendation, as appropriate, at once.

NATOPS FLIGHT MANUAL INTERIM CHANGES

Flight Manual Interim Changes are changes or corrections to the NATOPS Flight Manuals promulgated by CNO or NAVAIRSYSCOM. Interim Changes are issued either as printed pages, or as a naval message. The Interim Change Summary page is provided as a record of all interim changes. Upon receipt of a change or revision, the custodian of the manual should check the updated Interim Change Summary to ascertain that all outstanding interim changes have been either incorporated or canceled; those not incorporated shall be recorded as outstanding in the section provided.

NATOPS/TACTICAL CHANGE RECOMMENDATION
OPNAV FORM 3500/22 (5-69) 0107-722-2002   DATE

TO BE FILLED IN BY ORIGINATOR AND FORWARDED TO MODEL MANAGER

FROM (originator)	Unit
TO (Model Manager)	Unit

Complete Name of Manual/Checklist	Revision Date	Change Date	Section/Chapter	Page	Paragraph

Recommendation (be specific)

☐ CHECK IF CONTINUED ON BACK

Justification

Signature	Rank	Title

Address of Unit or Command

TO BE FILLED IN BY MODEL MANAGER *(Return to Originator)*

FROM	DATE

TO

REFERENCE
(a) Your Change Recommendation Dated _____

☐ Your change recommendation dated _____ is acknowledged. It will be held for action of the review conference planned for _____ to be held at _____ .

☐ Your change recommendation is reclassified URGENT and forwarded for approval to _____
_____ by my DTG _____ .

/S/ _____ MODEL MANAGER. _____ AIRCRAFT

CHANGE SYMBOLS

Revised text is indicated by a black vertical line in either margin of the page, adjacent to the affected text, like the one printed next to this paragraph. The change symbol identifies the addition of either new information, a changed procedure, the correction of an error, or a rephrasing of the previous material.

WARNINGS, CAUTIONS, AND NOTES

The following definitions apply to "WARNINGS", "CAUTIONS", and "NOTES" found through the manual.

WARNING

An operating procedure, practice, or condition, etc., which may result in injury or death, if not carefully observed or followed.

An operating procedure, practice, or condition, etc., which, if not strictly observed, may damage equipment.

Note

An operating procedure, practice, or condition, etc., which is essential to emphasize.

WORDING

The concept of word usage and intended meaning which has been adhered to in preparing this Manual is as follows:

"Shall" has been used only when application of a procedure is mandatory.

"Should" has been used only when application of a procedure is recommended.

"May" and "need not" have been used only when application of a procedure is optional.

"Will" has been used only to indicate futurity, never to indicate any degree of requirement for application of a procedure.

(This page intentionally left blank)

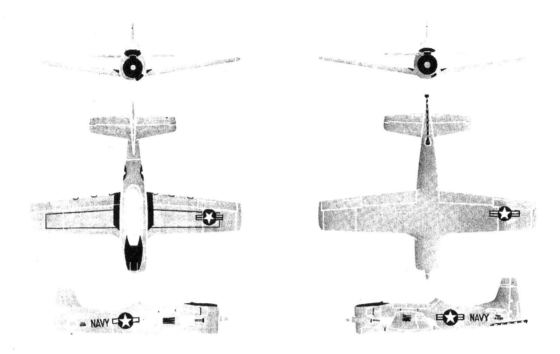

T-28B   **T-28C**

MODEL T-28 AIRCRAFT

T-28-1-00-4A

Figure 1-1

ALPHABETICAL INDEX

A

PAGE NUMBERS IN **BOLD** DENOTE ILLUSTRATIONS

PAGE NUMBERS IN **BOLD** DENOTE ILLUSTRATIONS

PAGE NUMBERS IN BOLD DENOTE ILLUSTRATIONS

PAGE NUMBERS IN **BOLD** DENOTE ILLUSTRATIONS

PAGE NUMBERS IN **BOLD** DENOTE ILLUSTRATIONS

PAGE NUMBERS IN BOLD DENOTE ILLUSTRATIONS

PAGE NUMBERS IN **BOLD** DENOTE ILLUSTRATIONS

PAGE NUMBERS IN BOLD DENOTE ILLUSTRATIONS

PAGE NUMBERS IN BOLD DENOTE ILLUSTRATIONS

PAGE NUMBERS IN BOLD DENOTE ILLUSTRATIONS

PAGE NUMBERS IN BOLD DENOTE ILLUSTRATIONS

☆U.S. GOVERNMENT PRINTING OFFICE: 1970-434-201/15504

PAGE NUMBERS IN BOLD DENOTE ILLUSTRATIONS

The Aircraft

section I

TABLE OF CONTENTS

PART 1 — GENERAL DESCRIPTION

THE AIRCRAFT

The T-28B and T-28C are straight-wing, high-performance, two-place trainers equipped with dual controls. The T-28C is a carrier version of the T-28B and maintains the same outward appearance except for the arresting hook. A speed brake is located on the bottom of the fuselage and, with a few exceptions, both cockpits contain identical controls and instruments. The cockpits were designed and arranged to be as much like fighter cockpits as practical. For armament training, machine guns, bombs, or rockets may be carried externally under each wing panel. When any configuration of armament is carried, a MK 6 Mod 0 fire control system and armament control panel with a MK 8 Mod 5 gunsight are installed in the front cockpit.

DIMENSIONS

Approximate overall dimensions are:

    Length ....33 feet
    Wing Span ....41 feet
    Height (to top of fin) ....13 feet

GENERAL ARRANGEMENT

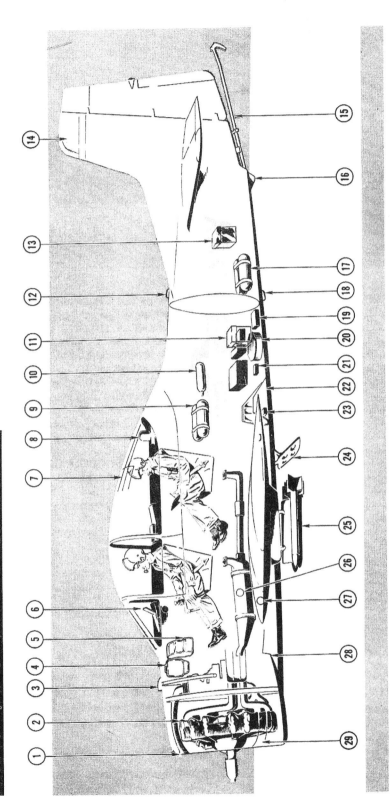

1. CARBURETOR AIR INTAKE
2. R-1820-86 OR -86A ENGINE
3. MAGNETO AIR INTAKE
4. ENGINE OIL TANK
5. HYDRAULIC RESERVOIR
6. MK-8 GUNSIGHT
7. AN/ARN-6 RADIO COMPASS SENSE ANTENNA
8. AN/ARN-6 RADIO COMPASS LOOP ANTENNA
9. OXYGEN CYLINDERS (T-28C)
10. CANOPY EMERGENCY AIR BOTTLE

11. BATTERY (T-28C)
12. UPPER ANTI-COLLISION LIGHT
13. BATTERY (T-28B)
14. UHF COMM/TACAN ANTENNA
15. ARRESTING HOOK (T-28C)
16. TAIL BUMPER
17. OXYGEN CYLINDERS (T-28B)
18. LOWER ANTI-COLLISION LIGHT
19. MARKER BEACON ANTENNA
20. AN/ARA-25 ADF ANTENNA

21. EXTERNAL POWER RECEPTACLE
22. BAGGAGE COMPARTMENT DOOR
23. DATA CASE (BAGGAGE COMPARTMENT)
24. SPEED BRAKE
25. ARMAMENT PACKAGE
    (2.25-INCH ROCKETS SHOWN)
26. COCKPIT HEATER COMBUSTION AIR OUTLET
27. COCKPIT HEATER COMBUSTION AIR INLET
28. OIL COOLER OUTLET
29. OIL COOLER INTAKE

T-28C-1-00-5C

Figure 1-2

DIFFERENCES

The only salient difference between B and C series aircraft is the T-28C arresting hook, including a cutout portion in the bottom of the rudder to provide clearance for the hook in the retracted position. The diameter of the T-28C propeller is 9 inches smaller and the blades are slightly wider than those of the T-28B. The smaller diameter propeller is used to provide greater deck clearance for arrested landings. Some T-28C aircraft have been modified to increase armament capabilities, having six external armament stations instead of the basic two stations.

NAVAIR NUMBER SUMMARY

T-28B AIRCRAFT

NAVAIR NUMBERS	MANUFACTURE SEQUENCE
137638 — 137810	1 — 173
138103 — 138367	174 — 438
140002 — 140052	439 — 489

T-28C AIRCRAFT

NAVAIR NUMBERS	MANUFACTURE SEQUENCE
140053 — 140077	1 — 25
140449 — 140666	26 — 243
146238 — 146293	244 — 299

AIRCRAFT CHANGES

The following table presents those outstanding aircraft changes considered essential for aircrew indoctrination. A complete list of aircraft changes can be found in NavSandA Publication 2002, Section VIII, Parts C and D. Changes listed include the following:

ASC	Aircraft Service Change (obsolete)
AFC	Airframe Change
AAC	Aircraft Armament Change
AVC	Avionics Change

AIRCRAFT CHANGE	SUBJECT AND PURPOSE	CATEGORY
ASC 20	Installation of AN/ARN-21 equipment, three-phase program	Routine
Phase I	Installation of provisions for AN/ARN-21, including installation of 300-ampere generator	Routine
Phase II	Removing AN/ARN-6 and AN/ARN-14E equipment and installing AN/ARN-21 equipment, keeping provisions for AN/ARN-6 and AN/ARN-14E systems intact	Routine
Phase III	Removing provisions for AN/ARN-6 and AN/ARN-14E retained in Phase II	Routine
ASC 36	Electrical — Modification of a-c and d-c control systems	Routine
ASC 63	Electrical — Modification of landing gear warning system to provide a visual wheels warning light and a propeller control switch in the warning circuit	Routine
AFC 97	Avionics — Installation of UHF COMM control panel having manual tuning capability	Routine
AFC 103	Engine controls — Installation of mixture control lever idle cutoff warning device	Urgent
AFC 105	Electrical — Installation of fuel boost pump test switch	Routine

LEFT CONSOLE (TYPICAL)

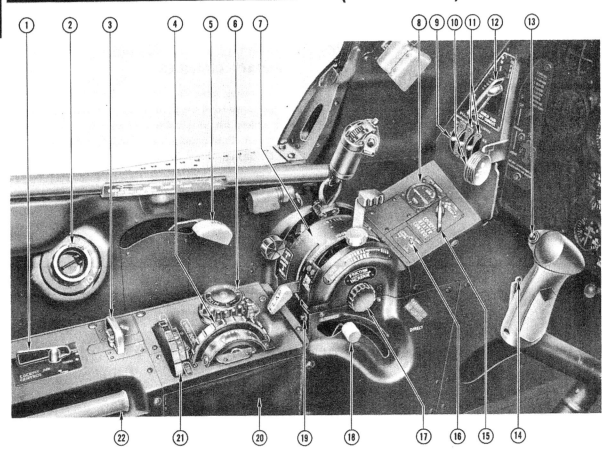

1. COCKPIT AIR CONTROL HANDLE
2. AIR OUTLET
3. FUEL SHUTOFF HANDLE
4. ELEVATOR TRIM WHEEL
5. CANOPY CONTROL HANDLE
6. RUDDER TRIM WHEEL
7. THROTTLE QUADRANT
8. HYDRAULIC SYSTEM PRESSURE GAGE
9. STALL WARNING TEST SWITCH (T-28C)
10. LANDING GEAR HANDLE
11. LANDING LIGHT SWITCHES

12. WINDSHIELD AND CANOPY DEFROST ◀ CONTROL HANDLE
13. BOMB RELEASE BUTTON ◀
14. ROCKET FIRING BUTTON ◀
15. COCKPIT HEATER CONTROL HANDLE ◀
16. COWL AND OIL COOLER FLAP SWITCH
17. FRICTION LOCK KNOB ◀
18. CARBURETOR AIR CONTROL
19. HORN SILENCER BUTTON (SOME AIRCRAFT)
20. FLIGHT REPORT HOLDER
21. AILERON TRIM WHEEL
22. HYDRAULIC HAND-PUMP ◀

◀ FRONT COCKPIT ONLY

T-28B-1-00-31C

Figure 1-3

COCKPIT - FORWARD VIEW

(TYPICAL)

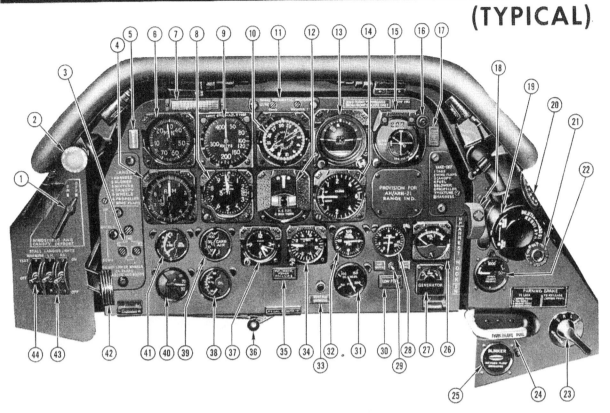

1. WINDSHIELD AND CANOPY DEFROST CONTROL HANDLE ◀
2. CANOPY EMERGENCY STOP BUTTON
3. LANDING GEAR POSITION INDICATORS
4. TACHOMETER
5. LANDING GEAR WARNING LIGHT (ASC 63)
6. MANIFOLD PRESSURE INDICATOR
7. AIRSPEED CORRECTION CARD
8. ALTIMETER
9. AIRSPEED INDICATOR
10. RADIO MAGNETIC INDICATOR
11. COMPASS ANNUNCIATOR
12. TURN-AND-BANK INDICATOR
13. GYRO HORIZON INDICATOR
14. VERTICAL SPEED INDICATOR
15. COURSE INDICATOR
16. MARKER BEACON LIGHT
17. COURSE SETTING CHANGE LIGHT
18. ARRESTING HOOK HANDLE (T-28C)
19. OXYGEN REGULATOR
20. FREE AIR TEMPERATURE INDICATOR ◀
21. OXYGEN REGULATOR EMERGENCY VALVE
22. OXYGEN PRESSURE INDICATOR
23. IGNITION SWITCH
24. PARKING BRAKE HANDLE ◀
25. OXYGEN FLOW INDICATOR
26. GENERATOR VOLTMETER
27. GENERATOR LOAD INDICATOR
28. FUEL QUANTITY INDICATOR
29. FUEL QUANTITY INDICATOR TEST SWITCH
30. FUEL LOW-LEVEL WARNING LIGHT
31. OIL PRESSURE INDICATOR
32. FUEL PRESSURE INDICATOR
33. SUMP PLUG WARNING LIGHT
34. ACCELEROMETER
35. FLIGHT INSTRUMENT POWER FAILURE WARNING LIGHT
36. RUDDER PEDAL RELEASE LEVER
37. CLOCK
38. OIL TEMPERATURE INDICATOR
39. CARBURETOR AIR TEMPERATURE INDICATOR
40. WING FLAP POSITION INDICATOR
41. CYLINDER HEAD TEMPERATURE INDICATOR
42. LANDING GEAR HANDLE
43. LANDING LIGHT SWITCHES
44. STALL WARNING TEST SWITCH (T-28C)

◀ FRONT COCKPIT ONLY

T-28B-1-00-20E

Figure 1-4

RIGHT CONSOLE (TYPICAL)

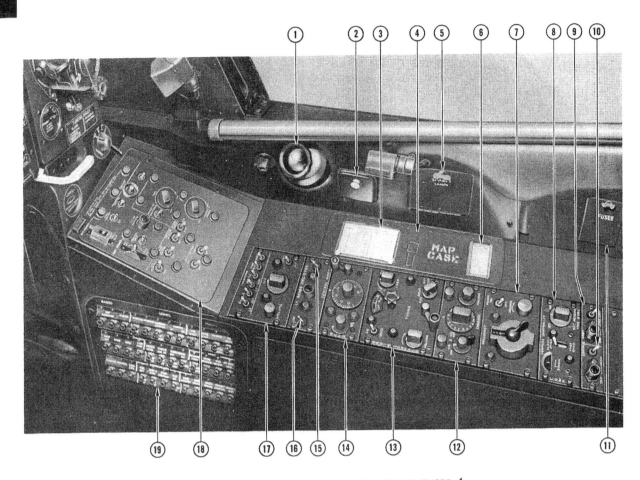

1. AIR OUTLET
2. ASH TRAY
3. CHANNELIZATION LOG
4. MAP CASE ◀
5. SPARE LAMPS ◀
6. COMPASS CORRECTION CARD
7. OMNIDIRECTIONAL RECEIVER
8. GYROCOMPASS CONTROL PANEL
9. NAV AND COMPASS CONTROL TRANSFER PANEL
10. COMMAND RADIO CONTROL SHIFT TRANSFER SWITCH

11. SPARE FUSES ◀
12. UHF RADIO CONTROL PANEL
13. RADIO COMPASS CONTROL PANEL
14. RANGE RECEIVER CONTROL PANEL
15. RANGE RECEIVER CONTROL SHIFT SWITCH
16. RANGE RECEIVER POWER SWITCH
17. INTERCOM CONTROL PANEL
18. ELECTRICAL SWITCH PANEL
19. CIRCUIT BREAKER PANEL ◀

◀ FRONT COCKPIT ONLY

T-28B-1-00-22E

Figure 1-5

RIGHT CONSOLE   FRONT COCKPIT

AFC 97 COMPLIED WITH

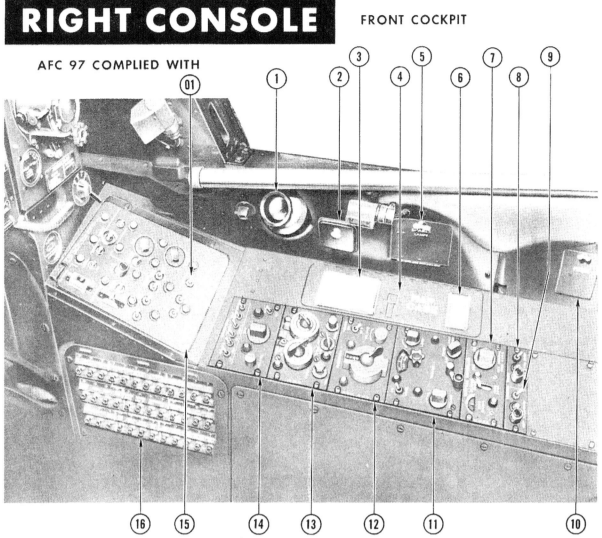

01. FUEL BOOST PUMP TEST SWITCH *◀

1. AIR OUTLET

2. ASH TRAY

3. CHANNELIZATION LOG

4. MAP CASE ◀

5. SPARE LAMPS ◀

6. COMPASS CORRECTION CARD

7. GYROCOMPASS CONTROL PANEL

8. NAV AND COMPASS CONTROL
TRANSFER PANEL

9. UHF COMMAND RADIO CONTROL
SHIFT SWITCH

10. SPARE FUSES ◀

11. RADIO COMPASS CONTROL PANEL

12. OMNIDIRECTIONAL RECEIVER
OR TACAN CONTROL PANEL

13. UHF RADIO CONTROL PANEL

14. INTERCOM CONTROL PANEL

15. ELECTRICAL SWITCH PANEL

16. CIRCUIT BREAKER PANEL ◀

◀ FRONT COCKPIT ONLY
* AIRCRAFT HAVING AFC 105 COMPLIED WITH

T-28B-1-00-44A

Figure 1-5A

PART 2 — SYSTEMS

ENGINE

Power is provided by a nine-cylinder, radial, air-cooled Wright Cyclone engine, Model R1820-86 or -86A. At take-off and military power, the engine develops 1425 horsepower. Engine exhaust outlets on each side of the cowl are designed to utilize the additional thrust available from the jet effect of the exhaust. The engine is equipped with a single-stage, two-speed, engine-driven supercharger, a direct-cranking starter, and an injection-type carburetor incorporating an electric primer valve.

ENGINE CONTROLS

Engine throttle, mixture, supercharger, and carburetor air controls are located on the left side of each cockpit and are interconnected between cockpits to move simultaneously. The individual shape of each control knob permits the pilot to identify it by feel. A friction lock knob on the inboard side of the quadrant in the front cockpit can be rotated to adjust friction on the quadrant controls. Cylinder head temperature and oil temperature are controlled simultaneously by electrically actuated cowl and oil cooler flaps.

THROTTLES

Each throttle (figure 1-6) is provided with a take-off stop in the quadrant so the pilot can feel when the throttle has been advanced to take-off power (at sea level). Pushing the throttle through the stop at sea level will cause the maximum allowable manifold pressure to be exceeded. At altitudes above sea level, the throttle may be pushed beyond the stop as long as the manifold pressure is kept below the maximum limit. Forward movement of the throttle actuates a mechanically linked carburetor accelerating pump. The throttle grip contains the SPEED BRAKE switch, a CALL (ICS) button, and the MIKE (microphone) button. The grip in the front cockpit can be rotated to provide manual ranging of the MK 8 sight when installed.

Note

The surface control lock in the front cockpit locks the throttle in the CLOSED position.

MIXTURE CONTROL LEVERS

The mixture control levers (figure 1-6), one in each cockpit, have three positions: RICH, NORMAL, and IDLE CUTOFF. The RICH position is used for all ground operation, take-off, climb, descent, and landing; the NORMAL position is used for all other normal flight conditions. The IDLE CUTOFF position shuts off fuel flow at the carburetor to stop the engine. On some aircraft,* a

spring detent is installed to provide a positive warning and "feel" when the lever is retarded to IDLE CUTOFF.

Note

Fuel is injected into the impeller section of the engine if the boost pump is operating and the mixture control is not in the IDLE CUTOFF position.

SUPERCHARGER HANDLES

Operating speed ratio of the two-speed supercharger is selected by the position of the supercharger control handle (figure 1-6), located on the throttle quadrant in each cockpit. When the handle is at the LOW (up) position, the supercharger is set at low blower; when the handle is at the HIGH (down) position, the supercharger is set at high blower.

CARBURETOR AIR CONTROL HANDLES

A carburetor air control (figure 1-6) is located below the throttle quadrant in each cockpit. With the handle at the ALTERNATE position, the ram-air duct is closed and heated air from the area aft of the engine is drawn into the carburetor. As the handle is moved toward the DIRECT position, heated air is mixed with cold ram air to obtain the desired carburetor air temperature. When

THROTTLE QUADRANT

Figure 1-6

*Aircraft having AFC 103 incorporated

the handle is in DIRECT, all carburetor air is admitted through the ram-air scoop in the top leading edge of the cowling.

IGNITION SWITCHES

A standard magneto ignition switch (23, figure 1-4) is located on the right instrument subpanel in each cockpit. Switch positions are BOTH, L, R, and OFF. The L and R positions are provided to individually check engine operation on the left or right ignition system.

STARTER BUTTONS

The direct-cranking electric starter is controlled by a guarded push button (figure 1-7) on the right console in each cockpit. Holding the STARTER button down operates the starter. The starter can be powered by the battery when external power is not available; however, this procedure causes a heavy current drain from the battery and should be used only when external power is not available. The starter can be operated only by the pilot who last actuated his electrical CONTROL SHIFT switch. The starter is powered by the primary d-c bus.

PRIMER BUTTONS

The engine fuel priming system for starting is controlled by a PRIMER button on the right forward console in each cockpit. See figure 1-7. Depressing this button opens an electric primer valve on the carburetor, permitting pressurized fuel from the carburetor to be injected into the engine blower section. Fuel pressure for priming is provided by the fuel booster pump. The system is very sensitive and care must be used to avoid overpriming. The primer system is powered by the primary d-c bus.

ENGINE INDICATORS

Identical engine indicators are installed on both instrument panels. The oil pressure and manifold pressure indicators read out pressure directly from the engine; the fuel pressure indicator reads out pressure directly from the carburetor. When the engine is not running, manifold pressure reading corresponds to barometric pressure. The tachometer is self-generating and does not require aircraft electrical power input. Oil, cylinder head, and carburetor air temperature indicators, however, depend upon 28-volt d-c power from the primary bus for operation. Two independent cylinder head temperature indicating systems are provided, one for each cockpit. The indicator in the front cockpit indicates the temperature of No. 6 cylinder and the indicator in the rear cockpit indicates the temperature of No. 5 cylinder. The front cockpit cylinder head temperature indicator will normally indicate slightly higher than the rear cockpit indicator.

PROPELLER

The engine drives a three-blade, constant-speed Hamilton Standard hydromatic propeller. A double-capacity

governor, controlled by mechanical linkage from the cockpit, maintains a selected rpm, regardless of varying airspeeds or flight loads. The governor and oil pump are contained within a constant-speed control assembly mounted on the nose section of the engine.

The dome of the three-blade propeller contains a piston-actuated geared cam, which is meshed to the gear teeth on the propeller blades. Engine oil pressure, boosted by the governor pump, moves the piston, which moves the propeller blades to the desired pitch. If the propeller is in an underspeed condition, the governor permits oil to drain from the outboard side of the piston. Then, the centrifugal twisting movement of the propeller blades can move the piston outboard, decreasing the blade angle and increasing the engine rpm.

If an overspeed condition exists, high-pressure oil from the governor is directed to the outboard side of the piston. This oil forces the piston inboard, increasing the blade angle and decreasing the rpm. During an on-speed condition, a difference in pressure is maintained by the governor to offset the centrifugal twisting movement of the blades. This holds the blades at the desired pitch.

The propeller is governed within the range of 1200 to 2700 rpm. Fast throttle bursts should be avoided with the propeller control set above 2500 rpm. Because of the extremely rapid acceleration of the engine, the engine will overspeed before sufficient high-pressure oil can be supplied by the governor to correct the overspeeding condition.

PROPELLER CONTROL LEVERS

Engine rpm is determined by the setting of the PROP control lever (figure 1-6), located on the throttle quadrant in each cockpit. The position of the lever determines the setting of the propeller governor.

OIL SYSTEM

Oil for engine lubrication is supplied from a 12.2 U.S. gallon oil tank. Of the total, 8.8 gallons are usable, with 3.4 gallons foam and expansion space. Lubrication is accomplished by a pressure system with a dry sump and scavenger pump return. Oil flows, by gravity, from the tank to the engine pressure pump, which forces it through the engine. Two scavenge pumps force the oil through either the oil cooler warmup jacket or through the oil cooler (depending on oil temperature), then back to the tank. The engine cowl and oil cooler flaps are manually controlled and driven by an electric motor. The two cowl flaps are located on each side of the engine cowling and the oil cooler flap is located on the lower left side of the cowling. When full-open, the oil cooler flap is open approximately 2½ inches more than the cowl flaps. In the closed position, the oil cooler flap will be approximately 5 degrees open when the cowl flaps are closed. This design balances the temperature differential between the cylinder heads and the oil cooler.

SWITCH PANELS (TYPICAL)

RIGHT CONSOLE

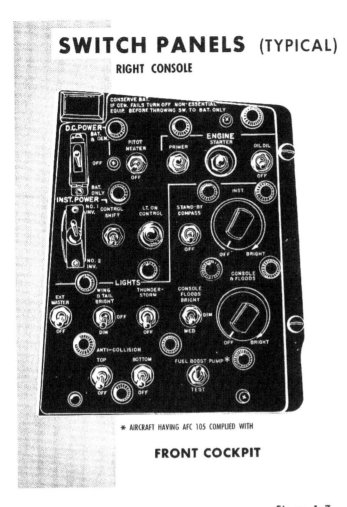

* AIRCRAFT HAVING AFC 105 COMPLIED WITH

FRONT COCKPIT

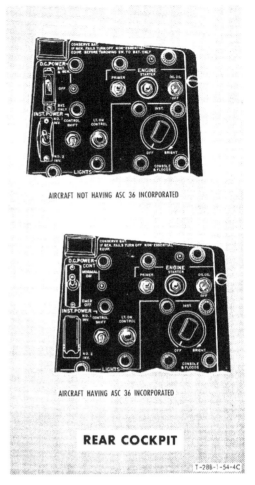

AIRCRAFT NOT HAVING ASC 36 INCORPORATED

AIRCRAFT HAVING ASC 36 INCORPORATED

REAR COCKPIT

T-28B-1-54-4C

Figure 1-7

OIL SYSTEM SUMP PLUG WARNING LIGHTS

A press-to-test light is located at the lower center of the instrument panel of each cockpit. The light will illuminate if foreign particles in the engine oil system become attached to the forward or the aft engine oil sump magnetic plug. Illumination of this light may be an indication of impending engine failure.

OIL SYSTEM CONTROLS

COWL AND OIL COOLER FLAP SWITCHES

Both the cowl flaps and the oil cooler flaps are operated simultaneously by means of a toggle switch (16, figure 1-3) on the left console forward of the throttle quadrant in each cockpit. Placing the switch at OPEN or holding it at the spring-loaded CLOSE position operates the cowl and oil cooler flaps. Intermediate positions are selected by returning the switch to the center (off) position. The cowl and oil cooler flaps can be operated only by

the pilot who has last actuated his electrical CONTROL SHIFT switch. No position indicator is necessary as the cowl flaps are visible from either cockpit. The cowl and oil cooler flaps are powered from the secondary d-c bus.

OIL DILUTION SWITCHES

An oil dilution system is provided for thinning engine oil with gasoline before engine shutdown whenever a cold-weather start is anticipated. The OIL DIL switch (figure 1-7), located on the right console switch panel in each cockpit, is spring-loaded to the OFF position and must be held at OIL DIL to dilute the oil. When the switch is held at OIL DIL, pressurized fuel from the carburetor is allowed to enter the oil line to the engine to lower the viscosity of the oil. For recommended oil dilution procedures, refer to OIL DILUTION, in Section VI. The oil dilution system is powered from the primary d-c bus.

ENGINE OPERATION

DETONATION

Detonation is the result of one type of abnormal combustion of part of the fuel-air mixture. The other prevalent form of abnormal combustion is preignition. When detonation occurs, combustion progresses normally during initial burning; then, at some point, the rate of combustion speeds up tremendously, resulting in an explosion or nearly instantaneous combustion. This explosion actually pounds the cylinder walls, producing "knock." This "knock" or pounding of the cylinder walls can cause an engine failure. In flight, the "knock" is not heard because of other engine and propeller noises. However, detonation can be detected by observation of the exhaust for visible puffs of smoke, glowing carbon particles, or a small, sharp, whitish-orange flame. In addition, a rapid increase in cylinder head temperatures often indicates detonation. When detonation is evident, throttle reduction is the most immediate and sure remedy. *When detonation occurs, power is lost.* Contributing causes of detonation are as follows:

1. Low-octane fuel.

2. High cylinder head temperature caused by too long a climb at too low an airspeed, or by too lean a mixture, or by cowl flaps not adjusted properly.

3. High mixture temperature caused by improper use of carburetor air control handle or by high outside air temperature.

4. Excessive manifold pressure with other conditions favorable to detonation.

5. Improper mixture caused by a faulty carburetor or lean mixture.

PREIGNITION

Preignition is closely related to detonation. In fact, detonation often progresses into preignition. When the engine gets too hot, the mixture is ignited before the spark occurs. When this happens, much of the power is wasted trying to push the piston down while it is still rising in the cylinder. The power impulses are uneven, horsepower falls off, and the engine can be damaged from excessive pressures and temperatures. Preignition is indicated by backfiring through the carburetor and possibly by a rapid increase in cylinder head temperatures. When preignition is encountered, the throttle should be retarded immediately.

USING PRIMER

Proper use of the electric primer during starting will greatly aid in quick engine starts with a minimum of "torching" or backfiring. The starting procedure in Section III states that the primer button should be depressed when starting the engine; also, the engine should be started with the throttle set to obtain approximately 1000 to 1200 rpm. To do this, the throttle position must vary to account for air density changes with

changes in ambient temperature. An easily remembered rule for starting engines is: If the air temperature is low, retard the throttle about 1/4 inch from the normal starting position. If the weather is hot, advance the throttle about 1/4 inch beyond the normal starting position. The engine should be operating smoothly on fuel from the primer before moving the mixture control from IDLE CUTOFF to RICH. Lean fuel-air ratios tend to cause backfire through the induction system and rich mixtures tend to foul spark plugs or cause "torching." Starting the engine on primer fuel and then slowly moving the mixture control toward RICH prevents lean mixtures and eliminates backfiring. When fuel from the carburetor adds to fuel from the primer, a rich mixture results. When engine rpm starts dropping because of this richness, the primer button may be released and the engine should continue to run smoothly.

CHANGING POWER SETTINGS

One of the basic limitations placed on engine operation is imposed by the amount of pressure developed in the cylinders during combustion. If this pressure becomes excessive, it can cause detonation and will result in eventual engine failure. Since improper coordination of the use of the throttle and PROP lever can cause these limitations to be exceeded, it is important to learn the correct sequence in which these controls should be used. *Whenever the engine power is to be reduced, retard the throttle first; then retard the PROP lever. Conversely, when increasing engine power, advance the PROP lever first; then advance the throttle.*

Note

The PROP lever and throttle should be advanced slowly and smoothly when changing power settings to prevent engine backfiring.

MIXTURE CONTROL

The MIXTURE control lever on the throttle quadrant is provided with two positions (NORMAL and RICH) for use during flight. The RICH position should be used only for ground operation, take-off, climb, descent, landing, and when operating at normal rated power and above with alternate air; the NORMAL setting should be used during all other conditions of flight. The injection-type carburetor on the R-1820 is equipped with an automatic mixture control to maintain the mixture setting selected, regardless of changes in altitude or temperature. No intermediate position between RICH and NORMAL, or between NORMAL and IDLE CUTOFF, should be selected to arbitrarily adjust the mixture. All performance data in Section XI (except Take-off Distances) are calculated for performance with the mixture control lever in the NORMAL position. Moving the lever between NORMAL and RICH will increase fuel consumption and decrease planned fuel reserve. Moving the lever between NORMAL and IDLE CUTOFF will lean the mixture and may seriously damage the engine by causing rough engine, backfiring, overheating, detonation, loss in power, or sudden engine failure.

SUPERCHARGER

The supercharger low position is used for ground operation, take-off, and during flight up to an altitude where it is more advantageous to operate with high blower (approximately 13,500 feet at military power or 15,000 feet at normal rated power). At the appropriate altitude, before shifting the supercharger to high, reduce the manifold pressure to less than 20 in. Hg and adjust prop control to obtain 1600 rpm. Supercharger shifts from low to high should be made rapidly to avoid wear on the clutch. When a shift is made, be sure that handle reaches the extremity of its travel to prevent clutch slippage. A slight increase in manifold pressure will indicate engagement of the high blower clutch. The supercharger should be shifted to low for all descents.

CAUTION

Do not shift from low to high blower at less than 5-minute intervals in order to prevent overheating the supercharger clutch. Shift from high to low, as desired, since no heat is generated.

HIGH-POWER OPERATION

TAKE-OFF AND MILITARY POWER

It is often asked what the consequences would be if the 5-minute limit at take-off power (rich mixture) or the 30-minute limit at military power (normal mixture) were exceeded. Another frequent inquiry is how long a period must be allowed after the specified time limit has elapsed until take-off power can again be used. These questions are difficult to answer, since the time limit specified does not mean that engine damage will occur if the limits are exceeded. It does mean that total operating time at high power should be kept to a reasonable minimum in the interest of prolonging engine life. It is generally accepted that high-power operation of an engine results in increased wear and necessitates more frequent overhaul than low-power operation. However, it is apparent that a certain percentage of operating time must be at full power. The engine manufacturer allows for this in qualification tests in which much of the running is done at take-off power to prove ability to withstand the resulting loads. It is established in these runs that the engine will handle sustained high power without damage. Nevertheless, it is still the aim of the manufacturer and to the best interest of the pilot to keep within reasonable limits the amount of high-power time accumulated in the field. The most satisfactory method for accomplishing this is to establish time limits that will keep pilots constantly aware of the desire to hold high-power periods to those as brief as the flight plan will allow, so that the total accumulated time at high-power settings and resulting wear can be kept to a

minimum. How the time at high power is accumulated is of secondary importance; i.e., it is no worse from the standpoint of engine wear to operate at take-off power for 1 hour straight than it is to operate in twelve 5-minute stretches, provided engine temperatures and pressures are within limits. In fact, the former procedure may even be preferable, as it eliminates temperature cycles which also aggravate engine wear. Thus, if flight conditions occasionally require exceeding time limits, this should not cause concern so long as constant effort is made to *keep the overall time at take-off power to the minimum practicable.*

MAP VS. RPM

Another factor, to be remembered in operating engines at high power, is that full military power is to be preferred over military power rpm with reduced manifold pressure. This procedure results in less engine wear for two reasons: first, the resulting high brake horsepower decreases the time required to attain the objective of such high-power operation; second, high rpm results in high loads on the reciprocating parts due to inertia forces. As these loads are partially offset by the gas pressure in the cylinders, the high cylinder pressures resulting from use of high manifold pressure will give lower net loads and less engine wear due to piston "slap" as seen at low MAP (manifold pressure). Sustained high rpm is a major factor producing engine wear. High rpm and low manifold pressure require more "rpm minutes" or "piston ring miles" to attain the desired objective of high-power operation.

TAKE-OFF POWER

The engine produces 1425 brake horsepower at sea level for take-off purposes. However, if maximum power is not required, NATOPS procedures recommend using 48 inches MAP with full increase rpm. The "piston miles" necessary to gain a given altitude at this power will normally be less than those obtained at 2700 rpm using a reduced MAP. Take-off power should be maintained until the recommended climbing speed and a safe altitude, considering the local terrain, are attained.

LOW-ALTITUDE OPERATION

With high-power operations, it is possible to overtemperature the engine without the overtemperature being observed in the cockpit. FCLP (field carrier landing practice) is an example of this condition; therefore, it is recommended that following each fifth FCLP pass, the aircraft should be flown at a safe gliding altitude at reduced power for at least 5 minutes to allow all parts of the engine to cool. High-power operations also require high fuel consumption. For this reason, great care must be exercised when operating at high power, especially at low altitude. For example, at military power at 1000 feet altitude, the fuel supply will be exhausted in approximately 45 minutes. Therefore, *when practicing take-offs and landings or when flying at high powers— keep an eye on fuel quantity.*

TEMPERATURE AND HUMIDITY EFFECTS

Temperature or humidity, above or below the standard operating conditions [dry air at 15°C (60°F)], will affect engine horsepower output. Engine horsepower output is proportional to the weight of air consumed by the engine. If air temperature is above 15°C (60°F), the weight of air will be less than the standard value because of the expansion of heated air, and engine power will decrease. Conversely, at temperatures below 15°C (60°F), power output will increase because the contracted cool air is denser. If air temperature is held constant, power output will decrease if water vapor is present, because the amount of air available for combustion is reduced by the water vapor which replaces some air. In addition, water vapor causes richer fuel-air ratios by reducing air intake volume. The carburetor cannot differentiate between water vapor and air, and meters fuel according to the pressure affecting the various diaphragms, regardless of what causes the pressure. Therefore, with a higher quantity of water vapor and, consequently, less air, the resulting fuel-air ratio will be richer than would occur with dry air. This also decreases engine output during operation at high power. The effects of temperature and humidity may be best illustrated by the following example:

Assume air temperature is 32°C (90°F), the relative humidity is 70 percent, and the engine is operating at take-off rpm and manifold pressure (2700 rpm, 52.5 in. Hg at sea level). Engine output will be approximately 1335 bhp (brake horsepower), or a 6.3 percent loss in power due to water vapor in the air. The air temperature increase will cause an additional 2.8 percent loss in power. The total bhp after correcting for both temperature and humidity will be 1295 or a total loss of 130 bhp. The available take-off power of the engine is more than adequate for any condition of humidity or temperature likely to be encountered. Humidity corrections are made only for take-off conditions. At high altitude, humidity effect is usually very small and the effects on engine performance are negligible.

ENGINE-PROPELLER SURGING

Under some flight conditions, usually at high altitudes, engine-propeller surging has been encountered. The surge, which takes the form of rhythmic rpm and manifold pressure variations, usually is noted at altitudes of 25,000 feet or above, although surge is sometimes encountered at lower altitudes. In most cases, the surge consists of stable oscillations; however, in some cases, the oscillations become more and more severe. The precise cause or causes of the surge have not yet been completely determined. However, in all known instances, effective corrective action has consisted of advancing the mixture control lever from NORMAL to RICH. It is recommended that this procedure be utilized when surge is experienced. Other corrective methods which may be effective in some cases are reduction of manifold pressure, increase in rpm, or a descent. When outside air temperature is low and icing conditions exist, the use of carburetor heat may be effective in eliminating surge. Since surge occurs in most cases at high altitudes where moisture content is so low that icing rarely occurs, the use of a rich mixture to eliminate surge is considered preferable to the use of carburetor heat. Of course, when a rich mixture is utilized to eliminate surge, fuel flow is increased. With mixture control at RICH, and in high blower, range will be reduced approximately 15 percent.

The engine-propeller surge described should not be confused with momentary propeller-engine instability which occurs in some instances when governor or throttle settings are changed. The instability resulting from such changes is usually of much lesser severity and automatically dampens itself in from 5 to 15 seconds.

ENGINE SHUTDOWN TEMPERATURES

Flight testing has shown that one of the most critical periods, with regard to adequate cooling of the power plant installation, is after the engine is shut down. A large amount of heat is generated during flight, and some of it is retained after shutdown. Since there is no longer any cooling airflow over the engine, the retained heat is conducted throughout the engine. Retained heat may be sufficient to raise the temperature of power plant components above their limits, and serious damage may result. Intake pipes may warp or crack, rocker box covers may warp (resulting in excessive oil leakage), insulation on electrical wires and magnetos or generators may be damaged, etc. For this reason it is very important to idle the engine until cylinder head temperatures have dropped to 150°C, or less, before shutting down. Cylinder heads will usually be cooled by the time the parking area is reached. This is not always the case, especially in hot weather. The cylinders should always be allowed to cool before the engine is stopped.

STOPPING ENGINE

THROTTLE POSITION

In the days of float carburetors, it was customary to stop the engine by turning off the fuel supply, and advancing the throttle so the maximum possible amount of fuel in the carburetor would be consumed in a short time. This practice was carried over to pressure injection carburetors, perhaps with little thought as to practical consequences. The correct method of stopping an engine equipped with pressure injection carburetion is simply to place the mixture control in IDLE CUTOFF *without* advancing the throttle. This method is specified in Section III. Advancing the throttle during the stopping procedure of an engine with a fuel injection system usually results in engine backfires, some mild and some severe. Such backfires can seriously damage the sensitive automatic control unit and, in some instances, can deform or break the air induction scoop, or the hot air door mechanism or castings. Such damage is often not immediately detected. At best, the consequences might mean a carburetor or air scoop change or, if the damaged part should fail in flight, the end results might very well cause a forced landing. Adherence to standardized procedures in this manual will prevent carburetor or air scoop damage from improper engine stopping.

STABILIZED RUN

It will also be noted that the engine shutdown procedure in Section III specifies 60 seconds of engine operation at 1200 rpm prior to stopping. The reason for this should be understood. In a radial engine, the lower cylinders are vulnerable to the flow of oil into the cylinder head when the engine is stopped. Such oil will flow from the crankcase into the lower cylinders and, in time, will seep past the piston rings. On the subsequent start, the oil which has collected in the cylinder may "liquid-lock" the piston. Severe bearing loads are imposed on the engine, and connecting rods have been bent when an attempt has been made to start a "liquid-locked" engine. The obvious solution to this problem is to remove the accumulation of oil in the engine crankcase prior to shutdown. Under normal operating conditions, the engine oil sumps are of sufficient volume to prevent accumulation of oil in the crankcase. In addition, at higher rpm, the scavenge oil pumps can easily return all oil accumulating in the engine sumps. However, at lower rpm, the scavenge pumps are relatively inefficient and may not be able to scavenge all the oil unless a sufficient period of time is allowed for this purpose. It has been found by tests that a period of 60 seconds running at approximately 1200 rpm will assure a clean shutdown; i.e., it will allow sufficient time for any excess oil in the crankcase or sumps to be fully scavenged and returned to the oil tank. Under such conditions, liquid lock from excess oil at the time of shutdown is prevented. As stated before, the consequences of liquid lock can be very serious. On many occasions, the effects of excessive internal loads are not apparent immediately, but cause an incipient failure which occurs with the accumulation of engine time. Usually, such failures occur when they can be least tolerated, such as with the use of high power for take-off or waveoff.

ENGINE ICING

INDUCTION ICE

There are several types of engine ice formation, and the effect of each on the engine is different. The most common form, induction icing, occurs in the air passages, carburetor, or carburetor air scoop. Low air temperature and high humidity are the primary cause of this icing, and the refrigerating effect of fuel vaporization aggravates the condition. Ice builds up until the air passages are sufficiently restricted to cause a reduction in airflow, with a resultant loss of power. This type of icing is indicated by a gradual decrease of manifold pressure

and engine power. The purpose of carburetor alternate air is to prevent ice from forming in these passages. If icing conditions are expected, move the carburetor air control to the ALTERNATE position *before* ice is encountered. This will provide a higher carburetor air temperature and prevent ice from forming in the carburetor air passages. If ice is already accumulated, move the carburetor air control to ALTERNATE and fly at a warmer altitude. Carburetor air temperature can be further increased by closing the cowl flaps to the greatest extent consistent with cylinder head and oil temperature limitations. Increasing rpm will also raise cylinder head temperatures, thereby providing more heat for the carburetor air supply in the alternate position.

Note

Induction ice will usually occur only under conditions resulting in general clear ice accumulation.

CARBURETOR ICE

Rich Mixture

The other forms of engine ice occur within the carburetor and can occur in clear air conditions, and, depending upon what portion of the carburetor is affected, can produce either extremely rich or extremely lean mixtures. If the mixture control bleeds between the carburetor air chambers become iced, a rich mixture will result. Loss of power, increased fuel flow, "torching," or black smoke out the exhaust is an indication of this condition. To control the fuel flow, it is necessary to gradually pull the mixture control toward IDLE CUTOFF until the engine operates normally. This type of ice may be stubborn and require full alternate air for some time before it is removed. When normal engine operation is restored, as evidenced by normal power when the mixture control is placed in NORMAL, the carburetor air control handle should be positioned to maintain carburetor air temperature above 15°C. As long as alternate air is being used, there will be very little danger of icing even though the carburetor air temperature goes below 15°C.

Lean Mixture

Ice forming in the impact pressure tubes or at the valve seat of the automatic mixture control unit will cause the carburetor to supply a very lean mixture. This form of ice will cause decreased fuel flow, loss of power, or backfiring. To increase the fuel flow, move the mixture control to RICH. If this does not provide a sufficiently rich mixture, intermittent priming may be used until the carburetor has thawed out. This form of ice is the most difficult to remove, since it is necessary to heat the metal of the impact tubes and the automatic mixture control unit to effect melting. The quickest relief will be to fly at a warmer altitude and use full alternate air until engine operation is normal. Free moisture (including rain and supercooled water droplets) is excluded from the carburetor, when using alternate air, by abrupt turning of the air into the carburetor mixing valve. This provides inertia separation which removes the heavier water particles from the air.

GENERAL RULES/USE OF ALTERNATE AIR

In general, icing conditions are usually not encountered above 25,000 feet. At lower altitudes, increasing or decreasing altitude will often effect escape from icing conditions. If icing in any form is encountered and the use of alternate air will not provide sufficiently high carburetor air temperature to remove it, change altitude to get out of the icing level.

Use caution in the use of the carburetor air control handle, as extremely high carburetor air temperatures contribute to detonation and resulting engine damage. In addition, engine power is reduced by use of alternate air, because airflow is decreased. Full engine power, therefore, is not available with the carburetor air control handle at ALTERNATE. When it is necessary to use alternate air to remove carburetor ice, the carburetor air temperature limits shown in Section I, Part 4, should be closely observed. At all other times, the carburetor air control handle should be in the DIRECT position.

FUEL SYSTEM

The aircraft fuel system is entirely automatic after being put into operation. Turning the fuel shutoff handle ON from either cockpit opens the fuel shutoff valve and starts the d-c powered boost pump in the sump tank located in the right wheel well. Fuel flows by gravity from the wing tanks into the sump tank, automatically, maintaining an equal fuel level in each wing. The boost pump forces fuel under a pressure of 19 to 24 psi through the fuel shutoff valve, the strainer, and the engine-driven fuel pump. The engine-driven fuel pump then boosts the fuel to an operating pressure of 21 to 25 psi. If the engine-driven fuel pump fails, the boost pump will still supply sufficient fuel for satisfactory operation. If failure of the boost pump occurs, the engine-driven fuel pump will enable the engine to operate up to 10,000 feet.

Two interconnected fuel cells are located in each wing. See figure 1-8. Port and starboard overboard vents are located in each wing flap to assist even fuel flow and to vent the tanks. As with most fuel systems of this type, prolonged unsymmetrical flight may cause uneven fuel flow or prevent fuel from flowing into the sump tank. If this occurs and the engine stops due to lack of fuel, immediately revert to normal flight and the engine should start. If the engine does not start, refer to AIR START procedures, in Section V. For fuel specifications, refer to Section I, Part 3, and for fuel quantity, see figure 1-9.

FUEL SYSTEM CONTROLS AND INDICATORS

FUEL SHUTOFF HANDLES

A fuel shutoff control handle (3, figure 1-3), located on

the left console of each cockpit, has two positions: ON and OFF. Each position operates the fuel shutoff valve and the boost pump simultaneously. No action by the pilot is necessary to maintain an equal fuel level in each wing other than normal flight and co-ordinated turns.

FUEL BOOST PUMP TEST SWITCH*

A fuel boost pump test switch is located on the electrical switch panel (15, figure 1-5A) in the forward cockpit. The test switch is wired in series with the boost pump switch on the fuel shutoff control handle. When held in the TEST position, power to the boost pump is interrupted, allowing the engine-driven fuel pump pressure to be checked.

FUEL QUANTITY INDICATORS

A fuel quantity indicator (28, figure 1-4) is located on the main instrument panel in each cockpit. The indicator system is electrically operated and measures the total fuel supply in pounds. The system automatically compensates for changes in fuel density so that the quantity indicator will always register the actual number of pounds of fuel in the tanks, regardless of fuel expansion or contraction due to temperature variation. The full mark on the indicator is set at 1040 pounds for a 25°C (77°F) fuel temperature. If the tanks are full but the temperature is above 25°C (77°F), the indicator will indicate less than full; if the tanks are full and the fuel temperature is below 25°C (77°F), the indicator will indicate above the full mark. The performance data in Section XI refers to fuel quantity by weight for accurate flight planning. The fuel quantity system is powered from the primary d-c bus.

Note

Fuel range per pound is the same regardless of fuel temperature.

Fuel Quantity Select Switch

A toggle switch (29, figure 1-4), located just below the indicator in each cockpit, is marked RIGHT WING and LEFT WING and is spring-loaded to a center (off) position. When the switch is depressed to the right, the indicator will show quantity in the right tank only. Holding the switch to the LEFT WING position will likewise give a reading of fuel remaining in the left tank. When the switch is released, the total fuel quantity will be indicated.

FUEL LOW-LEVEL WARNING LIGHT

A low-level warning light (30, figure 1-4) is located on the instrument panel in each cockpit. If fuel quantity falls below approximately 200 pounds, the light illuminates. If the fuel quantity indicator is not operating, the fuel low-level warning light should not be interpreted to mean there are exactly 200 pounds of fuel available, since its indication is only approximate.

ELECTRICAL SYSTEM
D-C POWER

The 28-volt d-c power system is powered by a 28-volt, 200-ampere engine-driven generator (30-volt, 300-

*Aircraft having AFC 105 complied with

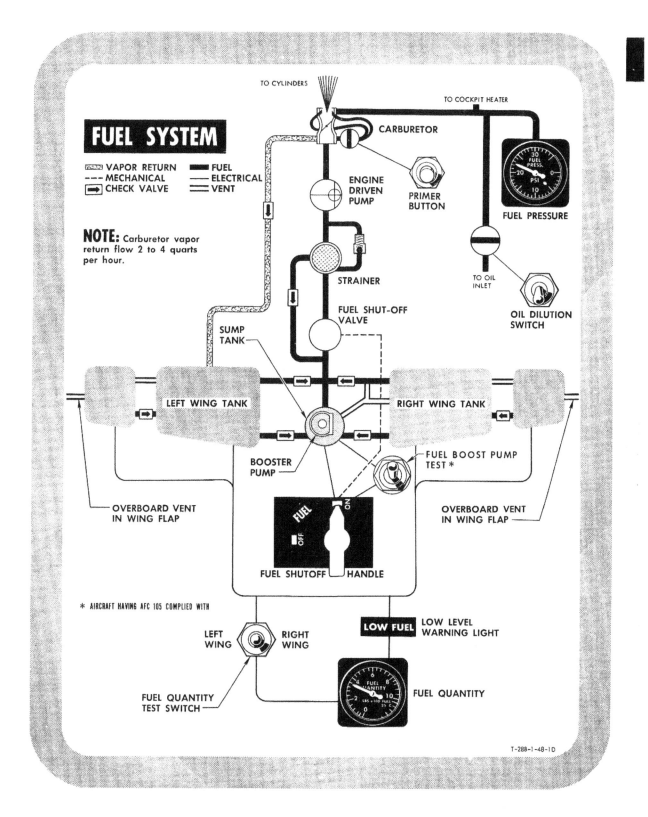

Figure 1-8

FUEL QUANTITY DATA

TANKS	PORT WING TANK	STARBOARD WING TANK	SUMP TANK
NUMBER	1	1	1
USABLE FUEL (EACH)	87.0	87.0	3.0
FULLY SERVICED (EACH)	87.5	87.5	3.0
EXPANSION SPACE (EACH)	2.0	2.0	
TOTAL VOLUME (EACH)	89.5	89.5	3.0

TOTAL USABLE FUEL, 177 U. S. GALLONS

NOTE: MULTIPLY GALLONS BY 6.0 TO OBTAIN POUNDS OF GASOLINE. FOR PURPOSE OF ROUGH WEIGHT CALCULATIONS, FUEL CAN BE ASSUMED TO WEIGH 6 POUNDS PER GALLON.

T-28C-1-48-2

Figure 1-9

ampere*) and a 24-volt storage battery serves as standby power. D-C power can also be supplied through an external power receptacle.

A-C POWER

Power for the a-c system is supplied by two inverters: a 750-volt-ampere inverter and a 250-volt-ampere inverter.

INTERCOCKPIT CONTROL

All instruments and controls essential to flight are provided in both cockpits. To provide independent and complete control of certain systems by one pilot at a time, a control shift is mounted on the right console in each cockpit. Momentary actuation of this toggle switch to the CONTROL SHIFT position transfers control of the battery, generator, inverters, starter, cowl and oil cooler flaps, speed brake, and all external lights. On some aircraft,† the d-c power and a-c inverter circuits have been removed from the cockpit control transfer relay. As a result, control of the battery, generator, and inverters has been removed from the control shift relay. Momentary actuation of the intercockpit control shift switch to the CONTROL SHIFT position, therefore, only transfers control of the starter, cowl and oil cooler flaps, speed brake, and all external lights. When control is shifted, the units will operate according to the positioning of the switches in the cockpit to which control is transferred. The shift switch in the rear cockpit can be held on to override operation of the switch in the front cockpit.

D-C POWER DISTRIBUTION

D-C power is distributed from four buses: battery, primary, secondary, and monitored. When the Aero 1A training armament kit is installed, an armament bus is powered from the secondary bus through an armament bus control relay. The battery bus is connected directly to the battery and is energized whenever the battery is installed. All four buses are powered from the generator through the d-c power switch. The primary bus is also energized by external power, and by battery power when the DC POWER switch is in either BAT. & GEN. or BAT. ONLY position. The secondary and monitored buses are energized through the primary bus by generator or external power. The secondary bus is also energized by the battery when the DC POWER switch is in the BAT. ONLY position or when the landing gear is down and the DC POWER switch is at BAT. & GEN. The monitored bus cannot be powered from the battery alone. For d-c power distribution, see figure 1-10.

A-C POWER DISTRIBUTION (BASIC)

Both the main inverter, 750 volt-amperes, and the standby inverter, 250 volt-amperes, are powered from the d-c distribution system. The main inverter receives power from the monitored bus and the standby inverter is powered from the primary bus. An instrument power switch is provided for manual selection of the inverters. The main inverter supplies power for the attitude gyros, the instrument power failure relay, the stall warning system (T-28C), and the radio magnetic indicator. If the main inverter fails, the standby inverter will supply power for the same equipment. For electrical power distribution, see figure 1-10.

A-C POWER DISTRIBUTION (MODIFIED‡)

Both inverters are powered by the d-c distribution system. The main inverter, 250 volt-amperes, receives power from the primary bus and the standby inverter, 750 volt-amperes, receives power from the monitored bus. An instrument power switch provides manual selection of either inverter. The standby inverter provides TACAN power and, if this inverter fails, there will be no power available to this equipment. TACAN power will also be lost if the instrument power switch in either cockpit is moved from the No. 1 to the No. 2 inverter. The front cockpit a-c bus can be powered by either inverter and supplies power to the front cockpit attitude gyro and instrument power failure relay, T-28C stall warning system, and both RMI indicators. The rear cockpit a-c bus can be powered by either inverter also, but only supplies power to the rear cockpit attitude gyro and instrument power failure relay. For electrical power distribution, see figure 1-10.

*Aircraft 140584 and subsequent and aircraft having ASC 20, Phase I complied with
†Aircraft 140584 and subsequent and aircraft having ASC 36 complied with
‡Aircraft having ASC 36 incorporated

EXTERNAL POWER

For starting the engine or for electrical ground checks, an external power source can be connected to the external power receptacle (figure 1-24) on the left side of the fuselage aft of the wing.

Note

There is no relay provided for the external power receptacle. Therefore, to prevent the plug from arcing, make sure the ground crew turns the power unit output off before disconnecting the external power plug.

ELECTRICAL SYSTEM CONTROLS AND INDICATORS

D-C POWER SWITCH (BASIC)

The DC POWER switch (figure 1-7), located on the right forward console in each cockpit, has BAT. & GEN., OFF, and BAT. ONLY positions. The switch cannot be moved to the BAT. ONLY position when the guard is down. With the switch at BAT. & GEN. position and the generator operating, power is supplied to all four d-c buses. With DC POWER switch OFF and the generator operating, the battery bus is energized by the battery and all other buses are inoperative. With the DC POWER switch at BAT. & GEN. and the generator not operating, the battery and primary buses are energized by the battery, and if the landing gear is extended, the secondary bus is automatically connected to the system. With the switch at the BAT. ONLY position and the generator inoperative, the battery, primary, and secondary buses are energized by the battery. Only the battery bus is energized if the switch is OFF and the generator is not operating.

Note

- The DC POWER switch should not be placed at BAT. & GEN. or BAT. ONLY when external power is applied.

- If it is necessary to use the battery simultaneously with external power, battery "on" time should be kept to a minimum since no ground ventilation is provided.

D-C POWER SWITCH (MODIFIED*)

See figure 1-7. The front cockpit DC POWER switch is marked: BAT. & GEN., OFF, and BAT. ONLY. The rear cockpit switch is a lever-lock type with two positions marked: NORMAL ON and EMER. OFF. The front cockpit switch cannot be moved to the BAT. ONLY position unless the guard is raised. The rear switch can be moved to either position by pulling up on the toggle before moving. With the front switch at BAT. & GEN. position and the generator operating, power is supplied to all four d-c buses. With this switch OFF and the generator operating, the battery bus is energized by the battery and all other buses are inoperative. With the DC POWER

switch at BAT. & GEN. position and the generator not operating, the battery and primary buses are energized by the battery and, if the landing gear is extended, the secondary bus is automatically connected to the system. With the switch in the BAT. ONLY position and the generator inoperative, the battery, primary, and secondary buses are energized by the battery. With the switch OFF and the generator not operating, only the battery bus will be energized. For normal operation, the d-c switch in the rear cockpit should always be in the NORMAL ON position. *If an emergency occurs, placing the switch in the EMER. OFF position will cut off all d-c power in the system except the battery bus.*

INSTRUMENT POWER SWITCH (BASIC)

The two-position instrument power switch (figure 1-7), located on the right console in each cockpit, controls the bus load from the main and the standby inverters. The switch can be operated only by the pilot who last actuated his control shift switch. The main inverter supplies current to the a-c bus when the switch is at the NO. 1 INV. position, and the standby inverter operates simultaneously under a dummy load. Moving the switch to NO. 2 INV. position connects the standby inverter to the a-c bus, and the main inverter then operates in an open circuit.

INSTRUMENT POWER SWITCH (MODIFIED*)

The instrument power switches have been removed from the transfer system. The aft cockpit switch cannot be moved to the NO. 2 INV. position unless the guard is lifted. The front cockpit inverter selector switch is used to select the power source, main or standby inverter, to all a-c equipment except the aft cockpit attitude gyro. The aft cockpit inverter selector switch is used to select the power source to the aft cockpit attitude gyro only. If TACAN is installed, it is powered by the 750-volt-ampere standby inverter only, and controlled by a relay which is actuated when both inverter selector switches are in the No. 1 position. If either switch is moved from the No. 1 position, power to the TACAN will be interrupted and the equipment will be inoperative.

INTERCOCKPIT CONTROL SHIFT SWITCHES

An intercockpit control shift switch is mounted on both right consoles (figure 1-7). The control shift system is energized by the battery bus and will function with the DC POWER switch OFF in both cockpits. If the DC POWER switch is positioned to either BAT. & GEN. or BAT. ONLY, or if external power is supplied, a light adjacent to the control switch in either cockpit marked LT. ON CONTROL will illuminate when the related switch is operated to take control.

CIRCUIT BREAKERS AND FUSES

All d-c circuits are protected from overloads by push-to-reset circuit breakers. Should an overload occur in a

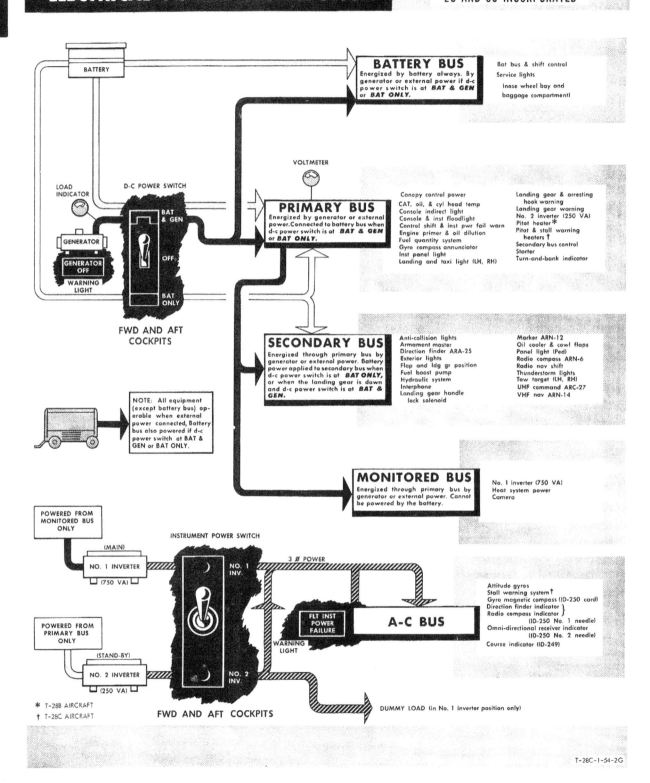

ELECTRICAL POWER DISTRIBUTION — AIRCRAFT NOT HAVING ASC'S 20 AND 36 INCORPORATED

Figure 1-10 (Sheet 1)

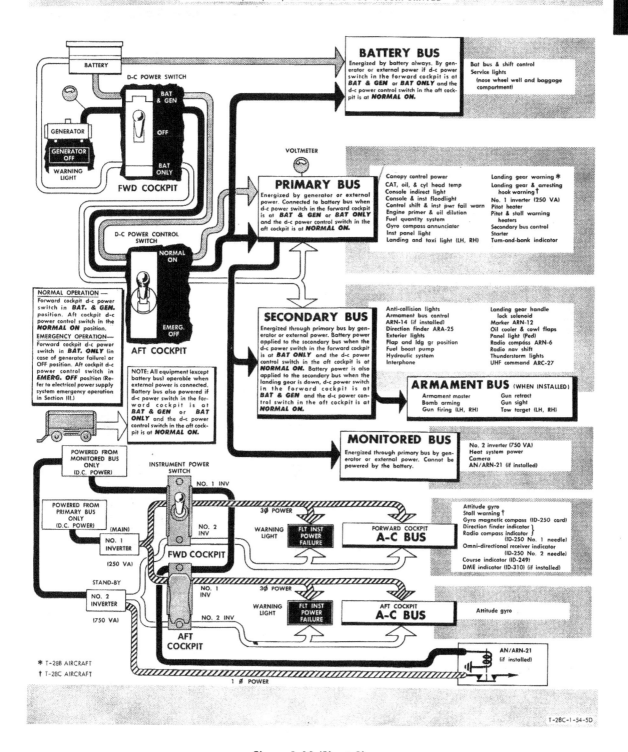

Figure 1-10 (Sheet 2)

FUSE AND CIRCUIT-BREAKER PANELS

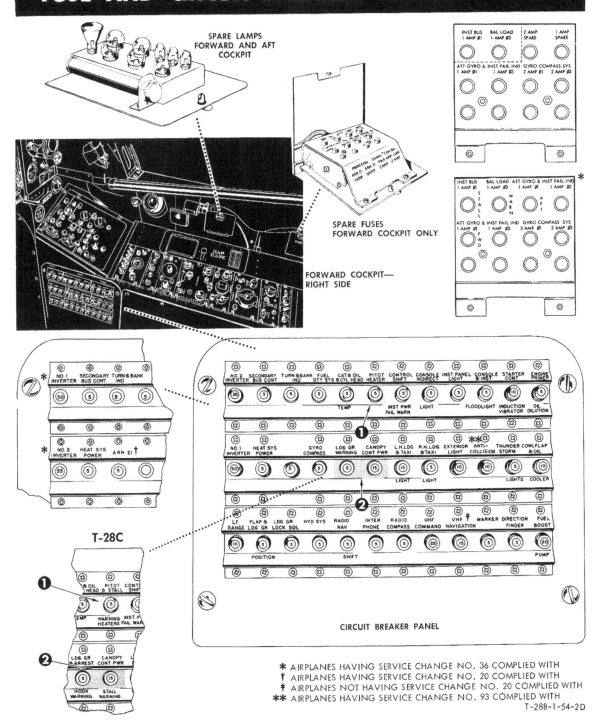

* AIRPLANES HAVING SERVICE CHANGE NO. 36 COMPLIED WITH
† AIRPLANES HAVING SERVICE CHANGE NO. 20 COMPLIED WITH
‡ AIRPLANES NOT HAVING SERVICE CHANGE NO. 20 COMPLIED WITH
** AIRPLANES HAVING SERVICE CHANGE NO. 93 COMPLIED WITH

T-28-1-54-2D

Figure 1-11

circuit, the resulting heat rise causes the circuit breaker to pop out and open the circuit. The circuit breaker may be pushed in again in an attempt to re-energize the circuit. However, the circuit breaker should not be held in if it opens the circuit a second time. The circuit-breaker panel (19, figure 1-5; figure 1-11) is located in the front cockpit below the right console. Alternating-current circuits are protected by fuses. The fuse panel can be reached through an access door in the front cockpit above the right console.

GENERATOR-OFF WARNING LIGHTS

A generator-off warning light (figure 1-7) is located on the right forward console in both cockpits. Illumination indicates that the generator is not operating and the battery or external power unit is supplying all power for the electrical system. To conserve the battery when the generator is inoperative, all unnecessary electrical equipment should be turned off or disconnected by pulling out related circuit breakers.

INSTRUMENT POWER FAILURE WARNING LIGHTS

A flight instrument power failure warning light (35, figure 1-4), mounted on both instrument panels, illuminates when the a-c bus is not energized or power is interrupted to the attitude gyro. Illumination with the instrument power switch at NO. 1 INV. position indicates that the attitude gyro or the main inverter is not operating. If the main inverter is inoperative, the attitude gyro and other a-c powered equipment will be inoperative. If the light goes out when the instrument power switch is moved to the NO. 2 INV. position, a-c power is being supplied to the bus by the stand-by inverter and failure of the main inverter is confirmed. Failure of the stand-by inverter also causes the light to illuminate, providing the switch is in the NO. 2 INV. position. If the light remains illuminated, regardless of the position of the instrument power switch, either both inverters are inoperative or the attitude gyro is not receiving a-c power. If one of the ATT GYRO & INST FAIL IND fuses (figure 1-11) is blown, the attitude gyro will be inoperative, but all other a-c powered equipment will be operative even though the warning light remains illuminated. Aircraft with ASC No. 36 incorporated have separate fuses for each cockpit attitude gyro and separate warning light circuits.

VOLTMETERS

A voltmeter (26, figure 1-4), located on the instrument panel, indicates voltage output of the generator battery, or external power unit. Normal voltage indication is approximately 27.7 volts.

LOADMETERS

A generator load indicator (27, figure 1-4) is mounted on both instrument panels. The indicator reflects the percent of generator output being used and is graduated in decimal fractions. An indication of 0.5 means the electrical system is using one-half of rated generator capacity.

HYDRAULIC SYSTEM

Hydraulic power is used to operate the landing gear, wing flaps, canopy, speed brakes, and, in T-28C aircraft, to retract the arresting hook. See figure 1-12. A variable-displacement, engine-driven pump supplies hydraulic pressure. When no hydraulic units are being operated in flight, the entire output of the pump is automatically diverted to the hydraulic reservoir through an electrically actuated bypass valve. When any hydraulic control is operated, the bypass valve is electrically deenergized and closes, allowing the hydraulic system to build up pressure for operation of the selected unit. The bypass valve is electrically energized to open and depressurizes the system only when all units are in their normal flight position, and the system is pressurized at all other times. System pressure is maintained whenever the speed brake or canopy are open and whenever the gear, T-28C arresting hook, or flaps are in any position other than up and locked. In the event of electrical failure, the bypass valve automatically closes, pressurizing the system. A standpipe in the reservoir retains enough fluid to supply the wheel brakes if all fluid is lost from the reservoir. A high-pressure air system is provided as an alternate for the hydraulic system to open the canopy in an emergency. A hydraulic pressure gage (8, figure 1-3) is located on the left console in each cockpit. The hydraulic system is d-c controlled from the secondary bus. For hydraulic system servicing, refer to Section I, Part 3.

HYDRAULIC HANDPUMP

A hydraulic handpump (22, figure 1-3) is provided in the front cockpit. The handpump is used primarily for ground check of the hydraulic system, but may be used in flight should the engine-driven pump fail. The handpump is merely a substitute for the engine-driven pump and does not provide separate fluid supply or lines to operate any part of the system.

FLIGHT CONTROL SYSTEMS

FLIGHT CONTROLS

The primary flight control surfaces (elevator, ailerons, and rudder) are operable from either cockpit by interconnected stick and rudder pedals. No hydraulic boost control system is provided. Cable-operated trim tabs on all control surfaces, except the right aileron tab, are manually positioned from trim tab control wheels located on the left consoles. Hydraulically operated, semislotted wing flaps are mounted on the trailing edge of each wing and are controlled by a lever on the throttle quadrants. A single, hydraulically operated, perforated speed brake, mounted on the bottom of the fuselage, may be extended at any speed. The rudder pedals are adjustable fore and aft and incorporate wheel brake control by pressure on the top of the pedals. All primary flight controls can be locked in a neutral position by a mechanical control lock in the front cockpit. This lock also secures the throttle in the closed position.

CONTROL STICKS

The control stick in both cockpits incorporates positive-grip handles. The stick grip in the front cockpit contains a gun trigger, a bomb release button marked B on top of the grip, and a rocket-firing button marked R on the side of the grip. The control sticks are mechanically connected to each other by a push-pull tube. The

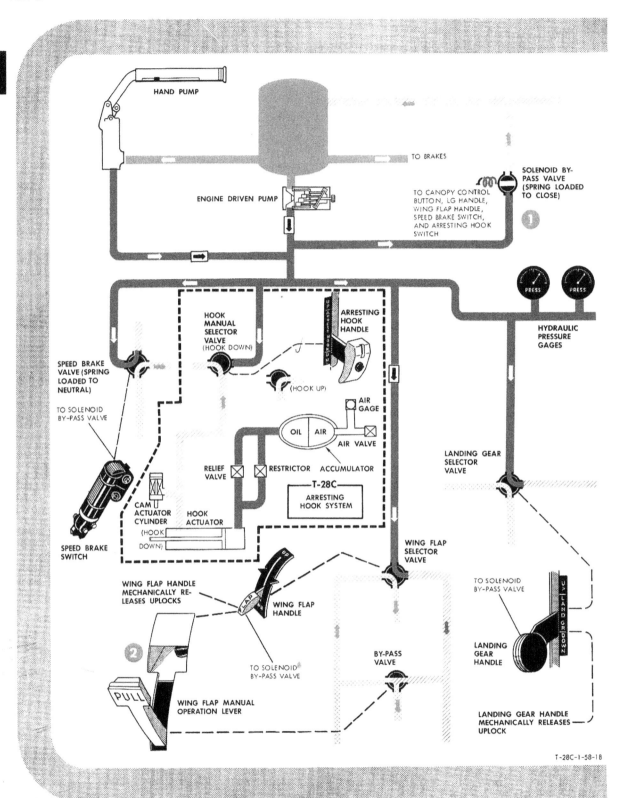

Figure 1-12 (Sheet 1)

HYDRAULIC SYSTEM

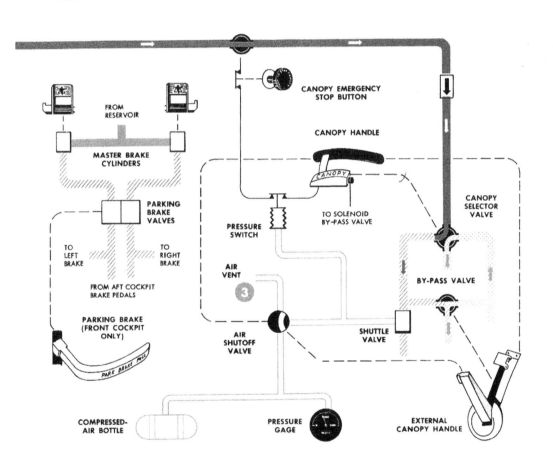

PRESSURE
DOWN, OPEN, OR ON
UP OR CLOSE
RETURN
SUPPLY
AIR LINE
ELECTRICAL CONNECTION
MECHANICAL CONNECTION
CHECK VALVE

1 Electrically actuated to by-pass when gear and flaps up, speed brake closed, and canopy handle button released.

2 To lower flaps on ground for use as step; also moves wing flap handle to **DOWN**.

3 Pressure is released when external canopy handle is moved from **EMERG** position.

FROM
RESERVOIR

CANOPY EMERGENCY
STOP BUTTON

CANOPY HANDLE

MASTER BRAKE
CYLINDERS

CANOPY

TO SOLENOID
BY-PASS VALVE

CANOPY
SELECTOR
VALVE

PARKING
BRAKE
VALVES

PRESSURE
SWITCH

BY-PASS VALVE

TO
LEFT
BRAKE

TO
RIGHT
BRAKE

AIR
VENT

3

FROM AFT COCKPIT
BRAKE PEDALS

PARKING BRAKE
(FRONT COCKPIT
ONLY)

AIR
SHUTOFF
VALVE

SHUTTLE
VALVE

PARK BRAKE PULL

COMPRESSED-
AIR BOTTLE

PRESSURE
GAGE

EXTERNAL
CANOPY HANDLE

T-28C-1-58-2

Figure 1-12 (Sheet 2)

elevator system incorporates a bungee and bobweight. The bungee provides satisfactory control "feel" during low-speed flight and landing, and the bobweight assists pilot effort during accelerated flight.

RUDDER PEDALS

A set of interconnected rudder pedals in each cockpit controls the rudder action through direct mechanical linkage to the rudder. The wheel brakes are actuated by pressure on the top rudder pedal plates. The rudder pedals can be adjusted for correct leg length.

Rudder Pedal Release Levers

A rudder pedal release lever (36, figure 1-4), located below the center of the instrument panel in each cockpit, permits individual adjustment of the pedals. Holding the lever to the right unlocks the pedals, allowing them to move full aft. Releasing the lever locks the pedals in the desired position. A cable running between the pedals prevents unequal adjustment.

Note

As the rudder pedals are spring-loaded to the aft position, have feet on the pedals when making adjustments.

TRIM CONTROL WHEELS

Cable-operated elevator, rudder, and aileron trim wheels (4, 6, and 21, figure 1-3) are located on the left console in each cockpit. Trim tab position is shown by a scale and pointer at each control. The left aileron trim tab is controlled by the aileron trim tab wheel. The right aileron trim tab can only be adjusted on the ground.

CONTROL LOCK

All surface controls and the throttle are locked by a control lock (figure 3-4), which is stowed on the floor of the front cockpit behind the stick. Pulling the plunger-type pin on the right side of the lock releases it from the stowed position on the floor. The lock can then be raised to engage the stick and rudder pedals in the neutral position. The plunger is then released to engage a hole in the side of the stick. When subsequently closed, the throttle is locked and will remain locked until the control lock is released.

WING FLAPS

Hydraulically operated, semislotted wing flaps extend from aileron to fuselage on each wing. The flaps are operable from either cockpit and a flap position indicator is provided on each instrument panel. No emergency system is provided for operating the flaps. However, if the hydraulic system fails, an attempt may be made to extend the flaps by operating the hydraulic handpump. The handpump will pressurize the system only when loss of pressure is caused by failure of the engine-driven pump. The flaps can be lowered manually on the ground from outside the aircraft and spring-loaded doors in the surface of the flaps may be used as steps up to the wing.

FLAP CONTROLS AND INDICATORS

FLAP HANDLES

The flaps are operated by means of a FLAP handle (figure 1-6) on the throttle quadrant in each cockpit. The handle is shaped in the form of an airfoil for easy

recognition by feel. Moving the handle to UP, 1/4, 1/2, 3/4, or DOWN electrically closes the solenoid bypass valve, which pressurizes the hydraulic system to operate the flaps, and mechanically positions the wing flap selector valve. When the desired flap position is obtained, the selector valve automatically returns to the neutral position. The flaps will lower 37 1/2 degrees when the FLAP handle is moved to DOWN. Detents hold the handle in the selected position. The flaps require approximately 7 to 12 seconds to extend and approximately 10 to 15 seconds to retract. The hydraulic system is pressurized as long as the flaps are in any position other than up and locked. The flaps are held in the up position by a mechanical overcenter lock and hydraulic lock and in any selected down position by the hydraulic locking action of the selector valve in the neutral position.

MANUAL FLAP LEVER (EXTERNAL)

The manual flap lever is located on the left side of the fuselage, above the wing trailing edge. The lever is provided to release the flap uplock and to open a bypass valve on the actuator, allowing the flaps to be pushed down manually to 50 degrees, enabling the pilot to reach the steps. If the engine is running when the lever is pulled, the flaps will lower hydraulically to 37 1/2 degrees, but must be manually pushed down to 50 degrees (with the lever still held out). When the lever is released, the flaps will return to 37 1/2 degrees if hydraulic pressure is available; the steps should not be used unless the flap is fully extended to 50 degrees. Lowering the flaps from the outside also moves the FLAP handles in the cockpits.

FLAP POSITION INDICATORS

A flap position indicator (40, figure 1-4), calibrated in degrees, is located on the instrument panel in each cockpit. Normal hydraulic flap travel is 37 1/2 degrees to the full down position. The flaps can be lowered manually to 50 degrees on the ground for access to the steps in the flaps. The flap position indicators are d-c powered from the secondary bus.

SPEED BRAKE

The hydraulically operated speed brake (figure 1-13) is essentially an additional flight control which is useful for making descents or moderate deceleration from high speeds. The brake can be opened at any airspeed up to maximum and, although brake opening causes a nose-up pitch, the forward stick pressure necessary to maintain the desired aircraft attitude is moderate up to 250 knots IAS. Above 250 knots, speed brake extension causes a nose-up pitch which requires large initial stick pressures to maintain a constant dive attitude. This stick pressure can be trimmed out at all speeds by adjustment of the elevator tab. Because of this excessive nose-up pitch, speed brakes should not be extended at the initiation of or during a high-speed pullout. Speed brakes should be extended prior to entering high-speed dives. Failure to observe these precautions may result in overstress during a pullout. Closing the brake, of course, causes a nose-down pitch. A limiter valve is incorporated in the speed brake hydraulic system to reduce the violence of the nose-up pitch and preclude possible overstress when the speed brake is opened at high airspeeds.

Changed 15 June 1970

SPEED BRAKE

T-28C-1-39-1

Figure 1-13

This valve reduces the pressure of the hydraulic fluid to the speed brake actuating cylinders and automatically allows the speed brake to extend to variable openings, dependent upon airspeed. Variable opening positions are maintained until the airspeed is reduced sufficiently to allow the limiter valve to overcome the force created by aerodynamic pressure and to fully open the speed brake. Conversely, if the speed brake is fully extended and high airspeed is attained, the limiter valve will automatically adjust degree of opening until airspeed has been reduced. The speed brake will then fully extend. When the speed brake is in use, the pilot has not positive control over the limiter valve other than airspeed control. Stick pressure to maintain a constant dive angle can be trimmed out at all speeds by adjustment of the elevator tab. When closing the speed brake, the limiter valve has no function in the system and the normal nose-down pitch will be experienced.

SPEED BRAKE SWITCHES

A speed brake switch (figure 1-6) is located on top of the throttle grip in each cockpit. The speed brake can be operated by the pilot who last actuated his control shift switch. The speed brake switch has only two fixed positions, OFF and ON, and no intermediate positions can be selected. When the switch is moved to ON, it energizes the speed brake selector valve, electrically closes the solenoid bypass valve, and pressurizes the hydraulic system. The hydraulic system remains pressurized as long as the brake is open. In event of an electrical failure while the speed brake is open, the speed brake automatically closes to a trail position, depending on airspeed. Should hydraulic failure occur while the brake is open, the brake will stay open until the speed brake switch is moved to OFF; air loads will then close the brake to a trail position.

CAUTION

Do not operate speed brake while the baggage compartment door is open. With the baggage compartment door open, the aft edge of the speed brake will not clear the baggage compartment door.

LANDING GEAR

The retractable tricycle landing gear is hydraulically operated. The main gear retracts inboard into the wing and fuselage; the nose gear retracts aft into the fuselage. Mechanically operated fairing doors cover the wheels in the retracted position. All fairing doors remain open when the gear is down. The gear is held up by mechanical locks and held down by overcenter side brace lockpins on each gear and by hydraulic pressure. The lockpins will hold the gear down should the hydraulic system fail. All uplocks are released by initial movement of the landing gear handle; consequently, in event of hydraulic failure, the gear can be unlocked by the gear handle. Once released, the main gear extends by its own weight, and the nose gear is extended fully by a spring bungee. A solenoid-operated downlock in the landing gear control system prevents inadvertent gear retraction when the aircraft is on the ground. Any landing gear position other than up and locked deenergizes the solenoid bypass valve and causes the hydraulic system to be pressurized. The full-swiveling nose wheel is equipped with a shimmy damper and automatic airborne centering. Brakes on the main wheels are used for directional control until the rudder becomes effective. A fixed tail skid is installed under the aft section of the fuselage.

LANDING GEAR CONTROLS AND INDICATORS

LANDING GEAR HANDLES

The landing gear handles (10, figure 1-3) are located at the left of the instrument panel in each cockpit. Moving either handle to UP or DOWN operates the gear selector valve, deenergizes the bypass valve which pressurizes the hydraulic system, and mechanically positions the gear uplocks. When the aircraft is on the ground, a solenoid-operated downlock (deenergized) prevents normal movement of the gear handles out of the DOWN position. The lock is automatically disengaged (electrically energized) when the aircraft is airborne. If an emergency requires gear retraction on the ground, pulling either handle up very sharply to UP overrides the solenoid-operated lock. In the event of hydraulic failure in flight, the gear can be lowered by moving the gear handle to DOWN, which mechanically releases the uplocks, allowing the main gear to drop. It may be necessary to yaw the aircraft to lock the main gear down. The nose gear is forced down and locked against air load by a spring bungee. With normal hydraulic system operation, the landing gear retracts in approximately 4 to 6 seconds and extends in approximately 6 to 10 seconds. To lock the gear handle at full UP or DOWN, it must be placed firmly in its extreme position. Any time the landing gear is not locked in the position required by the gear handle, a red light in the gear handle illuminates. Refer to LANDING GEAR AND WHEELS WARNING LIGHTS, in this section. Because of the gear handle location in the down position, care must be taken to avoid a gear retraction by inadvertently striking the handle with the knee.

Note

With the engine windmilling, prop control lever at full DECREASE RPM, the hydraulic system will maintain 1500 pounds pressure and the gear can be retracted in approximately 7 seconds and extended in approximately 4 seconds.

LANDING GEAR POSITION INDICATORS

Position of the landing gear is shown by three individual indicators (3, figure 1-4), one for each gear, located on the instrument panel in each cockpit. Each indicator shows crosshatching if the related gear is in any unlocked condition and in the absence of electrical power. The

word UP appears if the gear is up and locked, and a wheel shows if the gear is down and locked. The indicators are d-c powered from the secondary bus.

Note

The landing gear position indicators may stick and not fully return to the crosshatched deenergized position when the electrical system is turned off. However, the indicators will return to normal operation immediately when the electrical system is energized.

GROUND SAFETY LOCKS

Landing gear ground safety lockpins are provided for insertion in the side brace of each of the three landing gear struts to prevent accidental retraction of the landing gear on the ground. The pins must be removed before flight or the gear will not retract.

LANDING GEAR AND WHEELS WARNING LIGHTS

Additional warning of unsafe gear position is provided by a red light incorporated in the landing gear control

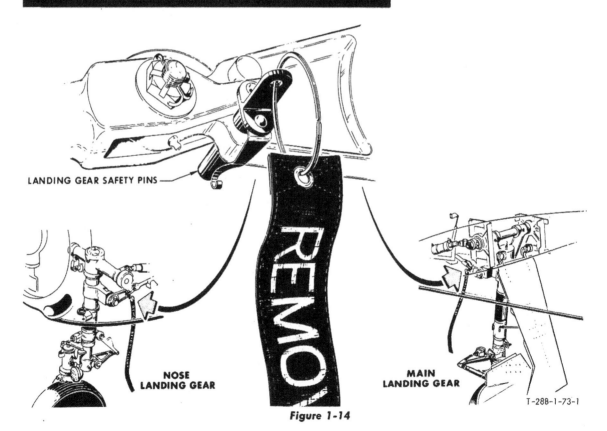

LANDING GEAR
GROUND SAFETY LOCKS

LANDING GEAR SAFETY PINS

REMO

NOSE
LANDING GEAR

MAIN
LANDING GEAR

T-28-1-73-1

Figure 1-14

handle and a flashing WHEELS warning light located at the top left corner of each instrument panel (5, figure 1-4). The WHEELS light will illuminate and flash whenever the throttle is retarded below approximate minimum cruise setting, with the flaps in any position other than fully retracted, and the landing gear not locked down. The WHEELS light will also provide a warning indication with the flaps fully retracted if the propeller control lever is at or above the 2500 rpm position. On aircraft equipped with the gear warning horn, the horn will be actuated when the throttle is retarded to approximately 15 inches MAP, regardless of flap position, if the landing gear is not down and locked. A horn silencer button is available and is located at the base of the throttle quadrant (figure 1-3). Both warning systems are d-c powered through the primary bus.

CAUTION

Some aircraft do not have the 2500 rpm propeller control lever switch installed. In these aircraft, when practicing no flap landings, the warning lights will not flash (flaps full up) and the only unsafe landing gear indication will be the position indicator and the warning light in the landing gear handle.

GEAR EXTERIOR POSITION LIGHTS

To aid in determining landing gear position from the ground at night, a white light is installed on each gear strut. Each light illuminates only when the related gear is down and locked and the EXT MASTER lights switch is turned ON.

ARRESTING HOOK (T-28C)

An arresting hook is installed on T-28C aircraft only. The hook is extended by bungee pressure and gravity and is retracted by hydraulic pressure. The hook can be lowered under most emergency conditions, as the uplock is mechanically connected to the control handle and the bungee action is positive and independent of any other system. If a hydraulic failure occurs and it is necessary to retract the hook, this can be attempted by placing the control lever in the UP position and operating the hand-pump. If there is hydraulic fluid in the reservoir and the hook retract system is intact, the hook should retract. An electrical failure will not affect hook operation in any way except for the unsafe indicator lights.

ARRESTING HOOK HANDLES

An arresting hook handle (18, figure 1-4) is located to the right side of each instrument panel, and is interconnected between cockpits. The handle has the shape of an arresting hook for identification by feel. The handle has two positions marked UP and DOWN, and movement of the handle is in a vertical plane.

ARRESTING HOOK UNSAFE LIGHTS

The arresting hook unsafe light, incorporated in the hook handles, receives power from the primary d-c bus. Only a complete electrical failure renders the light inop-

erative. The lights will illuminate whenever the hook is in any position other than full down or locked up.

When the hook is moving from one position to the other, the light will be on.

CAUTION

If the light does not go out when hook travel is completed, do not attempt an arrested landing until hook is visually checked for a safe condition.

WHEEL BRAKES

The main wheel brakes are of the manual, hydraulic, master cylinder type, operated by toe pressure on the rudder pedals. No boost is supplied by the aircraft hydraulic system, but fluid from the hydraulic system reservoir supplies the master cylinders. Should all fluid be lost from the reservoir, adequate fluid remains in the standpipe and lines to supply the brakes for normal operation. No emergency method of operating the brakes is provided. A parking brake handle (24, figure 1-4) is installed in the front cockpit only, to the right of the instrument panel. Parking brakes are set by depressing the pedals, rotating the parking brake handle, and then releasing pedal pressure. Brakes are subsequently released by depressing the pedals (front cockpit only).

STALL WARNING SYSTEM (T-28C)

The aircraft displays very little aerodynamic buffet prior to stall in the power approach and waveoff configurations; therefore, a mechanical stall warning device is incorporated to warn of impending stall approximately 7 or 8 knots above actual stall speed. This system consists of a transducer mounted on the right wing leading edge, a lift computer located in the nose wheel well, a rudder pedal shaker on the right rudder pedal in each cockpit, a landing gear switch on the right main gear strut, and a test switch on the left forward console in the front cockpit. The stall warning system functions on the principle that as aircraft angle of attack changes, so does the pressure distribution on the wing. The transducer is located so that just prior to the stall it senses the change of pressure and actuates the circuit to the rudder pedal shakers. The lift computer balances the circuit to maintain the margin of stall warning within the range between 105 and 115 percent of stall speed. Whenever the weight of the aircraft is on the landing gear, the switch on the right gear strut disrupts the circuit to make the pedal shakers inoperative. Operating the test switch on the left forward console will bypass the ground safety circuit and the pedal shakers will operate for a preflight check. The transducer is electrically heated when the pitot heater switch is ON.

INSTRUMENTS

All instruments are duplicated in both cockpits, with the exception of a free air temperature indicator and a magnetic compass, which are installed in the front cockpit only. For description of instruments that are a part of a particular system, refer to the applicable system.

PITOT-STATIC SYSTEM

The airspeed indicator, altimeter, and vertical speed indicator are operated by the pitot-static system. This system measures the difference between impact air pressure entering the pitot tube, mounted on the right wing, and static air pressure obtained at static ports on each side of the fuselage, aft of the wings. The airspeed indicator is connected to the pressure and static sides of the system. The altimeter and vertical speed indicator are connected to the static ports. Whenever the aircraft is parked, a cover must be placed over the pitot head to keep the pressure tube opening clean.

Note

The static ports on early aircraft* are located forward of those on later aircraft.† Differences in airspeed position error are covered in Section XI.

AIRSPEED INDICATORS

The airspeed indicators (9, figure 1-4) are calibrated from 40 to 400 knots. Graduations on the scale are provided logarithmically.

ALTIMETERS

A conventional three-pointer altimeter (8, figure 1-4), is installed on both instrument panels. A notched disk moves to expose warning stripes to give visual warning when altitudes under 16,000 feet are entered.

VERTICAL SPEED INDICATORS

A vertical speed indicator (14, figure 1-4) is installed on each instrument panel.

ACCELEROMETERS

A standard three-pointer accelerometer (34, figure 1-4) is installed on both instrument panels to indicate positive and negative accelerations. In addition to the indicating pointer, there are two recording pointers (one for positive g-loads and one for negative g-loads) which follow the indicating pointer to its maximum attained travel, and remain at the maximum travel positions reached by the indicating pointer. Pressing the button on the instrument returns the recording pointers to the normal (1-g) position.

STATIC PRESSURE SOURCE

T-28B AIRCRAFT, 137638
THROUGH 138189

T-28B AIRCRAFT 138190 AND
SUBSEQUENT AND ALL
T-28C AIRCRAFT

T-28B-1-51-2A

Figure 1-15

ATTITUDE INDICATORS

An MB-1 (H-6A) attitude indicator (13, figure 1-4) is installed on both instrument panels. The MB-1 gyro has a pitch scale that indicates pitch attitude within a range from 5 to 80 degrees in climb and dive. The instrument provides visual indications of dive, climb, and angle of bank, and it operates on alternating current supplied by either the main or standby inverter. The gyro is enclosed in a sphere, a portion of which is visible through the opening on the face of the instrument. Whenever the aircraft approaches a vertical climb or dive, as it would in a loop, the gyro precesses a controlled 180 degrees; this action is momentary and does not interfere with the indications. Thus, the pilot reads the same face of the sphere regardless of attitude. A manual caging device on the gyro horizon indicator provides quick erection for minimizing ground operation and for correcting characteristic in-flight turn errors. Because of acceleration forces which act upon the erection mechanism during turns, up to 5-degree errors may be noted in pitch and/or bank upon return to straight-and-level flight. The indicator begins to correct this lag immediately but manual caging may be used for quick erection. If errors greater than the 5-degree allowable tolerance are encountered, the instrument should be replaced. The indicator contains a power warning flag that is visible whenever the power supply is shut off, there is an improper phase rotation, or an open or short circuit in the instrument.

*T-28B aircraft 137638 through 137810 and 138103 through 138189
†T-28B aircraft 138190 and subsequent and all T-28C aircraft

The flag will disappear under normal circumstances indicating that the power supply is on and is satisfactory.

The pilot should not rely upon the indicator if the power warning flag is visible in the face of the instrument.

CAGING KNOB

Drawing the PULL TO CAGE knob smoothly away from the face of the instrument manually cages the gyro. A momentary stop is felt when the bank caging mechanism is engaged, and as the cage is pulled further, the pitch caging mechanism engages. As soon as the knob reaches the limit of its travel, it should be immediately released to uncage the gyro. Further travel or gyro precession indicates that the caging mechanism is not releasing properly or that the erection mechanism is not functioning properly.

STANDBY COMPASS

A standby magnetic compass is installed beneath the canopy bow to the left of the rearview mirror. A secondary-bus-powered switch on the right console switch panel (figure 1-7) controls standby compass lighting. The compass correction card is mounted on a spring-loaded overcenter hinged bracket on the forward side of the rearview mirror. When the card is not in use, it folds out of sight behind the mirror.

TURN-AND-BANK INDICATORS

The conventional turn-and-bank indicators (12, figure 1-4) are powered by the primary bus.

FREE AIR TEMPERATURE INDICATOR

The free air temperature indicator (20, figure 1-4) is installed in the front cockpit only, on the right side below the instrument panel shroud. This direct-reading indicator is calibrated to read from −50° to 50°C.

CLOCKS

The standard 8-day clocks (37, figure 1-4) incorporate a sweep second hand.

RADIO MAGNETIC INDICATORS

Refer to NAVIGATION INSTRUMENTS, in this section.

COURSE INDICATORS

Refer to NAVIGATION INSTRUMENTS, in this section.

SLAVED COMPASS SYSTEM

The S-2 compass system is normally slaved by a flux valve. The indications for compass headings are read from the rotating dial of the radio magnetic indicator. This section of the RMI can also be manually slaved or can operate as a free gyro compass. Compass readings of the instrument are indicated by the pointer at the top of the face. For operation in high latitudes, where the earth's magnetic fields converge rapidly or for areas of high magnetic disturbance, the system is provided with a gyro selector switch to disconnect the slaving action of the flux valve from the gyro. With the compass operating as a free gyro compass, the gyro spin axis will, in time, deviate from the magnetic north. To realign the spin axis, the system is provided with a manual slaving switch and a null indicating meter. Transfer of control between cockpits is accomplished by the VHF NAV-GYRO COMP control shift switch on the right console.

COMPASS CONTROLS AND INDICATORS

GYRO SELECTOR SWITCH

The gyro selector switch, located on the compass controller panel (figure 1-16) on the aft right console in each cockpit, controls the free-gyro feature of the compass. When the switch is at SLAVED GYRO, the compass is slaved by the flux gate valve system. Moving the switch to FREE GYRO electrically disconnects the slaving action of the flux valve and the compass operates on free gyro. For high-latitude operation (above 60 degrees), the gyro selector switch should be set at FREE GYRO.

MANUAL SLAVING KNOB

The spring-loaded manual slaving knob is located on the compass controller panel (figure 1-16) adjacent to the gyro selector switch. To rapidly precess the compass

COMPASS CONTROLLER PANEL

T-28B-1-72-1

Figure 1-16

to a new heading, the manual slaving knob should be momentarily held at either INC or DEC. If the null indicating meter indicates a "−" deflection, the manual slaving knob should be momentarily rotated to INC to zero the needle.

NULL METER

Any drift of the gyro spin axis after alignment is indicated on the null indicating meter. The null indicating meter, marked SYNC SIGNAL, is located on the compass controller panel (figure 1-16) on the right console in each cockpit. Normally, the needle is centered and any drifting is corrected by the flux valve. Should the needle indicate sustained "+" or "−" deflections, the gyro spin axis has precessed from magnetic north and the manual slaving knob should be used to correct it.

ANNUNCIATORS

The compass annunciator (11, figure 1-4), located at the top of the instrument panel in each cockpit, shows the words FREE or SLAVE as determined by the operating mode of the compass system. Crosshatching appears when power is off and the system is inoperative.

CARRIER-FIELD SWITCH (T-28C)

The carrier-field switch is located in the fuselage aft of the cockpit and is accessible only through the baggage compartment. The switch is normally lockwired in the FIELD position. With the switch in FIELD, the ground safety feature for the compass is bypassed and compass free or slaved mode selection is controlled by the position of the gyro selector switch regardless of the weight-on-gear conditions. When the switch is in the CARRIER position, the flux valve is automatically disengaged when the weight of the aircraft is on the landing gear and the free-gyro feature is in operation.

EMERGENCY EQUIPMENT

FIRST-AID KIT

A first-aid kit, installed between the cockpits, is mounted on top of the shroud over the rear cockpit instrument panel.

CANOPY

The canopy is divided into two sections, one for each cockpit, which move simultaneously. Normally, the canopy is operated hydraulically, but it may also be operated manually and, in an emergency, pneumatically. Mechanical locks automatically hold the canopy closed or full open and a hydraulic fluid lock is maintained to hold it in any selected intermediate position. The canopy can be operated during flight at any speed. The canopy is operable from either cockpit and externally from the left side of the fuselage by interconnected controls. The

external handle simultaneously moves the internal handles but is disconnected from the internal handles when in the stowed position. An external handle is provided on the lower frame of the aft section for moving the canopy manually.

CANOPY CONTROL HANDLES

Normal or emergency operation of the canopy is controlled by means of a canopy control handle containing an actuating button (figure 1-17) at the left side of each cockpit. Positions for each handle are EMERG OPEN, OPEN, LOCKED, CLOSED, and MANUAL. For normal hydraulic operation, the canopy handle must be moved to the desired operating position, OPEN or CLOSED, and the canopy handle button depressed. Moving the handle without depressing the button, except to the EMERG OPEN or MANUAL position, does not cause the canopy to move. When operated hydraulically, the canopy opens in approximately 3 seconds and closes in approximately 6 to 10 seconds. The canopy handle must be in the LOCKED position to hold the canopy partially open. Normal opening or closing of the canopy from the inside, without the engine running, can be accomplished as follows: Place DC POWER switch at BAT. ONLY and position the canopy handle as desired; then depress the canopy handle button while the hydraulic handpump is operated. The canopy can be operated manually when the canopy handle is moved to MANUAL to allow hydraulic fluid in the cylinder to be bypassed. In an emergency, pulling the canopy handle all the way back to the EMERG OPEN position opens the canopy fully in $1/2$ to $3/4$ second. The canopy handle button does not have to be depressed to actuate the system pneumatically in the EMERG OPEN position, although it is necessary to forcibly move the

CANOPY CONTROL

Figure 1-17

handle through a stop which normally prevents inadvertent operation of the emergency system. When the handle is moved to EMERG OPEN, air pressure from an air bottle is supplied to the canopy actuating cylinder through separate lines. To bleed the air overboard from the emergency system after pneumatic operation, the canopy handle is moved to OPEN (without pressing the canopy handle button) and left at OPEN for 30 to 45 seconds. Then operating the canopy through several complete cycles from closed to open will bleed any air from the normal canopy hydraulic system.

WARNING

After an emergency air opening, the canopy should not be closed until the system has been bled. If the canopy has been closed without this precaution, a subsequent emergency opening may be violent enough to damage the aircraft or cause injury to personnel in the canopy path.

Note

When locking the canopy after closing, if the locked position is inadvertently passed, move the handle to the closed detent and press the button. This will close the canopy tightly. Then release the button and carefully move the handle to the locked position. If this procedure is not followed when the handle is pushed past the locked detent toward the open detent, the canopy may open enough to admit exhaust fumes into the cockpit. In those cases where the canopy has a tendency to creep back ($1/4$ to $3/8$ inch), it is recommended that the control handle be moved to the CLOSED position and left there for flights with the canopy shut and that the LOCKED position be used for intermediate open settings. By following this procedure, hydraulic pressure will remain trapped in the system and provide a tightly closed canopy, thus eliminating the possibility of fumes entering the cockpit.

CANOPY HANDLE BUTTONS

A canopy handle button, on the forward face of the canopy handle in each cockpit, deenergizes the hydraulic system bypass valve and energizes the canopy system shutoff valve when depressed. This permits hydraulic pressure to enter the canopy system and open or close the canopy (canopy handle at OPEN or CLOSED). Depressing the button in flight deenergizes the hydraulic system bypass valve, permitting the hydraulic system to become pressurized. (Due to the extended landing gear, the system is always pressurized on the ground with engine running.) Releasing the button stops movement of the canopy by closing the canopy shutoff valve.

When the hydraulic handpump is used to pressurize the canopy system, the button must be held depressed to maintain the canopy shutoff valve in the open position. It is unnecessary to depress the button when the canopy handle is moved to the EMERG OPEN or MANUAL position.

CANOPY EXTERNAL HANDLE

A canopy external handle is provided on the left side of the fuselage above the wing trailing edge. Movement of the external handle accomplishes the same function as the internal handles for manual or emergency operation. (The canopy cannot be operated hydraulically by means of the external handle.) Pulling the canopy external handle out from the stowed position allows the handle to be turned forward to MANUAL for manual operation or aft to EMERG for pneumatic emergency canopy opening.

WARNING

When preparing to open the canopy by use of the external canopy handle, extreme caution should be exercised. To prevent accidental pneumatic emergency opening of the canopy, pull the handle full out before rotating it forward to the MANUAL position. Release the handle flush against the fuselage prior to returning it to the stowed position. If the external canopy handle is pulled only part way out and moved forward toward the MANUAL position, it can be rotated beyond the operating limit of the cockpit control handle. Then, if the overextended external handle is held out (engaged) during its return to the stowed position, the action will be duplicated by the internal (cockpit) control handle. As a result, the cockpit handle will be forced into the EMERG OPEN position, causing discharge of the pneumatic emergency canopy opening system. Accidental pneumatic emergency opening of the canopy through improper operation can result in injury to personnel in the canopy path or damage to the aircraft.

CANOPY MANUAL HANDLE

A canopy manual handle is provided on the lower frame of the aft canopy for externally moving the canopy manually.

CANOPY EMERGENCY STOP BUTTONS

A canopy emergency stop button (2, figure 1-4) is provided on the left side of the instrument panel shroud in each cockpit. This button is used in the event it is necessary to override the canopy handle (and button) and stop hydraulically operated movement. Pressing and *holding* either button while the canopy is moving closes the shutoff valve, thus disrupting the flow of hydraulic fluid to the actuating cylinder and stopping the canopy immediately. Canopy operation continues normally when the button is released.

CANOPY EMERGENCY AIR PRESSURE GAGE

A canopy emergency air pressure gage is located in the baggage compartment. For pressure requirements and servicing the canopy pneumatic system, refer to Section I, Part 3.

SEATS

The seats can be manually adjusted for height by means of a lever located at the right side of each seat. The seat is spring-loaded to the up position and has a vertical travel of approximately 7 inches. When the lever is pulled back, the pilot is assisted in raising the seat by the spring action. As the seat is raised, it will also move forward. A seat cushion is provided for each seat when a seat-pack parachute is not worn.

SHOULDER-HARNESS INERTIA REEL AND LOCK

An inerita reel for the shoulder harness is incorporated on the back of each seat. The lock handle for control of the reel is located on the left side of each seat. Fore and aft movement of the handle unlocks or locks the reel. A detent in the quadrant is provided to retain the handle in either selected position. In addition to manual locking, the reel automatically locks by inertia when the aircraft is subjected to a 2- to 3-g forward acceleration as in a crash landing. Consequently, it is necessary to manually lock the harness only during maneuvers and flight in rough air, or as an added safety precaution during take-off and landing.

Note

Manually pulling the shoulder straps out from the reel will not exert enough energy to serve as a check of the automatic locking feature of the reel.

If the harness is locked while the pilot is leaning forward, the harness will retract with him, moving into successive locked positions as he moves back against the seat. In order to unlock the harness, the tension must be removed from the reel. Therefore, if the harness is manually locked while the pilot is leaning back hard against the seat, he may not be able to unlock the harness without first releasing it momentarily at the safety belt or at the harness adjustment buckles. After the harness is automatically locked, it will remain locked until the locking lever is moved to the LOCKED position and then back to the UNLOCKED position. The

inertia reel is a self-contained unit and requires no power.

COCKPIT HEATING AND VENTILATING SYSTEM

AIR SOURCE

Air for heating and ventilating both cockpits is obtained from the oil cooler air duct just forward of the engine oil cooler. See figure 1-20.

COCKPIT HEATER

The combustion-type cockpit heater supplies heat by burning a fuel-air mixture. Heat produced is used for cockpit heat and for windshield and canopy defrosting. Fuel for heater operation is obtained from the carburetor through a cycling shutoff valve, and combustion air is taken in through an inlet in the left wing leading edge. The heater will not operate unless airflow is sufficient to provide combustion in the heater. Heaters in some aircraft* will operate up to approximately 25,000 feet altitude, while the heaters in later aircraft† provide satisfactory operation above 25,000 feet altitude. The heater cycles on and off as necessary to maintain the temperature selected in the cockpit. Should overheat occur (outlet temperature above 375°F), the heater electrical circuits and fuel supply will be turned off automatically. If automatic shutdown occurs, the heater should not be restarted until the cause of overheating has been determined. There are no provisions for emergency operation of the heating and ventilating system. The cockpit heating system is d-c powered from the monitored bus.

COCKPIT HEATER CONTROL HANDLE

Operation of the cockpit heater is controlled by a heater control handle (15, figure 1-3 and figure 1-18), located forward of the throttle quadrant in the front cockpit. To start the heater, open the cockpit air control handle and turn the heater control handle from OFF to ON. Heat output is increased by continued (clockwise) rotation of the handle.

COCKPIT AIR CONTROL HANDLES

A cockpit air control handle (1, figure 1-3 and figure 1-19) is located on the left console in each cockpit. The cockpit air control handles are interconnected. Control positions are EMERG. OFF, CLOSED, and OPEN. Moving either handle toward OPEN positions the system shutoff valve to increase the flow of hot or cold air to the air outlets and defrosting system in both cockpits. Turning either handle to CLOSED permits a small amount of air

*T-28B aircraft 137638 through 137792
†T-28B aircraft 137793 and subsequent and T-28C aircraft

LEFT FORWARD CONSOLE

T-28B-200-53-844C

Figure 1-18

to enter the cockpit for ventilation. When either handle is turned to EMERG. OFF, the heater electrical system is deenergized and the system shutoff valves are closed.

AIR OUTLETS

Manually controlled air outlets (2, figure 1-3 and 1, figure 1-5) are located on each side of both cockpits at waist level. Both outlets can be adjusted for desired volume of air and direction of airflow. Floor level air outlets are also provided in both cockpits. Airflow from the floor outlets in the front cockpit is controlled by the position of the cockpit air control handle. The rear cockpit floor air is controlled by a foot-operated valve on the outlet.

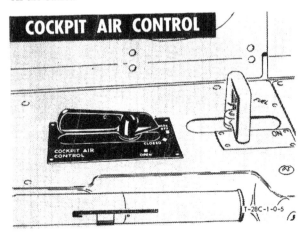

T-28C-1-0-5

Figure 1-19

COCKPIT HEATER OPERATION

Proper fuel-air ratios are necessary to obtain reliable operation of a heater of this type. To supply exactly the correct fuel-air ratio for all conditions of flight would require a carburetor or similar device. To avoid this complication, the heater fuel nozzle is a fixed size and the combustion air duct is designed to provide airflow that will give an acceptable fuel-air ratio at any flight condition expected in normal service. This arrangement somewhat compromises heater efficiency but provides a simple installation. Factors affecting airflow, such as altitude, airspeed, and outside air temperature, will affect heater operation. High speed at low altitude on a cold day may cause a very lean fuel-air ratio because of the high airflow. Conversely, very rich fuel-air ratios may occur at high altitude and low airspeed on a warm day. Either of these extremes may cause the heater to go out.

During a rapid descent or dive from high altitude, the windshield and canopy will fog if the necessary conditions of low temperature and high humidity occur. To prevent this, the cockpit heater control handle should be turned to full INC. TEMP, windshield and canopy defrost control handle turned ON, and the cockpit air control handle turned to OPEN several minutes before a descent or dive is started.

COCKPIT HEATER PROCEDURE

Before the heater can be started on the ground, the engine must be running above 1300 rpm to provide sufficient airflow for combustion and to actuate a ram-air pressure switch for starting and operating.

To obtain cockpit heat, open the cockpit air control handle and turn heater control handle to ON. The heater will begin operation within a few seconds and will maintain the temperature selected. For ground operation of the heater, maintain engine speed of at least 1000 rpm. To increase heat, rotate heater control clockwise toward the INC. TEMP position. For cockpit ventilation, open cockpit air control handle for desired volume of air and adjust cockpit outlets as necessary. If additional ventilation is required, turn windshield and canopy defrost handle to ON.

Heater Malfunctions

The first indication of a heater malfunction will be lack of heat. The heater may start itself again with no action by the pilot. However, it is good practice to turn the cockpit heater control handle OFF as soon as a heater failure is noted. Check the heater circuit breaker in. Wait a few minutes; then return the cockpit heater control handle ON. If the heater still will not start, reduce airspeed if flying at low altitude, or increase airspeed at high altitude. If the heater will not start after several attempts, turn the cockpit heater control handle to OFF and report the malfunction to the ground crew after landing.

When the heater goes out and cockpit heater control handle is left on, fuel fumes may be noted in the cockpit. If this occurs, turn the cockpit heater control

HEATING, VENTILATING, AND DEFROSTING SYSTEM

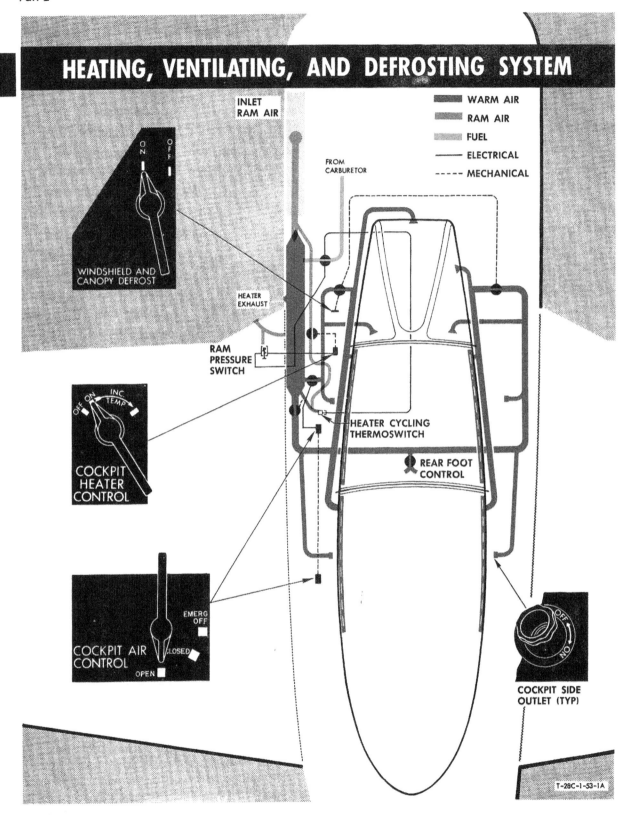

Figure 1-20

handle OFF and allow the fumes to clear before attempting to restart the heater. If the fuel fumes persist after the cockpit heater control handle is turned OFF, the heater is probably not at fault and the aircraft should be landed as soon as possible.

With the cockpit air control handle in the CLOSED position, a valve in the cockpit air supply duct is partially closed and a limited quantity of air is supplied to the cockpits. If the side air outlets in both cockpits and the foot outlets in the rear cockpit are closed, the air is directed into the front cockpit through the foot air outlets. Turning the cockpit air control handle to EMERG. OFF closes the air valves completely and no air is supplied. With this condition, carbon monoxide may accumulate in the cockpit. For this reason, the cockpit air control handle should not be placed in the EMERG. OFF position unless an emergency exists. When it is necessary to turn the cockpit air control handle to EMERG. OFF, an oxygen mask should be worn and 100% oxygen used.

DEFROSTING SYSTEM

Air for defrosting the windshield and canopy is obtained from the same source as cockpit heating and ventilating air. The cockpit air control handle must be open to supply air to the defrosting system and, if necessary, the cockpit heater control handle can be turned ON to heat the air. The defrosting system can be used with the cockpit heating and ventilating system, or heating and ventilating air outlets may be closed to direct most of the air to the defrosting system. There are no provisions for emergency operation of the defrosting system.

WINDSHIELD AND CANOPY DEFROST HANDLE

The windshield and canopy defrost handle (12, figure 1-3) is located on the left instrument subpanel in the front cockpit only. Turning the handle ON directs air (hot air if the cockpit heater control handle is ON, cold air if the cockpit heater control handle is OFF) to outlets at each side of the windshield and canopy.

Note

The cockpit heater control handle must be turned ON to heat the air before descent to prevent frost or fog on the windshield or canopy.

PITOT HEATER

The pitot tube is electrically heated to prevent erroneous pitot-static instrument readings due to icing.

PITOT HEATER SWITCH

The pitot heater switch (figure 1-7) is located on the right console switch panel in the front cockpit only.

CAUTION

To prevent burning out heater elements, the pitot heater switch should be OFF when the aircraft is on the ground.

ELECTRONIC SYSTEMS

The aircraft is equipped with radio communications and navigation systems as described in the following table of electronic equipment. Location of controls and actual equipment installed may vary between using commands, and will differ depending upon compliance with current Airframe and Avionics Changes. The equipment described should be considered "typical" for aircraft now being used by fleet operating activities.

TYPE	DESIGNATION	USE	RANGE
Interphone	NAA 10027-105 or NAA 60001-105	Intercockpit communication	
Radio compass*	AN/ARN-6	Position finding, homing, reception of voice and code communication	50 to 100 miles for range signals, 100 to 250 miles for broadcast signals
Marker beacon	AN/ARN-12	Reception of fan marker signal	
VOR*	AN/ARN-14E	Reception of VHF omni-range and voice facilities. Visual and aural navigation aid	30 miles at 1000 feet, 135 miles at 10,000 feet (line of sight)
TACAN†	AN/ARN-21	Reception of UHF TACAN beacon bearing and distance	Distance and bearing up to 195 miles (line of sight)
UHF communication	AN/ARC-27 or AN/ARC-27A	Two-way communication	30 miles at 1000 feet, 135 miles at 10,000 feet (line of sight)
LF range receiver	AN/ARC-5	Reception of range signals and voice	50 to 100 miles
Direction finder	AN/ARA-25	UHF homing, direction finding through AN/ARC-27	Same as AN/ARC-27

*Provisions or installation in some aircraft
†T-28C aircraft 140584 and subsequent and aircraft having all phases of ASC 20 incorporated (AN/ARN-6 ADF is not installed in these aircraft)

INTERCOMMUNICATIONS SYSTEM (ICS)

The ICS provides intercockpit communications through use of the CALL button on the throttle grips. The ICS control panels in early T-28B aircraft* do not incorporate an ICS VOL knob as found in subsequent T-28B and T-28C aircraft.

ICS CONTROLS

An ICS control panel is installed on the right console in both cockpits (2, figure 1-21).

Mixer Switches

Six ICS mixer switches (1, figure 1-21) are installed forward of the ICS control panels. Incoming signals from the various electronic systems may be selected for monitor (forward position) or turned off (aft position). These switches select ICS mixing as follows:

MIXER SWITCH	AUDIO CONTROLLED
LF RANGE	AN/ARC-5 (if installed)
ADF RANGE	AN/ARN-6 (if installed)
LF VOICE	AN/ARC-5 (if installed)
ADF VOICE	AN/ARN-6 (if installed)
VHF NAV	TACAN or VOR (as installed)
MARKER	AN/ARN-12

ICS/UHF Switch

The ICS/UHF switch (2, figure 1-21) allows the pilot to select ICS operation as desired. The switch normally rests at UHF, and must be held manually in ICS if used. The CALL buttons on the throttle grips may be used for the same purpose as desired. With either the switch or button actuated, continuous two-way (hot) communication capability is provided.

RADIO VOL Knob

The RADIO VOL knob (2, figure 1-21) is used to adjust audio volume of all receivers selected through the ICS mixer switches.

ICS VOL Knobs†

The ICS VOL knob (2, figure 1-21) may be used to adjust volume of received intercom audio as desired.

NORM/ALTR Switch

The NORM/ALTR switch (2, figure 1-21), which is normally left at NORM, allows selection of intercommunication through the AN/ARC-27 UHF communication set sidetone. Should intercockpit communications fail, selecting ALTR will route UHF sidetone directly to the headsets.

ICS OPERATION

Normal

1. DC POWER switch—BAT. & GEN. or BAT. ONLY, or external power on.
2. NORM/ALTR switch—NORM.
3. ICS mixer switches—as desired.
4. ICS VOL knob—Adjust as desired.
5. CALL button—Depress and check ICS operation.
6. ICS/UHF switch—Hold in ICS and check operation.

Alternate

Should the ICS fail, intercockpit communication may be reestablished as follows:

1. NORM/ALTR switch—ALTR.
2. RADIO VOL knob—Increase as required.
3. MIKE button—Depress for UHF sidetone.

Note

If all mixing switches are off (aft), the signal audible in the headset should be that of the UHF COMM receiver. If any mixing switch is forward, the related signal will also be heard. In this case, volume control is ineffective, except when the NORM/ALTR switch on the receiving panel is in the NORM position. When transmitting while operating either the CALL button or while holding the ICS/UHF switch in the ICS position, the signal should be audible at both stations with equal volume. This volume can be controlled by the ICS VOL at the station operating in NORM position.

UHF COMMUNICATIONS SET, AN/ARC-27

The AN/ARC-27 radio provides two-way voice communications within a frequency range of 225.0 to 399.0 megacycles on 18 preset frequencies. The radio also has a guard frequency that can be monitored alone or with another selected frequency. The control panel has a mode switch, a preset channel selector, and an audio volume control. On some aircraft,‡ the front cockpit has a UHF control panel with manual tuning capabilities (5, figure 1-21). The manual selection of frequencies may be obtained without disturbing any of the preset frequencies. The radio is powered by the secondary d-c bus.

UHF COMMUNICATIONS CONTROLS

UHF COMMAND CONTROL SHIFT Switches

The UHF COMMAND CONTROL SHIFT switch (8, figure 1-21), when positioned so as to illuminate the associated COMMAND indicator light, allows the pilot in either

*T-28B aircraft 137638 through 138317
†T-28B 146002 and subsequent and T-28C aircraft
‡Aircraft having AFC 97 incorporated

COMMUNICATIONS AND NAVIGATION CONTROLS

(TYPICAL)

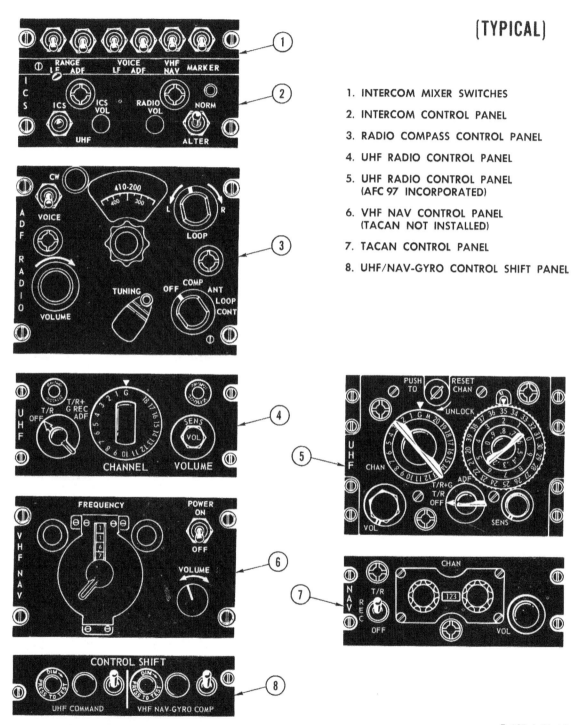

1. INTERCOM MIXER SWITCHES

2. INTERCOM CONTROL PANEL

3. RADIO COMPASS CONTROL PANEL

4. UHF RADIO CONTROL PANEL

5. UHF RADIO CONTROL PANEL
   (AFC 97 INCORPORATED)

6. VHF NAV CONTROL PANEL
   (TACAN NOT INSTALLED)

7. TACAN CONTROL PANEL

8. UHF/NAV-GYRO CONTROL SHIFT PANEL

T-28B-1-71-1D

Figure 1-21

cockpit to assume contr I of the AN/ARC-27 UHF communications set. The COMMAND light is on in the cockpit having control.

UHF COMM Control Panels

A UHF COMM control panel (4, figure 1-21) is installed on the right console in both cockpits. In some aircraft,* a UHF COMM control panel with manual tuning capabilities is installed in the front cockpit (5, figure 1-21). The panel contains a volume control, a vernier sensitivity control, function selector switch, channel selector switch, a manual tuning control, and a channel PUSH TO SET CHAN button. The volume control regulates the volume of incoming signals and the sensitivity control provides a vernier adjustment of the sensitivity. The channel selector switch has 20 channel positions, numbered 1 through 20, a G (guard) position, and an M (manual) position.

Mode Select Switch — The mode select switch has four positions, OFF, T/R, T/R + G REC, and ADF. The radio is turned on when the mode select switch is moved from OFF to any one of the other three positions. When the switch is at T/R, the radio operates on the frequency selected on the channel selector. With the switch at T/R + G REC, the radio operates on the selected frequency in addition to monitoring guard frequency. Moving the switch to ADF places the AN/ARA-25 direction finder in operation.

> **CAUTION**
>
> - If the mode select switch is moved from OFF to any other position, it must not be moved back to OFF within 10 seconds; otherwise, the radio will not have time to stabilize and a fuse may be blown.
> - If the mode select switch is moved to OFF, it must not be moved to any other position for 15 seconds. This allows the radio dynamotor to stop.

CHANNEL Knob — The CHANNEL knob has numbered positions 1 through 18, and a G position. Rotating the knob to any one of the numbered positions selects one of the 18 preset frequencies. The G position allows reception on guard frequency only. On some aircraft,* 1 through 20 preset frequencies are available with a G and an M position. The M position is provided for use of the manual frequency selection feature.

Manual Frequency Control* — The manual frequency control consists of three concentric dials that allow selection of any one of 1750 frequencies in the range from 225.0 to 399.9 megacycles. The outer dial is used to select the first two digits of the desired frequency, the center dial selects the third digit, and the inner dial selects the digit to the right of the decimal point. The channel selector knob must be placed at M before the selected frequency can be used.

> **CAUTION**
>
> Do not select frequencies below 225 megacycles because of possible damage to the equipment.

VOL Knob — The VOL knob controls the audio volume of the AN/ARC-27 receiver. Clockwise rotation of the knob increases the volume; counterclockwise rotation decreases the volume.

Sensitivity Control* — To ensure peak reception of UHF signals, the sensitivity control on the UHF control box should be set immediately below the point at which background noise occurs. This normally occurs with the SENS-knob index near the 1 o'clock position. If unable to create noise by a clockwise movement of this knob, or if unable to eliminate it by a counterclockwise movement, the internal sensitivity is not adjusted properly. The guard receiver has a separate sensitivity control which eliminates background noise on the guard receiver. The pilot has no control of this setting.

Push to Set CHAN Button* — The push to set CHAN button is provided to permit the pilot or ground crewman to change frequencies for the 20 channel positions. To accomplish this, increase the receiver sensitivity until there is noticeable background noise. Set the channel selector to the desired channel. Dial in the new frequency on the manual tuning control. Rotate the push to set CHAN button and depress it momentarily. Lift the press to set button to its original position and release. Upon completion of channeling, background noise should again be heard.

UHF COMMUNICATIONS OPERATION

1. UHF COMMAND CONTROL SHIFT switch—CONTROL SHIFT light on.

2. Mode select switch—T/R or T/R + G REC. T/R + G allows monitoring of an added independent re-receiver preset to a frequency that is guarded continuously.

3. Rotate CHAN knob to desired position. Reception and transmission will be on the frequency preset for that channel.

*Aircraft having AFC 97 incorporated

4. On aircraft with a manual frequency capability, if manual frequency selection is desired, place CHAN knob on preset frequency, set desired frequency manually, then move CHAN knob to M.

Note

Manual frequency selection with CHAN knob on M causes excessive cycling of cams and could damage the radio.

5. Adjust intercom volume with the ICS VOL knob and then adjust radio receiver volume with the UHF VOLUME knob.

Note

The UHF VOLUME knob should not be forced beyond its rotational travel, as intermittent or complete loss of UHF signal will result.

6. To transmit, depress MIKE button on throttle; to receive, release MIKE button.

7. To transmit on G channel, select G on CHAN knob and T/R on the MODE switch.

DIRECTION FINDER, AN/ARA-25

The direction finder, AN/ARA-25, indicates relative bearing, or homes on radio signals to facilities received by the AN/ARC-27 radio. Essentially, the AN/ARA-25

and AN/ARC-27 combine to form an automatic UHF radio compass. Direction finding information is displayed on the No. 1 pointer of the radio magnetic indicator. When the controls are properly positioned for the direction finding operation, ARA-25 will appear in the compass annunciator (11, figure 1-4), at the top of the instrument panel in each cockpit. The system is powered by the secondary d-c bus.

UHF/ADF OPERATION

To operate UHF ARA-25, move the UHF mode switch to ADF position and the No. 1 pointer will indicate the relative bearing to the originating station.

Note

UHF radio transmission during ADF operation is available when the MIKE button on the throttle is depressed. It is not necessary to move the UHF mode select switch from the ADF position.

RADIO COMPASS, AN/ARN-6

The radio compass system is a navigational aid which provides a visual indication of the direction to low-frequency transmitting facilities or commercial broadcasting stations for homing operations, and indicates bearing from a transmitting station for position-finding operations. When radio compass controls are properly positioned for ADF operation, the compass annunciator at the top of the instrument panel will read ARN-6. The system is powered by the secondary d-c bus.

Four separate frequency bands are available: 100 to 200 kilocycles, 200 to 410 kilocycles, 410 to 850 kilocycles, and 850 to 1750 kilocycles.

RADIO COMPASS CONTROLS

All controls for the AN/ARN-6 radio compass are located on the RADIO COMPASS control panel (3, figure 1-21) on the right console in both cockpits.

Function Knob

The radio compass function knob controls radio compass operation as follows:

POSITION	OPERATION
OFF	Secured
COMP	Automatic direction finding with No. 1 pointer of RMI

POSITION	OPERATION
ANT	Primary listen, tune, and voice monitor position
LOOP	Allows manual control of loop antenna for aural null operation and best listen during adverse conditions
CONT	Spring-loaded momentary position for taking or giving control of the system

Band Select Knob

The band select knob allows selection of any one of the previously described frequency bands for tuning.

TUNING Crank

The TUNING crank allows adjustment to desired frequency within the selected band.

VOLUME Knob

The VOLUME knob allows adjustment of audio signals received through the radio compass. A definite decrease in volume setting is usually required when COMP mode operation is selected, and an increase is required on selection of LOOP.

CW/VOICE Switch

The CW/VOICE switch allows selection of a beat frequency input (CW) or straight tone (unmodulated, or VOICE) input characteristics. CW/VOICE selection has no effect on COMP mode operation, and is used to effect aural null ambiguity and to identify certain types of radio beacon facilities not found within the United States. The CW position may also be used to aid in finely tuning radio compass frequency. Refer to RADIO COMPASS OPERATION, in this section.

LOOP Switch

The LOOP (L-R) switch allows manual rotation of the radio compass loop antenna with the mode knob in LOOP position only. The No. 1 pointer of the RMI can be considered oriented at 90 degrees to the plane of the loop antenna; therefore, the needle points to the selected station when the antenna detects no signal.

The loop is moved counterclockwise (left) or clockwise (right) with the LOOP switch.

RADIO COMPASS OPERATION

Automatic Direction Finding

1. Mixer switches—on (forward).

2. Move FUNCTION knob to LOOP and rotate No. 1 needle with LOOP switch. If needle does not move, switch FUNCTION knob to CONT position to gain control of radio. Then switch back to ANT for tuning.

Note

The ICS VOL knob has no effect upon radio compass audio signals when the function knob is in ANT or LOOP, but volume can be controlled through the VOLUME knob on the radio compass panel.

3. Rotate band select knob to desired frequency band.

4. Turn tuning crank to desired station frequency in kilocycles.

5. Listen for station identification to be sure correct station is being received. To finely tune desired frequency, wait until in fairly close proximity to station and move CW/VOICE switch to CW. Adjust volume as desired, then, using the tuning crank, adjust frequency until the tone falls below audible frequency or to minimum frequency attainable.

6. Select COMP position to obtain bearing indication from the No. 1 pointer on the RMI.

7. CW/VOICE switch to VOICE. (For aural identification of keyed "CW" stations, switch to CW).

8. To secure the radio compass, move function knob to OFF.

Aural Null

Should COMP position operation prove unreliable, low frequency facilities can be located as follows:

1. Accomplish steps 1 through 4 of AUTOMATIC DIRECTION FINDING.

2. Listen for station identification to be sure correct station is being received.

3. CW/VOICE switch—CW.

4. Mode knob—LOOP.

5. Retune for solid tone and maximum readability.

6. Adjust volume to attain a null equal to approximately 5 degrees of No. 1 pointer travel on the RMI.

VHF NAV SET, AN/ARN-14*

The VHF NAV set receives signals in the frequency band from 108.0 to 135.9 megacycles. When tuned to a VOR station, the set provides bearing to the station information which is displayed on the No. 2 needle. When set to an ILS frequency, the aircraft deviation from the localizer or final approach course is displayed on the ID-249. The ARN-14 is powered by the secondary d-c bus.

VHF NAV CONTROLS

All VHF NAV controls are located on the VHF NAV panel (6, figure 1-21), on the right console in both cockpits.

POWER Switch

The VHF NAV POWER switch is used to turn AN/ARN-14 power ON and OFF.

VOLUME Knob

The volume of VOR station identification audio and voice advisories may be adjusted through use of the VOLUME knob on the VHF NAV control panel.

Frequency Select Knobs

Desired VOR or ILS station frequency may be set by using the frequency select knobs. The first digit (one-hundred) is fixed. The tens and units digits are set by using the concentric grip-dial which surrounds the raised portion of the selector. Tenths of megacycles are selected by positioning the key-shaped select knob on top of the selector.

VHF NAV OPERATION

1. To assume control of receiver, operate VHF NAV-GYRO COMP control shift switch—check to see that control light comes on.

Note

- The OBTAIN COURSE SETTING FROM OTHER COCKPIT light on the instrument panel is off in the cockpit that has control of the AN/ARN-14.

- When control is transferred during flight, be sure to obtain the course setting from the other pilot and set the course window on your indicator to correspond.

2. POWER switch—ON.

3. Select desired frequency.

4. VHF NAV mixer switch—forward.

5. VOLUME knob—Adjust as desired.

6. Bearing information displayed by No. 2 needle (VOR only); course information displayed on course indicator (VOR and ILS).

7. To secure VHF NAV, move POWER switch to OFF.

*Aircraft not having TACAN installed

TACAN SET, AN/ARN-21*

The TACAN (tactical air navigation) set is a navigational aid capable of providing bearing and slant range to a surface beacon. The set transmits an interrogation signal to the selected surface station beacon, which receives the same signal and retransmits to the set. The equipment in the aircraft accepts only the answer to its interrogation signal. Slant range in nautical miles to the surface beacon is computed by electronic measurement of elapsed time and is shown on a range indicator. The surface beacon also transmits a Morse code identification signal every 38 to 75 seconds. The audio signal is directed through the ICS amplifier. The TACAN system has a line-of-sight range of about 195 miles. The ARN-21 is d-c powered from the monitored bus and a-c powered from the standby inverter.

TACAN CONTROLS AND INDICATORS

All TACAN controls are located on the TACAN panel (7, figure 1-21) on the right console in both cockpits.

Function Switch

When the function switch is at T/R, the system transmits an interrogation signal to the surface beacon for range information and receives bearing information from the surface beacon. Moving the function switch to REC stops the transmitting of the interrogation signal and only bearing information is received from the surface beacon. When the function switch is moved to OFF, the TACAN system is turned off and a red bar drops across the range indicator.

CHAN Select Knobs

The CHAN select knobs permit selection of any of the 126 channels for air-to-ground transmissions. These channels cover 1025 to 1150 megacycles with a 1-megacycle separation. Any combination of channels from 001 to 126 can be set up in the channel window.

CAUTION

Do not attempt to select channels above 126 or below 01. Such selection can cause damage to the equipment.

Note

Allow about 12 seconds after channel selection for the TACAN bearing pointer and the range indicator to correctly indicate the new information.

VOL Knob

The VOL knob adjusts the audio signal strength of the surface beacon identification tone. The knob should be rotated clockwise to increase the tone.

Bearing Pointer

The TACAN bearing pointer (RMI double-barred pointer) indicates magnetic bearing to the surface beacon from the aircraft. The pointer provides radio bearing information which is read directly from the indicator as magnetic bearing to the beacon. The indicator operates when the function switch is at either REC or T/R. If the bearing signal is lost or blanked out, such as during a steep bank which might place the antenna away from the surface beacon, a memory circuit in the receiver maintains the last bearing received for about 3 seconds. If the signal is still disrupted after the time limit, the bearing pointer spins counterclockwise until the signal is picked up again. If the aircraft is above a 40-degree angle from the surface beacon, the bearing pointer keeps spinning until the aircraft is back within this limit. During a channel change or when the equipment is first turned on, the bearing pointer may falsely lock-on momentarily to a bearing, but as the correct data is fed into the system, the pointer will swing to the correct bearing. Therefore, wait a few seconds after a lock-on before relying on the bearing indicated.

Range Indicator

An ID-310 range indicator is installed on both instrument panels in aircraft having TACAN installed. This indicator displays slant range in nautical miles from the aircraft to the surface beacon by means of figures displayed in a small window in the center of the instrument. The indicator operates only when the function switch is at T/R. When the indicator is inoperative or when the channel is being changed, a red bar drops down and covers the figures. If the return signal from the surface beacon is lost because of interference or because the aircraft is beyond range of the station, a memory circuit retains for about 10 seconds the last distance before the interruption; then the red bar drops across the figures. When the aircraft is back within range, the range indicator corrects itself and the red bar disappears automatically. There will be a momentary false indication when the equipment is first turned on or when changing channels. However, wait a few seconds to ensure that the indication can be relied upon.

Course Indicator

Refer to NAVIGATION INSTRUMENTS, in this section.

*Aircraft having ASC 20, Phases I and II, complied with

TACAN OPERATION

1. VHF NAV-GYRO COMP control shift switch—control light comes on.

Note

- The course setting change indicator light on the instrument panel is off in the cockpit having control.

- When control is transferred in flight, be sure to obtain the course setting from the pilot in control and set the course window on your indicator to correspond.

2. Function switch—REC.

   To read slant range, select T/R.

3. Select desired beacon channel.

4. VHF NAV mixer switch—forward.

5. VOL knob—Adjust as desired.

6. Read bearing to station with RMI No. 2 pointer; course deviation through course indicator; distance to station on range indicator.

7. To secure TACAN, move function switch to OFF.

Note

TACAN will occasionally lock-on to a false bearing which will be 40 degrees, or any multiple of 40 degrees, in error on either side of the correct bearing. Switching to another channel and then returning to the desired channel should recycle the search mode. This deficiency does not affect the distance indication provided by the TACAN unit.

MARKER BEACON RECEIVER, AN/ARN-12

The AN/ARN-12 marker beacon receiver is a fixed-tuned set used for navigational purposes. A marker beacon light on the upper right corner of the course indicator on both instrument panels illuminates when the aircraft is over or in close proximity to marker beacons. The equipment is in the standby (on) condition at all times when secondary d-c bus power is available. To listen to marker beacon signals, place the MARKER mixer switch forward (on).

NAVIGATION INSTRUMENTS

RADIO MAGNETIC INDICATOR (RMI)

An ID-250 radio magnetic indicator (10, figure 1-4) on each instrument panel is in reality four instruments in one. The compass card is used as the gyro magnetic compass and revolves, using the large index mark at the top of the instrument as a lubber line. The No. 2 pointer is used with the VOR or TACAN to indicate magnetic bearing to stations, in conjunction with the vertical bar of the course indicator. The No. 1 pointer is used with the AN/ARA-25 and AN/ARN-6 as an ADF or homing indicator. The position of the mode select switch on the UHF radio panel (figure 1-21) selects which receiver will control the needle. Direct current is necessary for power and alternating current if necessary for operation of the compass dial of the RMI. All other portions of the RMI operate on alternating current.

POINTER 1 COMPASS ANNUNCIATOR

The mode of operation (direction finding or radio compass) of the No. 1 pointer of the radio magnetic indicator is displayed on the POINTER 1 compass annunciator (11, figure 1-4) at the top of the instrument panel. The annunciator will read ARA-25 when the AN/ARA-25 direction finder is in operation, and in aircraft having the radio compass installed, ARN-6, when the AN/ARN-6 radio compass system is in operation. The annunciator is powered by the secondary d-c bus.

COURSE INDICATOR

The ID-249 course indicator (15, figure 1-4) on each instrument panel consists of vertical and lateral crossbars, a magnetic heading pointer, a "TO-FROM" window, and the "COURSE" window. The vertical crossbar moves laterally to indicate lateral deviation from a selected VOR, TACAN, or ILS course. The horizontal crossbar is used in conjunction with ILS glide slope receivers, and is inoperative in this installation. Whenever the vertical crossbar is off center (off set course), the aircraft heading is changed in the direction of the crossbar to resume on-course flight. A red signal flag, marked "OFF," appears at the bottom of the vertical crossbar whenever signal levels decrease to the extent that they are not reliable. The magnetic heading indicator, identified by the white circle on the needle below the point, indicates the angle between compass heading and the course set into the course indicator. Its travel is calibrated to 45 degrees from each side of center at both the top and bottom of the instrument. The indicator facilitates reading for wind correction and desired track. The "TO-FROM" window indicates whether the selected course is to or from the station being received. In the event of signal failure, this window will not show either indication. A marker light, with press to test and dim features, is in the upper right corner of the instrument, and a knob marked SET is in the lower left corner of the instrument. The light comes on when the aircraft is directly over marker beacon facilities, and the knob is used to set to the selected course in the course window. The course indicator is powered by the secondary d-c bus.

Note

For detailed procedures and instructions concerning VOR, ILS, TACAN, and ADF navigation, refer to the ALL-WEATHER FLIGHT MANUAL.

CONTROL SHIFT SWITCHES

Control of the UHF radio, VOR, or TACAN, and the gyro compass system can be transferred from one cockpit to the other by two control shift switches (8, figure 1-21), located on the right console in each cockpit. The switch labeled UHF COMMAND will transfer the UHF radio, and the switch labeled VHF NAV-GYRO COMP will transfer the VOR or TACAN radio and the gyro compass system. Indicator lights adjacent to the control shift switches will illuminate when control of the related equipment is obtained. The switches for transfer of the radio and gyro compass equipment in the rear cockpit will not override the corresponding switches in the front cockpit. In aircraft having a radio compass, control is transferred by positioning the function switch on the radio compass control panel momentarily in the CONT position.

LIGHTING SYSTEMS

EXTERIOR LIGHTS

The wing and tail position, landing and taxi, and anti-collision lights may be controlled from either cockpit. Control command for exterior lights, however, is assumed by the pilot having electrical control.

EXTERIOR LIGHTS CONTROLS

EXT MASTER Light Switches

An EXT MASTER light switch (figure 1-7), located on the right console in each cockpit, has two positions: ON and OFF. The switch must be in the ON position before any of the external lights, except the anti-collision lights, can be turned on.

Landing Light Switches

Two landing light switches (LH, RH, 43, figure 1-4), located on the left instrument subpanel, control two retractable lights installed near the leading edge of each wing. Moving the switches to ON (EXT MASTER light switch ON) extends and illuminates the lights. When the switches are positioned to OFF, the lights retract into the wing and are turned off.

WING & TAIL Lights Switches

The wing tip and tail position lights are controlled through the OFF, DIM, and BRIGHT positions of the WING & TAIL lights switch. With the EXT MASTER light switch on, the exterior gear-down lights illuminate when the landing gear is down and locked. A 1/4-inch Lucite rod transmits light from the wing tip light to a point on the top surface of the wing tip, enabling the pilot to check illumination. On T-28C aircraft, the right wing tip position light has been moved forward so as to be visible to the Landing Signal Officer during night carrier approaches. The Lucite indicator on the top surface of the right wing, which enables the pilot to check the illumination of this light, will be observed to be forward of the wing position light indicator for the left wing.

ANTI-COLLISION Lights Switches

The rotating anti-collision lights are controlled through the TOP and BOTTOM ANTI-COLLISION lights switches. These lights may be selected separately and are independent of the EXT MASTER lights switch.

INTERIOR LIGHTS

Interior lighting consists of instrument panel red individual lighting, console edge lighting and floodlighting, thunderstorm lights, and utility extension lights.

INTERIOR LIGHTS CONTROLS

All interior lights controls are located on the switch panel on the right console in each cockpit. Control of interior lights is independent of the opposite cockpit control.

INST Lights Knobs

Each indicator on the main instrument panel in both cockpits is illuminated individually by red lights. The lights are turned on and adjusted for brilliancy by an INST lights knob (figure 1-7) on the right console switch panel in each cockpit. Selecting a position out of OFF in the front cockpit dims the standby compass light.

Note

Selecting a position other than OFF with the instrument lights knob in either cockpit reduces the potential brightness of all warning lights and advisory indicators, except sump plug warning lights.

CONSOLE & FLOODS Knobs

Brightness of the red edge lights in the Lucite panels on the right console is controlled by the CONSOLE & FLOODS lights knob on the right console switch panel. Floodlights mounted above each console are turned on by moving the CONSOLE & FLOODS knob from the OFF position.

CONSOLE FLOODS Light Switches

Brilliancy of the floodlights mounted above the consoles and the instrument panel is controlled by a CONSOLE FLOODS light switch (figure 1-7) on the right console switch panel in each cockpit. After the console floodlights have been turned on by initial movement of the CONSOLE & FLOODS, the CONSOLE FLOODS switch can be moved to BRIGHT, MED, or DIM as desired. When the switch is moved to BRIGHT, floodlights above the instrument panel also illuminate.

THUNDERSTORM Light Switches

A high-intensity white floodlight is mounted on each side of each cockpit for use when flying in or near thunderstorms to protect the pilot's vision from lightning flashes. The THUNDERSTORM light switch (figure 1-7), located on the right console switch panel in each cockpit, turns on the light when moved from OFF to THUNDER-STORM.

STANDBY COMPASS Light Switch

Illumination of the standby compass in the forward cockpit is controlled by a STANDBY COMPASS light switch (figure 1-7) on the right console switch panel in the front cockpit.

Utility Lights

A utility extension light is provided above the right console in each cockpit. The light is turned on and adjusted for brilliance by a rheostat on the light assembly. The light has a coiled cord and swivel base which allow the light to be pointed in any direction. The red filter may be removed if a white light is desired. The light assembly can be removed and placed in a bracket further forward above the right console.

APPROACH LIGHT (T-28C)

The approach light is mounted on the leading edge of the left inboard wing panel. The light is controlled through the EXT MASTER lights switch. Normally, this light will operate only when the arresting hook is down. However, a bypass switch can be actuated to activate the light for practice carrier landings. The approach light consists of a tri-colored prismatic lens over a single bulb. When the aircraft is approaching at the proper airspeed (angle-of-attack), an amber lens will be visible to the Landing Signal Officer. If the approach is too slow the lens will show green, and if the approach is too fast the lens will show red.

APPROACH LIGHT BYPASS SWITCH

The APPROACH LIGHT BY-PASS switch is located in the nose wheel well. When this switch is moved to ON, it bypasses the normal operating circuit which is actuated by the arresting hook. If the switch is placed ON for field carrier landing practice, the approach light will illuminate whenever the EXT MASTER lights switch is on. For all normal operation, the switch should remain in the OFF position.

LANDING GEAR POSITION LIGHTS

To aid ground observers at night, a small white light on each gear strut automatically illuminates when the landing gear is down and locked if the EXT MASTER lights switch is ON.

BAGGAGE COMPARTMENT LIGHT

A light is located in the rear fuselage section to provide illumination of the baggage compartment. The light switch is wired directly to the battery, so that it receives power, regardless of DC POWER switch position.

NOSE WHEEL WELL LIGHT

A service light is provided in the nose wheel well for ground use. The light switch is wired directly to the battery, so that it receives power, regardless of DC POWER switch position.

OXYGEN SYSTEM

A high-pressure oxygen system is installed for use on flights above 10,000 feet. Oxygen pressure is supplied by two 514-cubic-inch bottles. A diluter-demand oxygen regulator, a flow indicator, and a pressure gage are installed in each cockpit. Location of the oxygen filler valve is shown in figure 1-24. The approximate oxygen duration for a crew of two is given in figure 1-22. If flying solo, double the given time.

OXYGEN REGULATORS

A diluter-demand oxygen regulator (19, figure 1-4) is located on the right instrument subpanel in the front cockpit and above the right console in the rear cockpit. The regulator automatically supplies the proper mixture of air and oxygen at all altitudes.

OXYGEN CONTROLS AND INDICATORS

DILUTER LEVERS

The diluter levers (19, figure 1-4) should always be set at the NORMAL OXYGEN position except under emergency conditions. With the diluter lever set at 100% OXYGEN, 100 percent oxygen is supplied at all altitudes and oxygen system duration is considerably reduced.

EMERGENCY VALVES

The emergency valves (21, figure 1-4) should be opened only in an emergency. Turning the knob on the regulator counterclockwise opens the valve, directing a steady stream of oxygen into the mask and considerably reducing the oxygen system duration.

OXYGEN PRESSURE INDICATORS

Oxygen cylinder pressure is indicated by a pressure gage (22, figure 1-4), located on the right instrument subpanel in each cockpit.

Note

At high altitudes, where ambient temperature is normally quite low, the oxygen cylinders become chilled. As the cylinders grow colder, oxygen pressure is reduced, sometimes rather rapidly. With a 38°C (100°F) decrease in temperature in the cylinders, oxygen pressure can be expected to drop 20 percent. This rapid fall in pressure is occasionally a cause for unnecessary alarm. All the oxygen is still there and, as descent to warmer altitudes is made, the pressure will tend to rise again so that the rate of oxygen usage may appear to be slower than normal. A rapid fall in oxygen pressure, while the aircraft is in level flight or while it is descending, is not ordinarily due to falling temperature, of course. When this happens, leakage or loss of oxygen must be suspected.

CAUTION

If oxygen is used when the pressure is below 15 psi, the bottles will have to be purged before they can be refilled.

OXYGEN FLOW INDICATORS

The flow indicators (25, figure 1-4) are located on the right instrument subpanel in each cockpit. The flow indicators show that oxygen is flowing through the regulator. It does not indicate how much oxygen is flowing. The "eye" of the indicator blinks with each breath of the user. When the emergency valve is opened, the indicator does not blink but remains open.

OXYGEN SYSTEM OPERATION

PREFLIGHT CHECK

Before each flight requiring use of oxygen, check oxygen system as follows:

1. The oxygen pressure gage should read 1800 psi.
2. Check oxygen mask for fit and leakage.

CAUTION

Some oxygen regulators may have been changed by individual commands. Make sure that your mask is the type recommended for the regulator installed.

3. Connect mask hose to regulator hose. Check connection for tightness. Attach clip to shoulder harness high enough to permit free movement of head without pinching or pulling hose.

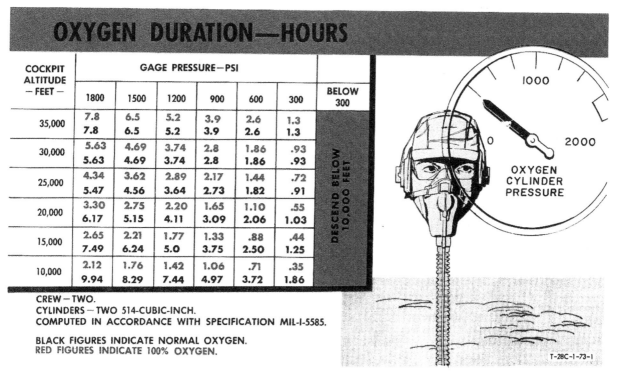

OXYGEN DURATION—HOURS

COCKPIT ALTITUDE — FEET —	GAGE PRESSURE—PSI						BELOW 300
	1800	1500	1200	900	600	300	
35,000	7.8 / 7.8	6.5 / 6.5	5.2 / 5.2	3.9 / 3.9	2.6 / 2.6	1.3 / 1.3	DESCEND BELOW 10,000 FEET
30,000	5.63 / 5.63	4.69 / 4.69	3.74 / 3.74	2.8 / 2.8	1.86 / 1.86	.93 / .93	
25,000	4.34 / 5.47	3.62 / 4.56	2.89 / 3.64	2.17 / 2.73	1.44 / 1.82	.72 / .91	
20,000	3.30 / 6.17	2.75 / 5.15	2.20 / 4.11	1.65 / 3.09	1.10 / 2.06	.55 / 1.03	
15,000	2.65 / 7.49	2.21 / 6.24	1.77 / 5.0	1.33 / 3.75	.88 / 2.50	.44 / 1.25	
10,000	2.12 / 9.94	1.76 / 8.29	1.42 / 7.44	1.06 / 4.97	.71 / 3.72	.35 / 1.86	

CREW—TWO.
CYLINDERS—TWO 514-CUBIC-INCH.
COMPUTED IN ACCORDANCE WITH SPECIFICATION MIL-I-5585.

BLACK FIGURES INDICATE NORMAL OXYGEN.
RED FIGURES INDICATE 100% OXYGEN.

1000
0
2000
OXYGEN CYLINDER PRESSURE

T-28C-1-73-1

Figure 1-22

4. Breathe normally several times with diluter lever at NORMAL OXYGEN and 100% OXYGEN to check flow from oxygen regulator and to check operation of flow indicator.

5. Check oxygen regulator to see that emergency valve is closed and diluter lever is in NORMAL OXYGEN position.

NORMAL OPERATION

Unit doctrine sometimes dictates the use of 100 percent oxygen for take-off, switching to NORMAL oxygen between 3000 and 5000 feet, and reversing the procedure for landing. The only disadvantage in this is the high rate of flow of oxygen at low altitude. At sea level, oxygen is consumed at a rate three or four times faster than at high altitudes. The advantage in using 100 percent oxygen from take-off to a safe altitude is, if for any reason smoke or fumes form in the cockpit, 100 percent oxygen will eliminate the possibility of the pilot breathing this contaminated air at critical periods of flight, such as take-off and landing. In the event ditching becomes mandatory, 100 percent oxygen will enable the pilot to breathe for several minutes even if submerged. This additional time may enable the pilot to free himself from the cockpit. With the diluter lever at NORMAL, breathing would be stopped when the water level reached the oxygen regulator. If the flight is to be made at any altitude below 10,000 feet, the regulator can be turned OFF when selected altitude is reached.

During flight, check oxygen system as follows:

1. Diluter lever at NORMAL OXYGEN.

2. Check connection of mask hose to regulator hose.

3. Check flow indicator frequently for flow of oxygen.

4. Check pressure gage frequently for oxygen system pressure and determine duration.

EMERGENCY OPERATION

When symptoms of hypoxia occur or smoke or fuel fumes enter the cockpit, immediately set diluter lever to 100% OXYGEN. Should the oxygen regulator become inoperative, open emergency valve by turning red emergency knob counterclockwise.

CAUTION

After the emergency is over, set the diluter lever to NORMAL OXYGEN and close the emergency valve.

EMERGENCY CONDITIONS

HYPERVENTILATION

Safety studies have determined that some of the so called "unexplained" accidents have been caused by a physiological condition known as hyperventilation. This is not to be confused with hypoxia. Hyperventilation is a result of the respiratory system discharging carbon dioxide too rapidly, thus starving the blood of this much needed factor. Hyperventilation can occur at any altitude, with or without a supply of breathing oxygen. It will be most common when blood-sugar count is low. This deficiency can be greatly eliminated by a high protein diet, particularly for breakfast, before a morning flight. The condition is brought on by rapid breathing such as occurs during excitement or extreme tension. The first symptoms will be a tingling in the fingers and toes which will get progressively worse until spasms occur in these areas. If no preventive action is taken, these symptoms will be followed by extreme tensioning of all muscles, soon followed by unconsciousness. During this period, your breathing will return to its normal rate and, in 1 or 2 minutes, consciousness will return. If, at any time, you feel the preceding symptoms, hold your breath for as long a period as possible to allow the carbon dioxide in your bloodstream to build up to normal. The result will be felt almost immediately. Continuing to hold the breath for long periods, or forcing yourself to breathe very slowly, will soon eliminate this condition.

HYPOXIA

A lack of adequate oxygen in the bloodstream causes the physiological condition called hypoxia. This condition probably never will occur below 10,000 feet. It can be caused by a leaking oxygen system, mask, shortage of oxygen, or a faulty regulator. Though no two persons are identical in visible symptoms, the onset of hypoxia is seen as a noticeable blue coloring of the fingernails, a headache, and/or a feeling of giddiness. The only remedy for hypoxia is to select 100 percent oxygen at once or immediately descend to an altitude where oxygen is not required. If it is thought that either hyperventilation or hypoxia is occurring and you are not sure which one it is, it should be assumed that it is hypoxia since this is usually more dangerous than hyperventilation. Immediately move the oxygen control to 100 percent and take three quick breaths. If immediate relief is not experienced, start holding your breath for extended periods to offset the effects of hyperventilation.

ARMAMENT SYSTEMS

Refer to Section VIII.

MISCELLANEOUS EQUIPMENT

ANTI-G SUIT PROVISIONS

Provisions for installation of an anti-g suit system are available on the aircraft.

FLIGHT REPORT HOLDER

A canvas flight report holder (20, figure 1-3) is located in each cockpit on the side of the left console next to the seat.

MAP CASE

A map case (4, figure 1-5) is provided in the front cockpit outboard of the right console.

CHECK LISTS

Take-off and landing check lists are mounted on the instrument panel in each cockpit.

INSTRUMENT-FLYING HOOD

An instrument-flying hood (figure 1-23) is mounted behind the seat in the rear cockpit. The hood is stowed at the back of the cockpit when not in use. The cockpit can be enclosed for instrument flight training by pulling the hood forward and engaging it with the snap below the handhold on the instrument panel shroud. The hood is provided with a spring to hold it in the stowed position.

RELIEF TUBE

A relief tube is stowed under each seat.

ASH TRAY

Each cockpit is provided with an ash tray (2, figure 1-5) which is located under the right canopy track.

REARVIEW MIRROR

A rearview mirror is installed at the top of the windshield in the front cockpit.

BAGGAGE COMPARTMENT

The baggage compartment is reached through a door in the bottom of the fuselage. Two levers on the door must be pulled down to open the door. The compartment is made of fabric, with the bottom of the fuselage as the floor. Zippers in the fabric provide an entrance into the baggage compartment. A baggage tie-down loop is provided on the floor in each corner of the compartment. A baggage compartment light is provided for night illumination of the compartment. The light is powered

INSTRUMENT FLYING HOOD

PULL HOOD FORWARD AND ATTACH STRAP TO INSTRUMENT PANEL SHROUD BELOW HAND-HOLD. THE HOOD IS SPRING-LOADED TO THE STOWED POSITION.

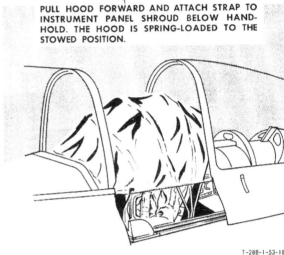

T-28B-1-53-1B

Figure 1-23

from the battery bus and controlled by a switch on the light. The canopy emergency air pressure gage is located in the baggage compartment.

MOORING KIT

Equipment for mooring is contained in a kit which is stowed in the baggage compartment.

Note

Remove mooring kit prior to flights involving unusual attitudes.

PART 3 — AIRCRAFT SERVICING

MATERIAL SPECIFICATIONS

The following materials are required to service the aircraft:

MATERIAL	SPECIFICATION	NATO CODE
Fuel		
Recommended—115/145	MIL-G-5572	F-22
Emergency—100/130	MIL-G-5572	F-18
Oil		
Primary—Dispersant	MIL-L-22851	None
Alternate—Grade 1100	MIL-L-6082	O-117
Cold Alternate— Grade 1065 (below +25°F)	MIL-L-6082	O-113
Hydraulic Fluid	MIL-H-5606	H-515
Oxygen, High-pressure Gaseous Oxygen	MIL-O-21749, Type I	None
Alternate	MIL-O-27210 (USAF)	None
Nitrogen, High-pressure	MIL-N-6011	None

ELECTRICAL POWER UNITS

External power units must be capable of producing 28-volt d-c power at a minimum of approximately 250 amperes for starting. The following standard units are acceptable for use:

NAVY UNITS	USAF UNITS	
NC-2A	A-1	C-26
NC-5	A-3	MD-3, -3A
NC-6	A-4	MD-3M
NC-7		
NC-8	A-7	MC-1
NC-10	AF-M32A-10	MA-1MP
NC-12	B-10A	MA-2MP
	B-10B	MA-3MP
	C-22	

HIGH-PRESSURE AIR UNITS

Dry air at high pressures is required for servicing tires, struts, and the canopy emergency pneumatic system. The following units are suitable for supplying high-pressure air:

NAVY UNITS	USAF UNITS	
Joy 515PH3MS1	ACE-37A	MA-1MP
Ingersol P4R156-B	MC-1 (Joy)	MA-2MP
	MC-11 (Ingersol)	MA-3MP

SYSTEMS SERVICING

REFUELING

To refuel the aircraft, proceed as follows:

1. Check for proper grounding.

2. Ground refueling hose nozzle to wing fuel cap grounding receptacle.

3. Remove cap (1, figure 1-24) and fill cell to filler neck lip.

4. Replace cap securely and remove grounding plug.

5. Repeat steps 2 through 4 for opposite wing.

OIL SYSTEM

1. Open access door (8, figure 1-24) and remove filler cap.

2. Check oil level with dipstick (minimum 8 gallons).

3. Add oil as necessary to spillover level.

4. Reinstall cap and dipstick.

5. Lock dipstick and close access door.

ARRESTING HOOK SNUBBER (T-28C)

1. Open access (4, figure 1-24) and check gage.

2. Service with nitrogen only to 350—450 psig (hook up).

3. Close access door.

LANDING GEAR STRUTS

Landing gear struts should be serviced with MIL-H-5606 hydraulic fluid and compressed, dry nitrogen (MIL-N-6011). If nitrogen is not available and field-carrier landing practice is not anticipated, dry, high-pressure air (PRESAIR) may be used. Struts should be serviced to the following extension in inches:

	FIELD	FCLP
Nose Gear	3.25 (± ⅛)	3.25 (± ⅛)
Main Gear	2.50 (± ⅛)	2.50 (± ⅛)

OXYGEN SYSTEM

The oxygen bottles, when serviced, should be filled with MIL-O-21749 (Type I) high-pressure gaseous oxygen. To service the system, proceed as follows:

1. Check regulator emergency valves closed.

2. Check regulator "SAFETY PRESS" plungers out.

3. Locate oxygen filler valve:

   (a) T-28B — left fuselage.

   (b) T-28C — centerline in baggage compartment.

4. Open supply cart regulator adjust screw and slowly open supply cylinder valve.

5. Close adjust screw until supply gage reads 1900 to 1950 psig.

SERVICING

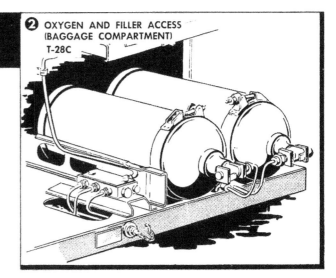

② OXYGEN AND FILLER ACCESS
(BAGGAGE COMPARTMENT)
T-28C

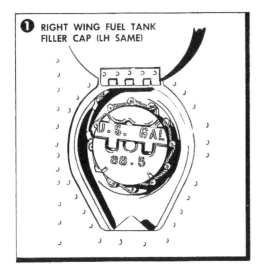

① RIGHT WING FUEL TANK
FILLER CAP (LH SAME)

U.S. GAL
88.5

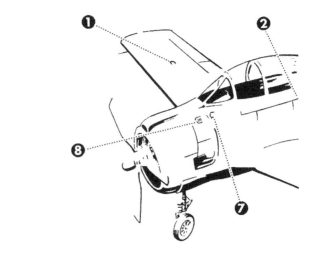

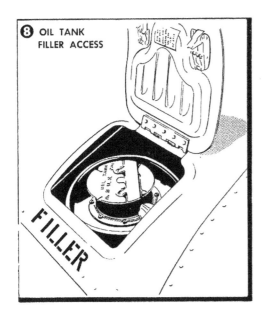

⑧ OIL TANK
FILLER ACCESS

FILLER

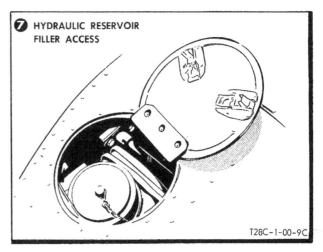

⑦ HYDRAULIC RESERVOIR
FILLER ACCESS

T28C-1-00-9C

Figure 1-24 (Sheet 1)

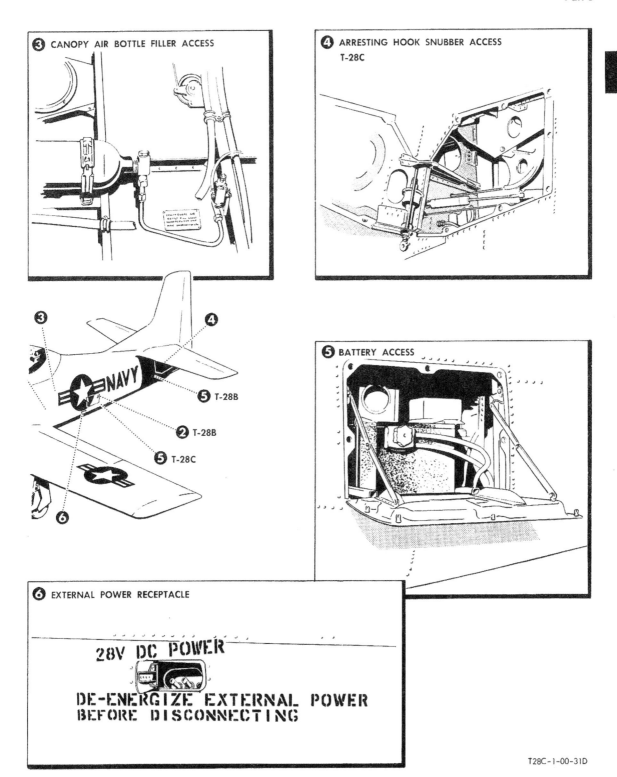

③ CANOPY AIR BOTTLE FILLER ACCESS

④ ARRESTING HOOK SNUBBER ACCESS
T-28C

⑤ BATTERY ACCESS

⑥ EXTERNAL POWER RECEPTACLE

28V DC POWER

DE-ENERGIZE EXTERNAL POWER
BEFORE DISCONNECTING

③
④
⑤ T-28B
② T-28B
⑤ T-28C
⑥

T28C-1-00-31D

Figure 1-24 (Sheet 2)

6. Remove filler valve cap and attach nozzle of supply hose to filler valve.

7. Open supply shutoff valve and fill slowly until both cockpit quantity indicators read 1900 to 1950 psig.

8. Turn off supply valve and disconnect nozzle from filler valve.

CAUTION

Hold filler hose firmly during removal as pressure may exert considerable force.

9. Check filler valve for leakage and replace cap.

CANOPY EMERGENCY AIR SYSTEM

The canopy emergency air bottle is located in the baggage compartment (3, figure 1-24). Service as follows:

1. Check pressure gage and service with dry air to 1980 psig.

2. Tighten swivel nut to 50—70 inch-pounds.

TIRES

For normal field operations, tires may be filled with dry air. For FCLP operation, dry nitrogen should be used. Tire pressures should be checked regularly and maintained as follows:

	TIRE PRESSURE — PSI	
	FIELD	FCLP
Nose Wheel	80	150
Main Wheel	55	110

BATTERY

For normal operation, full charge hydrometer reading should fall between 1.275 and 1.300. If less than 1.240, replace the battery. The following electrolyte temperature correction must be used to arrive at the correct hydrometer reading:

ELECTROLYTE TEMP (°F)	CORRECTION FACTOR
140	+0.024
120	+0.016
100	+0.008
80	Zero

ELECTROLYTE TEMP (°F)	CORRECTION FACTOR
60	−0.008
40	−0.016
20	−0.024
0	−0.032
−20	−0.040

HYDRAULIC SYSTEM

The hydraulic reservoir access is located on the left forward fuselage, adjacent to the engine oil tank filler access (7, figure 1-24). The hydraulic system is serviced as follows:

1. Open access door and check sight gage level.

2. If low, proceed as follows:

   (a) Check flaps — DOWN.

   (b) Canopies — OPEN.

   (c) Speed brake — CLOSED.

   (d) Arresting hook (T-28C) — UP.

   (e) Remove filler cap and add hydraulic fluid until sight gage reads "FULL."

   (f) Replace cap and close access door.

SYSTEMS CAPACITIES

FUEL SYSTEM

TANK	U.S. GAL.	IMP. GAL.	LITERS
Wing (each)	87.5	72.9	330.2
Sump	3.0	2.5	11.4
Total	178.0	148.3	671.8

OIL TANK

	U.S. GAL.	U.S. QUARTS	IMP. GAL.	LITERS
Usable	8.8	35.2	7.3	33.3
Unusable	3.4	13.6	2.8	12.9
Total	12.2	48.8	10.1	46.2

HYDRAULIC SYSTEM

	U.S. GAL.	IMP. GAL.	LITERS
Reservoir	2.5	2.1	9.5
System total	4.5	3.7	17.0

PART 4 — AIRCRAFT OPERATING LIMITATIONS

INTRODUCTION

This part includes the engine and aircraft limitations that must be observed during normal operation. Instrument markings showing the various operating limitations are illustrated in figure 1-25. Some markings are self-explanatory and are not discussed. Operating limitations not indicated on the cockpit instruments are discussed.

MINIMUM CREW REQUIREMENTS

The aircraft can be flown solo from the front cockpit only. Solo flight from the rear cockpit is prohibited because of a marginal CG condition. The cockpit heater control and the circuit-breaker panel are not duplicated in the rear cockpit.

ENGINE LIMITATIONS

All normal engine limitations are shown in figure 1-26. Full take-off power is 52.5 in. Hg MAP and 2700 rpm at sea level with rich mixture and is limited to 5 minutes. For other recommended maximum manifold pressures, see figure 1-26.

Note

If high blower is used above 10,000 feet with alternate air ON, use rich mixture for normal rated power settings and above.

OVERBOOST LIMITS

Concerted effort should be made at all times to stay within established engine limitations. Overboost may cause detonation and/or preignition, with resulting engine damage. Refer to the latest revision to General Reciprocating Engine Bulletin No. 197 for overboost MAP and time limitations which are cause for inspection and/or removal of the engine. If overboost occurs, make Yellow Sheet entry of duration, RPM, CHT, CAT, MAP, oil pressure, and oil temperature.

HIGH RPM/LOW MAP OPERATION

Operation at high rpm and low MAP is one of the major causes of master rod bearing, piston, and ring failures. Therefore, a minimum of 1 inch MAP for each 100 rpm should be maintained during descents.

RPM LIMITS

If severe engine overspeeding occurs, land as soon as practicable. Note all conditions and duration of overspeeding on the Yellow Sheet. If engine rpm is between 3000 and 3200, the engine must be inspected before the next flight. If engine rpm exceeds 3200,

the engine must be changed prior to the next flight. Refer to General Power Plant Bulletin No. 10.

CAUTION

To prevent engine overspeed, do not throttle burst above 2500 rpm. Fast throttle bursts should be made only while governing at 2500 rpm or less.

PROPELLER LIMIT (T-28C ONLY)

The propeller is restricted from ground operation in the range between 1900 and 2200 rpm. There are no limitations on the propeller, in flight, other than the maximum overspeed of the engine. Ground operation within this range should be avoided.

AIRSPEED LIMITATIONS

The maximum permissible indicated airspeeds are as follows:

In smooth or moderately turbulent air—
With arresting hook, landing gear, and wing flaps retracted, canopy open or closed, and speed brakes retracted or extended . . . as shown in figure 1-27.

Note
For variable effectiveness of speed brake, refer to SPEED BRAKE, in Section I, Part 2.

With landing gear, arresting hook
and/or wing flaps extended.........................140 knots
With landing lights extended...........................120 knots

In severe turbulence, indicated airspeeds in the range from 125 to 185 knots are recommended.

ALLOWABLE MANEUVERS

The following maneuvers are permitted:

Inverted flight (not to exceed 10 seconds)
Loop
Immelmann turn
Aileron roll
Wing-over
Chandelle
Spin (except that intentional inverted spins are not permitted)
Barrel roll
One-half cuban eight

ACCELERATION LIMITATIONS

The maximum permissible accelerations for flight in smooth air, at weights of 8050 pounds or less, are shown

INSTRUMENT MARKINGS

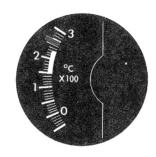

MANIFOLD PRESSURE

18 in. Hg	Min. recommended in flight
18-47 in. Hg	Continuous
47 in. Hg	Max. continuous operation above this pressure limited)
51.5 in. Hg	Military (30 min max)
52.5 in. Hg	Take-off at sea level

TACHOMETER

1400 rpm	Min. recommended in flight
14-2500 rpm	Continuous
2500 rpm	Max. continuous operation above this rpm limited)
2600 rpm	Military high blower max (30 min limit)
2700 rpm	Military low blower max (30 min limit)

CYLINDER HEAD TEMPERATURE

150°C-230°C	Desired continuous
245°C	Max. continuous operation above this temperature limited)
260°C	Maximum military (30 min) and take-off

CARBURETOR AIR TEMPERATURE

—10° to +5°C	Danger of icing
+15° to +38°C	Continuous
+38°C Max	Desired maximum (low blower)
+15°C Max	Desired maximum (high blower)

OIL TEMPERATURE

GRADE 1100 OIL OR MIL-L-22851 OIL		GRADE 1065 OIL
40°C	Minimum	40°C
75°C—90°C	Normal	65°C—75°C
95°C	Maximum	80°C

OIL PRESSURE

65 psi	Minimum for flight
65-75 psi	Continuous operation
90 psi	Maximum

FUEL PRESSURE

21-25 psi	Continuous operation

HYDRAULIC PRESSURE

0-100 psi	Normal (system depressurized)
1250-1650 psi	Normal (system pressurized)
1650 psi	Maximum

CANOPY EMERGENCY AIR PRESSURE

1300 psi	Minimum air pressure (one operation only)
1600-1800 psi	Normal
1980 psi	Maximum

T-28C-1-51-2G

Figure 1-25

in figure 1-27. Accelerations at which buffeting is encountered shall not be exceeded. When flying in conditions of moderate turbulence, it is essential that accelerations, because of deliberate maneuvers, be limited to 4 g's, at a gross weight of 8050 pounds, in order to minimize the possibility of overstress as a result of the combined effects of gusts and maneuvering loads. As gross weights are increased above 8050 pounds, the permissible accelerations decrease. To determine the maximum permissible accelerations at gross weights in excess of 8050 pounds, multiply the accelerations shown in figure 1-27 for smooth air or that given for moderate turbulence by the ratio of 8050 pounds to the new gross weight.

On aircraft equipped with strakes, the maximum permissible acceleration is 5.7 g's when carrying stores. However, when stores are carried in turbulent air, the maximum permissible acceleration is 3.7 g's. This limit is necessary so that the 5.7-g limit will not be exceeded when severe gusts are encountered.

Because rolling pullouts impose additional stress, maximum permissible acceleration is two-thirds the maximum permissible acceleration for a normal pullout.

At indicated airspeeds between 170 and 210 knots, critical combinations of acceleration and buffet can cause overstress. In the clean configuration, the maximum permissible acceleration for flights in smooth air (dynamic stall line) is 5 g's at 170 knots IAS and 6 g's at 210 knots IAS, varying linearly from 170 to 210 knots as shown in figure 1-27. Stick back pressure should be relaxed at the onset of buffet in the 170- to 210-knot speed range.

ARMAMENT (MODIFIED T-28C)

1. On modified T-28C aircraft with six store stations, figure 1-28 establishes maximum permissible accelerations for symmetrically loaded store configurations at 2500 feet or less at a maximum airspeed of 295 knots in smooth air. However, when stores are carried in turbulent air, reduce the maximum acceleration shown in figure 1-28 by 2 g's.

2. The maximum permissible acceleration for store loadings heavier than 100 pounds asymmetrically is 3.2 g's at 9500 pounds gross weight or greater and 3.7 g's at less than 9500 pounds gross weight.

3. Rolling pullouts for all configurations may be performed at two-thirds the symmetrical flight limits. Lateral stick deflections are limited to half throw when stores over 250 pounds are carried at stations 2 and 5.

4. High sink speed landings are prohibited for all store configurations other than 150 pounds maximum at store stations 3 and 4.

CENTER-OF-GRAVITY LIMITATIONS

For center-of-gravity limitations, refer to the Handbook of Weight and Balance (AN01-1B-40). Solo flight must be made from the front seat. If solo flight is made from the rear seat, an aft CG condition may occur which would make it possible for the aircraft to flat spin.

WEIGHT LIMITATIONS

1. For take-off weights and distances, refer to Section XI.

2. Maximum recommended gross weight for carrier landings is 8300 pounds.

3. Maximum recommended gross weight for field landings is 10,900 pounds (T-28C) and 8600 pounds (T-28B).

4. Maximum allowable baggage weight is 90 pounds.

STORES LIMITATIONS

External stores may be carried and all except gun packages released, singly or in combination, under the same restrictions on flight that apply without such stores, except as follows:

1. When carrying stores on T-28C aircraft, strakes must be installed.

2. When carrying stores, intentional spins are not permitted.

3. When carrying stores, the maximum permissible indicated airspeeds in smooth or moderately turbulent air—are as follows:

2,500 feet or less	295 knots
15,000 feet	270 knots
25,000 feet	240 knots
35,000 feet	190 knots

4. When carrying stores, the maximum permissible acceleration is 6.0 g's (5.7 g's on T-28C). Maximum permissible accelerations for modified T-28C aircraft are as shown in figure 1-28. However, when stores are carried in turbulent air, the maximum permissible acceleration is reduced by 2 g's. This limit is necessary so the maximum g limit will not be exceeded when severe gusts are encountered.

CARRIER OPERATION LIMITATIONS (T-28C)

1. Carrier operation with barriers or barricades rigged is not permitted.

2. Maximum permissible arresting hook load is 29,627 pounds and the maximum permissible longitudinal deceleration for arrested landing is 4.2 g's.

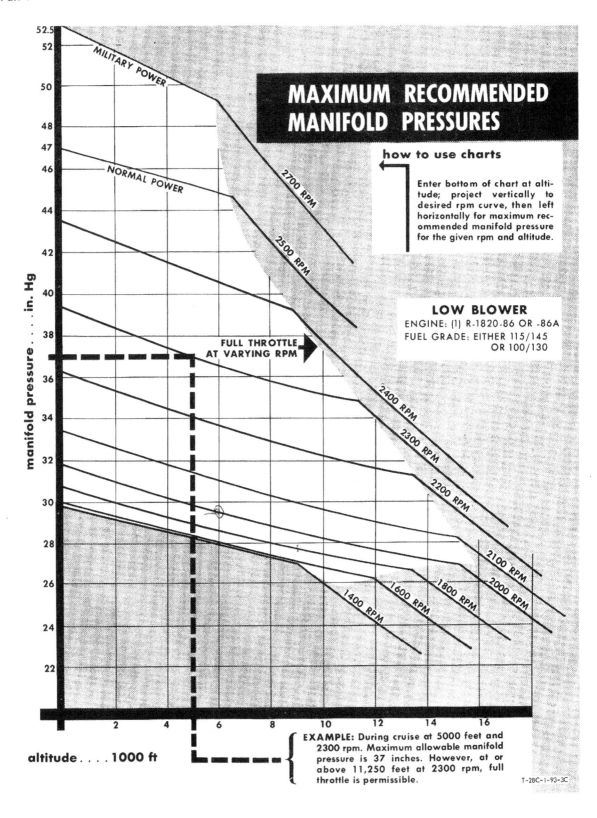

MAXIMUM RECOMMENDED MANIFOLD PRESSURES

how to use charts

Enter bottom of chart at altitude; project vertically to desired rpm curve, then left horizontally for maximum recommended manifold pressure for the given rpm and altitude.

LOW BLOWER
ENGINE: (1) R-1820-86 OR -86A
FUEL GRADE: EITHER 115/145 OR 100/130

MILITARY POWER

NORMAL POWER

2700 RPM

2500 RPM

FULL THROTTLE AT VARYING RPM

2400 RPM

2300 RPM

2200 RPM

2100 RPM

2000 RPM

1800 RPM

1600 RPM

1400 RPM

manifold pressure . . . . in. Hg

altitude . . . . 1000 ft

EXAMPLE: During cruise at 5000 feet and 2300 rpm. Maximum allowable manifold pressure is 37 inches. However, at or above 11,250 feet at 2300 rpm, full throttle is permissible.

T-28C-1-93-3C

Figure 1-26 (Sheet 1)

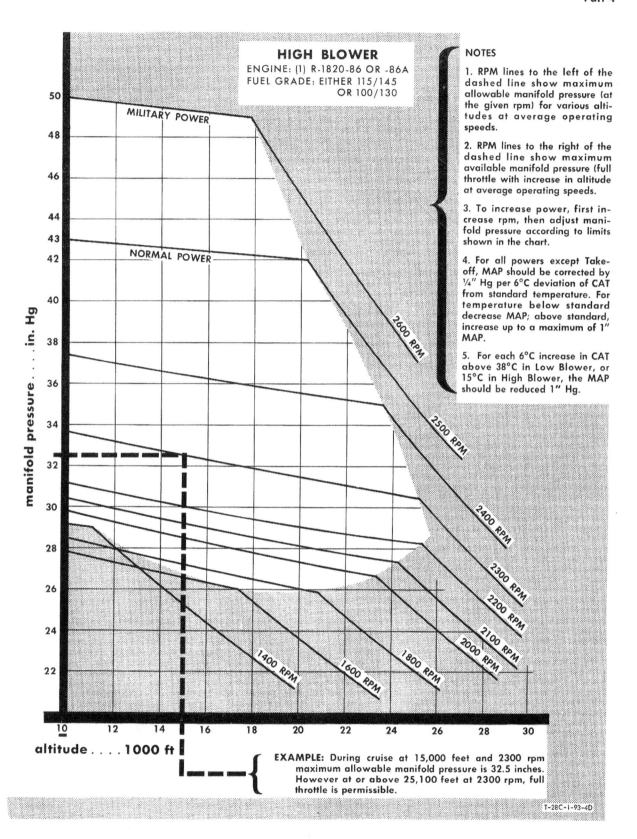

HIGH BLOWER
ENGINE: (1) R-1820-86 OR -86A
FUEL GRADE: EITHER 115/145
OR 100/130

NOTES

1. RPM lines to the left of the dashed line show maximum allowable manifold pressure (at the given rpm) for various altitudes at average operating speeds.

2. RPM lines to the right of the dashed line show maximum available manifold pressure (full throttle with increase in altitude at average operating speeds.

3. To increase power, first increase rpm, then adjust manifold pressure according to limits shown in the chart.

4. For all powers except Take-off, MAP should be corrected by ¼" Hg per 6°C deviation of CAT from standard temperature. For temperature below standard decrease MAP; above standard, increase up to a maximum of 1" MAP.

5. For each 6°C increase in CAT above 38°C in Low Blower, or 15°C in High Blower, the MAP should be reduced 1" Hg.

EXAMPLE: During cruise at 15,000 feet and 2300 rpm maximum allowable manifold pressure is 32.5 inches. However at or above 25,100 feet at 2300 rpm, full throttle is permissible.

T-28C-1-93-4D

Figure 1-26 (Sheet 2)

OPERATING FLIGHT STRENGTH
GROSS WEIGHT-8050 POUNDS

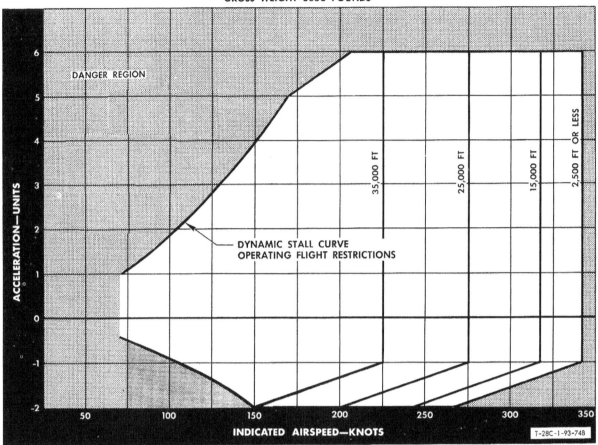

Figure 1-27

OPERATING FLIGHT STRENGTH
MODIFIED T-28C WITH STORES ABOARD

MAXIMUM ACCELERATION "G"	MAXIMUM STORE LOADS AT EACH STATION—POUNDS					
	1	2	3	4	5	6
3.8	150	500*	500	500	500*	150
4.0	150	250	500	500	250	150
4.2	150	250	250	250	250	150
4.3	150	150	250	250	150	150
4.4		150	150	150	150	
4.3		500*	500	500	500*	
4.5		250	500	500	250	
4.8		250	250	250	250	
4.9		150	250	250	150	
5.0		150	150	150	150	
5.1			500	500		
5.4			250	250		
5.5			150	150		
5.8	CLEAN AIRPLANE AND TWO CREWMEN					

*IF 500 POUND STORES ARE CARRIED AT STORE STATIONS 2 & 5 LATERAL STICK DEFLECTION IS LIMITED TO HALF THROW.

T-28C-1-93-88

Figure 1-28

section II

Indoctrination and Training

T 28B 1 50-13A

TABLE OF CONTENTS

INTRODUCTION

The purpose of this section is to standardize ground and flight training for pilots *initially* checking out in the T-28, to establish first pilot currency requirements, and to list minimum personal flight equipment required.

GROUND TRAINING SYLLABUS

INTRODUCTION

T-28 currency requirements. Personal flying equipment required. Description of aircraft.

ENGINEERING AND AIRCRAFT SYSTEMS

Engine, propeller, oil, fuel, electrical and hydraulic systems, instruments, electronic communication/navigation equipment, aircraft operating limitations, servicing requirements.

NATOPS PROCEDURES

Normal operating procedures. Flight procedures and aircraft characteristics. Emergency procedures. All-weather procedures.

NATOPS GROUND EVALUATION

Open book examination. Closed book examination.

FLIGHT SYLLABUS

The flight training syllabus will consist of five flights with a total flight time of approximately 7.5 hours. Where recent experience in similar model warrants, unit commanders can waive, by unit instruction, all but 3 hours of dual instruction prior to flight evaluation.

1. Flight One—Instructor pilot introduces and student pilot practices: preflight, start, take-off, climb, descent, slow flight, landing attitude maneuver, approach turn stall, simulated engine failure (high altitude), and full-flap landings.

2. Flight Two—Instructor pilot introduces and student pilot practices: simulated engine failure (low altitude), no-flap landings, spin, and previously introduced maneuvers.

3. Flight Three—Student pilot practices previously introduced maneuvers.

4. Flight Four — Student pilot demonstrates proficiency in essential instrument procedures to include holding, penetration, low approach, GCA, and emergency procedures.

5. Flight Five—NATOPS evaluation flight.

FLIGHT CREW REQUIREMENTS

PILOT IN COMMAND CURRENCY REQUIREMENTS

To be currently qualified, a pilot must have:

1. Successfully completed a NATOPS evaluation in the last 12 months.

2. A current instrument rating.

3. Made at least two (2) take-offs and landings and logged five (5) hours of flight time in the T-28 within the preceding 90 days. Pilots who fail to meet the above requirements shall be considered no longer currently qualified and are required to requalify in accordance with OPNAVINST 3710.7 series and this manual.

PASSENGER REQUIREMENTS

1. Must be familiar with the operation of the intercom system, emergency equipment, and bailout procedures.

2. Must have required personal flying equipment.

PERSONAL FLYING EQUIPMENT

The following equipment shall be worn or carried on all flights in T-28 aircraft unless safety or mission considerations or design characteristics of model aircraft dictate otherwise:

1. Flame retardant flight suit.

2. Identification tags.

3. Flight gloves.

4. Flight safety boots/field shoes (ankle-high lace type).

5. Protective helmet—latest available approved type.

6. Life preserver on all overwater flights. The preserver will be equipped in accordance with the applicable BuWeps technical bulletins.

7. An approved survival knife and sheath.

8. Personal survival kit.

9. Parachute.

10. Oxygen mask.

11. Anti-exposure suit in accordance with 3710.7 series.

12. A pistol with tracer ammunition for all flights overwater, at night, or over sparsely populated areas. An approved signaling device is authorized as a substitute for the pistol, when operational and/or security conditions warrant.

13. Flashlight for all night flights.

Note

All survival equipment will be secured in such a manner that it is easily accessible and will not be lost during an emergency.

FLIGHT TEST

TEST PILOT REQUIREMENTS

Aviators appointed as test pilots should meet the following requirements:

1. Logged 50 hours in T-28 aircraft within the preceding 6 months. Commanding Officers are authorized to waive this requirement, in writing, when individual pilot proficiency warrants.

2. Designated as qualified test pilot in writing by Commanding Officer.

Normal Operating Procedures

section III

TABLE OF CONTENTS

PART 1 — BRIEFING AND DEBRIEFING

BRIEFING

The flight leader or pilot in command will ensure that each flight is preceded by a thorough briefing. Each pilot will maintain a kneepad and record all data necessary to successfully complete the assigned mission. The briefing will include the following items:

COMMUNICATIONS

1. Frequencies.
2. Radio procedures and discipline.
3. Navigational aids.
4. Identification and ADIZ procedure.

WEATHER

1. Local area.
2. Local area and destination forecast.
3. Weather at alternate.

NAVIGATIONAL AND FLIGHT PLANNING

1. Climb-out.
2. Mission planning, including fuel/oxygen management.
3. Penetration.
4. GCA.
5. Recovery.

EMERGENCIES

1. Aborts.
2. Divert fields.
3. Minimum and emergency fuel.
4. Waveoff pattern.
5. Radio failure.
6. Loss of visual contact with flight.
7. Downed pilot and aircraft emergencies.
8. System failures.

The flight leader will inspect all flight members for the proper flight equipment.

DEBRIEFING

Each flight shall be followed with a thorough debriefing by the flight leader or pilot in command as soon as is practical. All areas of flight should be covered, paying particular attention to those areas where difficulty was encountered. The debriefing area may quite possibly be the most beneficial nonflying portion of the flight, for it is here that errors committed are reviewed, the proper techniques discussed, and these associated with past performance.

PART 2 — MISSION PLANNING

MISSION PLANNING

Mission planning is the responsibility of the first pilot or flight leader and will cover all matters pertinent to the mission to be flown. Every task which can be completed prior to take-off will contribute to the ease and success with which the actual flight is conducted.

WEATHER

A complete weather briefing and an understanding of the weather picture is a prerequisite of successful mission planning. Enroute weather will dictate the probable altitude assignments and whether or not those altitudes assigned will be acceptable. Destination weather will determine expected delays in letdown and landing procedures, and a good weather alternate or alternates are a must to save the day in unforeseen circumstances. All of this weather picture affects fuel planning and flight procedures.

PLANNING DATA

Data and information required for determining the operational parameters and the mission requirements are found in Section XI.

PART 3 — SHORE-BASED PROCEDURES

SCHEDULING

Flight scheduling is the responsibility of the Commanding Officer or his designated representative. The primary function of schedules is to provide a smooth, orderly utilization of pilots and aircraft. Commanding Officers having aircraft custody are responsible for the determination of pilot qualification for schedule purposes.

LINE OPERATIONS (MANNING AIRCRAFT)

The pilot in command will not accept the aircraft until he is assured that the aircraft is ready for safe flight. The two steps to be taken prior to acceptance of the aircraft are a careful examination of recent discrepancies and a thorough preflight inspection.

YELLOW SHEETS

At least the last ten discrepancy sections of the yellow sheet will be made available to the pilot for his examination. The pilot in command will ensure that the plane captain has conducted a preflight inspection, that all servicing entries have been made, and the yellow sheet has been signed off. When satisfied that all required information has been stated, the pilot in command will sign the yellow sheet.

PREFLIGHT INSPECTION

The pilot in command will cause a proper preflight inspection to be accomplished. A satisfactory preflight inspection will consist of completing both the cockpit safety check and the exterior inspection (figure 3-1).

COCKPIT SAFETY CHECKS

The canopy can be opened from the left side of the aircraft only. See figure 3-3.

FRONT COCKPIT

The following items will be inspected prior to performing the exterior inspection.

1. Fuel shutoff—OFF.
2. Trim tabs—zero.
3. MIXTURE control—IDLE CUTOFF.
4. Landing gear handle—full DOWN.
5. Accelerometer within limits (+6/−2).
6. IGNITION switch—OFF.
7. Oxygen pressure—1000 psi minimum (hose stowed).
8. Radios—OFF.
9. No. 1 and No. 2 inverter circuit breakers—out.
10. Landing light circuit breakers—out.
11. DC POWER switch—BAT. & GEN.

    (a) Check voltage—22 volts minimum.

    (b) Sump warning light—Press to test.

    (c) Gear position indicators—all down (wheels).

    (d) COWL & OIL COOLER FLAPS switch—OPEN.

12. DC POWER switch—OFF.
13. Controls unlocked (check control lock secured).
14. Fire wall door closed. (All dzus buttons parallel with outer edge of door.)
15. Canopy—check for cracks.

If night flying is anticipated, the following additional checks should be made:

1. With aid of outside observer, test operation of wing and tail, anti-collision, approach (if applicable), landing and taxi, and exterior gear-down lights.
2. Check operation of instrument panel, console, and extension lights.
3. Be sure you have a flashlight.

REAR COCKPIT

1. INST POWER switch—NO. 1 INV.
2. DC POWER switch—OFF (NORMAL ON*).
3. If solo:

    (a) All other switches—OFF.

    (b) Oxygen equipment—secure.

    (c) Safety belt and shoulder harness—secure.

EXTERIOR INSPECTION

Make an exterior inspection, starting at the front cockpit and moving clockwise as shown by figure 3-1.

1. Port Nose Section.

    (a) Inspect the hydraulic reservoir. Fluid level should be above the "FILL" line. Maximum fluid level should permit an air bubble at the top of the sight gage. Check the hydraulic filler cap for proper security.

    (b) Inspect the oil quantity by removing the dipstick, which should be a minimum of 8.0 gallons. *Make certain the dipstick retaining wire is properly seated* after replacing the dipstick. See that the oil filler cap is properly secured.

2. Port Wing, Upper Surface.

    (a) Inspect the top surface of the wing, making certain access plates and doors are secured.

    (b) Visually check the fuel quantity. The tank should be full. Check the fuel filler cap gasket for proper seating.

*Aircraft 140584 and subsequent and aircraft having ASC 36 incorporated

EXTERIOR INSPECTION

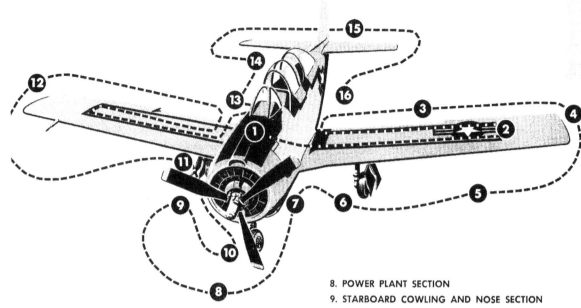

8. POWER PLANT SECTION
9. STARBOARD COWLING AND NOSE SECTION
1. PORT NOSE SECTION
2. PORT WING, UPPER SURFACE
3. TRAILING EDGE OF PORT WING
4. PORT WING TIP
5. LEADING EDGE, PORT WING
6. PORT GEAR AND WHEEL WELL
7. PORT COWLING AND WING ROOT
10. NOSE WHEEL WELL
11. STARBOARD GEAR AND WHEEL WELL
12. STARBOARD WING
13. BAGGAGE COMPARTMENT
14. FUSELAGE, STARBOARD SIDE
15. EMPENNAGE
16. FUSELAGE, PORT SIDE

T-28B-1-00-6C

Figure 3-1

Note

Excess fuel should be allowed to drain at this time to avoid a siphoning effect which could occur during engine run-up or on take-off roll.

3. Trailing Edge, Port Wing.
    (a) Check that the flap turnbuckle linkage is straight, locknuts cotter-keyed, and the turnbuckle safety-wired.
    (b) Check flaps for excessive play by pulling up on the trailing edges. A maximum of 1½ inches play is allowed.
    (c) Check aileron trim tab for flush alignment with the aileron in the neutral position. Check aileron for freedom of movement, cables properly riding on pulleys, and turnbuckles safety-wired and moving freely past wing rib ends.
    (d) Check static discharge wicks for proper length and security, (minimum of 6 inches with 1 inch of fray).
    (e) Check hinges for cracks and bonding braids attached.

4. Port Wing Tip.
    (a) Inspect the wing tip and aileron tip for breaks or scratches. Do not push or pull on the port tip, as it is made of fiberglass and could be broken.
    (b) Check the condition of the wing light.

5. Leading Edge, Port Wing.
    (a) Examine the leading edge for breaks or bulges and proper contour.
    (b) Check the landing light fully retracted.
    (c) Check the tie-down eye for security.
    (d) Ascertain that there is no leakage from the port fuel tank drain.
    (e) Check the port and starboard fuel tank vent outlets (located on the inboard, bottom surface of port and starboard wing flaps). These outlets should be similarly cut off, i.e., at a 25-degree angle to the flap skin and protruding an equal distance below the flap skin. If these outlets are not similarly cut or if one is obstructed, uneven fuel flow will result.

6. Port Main Landing Gear and Wheel Well.

The following can be checked in the minimum amount of time by following the prescribed order:

(a) Wheel properly chocked.

(b) Wheel and strut fairings secure and not bent.

(c) Main wheel retaining nut cotter-keyed.

(d) Tire properly inflated and no cord showing.

(e) Striker plate set at the proper angle.

(f) Uplock roller secure and free to roll.

(g) No hydraulic leaks in brake lines.

(h) Outboard brake pucks no thinner than $\frac{1}{16}$ inch (thickness of a dime).

(i) Brake disk not warped or scored.

(j) Brake disk keys fastened securely and free of cracks.

(k) Oleo extended a minimum of 2.5 inches (three finger widths).

(l) Shock strut scissors retaining nut cotter-keyed. Ground safety switch securely fastened to shock strut scissors.

(m) Landing gear position indicating light clean and not broken.

(n) No cracks in shock strut, trunnion fitting, and trunnion pin.

(o) Downlock switch and actuating arm securely fastened to overcenter side brace and mechanical locking pin.

(p) Downlock bungee actuating rod not bent.

(q) Check wheel well for hydraulic or fuel leaks and/or loose lines.

(r) Wheel door retracting roller free to roll.

(s) Check wheel door for ease of movement to the full retract position. Make certain the door braces are not rubbing or chafing the fuel line.

(t) Main gear uplock hook and turnbuckle not bent or cracked and turnbuckle safety-wired. Spring properly secured to the turnbuckle.

7. Port Cowling and Wing Root Fuselage Area.

(a) Check the heater ram-air intake (located in the leading edge of the port wing root) clear of obstructions.

(b) Check wing root rubber seal (top and bottom) in place.

(c) Check the heater exhaust outlet clear of obstructions.

(d) Check that the fuel strainer drain and the two heater drains are not leaking fuel.

(e) Check that the pullout step is in.

(f) Make certain the rear of the port cowling is flush with the fuselage, the cowling release handle is flush with the cowling, and the release handle dzus button is vertical. When not properly secured, the port cowling may break off in flight and tear the canopy off.

(g) Check exhaust stacks for cracks, security, and covers removed.

(h) Check the cowl flap for security and the cowl flap actuating rod straight and properly secured to the cowl flap.

(i) Check the oil cooler flap for proper security and the oil cooler flap actuating rod straight and properly secured to the oil cooler flap. See that there are no excessive oil leaks in the rear of the oil cooler and there are no obstructions to the rear of the oil cooler.

8. Power Plant Section.

CAUTION

Do not pull engine through by hand before rotating with starter as engine can be damaged by hydraulic lock.

(a) Check that the oil cooler air scoop, carburetor air scoop, and generator air intake are clear of obstructions.

(b) Check that the prop dome cap is cotter-keyed to the prop dome.

(c) Check that one of the four dome retainer nut lockscrews is safety-wired to the prop dome.

(d) Check for oil leaks around the prop dome and the prop blade hub assembly.

(e) Check the three prop blades for cracks or excessive nicks.

(f) Check the prop governor for the following:

(1) No oil leaks.

(2) Prop control cable seated properly on the governor pulley and sufficient tension on the control cable. Cable turnbuckle safety-wired.

(3) Cotter keys in two of the three locknuts on the governor pulley and washer on shaft.

(g) The cowling consists of five separate panels, two of which are fixed, while three are hinged to permit access to the engine. These five panels are held together by five shear pins. Make certain the shear pins are properly secured to the shear pin receptacles. When properly secured, about $\frac{3}{8}$ inch of the rounded end of the shear pin protrudes through the shear pin receptacle.

(h) Check the ignition harness for cracks and security. Do not pull on the harness excessively.

(i) Check that all ignition leads are properly secured to spark plugs.

(j) Check push rod housings and rocker box covers for excessive oil leaks, cracks, and proper security.

(k) Check cylinder heads and bodies for excessive oil leaks and cracks.

(l) Check cylinder cooling fins for security.

(m) Check the engine sump tank for the following:

    (1) Excessive oil leaks.

    (2) Magnetic drain plug safety-wired.

    (3) Sump warning light Cannon plug and lead properly secured.

(n) Check the area below the sump for excessive amount of oil, rags, tools, etc.

9. Starboard Cowling and Nose Section.

(a) Exhaust stacks—same as port side.

(b) Cowl flaps—same as port side.

(c) Cowl release handles—same as port side. There are *two* cowl release handles on the starboard side.

(d) Check to see that the fire extinguisher door is not stuck shut.

(e) Check fuel, oil, and hydraulic drains. See figure 3-2.

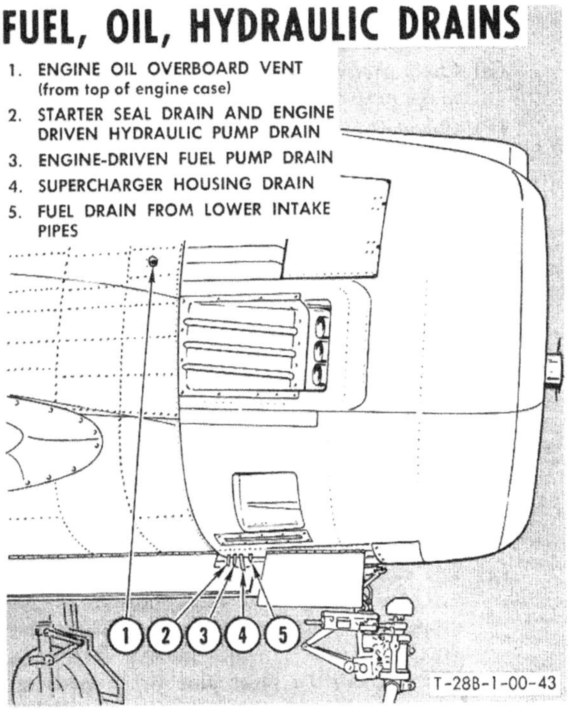

FUEL, OIL, HYDRAULIC DRAINS

1. ENGINE OIL OVERBOARD VENT (from top of engine case)
2. STARTER SEAL DRAIN AND ENGINE DRIVEN HYDRAULIC PUMP DRAIN
3. ENGINE-DRIVEN FUEL PUMP DRAIN
4. SUPERCHARGER HOUSING DRAIN
5. FUEL DRAIN FROM LOWER INTAKE PIPES

T-28B-1-00-43

Figure 3-2

10. Nose Wheel Well.

The following can be checked in the minimum amount of time by following the prescribed order:

(a) Ground wire in place and touching ground.

(b) Nose wheel retaining nut cotter-keyed.

(c) Tire properly inflated and no cord showing.

(d) Landing gear position indicating light clean and not broken.

(e) Oleo extended a minimum of 3.25 inches (four finger widths).

(f) Shock strut scissors retaining nut cotter-keyed.

(g) Check striker plate for excessive gouges or roughness.

(h) Uplock roller secure and free to roll.

(i) Uplock solenoid actuating arm in the vertical position.

(j) Check that the shimmy damper fluid level indicator is between the full and refill marks.

(k) No cracks in shock strut, trunnion fitting, or trunnion pin.

(l) Spring bungee not cracked.

(m) Excessive oil leaks in the top forward section of the nose wheel well.

(n) Nose gear uplock hook not bent or cracked.

(o) Ground safety pin in place and not being pinched by the overcenter side brace.

(p) Downlock switch and actuating arm securely fastened to the overcenter side brace and mechanical locking pin.

(q) Downlock bungee actuating rod not bent.

(r) Check the nose gear torque box for cracks. Check torque box bolts and rivets for sign of looseness.

(s) Check security of the five dzus fasteners on the lower cowling access plate just forward of the nose wheel well.

(t) No hydraulic leaks around nose gear actuating cylinder.

(u) Check the scissors formed by the wheel well door actuating arms for excessive gouges.

(v) Check the three springs attached to the wheel well doors, the doors themselves, and the door actuating arms for proper security or cracks.

(w) Hydraulic system drain for leaks.

(x) Open defueling valve access door; check valve safety-wired and not leaking.

(y) Check all access doors closed.

(z) Check dust cover secured and dzus button slots parallel to the ground.

11. Starboard Main Landing Gear and Wheel Well.

(a) Same as port gear and wheel well.

(b) Fuel sump tank for leaks, especially in the tank drain area.

12. Starboard Wing.

(a) Same as port wing.

(b) Make certain the pitot cover is removed from the pitot tube and the tube clear of obstructions.

(c) The starboard aileron trim tab is mechanically set on the ground and will not necessarily be flush with the aileron.

13. Baggage Compartment.

(a) Check that the data case (inner side of baggage compartment door) is empty of any articles.

(b) Visually inspect the baggage compartment door seal for tears or excessive wear. If this seal is not in place, there is a good possibility of carbon monoxide entering the compartment and then passing up into the cockpits.

(c) Make certain the two baggage compartment latches are over the latch rollers and the latch spring attached. With the speed brake extended, the forward section of the baggage compartment will fall down if the latches are not in place.

(d) Check the aileron yoke assembly for full throw, cracks, and proper security at all fittings.

(e) Check the elevator control system for the following:

(1) Full throw.

(2) Cracks and proper security at all fittings.

(3) Bobweight clearing control cables and not touching the compartment wall when at the full forward position.

(4) Bobweight bungee for cracks in the housing or rod.

(5) Elevator control cables for proper tension and security.

(f) Inspect all hydraulic lines for leaks, paying particular attention to the hydraulic panel located on the port side and the canopy actuating cylinder located in the top of the compartment.

(g) Check security of gear in the baggage compartment.

(h) The boots on the two speed brake actuating cylinders are snapped in place.

(i) The canopy emergency air pressure is within limits (1300 to 1980 psi).

(j) The elevator cable chafing strip is installed. This strip prevents the elevator cable from rubbing or looping over the ARN-14 dynamotor.

(k) All control cables free of obstructions and for proper tension.

(l) Check (by trying to move) all radio boxes, oxygen bottles (in T-28C), battery (in T-28C), inverters, and canopy air bottle for proper security. Some of the radio boxes are shock-mounted and will, therefore, display some give.

(m) Check the UHF control box for the following: The GUARD-BOTH-COMD switch is on BOTH. The LOCAL-REMOTE switch is wired to REMOTE (you will not be able to switch UHF channels in the cockpit if it is on local) and the TONE-VOICE switch is wired to VOICE.

(n) Turn off the baggage compartment service light.

(o) Assure that the baggage compartment is properly locked.

14. Fuselage, Starboard Side.

(a) Make certain the canopy seal is in place.

(b) Check that the static vent is unobstructed.

(c) Check the condition of the fuselage anticollision lights.

15. Empennage.

(a) Visually inspect the skin of the vertical and horizontal stabilizers for cracks.

(b) Check the leading edge of the horizontal stabilizer for breaks, bulges, and proper contour.

(c) Check the elevator for the following:

(1) Freedom of movement.

(2) Hinges for cracks and bonding braids attached.

(3) Check security of the two counterweights installed in each elevator, one at each end. Each counterweight is held in place by two screws on the leading edge of the elevator and two bolts near the elevator hinge. If these screws/bolts worked loose in flight, the elevator could be jammed.

(4) Static discharge wicks for proper length and security.

(5) Elevator trim tab flush with elevator when the elevator is in a neutral position.

(6) Elevator trim tab actuating rod locknut tight.

(7) Trim tab hinge pin in place.

(d) Check the rudder for the following:

(1) Freedom of movement.

(2) Hinge for cracks and bonding braids attached.

(3) Static discharge wicks for proper length and security.

(4) Rudder trim tab flush with rudder when the rudder is in the neutral position.

(5) Rudder trim tab actuating rod locknut tight.

(6) Trim tab hinge pin in place and bent end of pin secured in hole.

(7) Drain hole (located on the bottom edge of the rudder) clear. If this hole were plugged, the rudder would fill with water and affect the center of gravity of the aircraft.

(8) Condition of tail light.

(9) If a tail hook is installed (T-28C only), make certain it is locked up.

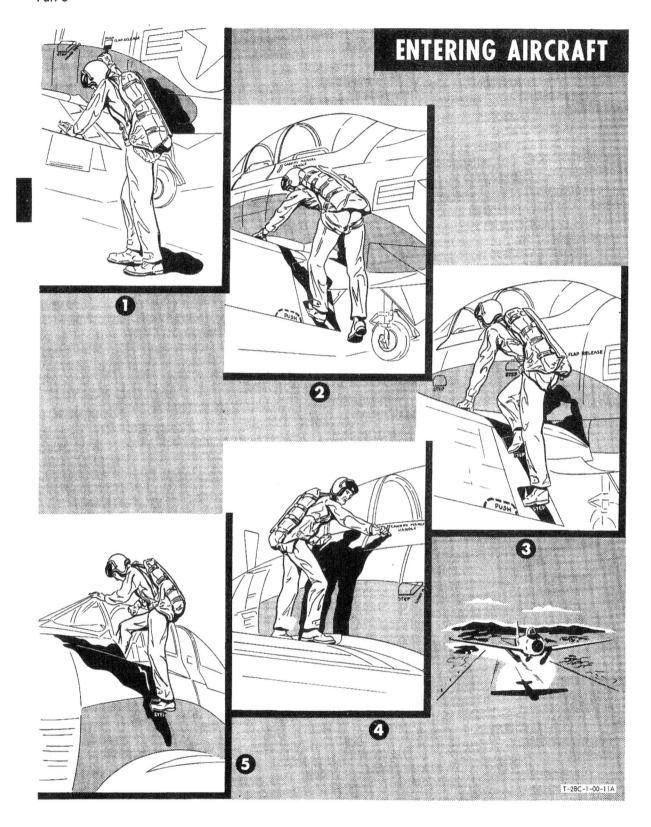

ENTERING AIRCRAFT

Figure 3-3

16. Fuselage, Port Side.

(a) Same as starboard side.

(b) Make certain the empennage surface control access door is secured.

(c) See that the battery access door is secured. In the T-28B, the door is located just forward of the leading edge of the horizontal stabilizer. In the T-28C, it is located about 6 feet forward of the leading edge of the horizontal stabilizer.

(d) See that the oxygen filler valve access door is secured in the T-28B. The filler valve is located inside the baggage compartment on the upper rack in the T-28C.

PRESTART CHECK LIST

1. Rudder pedals and seat—Adjust and Lock.

Note

Assure that the seat adjust lever is full forward.

2. Controls—free.
3. Control lock—stowed.
4. COCKPIT AIR CONTROL—OPEN.
5. FUEL shutoff—ON.
6. Trim tabs—Set (0, 0, 5 right).
7. Supercharger—LOW.
8. Mixture—IDLE CUTOFF.
9. PROP lever—Full INCREASE RPM.
10. Throttle—cracked (¾ inch).
11. SPEED BRAKE—OFF.
12. Carburetor air—DIRECT.
13. COWL & OIL COOLER FLAPS switch—OPEN.
14. COCKPIT HEATER handle—OFF.
15. Landing gear handle—DOWN.
16. LANDING LIGHTS switches—OFF.
17. CANOPY DEFROST handle—ON.
18. Oxygen pressure—1000 psi minimum.
19. Oxygen diluter lever—100%.
20. IGNITION switch—OFF.
21. DC POWER switch—OFF.
22. PITOT HEATER switch—OFF.
23. INST POWER switch—NO. 1 INV.
24. CONTROL SHIFT switch—energized.
25. Navigation and cockpit lights—as desired.
26. Circuit breakers—check.

Note

Check inverter circuit breakers out; landing light circuit breakers out for day flights.

27. Radios—off.
28. DC POWER switch—BAT. & GEN.
29. Gear position indicators—DOWN.
30. Sump plug warning light—Press to test.

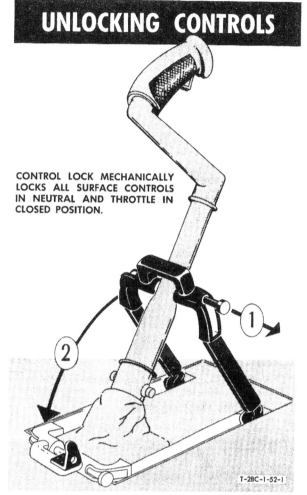

UNLOCKING CONTROLS

CONTROL LOCK MECHANICALLY LOCKS ALL SURFACE CONTROLS IN NEUTRAL AND THROTTLE IN CLOSED POSITION.

T-28C-1-52-1

Figure 3-4

31. Fuel pressure—13 psi minimum.
32. Battery voltage—22 volts minimum.
33. DC POWER switch—OFF.
34. Gear pins—removed.
35. Field barometric pressure—check.

STARTING PROCEDURE

1. DC POWER switch—BAT. & GEN. (OFF if external power used).

2. STARTER button—Depress.
   Turn propeller through at least eight blades.

3. IGNITION switch—BOTH.

4. PRIMER button—Depress.

CAUTION

If engine fails to start after 30 seconds of continuous cranking, let starter cool for 3 minutes before repeating starting procedure.

5. When engine starts, STARTER button—Release.
Continue steady priming and adjust throttle until engine is running smoothly between 1000 and 1200 rpm.

6. Mixture control—RICH.
When rpm drops slightly, indicating that carburetor is supplying fuel, release primer button. Check oil pressure; if it does not register in 10 seconds or rise to 40 psi in 20 seconds, secure engine and investigate.

7. If APU is used, disconnect, then DC POWER switch —BAT. & GEN.

8. INVERTER circuit breakers—in.

CAUTION

● During cold weather operations, if oil dilution has been used prior to engine shutdown, refer to COLD WEATHER OPERATIONS, in Section VI, for engine warmup procedures.

● Keep the cowl and oil cooler flaps open for warmup and all ground operation. Do not attempt to hurry the warmup period.

PRETAXI CHECK

While the engine is warming up (between 1200 and 1600 rpm), perform the following:

1. Radio equipment—as desired.

2. FLAP handle—UP.

3. Hydraulic pressure—1250 to 1650 psi.

4. Altimeter—Set to field elevation.

5. Clock—Set.

6. Engine instruments—check.

7. Fuel quantity—check total, LEFT WING and RIGHT WING.

8. Attitude gyro—erected. (Cage and Release.)

9. Gyro compass—SLAVED and aligned.

10. INST POWER switch—NO. 2 INV., check, return to NO. 1 INV.

11. Engine fuel pump—check at 1200 rpm. Pull FUEL BOOST PUMP circuit breaker, or (hold FUEL BOOST PUMP switch to TEST*), check fuel pressure 21 to 25 psi, and reset circuit breaker.

12. Ignition check—At approximately 750 rpm, turn IGNITION switch to L, R, and OFF momentarily and then to BOTH. The engine should run on L and R and cease firing on OFF. If engine ceases to fire on L or R, or does not cease to fire on OFF, shut down the engine and have a troubleshooter investigate.

CAUTION

Perform this check as rapidly as possible to prevent severe backfiring when switch is returned to BOTH.

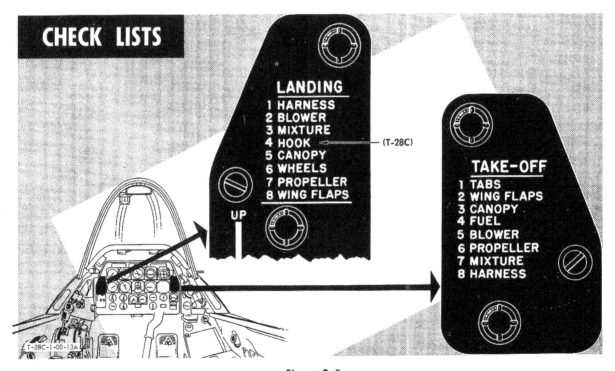

Figure 3-5

*Aircraft having AFC 105 complied with

TAXI, TAKE-OFF, AND LANDING

TAXI PROCEDURES

Observe the following instructions and procedures:

1. At idle, apply brakes and signal for chocks to be removed.

CAUTION

Avoid prolonged standing with engine idling, or taxiing with exhaust to windward, as dangerous concentrations of carbon monoxide may rapidly accumulate.

2. Release brakes and allow aircraft to roll straight ahead. Apply brakes evenly and firmly to check for adequate braking action. Do not ride brakes, as they will heat rapidly.

3. Under normal conditions, 750 to 950 rpm will be sufficient for taxiing.

4. Check turn-and-bank indicator and gyro magnetic compass during turns.

5. Whenever the aircraft is stopped, operate at 1200 rpm. This prevents plug fouling, creates propeller blast for engine cooling, and ensures proper operation of the d-c generator.

6. Taxi only on hard-surfaced areas.

7. Turn into the wind to provide maximum cooling and steady rpm for engine runup.

BEFORE TAKE-OFF

ENGINE RUNUP

Before engine runup, check engine instruments within normal operating range.

INTERIM CHANGE #36

Note

While performing checks requiring rpm reading, it may be necessary to tap instrument panel to prevent tachometer sticking, especially in cold weather. Do not strike instrument glass.

1. Check propeller control at full INCREASE RPM position.

2. Propeller check—At 1600 rpm, pull propeller control back to full DECREASE RPM and note rpm drop of approximately 400 rpm. Return control to full INCREASE RPM and check for full recovery of rpm.

3. Loadmeter and voltmeter check—Above 1300 rpm with the DC POWER switch in the BAT. & GEN. position and the INST POWER switch in the NO. 1 INV. position, check the loadmeter and voltmeter to

ensure proper operation of the d-c generating system.

Note

The loadmeter is graduated in percent and will indicate the relative load incurred, dependent upon the electrical equipment in use. The normal range is 0.3 to 0.5. The voltmeter is graduated in d-c volts and should indicate approximately 27.7 volts.

4. Supercharger check—At 1600 rpm with propeller control at full INCREASE RPM, move supercharger control handle to HIGH. A sudden decrease in engine rpm will indicate that the high ratio clutch has engaged. Advance throttle to obtain 30 in. Hg. Return supercharger control handle to LOW. A sudden decrease in manifold pressure indicates that the two-speed supercharger mechanism is working properly.

Note

One daily operation of the supercharger clutch, during preflight engine check, is satisfactory.

CAUTION

Do not shift from low to high supercharger ratio at less than 5-minute intervals, in order to prevent overheating of supercharger clutch. Shift from high to low ratio as desired, since no heat is generated.

5. Power check—Adjust throttle to obtain manifold pressure equal to field barometric pressure (as read on manifold pressure gage before starting engine) and check for 2275 (±75) rpm in the T-28C, 2250 (±50) rpm in the T-28B.

Note

If rpm is too low for given manifold pressure, engine is not developing sufficient power and should be checked before flight.

6. Ignition system check—With throttle adjusted to obtain 2300 rpm in the T-28C, manifold pressure equal to field barometric in the T-28B, check ignition system with IGNITION switch at L and R for maximum drop of 75 rpm. Return IGNITION switch to BOTH, between checks, to allow speed to stabilize.

CAUTION

Restrictions on the propeller prohibit prolonged ground operation between 1900 and 2200 rpm in the T-28C.

If drop exceeds 75 rpm, return ignition switch to BOTH and perform the following burnout procedure if plug fouling is suspected:

    (a) Set rpm at 2250.
    (b) Mixture—normal.
    (c) Maintain 2250 rpm for 1 minute or 200°CHT whichever occurs first.
    (d) Mixture—RICH.
    (e) Repeat ignition system check.

7. At 1800 rpm; check oil pressure—65 psi minimum. Close throttle; check for idling speed of approximately 750 rpm.
8. Radios—tuned and checked.
9. Pitot heat—checked and as desired.
10. Flight instruments—checked.

TAKE-OFF CHECK LIST

Before take-off, complete take-off check list as follows:
1. Trim tabs—0, 0, 5 degrees right rudder.
2. Flaps—FLAP handle UP, and visually check flaps up.
3. Canopy—check FULLY CLOSED.
4. Fuel—FUEL SHUTOFF ON, fuel pressure, full fuel load, FUEL BOOST PUMP circuit breaker in.
5. Supercharger—handle in LOW blower position.
6. PROP lever—full INCREASE RPM position.
7. Mixture—RICH position.
8. Harness—tight and LOCKED.

Note

Prior to take-off, close the cowl and oil cooler flaps to the one-fourth open position. Check controls for free proper movement, and carburetor air control DIRECT unless icing is anticipated.

TAKE-OFF

NORMAL FIELD TAKE-OFF

1. Roll into the take-off position and align nose wheel with runway.
2. Advance the throttle to 30 inches MAP while holding the brakes.
3. Check the engine instruments for proper indications.
4. Release the brakes and smoothly advance throttle to take-off power—48 inches. (52.5 in. Hg MAP is maximum allowable at sea level.)
5. Maintain directional control during first part of take-off run by use of rudder and differential braking if necessary. The rudder is effective for directional control above approximately 30 KIAS.
6. When the elevator becomes effective, raise the nose to the take-off attitude. Maintain the take-off attitude and allow the aircraft to fly itself off at 85 to 90 knots.

MINIMUM RUN OR OBSTACLE TAKE-OFF

A minimum run take-off is in maximum performance maneuver with the aircraft near stalling speed. It is directly related to slow flying and flaps-down stalls. Complete the normal before take-off checks and proceed as follows:

1. Complete take-off check list with flaps one-half down.
2. Roll into take-off position and align nose wheel with runway.
3. Advance the throttle to 30 inches MAP while holding the brakes.
4. Check the engine instruments for proper indications.
5. Advance throttle smoothly to take-off power; release brakes and apply full aft stick simultaneously; maintain directional control by differential braking, but discontinue using brakes as soon as rudder becomes effective.
6. The aircraft will fly off at approximately 60 KIAS.
7. When definitely airborne, ease stick forward to the position which will produce the airspeed for best angle of climb as determined from figure 11-60 in Section XI.
8. Apply brakes to stop rotation of wheels and raise gear.
9. When clear of obstacle, accelerate to normal climb speed, raise flaps, and reduce power for normal climb.

CROSS-WIND TAKE-OFF

The following procedure is recommended for cross-wind take-off:

1. Align aircraft straight down runway and advance throttle to take-off power. Hold nose straight down runway.
2. Continue as in a normal take-off, applying sufficient aileron pressure to maintain level attitude. Refer to take-off and landing cross-wind chart (figure 11-11) for minimum nose wheel liftoff speed.
3. At precomputed nose wheel liftoff speed, apply sufficient stick pressure to make a positive break with the ground.
4. After becoming airborne, correct for drift by making a coordinated turn into the wind.

NIGHT TAKE-OFF

Proceed as for normal field take-off.

Note

The cockpit lights should be at a low intensity and a serviceable flashlight should be readily accessible.

FCLP/CARRIER TAKE-OFF

Refer to Part IV of this section.

AFTER TAKE-OFF

1. When comfortably airborne, apply brake to stop wheels and then retract the landing gear.

2. Reduce power to 36 inches MAP and 2400 rpm.

3. Accelerate to normal climb speed.

CLIMB

Normal climb at sea level is 140 knots, 36 inches, and 2400 rpm. Maintain 36 inches but allow the airspeed to decrease at a rate of 1 knot per thousand feet. More efficient performance may be required immediately after take-off for obstacle clearance, climbout commitments, etc, and is allowable. Refer to Section XI for maximum performance climbs. During climbs, proceed as follows:

1. Advance throttle to maintain manifold pressure during climb.

2. Adjust cowl and oil cooler flaps as necessary to maintain desired cylinder head and oil temperatures.

3. Upon reaching the altitude where it is more advantageous to operate with high blower (approximately 13,500 feet for military power and 15,000 feet for normal rated power), shift supercharger to high blower as follows: (a) Retard throttle to obtain less than 20 in. Hg. (b) Move propeller control to 1600 rpm. (c) Move supercharger control handle rapidly to HIGH. (d) Readjust propeller control and throttle to give desired power setting.

CAUTION

Do not shift from low to high supercharger ratio at less than 5-minute intervals in order to prevent overheating of supercharger clutch. Shift from high to low ratio as desired, since no heat is generated.

4. Move mixture control to NORMAL after reaching the desired cruising altitude.

CRUISE

For NATOPS Evaluation Flight purposes, normal cruise is 170 KIAS below 10,000 feet and 155 KIAS above 10,000 feet.

During extended cruise at low power settings, clear engine every 30 minutes by operating for approximately 3 to 5 minutes at normal rated power.

FLIGHT PROCEDURES AND CHARACTERISTICS

All data on flight procedures and characteristics are presented in Section IV.

DESCENT

Shift supercharger handle to LOW at any cruise rpm to preclude the possibility of subsequent overboosting of engine at low altitudes. Use rich mixture to minimize possibility of engine backfire or cutout if sudden application of power is required. Close cowl flaps to minimize overcooling of engine.

Note

To prevent possible fogging of the windshield during a descent from high altitude, turn windshield and canopy defrost handle and cockpit heater control handle to ON prior to descent.

Use of low cruise rpm and highest manifold pressure, consistent with desired airspeed and engine manifold air pressure limits, is preferable to idle power descent or high rpm, low power descent, as "loading up" of engine will be minimized and engine temperatures can be maintained at desired values. Clear the engine periodically during descent by momentarily advancing the throttle.

For NATOPS Evaluation Flight purposes, descents normally will be accomplished at 170 KIAS with the speed brake retracted or extended. Maintain at least 1 inch of manifold pressure for every 100 rpm. Long distances can be covered during a descent with minimum power with gear and flaps up if a glide speed of 130 knots IAS is established. Lowering flaps or landing gear greatly steepens the gliding angle and increases rate of descent.

LANDING

LANDING CHECK LIST

Before entering the break or landing pattern, set carburetor air control as required and check:

1. Harness—locked.

2. Blower—low.

3. Mixture—rich.

4. Hook—as desired (T-28C).

5. Canopy—closed.

6. Wheels, propeller, wing flaps to go (propeller setting of 2200 rpm is recommended).

BREAK

1. Roll into the desired angle of bank.

2. Retard throttle to 15 inches or gear warning.

3. SPEED BRAKE switch—ON (extended).

4. Lower landing gear at 140 knots.

5. SPEED BRAKE—OFF (retracted).

6. Slow to, and maintain, 120 knots.

7. Propeller control—2400 rpm.

FULL FLAP LANDING

See figure 3-6.

1. Just prior to reaching a point abeam the intended point of landing, retard the throttle to 20 inches, put the propeller to the full low pitch position, and lower full flaps.

2. Abeam the intended point of landing, start the approach so as to arrive at the 90-degree position at 100 knots.

3. Intercept the landing line with 150 to 200 feet of altitude and approximately 1200 feet of straight-away to the touchdown point.

4. Level the wings and transition to the 90-knot attitude.

5. Commence the "flareout" at 5 to 10 feet of altitude.

6. On the rollout, lower the nose wheel to the runway as the elevator loses its effectiveness.

See figure 3-7 for full flap touch-and-go pattern.

NO FLAP LANDING

1. Just prior to reaching a point abeam the intended point of landing, retard throttle to 18 inches and put the propeller to the full low pitch position.

2. Abeam the intended point of landing, start the approach so as to arrive at the 90-degree position at 110 knots.

3. Intercept the landing line with 150 to 200 feet of altitude and approximately 1200 feet of straight-away to the touchdown point.

4. Level the wings and transition to the 100-knot attitude.

5. As the aircraft approaches the intended point of landing, close the throttle and transition to the landing attitude.

6. On the rollout, lower the nose onto the runway as the elevator loses its effectiveness.

See figure 3-8 for no flap touch-and-go pattern.

CROSS-WIND LANDING

No special technique is required in a cross-wind landing. Use the wing-low method.

1. Allow for drift while turning on final approach so that you will not overshoot or undershoot the approach leg.

2. Establish drift correction as soon as drift is detected.

3. Velocity and direction of the wind will determine the amount of flaps used for the landing.

Note

Since on the ground the aircraft acts like a weather vane, it attempts to swing into the wind. Flaps increase this weather-vaning tendency, so use a minimum degree of flaps in a cross wind. See take-off and landing cross-wind chart (figure 11-11) for minimum touchdown speed.

4. Use ailerons as necessary to counteract a wing-low condition during flare and touchdown.

WAVEOFF

The power required depends on the position of the aircraft in the approach, etc, but never raise the flaps below 300 feet.

1. Advance throttle smoothly. Do not exceed 52.5 in. Hg.

2. Establish climb attitude.

3. Landing gear handle—up.

4. Cowl flaps—open as necessary.

5. Raise wing flaps at 300 feet or above.

APPROACH AND LANDING PROCEDURE

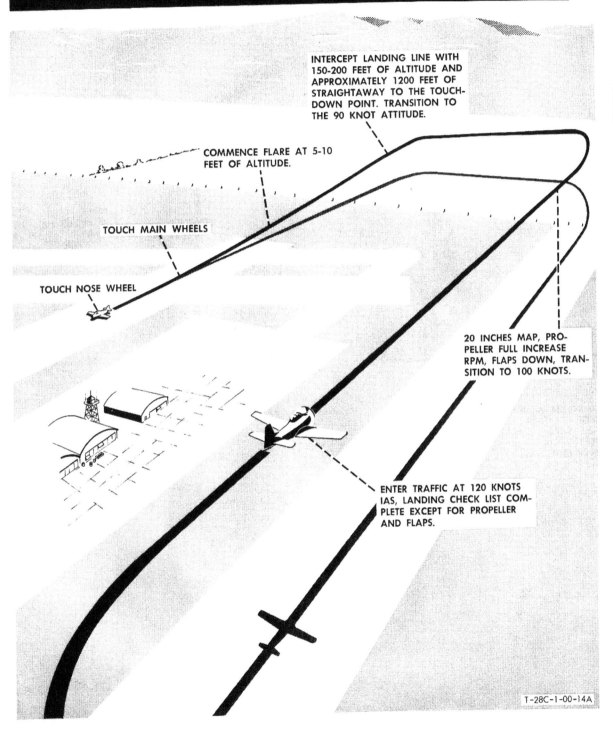

INTERCEPT LANDING LINE WITH 150-200 FEET OF ALTITUDE AND APPROXIMATELY 1200 FEET OF STRAIGHTAWAY TO THE TOUCHDOWN POINT. TRANSITION TO THE 90 KNOT ATTITUDE.

COMMENCE FLARE AT 5-10 FEET OF ALTITUDE.

TOUCH MAIN WHEELS

TOUCH NOSE WHEEL

20 INCHES MAP, PROPELLER FULL INCREASE RPM, FLAPS DOWN, TRANSITION TO 100 KNOTS.

ENTER TRAFFIC AT 120 KNOTS IAS, LANDING CHECK LIST COMPLETE EXCEPT FOR PROPELLER AND FLAPS.

T-28C-1-00-14A

Figure 3-6

FULL-FLAP TOUCH-AND-GO PATTERN

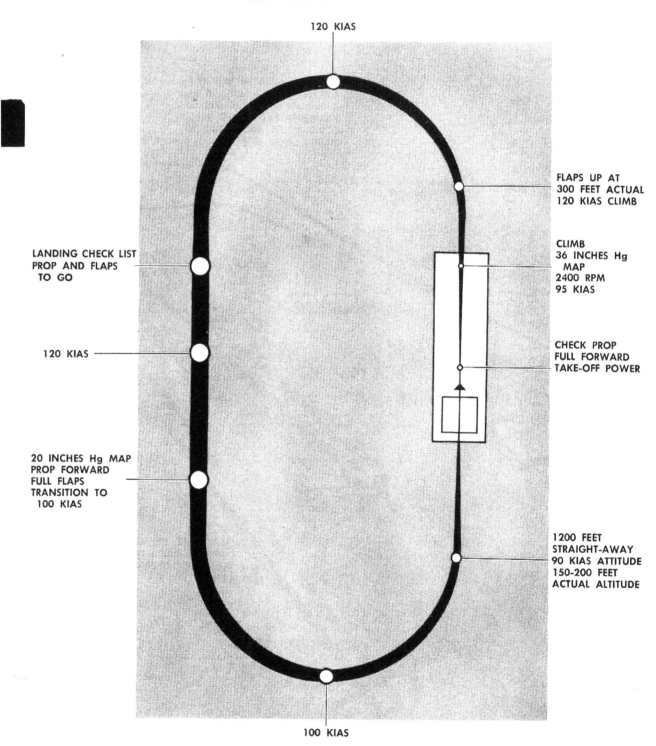

120 KIAS

FLAPS UP AT
300 FEET ACTUAL
120 KIAS CLIMB

CLIMB
36 INCHES Hg
MAP
2400 RPM
95 KIAS

LANDING CHECK LIST
PROP AND FLAPS
TO GO

CHECK PROP
FULL FORWARD
TAKE-OFF POWER

120 KIAS

20 INCHES Hg MAP
PROP FORWARD
FULL FLAPS
TRANSITION TO
100 KIAS

1200 FEET
STRAIGHT-AWAY
90 KIAS ATTITUDE
150-200 FEET
ACTUAL ALTITUDE

100 KIAS

T-28B-1-00-33A

NO-FLAP TOUCH-AND-GO PATTERN

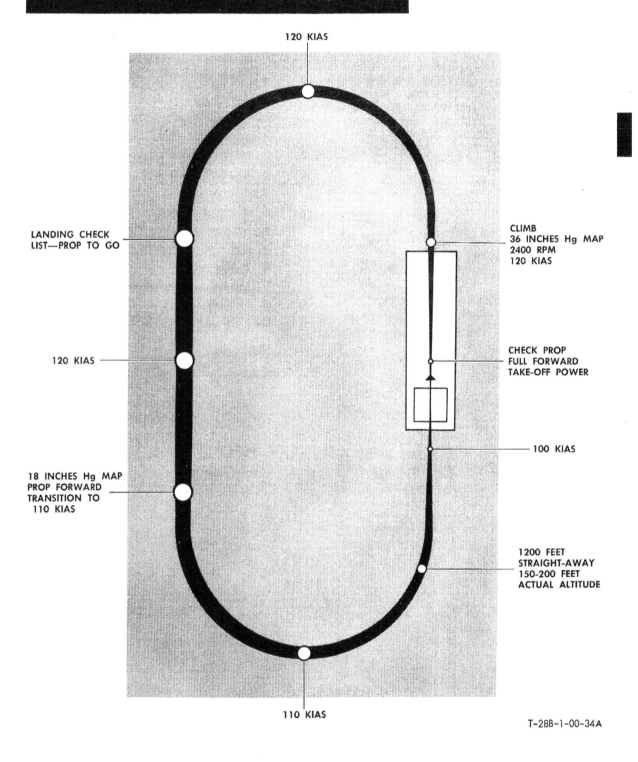

120 KIAS

LANDING CHECK
LIST—PROP TO GO

CLIMB
36 INCHES Hg MAP
2400 RPM
120 KIAS

CHECK PROP
FULL FORWARD
TAKE-OFF POWER

120 KIAS

18 INCHES Hg MAP
PROP FORWARD
TRANSITION TO
110 KIAS

100 KIAS

1200 FEET
STRAIGHT-AWAY
150-200 FEET
ACTUAL ALTITUDE

110 KIAS

T-28B-1-00-34A

Figure 3-8

FIELD BARRIER

If the field barrier is to be engaged, the aircraft should be in a three-point attitude with the engine secured. Aim for the center of the barrier.

AFTER LANDING

After landing, allow the aircraft to roll out toward the turn-off area. Commence braking soon enough so that a moderate amount of braking is all that is required to slow to a safe turn-off speed. When braking is needed, apply smooth, even, continuous pressure to the pedals and ease the stick to the full aft position to avoid undue stress to the nose strut and wheel. Release the brakes momentarily every few seconds to allow brake disc cooling. Do not pump the brakes. After the roll-out, clear the runway immediately. Before taxiing to the line:

1. Cowl flaps—full OPEN.

2. PITOT HTR switch—OFF.

3. Canopy—as desired.

ENGINE SHUTDOWN

When a cold weather start is anticipated for the next use of the aircraft, dilute oil as required by the lowest temperature expected. Refer to Section VI.

1. Cowl flaps—OPEN.

2. Ignition ground—checked.

3. Idle mixture—checked.

4. Scavenge engine at 1200 rpm for 60 seconds. Allow cylinder head temperature to stabilize.

5. Pull mixture to IDLE CUTOFF and throttle to CLOSED position.

Do not advance throttle after placing mixture control in IDLE CUTOFF. Refer to STOPPING ENGINE, in Section I, Part 2.

After propeller stops rotating:

1. FUEL shutoff—OFF.

2. DC POWER switch—OFF.

3. IGNITION switch—OFF.

4. Gear pins—in.

5. Accelerometer—within limits.

6. Oxygen—minimum 1000 psi.

7. Light switches—off.

8. Radios—off.

9. Inverter circuit breakers—pulled.

10. Controls—locked.

11. Trim tab controls—NEUTRAL.

POSTFLIGHT

Inspect aircraft for hydraulic, fuel, and oil leaks.

Do not set the parking brakes if wheel brakes are overheated.

PART 4 — CARRIER-BASED PROCEDURES

CARRIER OPERATIONS

Only those procedures differing from shore-based procedures are contained herein.

DECK LAUNCH

For carrier take-off (deck launch), the aircraft will be configured with flaps full down, canopy open, and trim settings of 0 degrees elevator, 0 degrees aileron, and 8 degrees of right rudder. When aligned for take-off and upon receipt of the two fingers turn-up signal, advance power to approximately 30 inches of MAP, scan the engine instruments, especially the oil pressure and sump warning light. If everything is normal, give a positive head nod to the launching officer. When given the launch signal release the brakes, simultaneously advancing the power to 48 inches MAP. On the take-off roll, proper use of rudders will generally be all that is necessary to maintain directional control. As elevator control is attained, raise the nose to the take-off attitude and allow the aircraft to fly off the deck. Following take-off, if departing the pattern, raise the landing gear. Flaps should not be raised below 100 KIAS and 250 feet of altitude.

MIRROR/LENS APPROACH

A typical mirror/lens approach for an angled deck carrier is shown in figure 3-9. The downwind leg is flown at 82 KIAS, configured with full increase rpm, gear down, hook down (arrested), full flaps, speed brake down, and canopy opened. The abeam position is 1000—1200 yards at 325 feet actual altitude. Abeam the LSO platform, a level turn is commenced utilizing 20—22 degrees angle of bank. At meatball pickup, or about the 70-degree position, power is reduced to commence the glide slope rate of descent (approximately 25—28 inches manifold pressure). Airspeed is maintained at 82 KIAS throughout the approach. Near the ramp, the LSO will give the cut signal. Following the cut, the 82 KIAS attitude will be maintained and the aircraft will touch down with the nose wheel 10—12 inches off the deck. The throttle is closed at the cut signal and remains closed throughout the landing rollout. In the event of a bolter, simultaneously lower the nose to the deck, add full power, retract the speed brake, and effect a touch-and-go landing.

WAVEOFF

A waveoff is a critical situation. The proper procedure is to add full power, level the wings, stop the rate of descent, and retract the speed brake. If waving off in close, (the last 5—6 seconds), continue straight ahead up the angle deck. Turn to parallel the ship's course when abeam the bow. If waving

off from an overshoot, fly up the starboard side of the deck (runway). Under no circumstances exceed 30 degrees angle of bank in the carrier landing pattern (FCLP pattern).

FIELD CARRIER LANDING PRACTICE

The FCLP pattern is basically the same as the 180-degree precision landing pattern with some changes in speed altitude, and groove length. The pattern is the familiar racetrack pattern with an extended downwind leg. The delay in initiating the 180-degree turn is to allow for a 20—25 second groove. See figure 3-10.

ENTRY INTO PATTERN

Break interval between aircraft will normally be 10 seconds. At the break, use 45 degrees of bank, reduce power to 15 inches manifold pressure, and open cowl and oil cooler flaps. As airspeed reaches 140 KIAS, lower the gear, advance the propeller to full increase rpm, and lower full flaps. When the airspeed reaches 100 KIAS, add power to maintain level flight at 90 KIAS. When established wings level downwind, 325 feet actual altitude, extend the speed brake and slow to 82 KIAS.

APPROACH

The 180-degree position should be 1000—1200 yards abeam (slightly more than a wingtip distance), 325 feet actual altitude, and 82 KIAS. Timing past the intended point of landing will vary from 10—20 seconds, depending upon the wind. The approach turn is level utilizing approximately 20 degrees angle of bank until intercepting the meatball at approximately the 90 degree position. At meatball pickup, reduce power to approximately 26 inches MAP to start the glide slope rate of descent which will vary from 350—500 feet per minute, depending upon the wind, and maintain 82 KIAS. As the aircraft rolls wings level in the groove, normally another power reduction will be necessary to preclude accelerating out of the turn. In the groove, if crosswind corrections are necessary, the standard wing down-top rudder method will be used. When the cut light is flashed, close the throttle, shift scan to the landing area, and flare as necessary to land with the nose wheel 10—12 inches off the deck. Upon touchdown, lower nose wheel to deck. For touch-and-go landings, add full power (48 inches MAP), raise the speed brake, raise the nose to take-off attitude, and smoothly fly the aircraft off the deck (75—85 KIAS). When a positive rate of climb has been established, make a gentle clearing turn to the starboard, transition to 90 KIAS in the climb, and climb out straight ahead to the pattern altitude of 325 feet actual altitude, using 36 inches MAP and full increase rpm. Normal interval is established by commencing the upwind turn when the aircraft ahead is abeam the port wingtip if he is still in the turn, or 20 degrees ahead of the wingtip if he is wings level downwind. The upwind turn is flown at 90 KIAS using approximately 20 degrees angle of bank.

CARRIER LANDING PATTERN

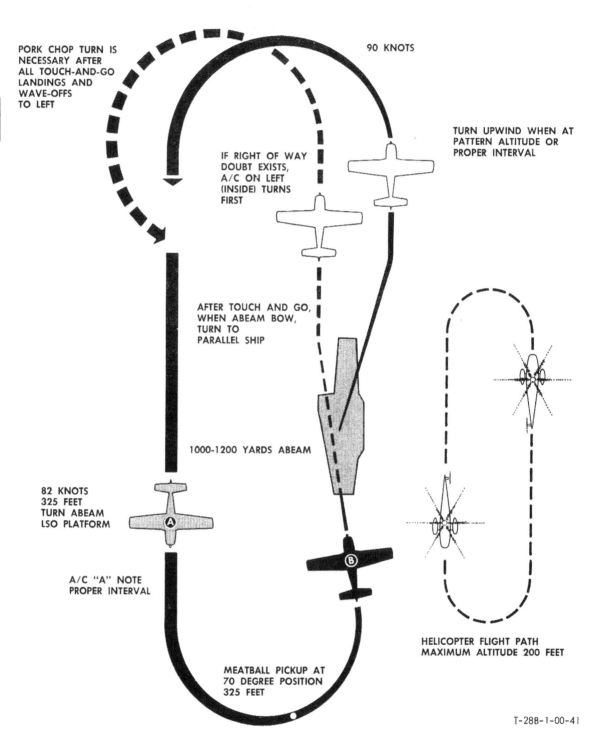

PORK CHOP TURN IS
NECESSARY AFTER
ALL TOUCH-AND-GO
LANDINGS AND
WAVE-OFFS
TO LEFT

90 KNOTS

IF RIGHT OF WAY
DOUBT EXISTS,
A/C ON LEFT
(INSIDE) TURNS
FIRST

TURN UPWIND WHEN AT
PATTERN ALTITUDE OR
PROPER INTERVAL

AFTER TOUCH AND GO,
WHEN ABEAM BOW,
TURN TO
PARALLEL SHIP

1000-1200 YARDS ABEAM

82 KNOTS
325 FEET
TURN ABEAM
LSO PLATFORM

A/C "A" NOTE
PROPER INTERVAL

MEATBALL PICKUP AT
70 DEGREE POSITION
325 FEET

HELICOPTER FLIGHT PATH
MAXIMUM ALTITUDE 200 FEET

T-28-1-00-41

Figure 3-9

TABLE OF CONTENTS

FLIGHT PROCEDURES

Procedures outlined herein will be adhered to during the initial checkout and while maintaining continuing flight proficiency. Knowledge of, and compliance with these procedures will be demonstrated during the initial checkout and the annual NATOPS evaluation flight. Criteria for grading the initial checkout and the annual NATOPS Evaluation Flight is found in Section X of this manual.

TRANSITION OR FAMILIARIZATION

TAKE-OFF
Refer to Section III.

NORMAL CLIMB
Refer to Section III.

NORMAL CRUISE
Refer to Section III.

DESCENT
Refer to Section III.

NORMAL LANDING
Refer to Section III.

FULL-FLAP LANDING
Refer to Section III.

NO-FLAP LANDING
Refer to Section III.

CROSS-WIND LANDING
Refer to Section III.

WAVEOFF
Refer to Section III.

AFTER LANDING
Refer to Section III.

EMERGENCIES
Refer to Section V.

SLOW FLIGHT

Slow flight will be performed while maintaining a constant heading and altitude. Enter slow flight from normal cruise as follows:

1. Mixture to RICH.

2. Increase rpm to 2400.

3. Retard throttle to 15 inches.

4. Extend speed brake.

5. At 140 knots, lower the landing gear and retract the speed brake.

6. Lower full flaps in one increment.

7. As the airspeed approaches 90 knots, increase throttle to approximately 25 inches and maintain 90 knots.

8. To return to normal cruise, advance throttle to 36 inches and retract the landing gear. When the gear indicates up, raise the flaps in one increment. At 170 knots, reduce power to normal cruise power setting and mixture to normal.

CLEARING TURNS

Clearing turns will be performed prior to any stall, spin, or acrobatic maneuver. Clearing turns will consist of two 45-degree, angle-of-bank turns for 90 degrees or one 180-degree turn.

STALLS

STALL CHECK LIST

A stall check list will be performed prior to any stall maneuver, as follows:

1. Mixture to RICH.

2. 2400 rpm.

3. Check bilges for loose gear.

4. Seat belt and shoulder harness locked.

APPROACH TURN STALL

1. Transition to slow flight.

2. Complete the clearing turns with 20 inches and establish a 90-knot approach attitude.

3. Roll into a 30-degree angle-of-bank turn and maintain 90 knots.

4. Simultaneously raise the nose to the landing attitude and close the throttle. Maintain 30-degree angle of bank and the landing attitude until the aircraft stalls.

5. Recover by reducing the angle of attack and leveling the wings. Simultaneously add throttle to maximum allowable. When flying speed is attained, raise the nose to stop loss of altitude.

LANDING ATTITUDE MANEUVER

1. Transition to slow flight.

2. Complete the clearing turns with 20 inches and establish a 90-knot approach attitude and trim for this attitude.

3. Raise the nose to the landing attitude, simultaneously closing the throttle.

4. Recover prior to a stall by applying maximum allowable manifold pressure and maintaining the landing attitude. Fly the aircraft out of the near stalled condition in balanced flight without a loss of altitude. As the airspeed increases, lower the nose and return to normal slow flight.

SPINS

Before commencing spins, perform clearing turns and proceed as follows:

1. During the last half of the clearing turns, simultaneously retard the throttle to idle and the propeller control to full decrease rpm.

2. Complete the clearing turn with approximately 120 knots.

3. Raise the nose 30 degrees above the horizon.

4. As the aircraft approaches the stall, lead with rudder in the desired direction.

5. As the nose begins to move in the desired direction and as the aircraft stalls, apply full rudder and smoothly bring the stick straight back.

6. Hold full back stick and full rudder into the spin.

7. Recover after one and one-half turns by applying full opposite rudder and forward stick (slightly ahead of neutral).

8. When rotation stops, neutralize the flight controls and start a smooth pullout.

9. When the nose is above the horizon, adjust propeller control to the 2400 rpm position and, oil pressure permitting, add throttle.

ACROBATICS

All acrobatic maneuvers originate from acrobatic cruise, which is 180 KIAS, mixture rich, rpm 2200, with throttle setting at required manifold pressure to maintain airspeed. Prior to starting acrobatics, complete the acrobatic check list. Do not retrim the aircraft during acrobatics. Details of maneuvers themselves will not be discussed in this section since acrobatics are the same for all aircraft with the exception of power settings and airspeeds.

ACROBATIC CHECK LIST

1. Mixture to RICH.

2. 2200 rpm.

3. Bilges clear.

4. Seat belt and shoulder harness locked and tight.

BARREL ROLL

Barrel roll entry airspeed is 180 knots. When inverted, and after 90 degrees of heading change, airspeed is approximately 100 knots. Recover on the original heading with 180 knots.

WING OVER

Wing-over entry airspeed is 200 knots. The airspeed should be 100 knots after completing 90 degrees of turn. Recover 180 degrees from the original heading with 200 knots.

LOOP

Loop entry and recovery airspeed is 220 knots. Make a 3½-g pullup.

IMMELMANN

Immelman entry airspeed is 240 knots. Make a 3½-g pullup and recover with approximately 100-120 knots in level flight.

ONE-HALF CUBAN EIGHT

One-half Cuban Eight entry airspeed is 240 knots. Make a 3½-g pullup. Recover on the entry altitude and 180 degrees from the original heading.

INSTRUMENTS

The T-28 is equipped with all necessary instruments for instrument flying. Considerable pilot effort is required to maintain precise altitude and heading. Flight into high density traffic areas in instrument weather conditions with only one pilot should be avoided. Flight in icing conditions will not be attempted as there are no provisions for structural or propeller deicing. Refer to COLD WEATHER OPERATIONS in Section VI.

CLIMB, CRUISE, AND DESCENT

Climb, cruise, and descent in instrument flight will be the same as VFR procedures described in NORMAL OPERATING PROCEDURES in Section III.

HOLDING

Holding airspeed is 130 knots, 1800 rpm, MAP as required, mixture NORMAL.

PENETRATION

1. Departing the initial approach fix, extend speed brake and descend at 210 KIAS, 20 inches MAP, and 1800 rpm.
2. Upon level-off, slow to 130 KIAS, retract the speed brake, and advance the throttle to hold 130 KIAS.
3. Inbound to low station, advance rpm to 2400 rpm, MAP to 24 inches, lower landing gear, lower one-half flaps, slow to and maintain 120 KIAS.

LOW-ALTITUDE APPROACH

1. Descend at 130 KIAS, 1800 rpm, 20 inches MAP, speed brake extended, mixture RICH.
2. Upon level-off, retract speed brake, MAP as necessary to maintain 130 KIAS.
3. Inbound to low station, advance rpm to 2400, MAP to 24 inches, lower landing gear, lower one-half flaps, slow to and maintain 120 KIAS.
4. At low station, reduce MAP 22 to 24 inches and descend at 120 KIAS (standard rate descent).
5. Prior to landing, propeller full INCREASE RPM and flaps as desired.

GCA

Power settings and aircraft configuration for downwind, base, and final legs are shown in figure 4-1.

MISSED APPROACH

1. Advance throttle smoothly. Do not exceed maximum allowable MAP.
2. Establish a climbing attitude.
3. Landing gear up.
4. Flaps up if above 300 feet and in a wings-level attitude.
5. Comply with the published instructions.

FORMATION AND TACTICS

The discussion of the fundamentals of formation flying will not be elaborated here. However, it is imperative that each aviator in the flight be briefed as to his particular part in the flight.

FLIGHT TEST PROCEDURES

Safety shall be the governing factor on all test flights, and the following general rules shall apply:

1. No aircraft shall be test flown until all safety-of-flight discrepancies have been corrected and signed off by a designated inspector.
2. All test flights shall be conducted under OPNAV, FAA, and local rules for contact flying. OPNAV Instruction 3710.7 (series) is particularly pertinent.
3. Radio communication with the control tower shall be maintained at all times.
4. Test flights will be flown in a designated area where an emergency landing can be made on a hard-surfaced runway.

FLIGHT CHARACTERISTICS

The aircraft has excellent stability and control characteristics under all conditions of speed, power, load factor (G), and altitude. The controls are effective throughout the speed range (stall to limit dive speed) and aircraft response to control movement is quite rapid. Satisfactory handling characteristics, in both accelerated and unaccelerated flight, have been effectively aided by tilting the thrust axis of the engine down 5 degrees. This also eliminates a large amount of the destabilizing effect of power. The majority of this correction is due to the fact that the tilted thrust axis

GCA PATTERN

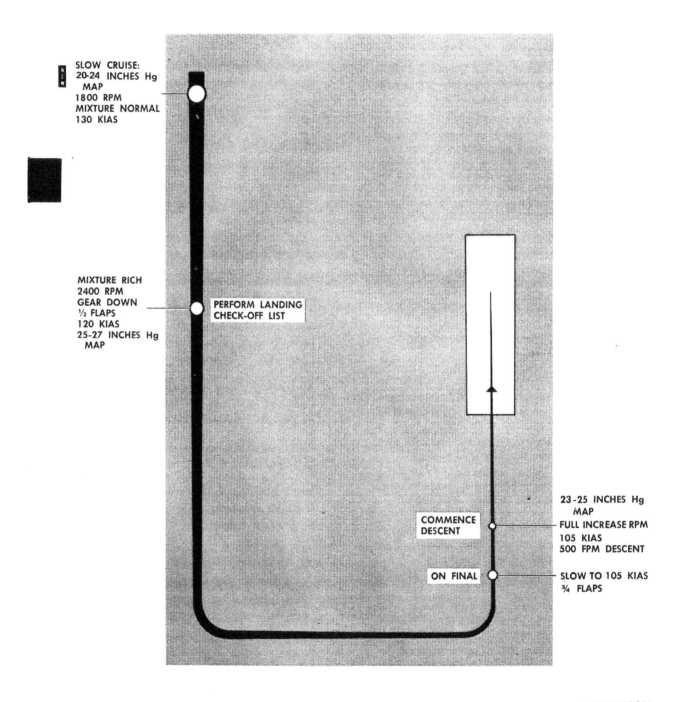

SLOW CRUISE:
20-24 INCHES Hg
MAP
1800 RPM
MIXTURE NORMAL
130 KIAS

MIXTURE RICH
2400 RPM
GEAR DOWN
½ FLAPS
120 KIAS
25-27 INCHES Hg
MAP

PERFORM LANDING
CHECK-OFF LIST

COMMENCE
DESCENT

23-25 INCHES Hg
MAP
FULL INCREASE RPM
105 KIAS
500 FPM DESCENT

ON FINAL

SLOW TO 105 KIAS
¾ FLAPS

T-28B-00-35D

Figure 4-1

TYPICAL INSTRUMENT APPROACH

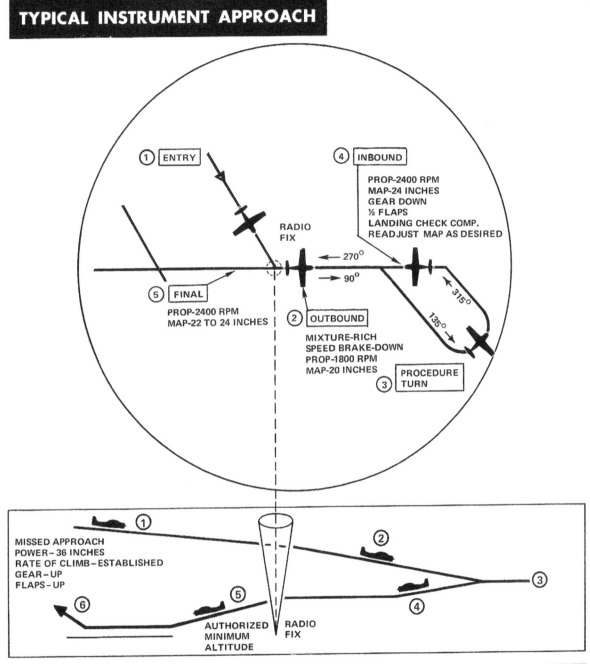

Figure 4-1A

NORMAL APPROACH AIRSPEED—KIAS	ENTRY ①	* OUTBOUND ②	PROCEDURE TURN ③	INBOUND ④	** FINAL ⑤	MISSED APPROACH ⑥
	AS DESIRED	130	130	120	120	140

* MAINTAIN ALTITUDE UNTIL OBTAINING 130 KNOTS, THEN DESCEND

** FULL INCREASE RPM AND FLAPS AS DESIRED FOR LANDING

T-28-1-0-10

passes further above the center of gravity than the untilted axis, thus increasing the stabilizing moment from the thrust forces. The tilted axis also improves the effect of the slip stream over the tail surfaces. The 100-degree-per-second rate of roll is comparable to that normally found only in fighters. The trim tabs are also effective at all speeds so that the aircraft may be easily trimmed to fly "hands off." Operation of the gear, arresting hook (T-28C), wing flaps, canopy, and cowl flaps, as well as changes in power setting, affects longitudinal trim (causes aircraft to pitch up or down) only slightly, thus requiring a minimum of stick movement to maintain flight attitude. The effects of speed brake operation are covered under USE OF SPEED BRAKE, in this section.

FLIGHT WITH EXTERNAL LOADS

The addition of external stores has little effect on flight characteristics. However, maximum allowable dive speed and "g" are lower than for the clean aircraft. Refer to STORES LIMITATIONS, Section I, Part 4, for unmodified aircraft and figure 1-28 for modified aircraft. The T-28C aircraft requires the installation of strakes, to aid spin recovery, when carrying external stores. In addition, as a result of the increased drag and weight, take-off distances are increased, and rate of climb and acceleration are reduced.

Change #38

STALLS

POWER-OFF STALLS

Power-off stalls in this aircraft are very mild. Along with the mechanical stall warning, you will be warned of an approaching stall by a light vibration caused by aircraft buffet which begins 2 or 3 knots above the actual stall. Sometimes mild pitching may accompany the buffet. When the stall occurs with flaps up, the aircraft pitches nose-down and straight ahead, with no tendency to roll. With flaps down, a slight roll to the left may accompany the nose-down pitch. See figure 4-2 for stalling speeds and figure 4-3 for items affecting stalling speeds and characteristics.

POWER-ON STALLS

Power-on stalls are also relatively mild. During the approach to a power-on stall, however, you will find it necessary to use a moderate amount of aileron to

keep the wing level and rudder as required to maintain desired heading. No appreciable buffeting occurs prior to actual stall. At the stall, the aircraft characteristically rolls left, although not violently, and, as in the power-off stalls, pitches nose-down.

Note

Gear position produces no noticeable effect on stall characteristics.

STALL RECOVERY

Stall recovery in this aircraft is accomplished in the conventional manner as follows:

1. Drop nose immediately by releasing back pressure on stick.

2. Use aileron and rudder, as required, to regain straight-and-level attitude.

3. At the same time, advance throttle smoothly. Do not exceed recommended manifold pressure for rpm setting.

4. After the nose is lowered, speed will increase rapidly. When you attain safe flying speed, raise nose with steady back pressure.

5. Retard throttle to cruising power.

INVERTED STALLS

Intentional inverted stalls are not permitted.

SPINS

SPINS—CLEAN

The aircraft has satisfactory spin characteristics with the gear and flaps up or down. A spin may be entered from a stall by applying full rudder in the desired direction of the spin and maintaining full back stick. If the spin is entered with the power on, reduce power to IDLE before starting recovery. If the controls are released after one turn in a spin to the left, the aircraft will recover itself; however, after two turns to the left or one turn to the right, the aircraft will continue to spin if the controls are released. Recovery from the spin will be characterized by a tightening up and acceleration in rate of spin immediately following application of controls for recovery, with the spin stopping rather abruptly at recovery. The spin characteristics are as presented in figure 4-4.

SPINS WITH EXTERNAL STORES ATTACHED (T-28C)

When gun packages or other external stores are installed (figure 4-5), strakes must be attached to each

STALL SPEEDS

KNOTS — IAS

GEAR AND FLAPS — UP

	GROSS WEIGHT — POUNDS				ANGLE OF BANK	LOAD FACTOR "G"	GROSS WEIGHT — POUNDS			
	7500	8000	8500	9000			9500	10,000	10,500	11,000
POWER ON MAXIMUM CONTINUOUS RPM — 2500 MAP — 47" Hg	69	72	76	79	0°	1.0	82	85	89	92
	75	78	82	85	30°	1.2	88	91	95	98
	89	94	99	102	45°	1.4	107	110	114	118
POWER OFF WINDMILLING PROPELLER	79	82	84	86	0°	1.0	89	91	93	96
	85	87	90	92	30°	1.2	95	97	100	103
	95	98	101	103	45°	1.4	106	109	112	115

GEAR AND FLAPS — DOWN

	GROSS WEIGHT — POUNDS				ANGLE OF BANK	LOAD FACTOR "G"	GROSS WEIGHT — POUNDS			
	7500	8000	8500	9000			9500	10,000	10,500	11,000
POWER ON APPROACH POWER RPM — 2500 MAP — 28" Hg	59	62	64	67	0°	1.0	69	72	74	77
	65	67	70	72	30°	1.2	74	77	80	82
	74	77	80	83	45°	1.4	86	89	92	95
POWER OFF WINDMILLING PROPELLER	68	70	72	74	0°	1.0	77	79	81	83
	73	75	78	80	30°	1.2	82	85	87	90
	81	84	86	89	45°	1.4	92	95	97	100

Figure 4-2

T-28B-1-93-6E

side of the forward portion of the fuselage. With the packages and strakes installed, spin entry and spin recovery are normal; however, intentional spins are not permitted. Installation of the strakes does not change the stall characteristics or the stall speeds of the aircraft. For aircraft flight restrictions when carrying external stores, refer to STORES LIMITATIONS, in Section I, Part 4.

SPIN RECOVERY

To effect the spin recovery, apply opposite rudder and move the stick slightly forward of neutral while maintaining neutral ailerons. Rotation will not stop completely until the stick is moved forward; however, if stick is moved forward too soon (during rapid rotation),

ITEMS AFFECTING STALLING SPEEDS AND CHARACTERISTICS

ITEM	STALL CHAR-ACTERISTICS	STALL SPEEDS
ABRUPT CONTROL MOVEMENT	X	X
ALTITUDE		
CG LOCATION	X	
COORDINATION	X	X
COWL FLAPS	X	
GROSS WEIGHT		X
LANDING GEAR		
POWER	X	X
SPEED BRAKE	X	
TURNS	X	X
WING FLAPS	X	X

T-28C-1-93-7A

Figure 4-3

aileron snatch and a resultant roll may occur. As the spin develops, rate of rotation increases and the ailerons may be difficult to hold in neutral as they have a tendency to float with the spin. If the ailerons are in the pro-spin or anti-spin position, recovery will be slower. The aircraft will recover from the spin almost immediately after forward stick is applied. The recovery will be in a steep, nose-down attitude and the stick should be immediately eased back to the neutral position to effect a normal recovery from the dive. After recovery controls are applied, the spin may tighten up for the first turn, but will stop rather abruptly in an additional one-half to one turn.

Note

Spins with external stores tend to be flatter and less oscillatory in nature and require more turns to recover.

CAUTION

Because of the steep diving attitude assumed by the aircraft during recovery, be careful when gear and flaps are down not to exceed the gear and flaps-down limit airspeed.

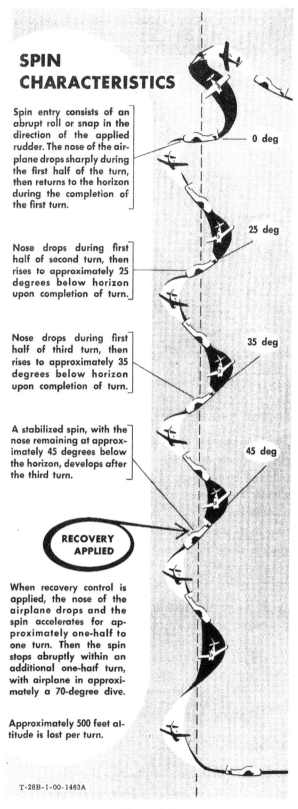

SPIN CHARACTERISTICS

Spin entry consists of an abrupt roll or snap in the direction of the applied rudder. The nose of the airplane drops sharply during the first half of the turn, then returns to the horizon during the completion of the first turn.

— 0 deg

Nose drops during first half of second turn, then rises to approximately 25 degrees below horizon upon completion of turn.

— 25 deg

Nose drops during first half of third turn, then rises to approximately 35 degrees below horizon upon completion of turn.

— 35 deg

A stabilized spin, with the nose remaining at approximately 45 degrees below the horizon, develops after the third turn.

— 45 deg

RECOVERY APPLIED

When recovery control is applied, the nose of the airplane drops and the spin accelerates for approximately one-half to one turn. Then the spin stops abruptly within an additional one-half turn, with airplane in approximately a 70-degree dive.

Approximately 500 feet altitude is lost per turn.

T-28B-1-00-1463A

Figure 4-4

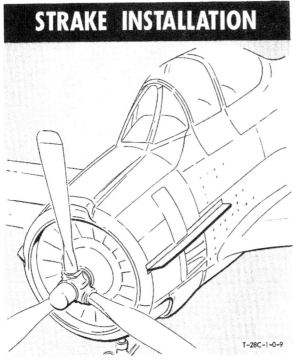

STRAKE INSTALLATION

T-28C-1-0-9

Figure 4-5

INVERTED SPIN RECOVERY

To effect recovery from an inverted spin, reduce the power to idle and apply hard, full, opposite rudder, followed by full back stick while maintaining neutral aileron. The recovery will be in an extreme nose-down attitude. Recovery can be completed as the last half of a loop or as the last half of a roll depending upon the attitude of the aircraft and the altitude available.

Note

If an inverted spin is entered with power on, reduce power to idle immediately.

CAUTION

Intentional inverted spins are prohibited.

DIVING

In dives to limit airspeed, the handling characteristics of the aircraft are good. All control movement is easy and effective, and the aircraft responds rapidly. If the aircraft is trimmed for level flight, stick push forces will be high in a dive. Trimming the aircraft to the dive with the speed brake open, will effectively reduce these forces below 280 knots IAS. Above this speed, the forces will be quite high. With the speed brake closed, the push forces will be lighter. However, if recovery from a clean dive is attempted by use of the speed brake, an additional 2- to 3-g load will be imposed upon the aircraft when the speed brake opens. This sudden increase in push forces may be quite difficult to control and the added g load may exceed the structural limits and result in damage to the aircraft. Therefore, it is recommended that the speed brake be opened before starting a dive. In diving the aircraft, remember that maximum permissible airspeed varies with altitude. The red line on the airspeed indicator marks the limit at sea level only. The altitude scale on the airspeed indicator light shield should be used to determine the limit dive speed for the clean aircraft at various altitudes. Refer to AIRSPEED LIMITATIONS, in Section I, Part 4, for complete listing of airspeed limits. Use the following procedure in a dive:

1. Check canopy closed before starting dive.

2. Adjust cowl and oil cooler flaps to prevent too rapid cooling in dive.

3. Carburetor air control adjusted as required to maintain normal carburetor air temperature.

4. Mixture control to RICH.

5. Decrease rpm as necessary.

6. Use speed brake when desired. Refer to USE OF SPEED BRAKE, in this section.

7. Do not allow engine to overspeed during dive.

CAUTION

Open throttle slowly to prevent partly cooled engine from cutting out at completion of dive.

USE OF SPEED BRAKE

The speed brake is essentially an additional flight control, which you will find useful for making descents or moderate deceleration from high speed. The brake can be opened at any airspeed up to limit speed, but should be extended prior to entering high-speed dives.

Although brake opening causes a nose-up pitch, the forward stick pressure necessary to maintain the desired aircraft attitude is moderate up to 250 KIAS. Above 250 knots, extension of the speed brake is accompanied by nose-up pitch, which can be corrected by a large forward stick pressure to maintain constant dive attitude. This stick pressure can be trimmed out to within approximately 10 pounds at speeds up to 280 knots by adjustment of the elevator tab. Closing the brake causes a nose-down pitch.

CAUTION

Do not extend speed brake at the initiation of, or during a pull-out.

ALTITUDE LOSS IN DIVE RECOVERY

The altitude lost during dive recovery is determined by four independent factors: angle of dive, altitude at start of pullout, airspeed at start of pullout, and acceleration maintained during pullout. Because these factors must be considered collectively in estimating altitude for recovery from any dive, their relationship is best presented in chart form as shown in figure 4-6.

Note that the charts are based on a constant 4- or 6-g pullout. Remember that a value obtained from either chart is the altitude lost during recovery, not the altitude at which recovery is completed. Therefore, in planning maneuvers which involve dives, first consider the altitude of the terrain and then use the respective chart to determine the altitude at which recovery must be started for pullout with adequate terrain clearance.

In using the charts, you should allow for the fact that, without considerable experience in this aircraft, you cannot determine exactly what your dive angle and speed are going to be at the start of the pullout. If you come out of a split "S" or other high-speed maneuver in a near vertical dive, speed builds up rapidly. Consequently, until you know the aircraft well, go into the chart at the highest speed and dive angle you might expect to reach after completing your maneuvers. If, for instance, you are in a 90-degree dive at an airspeed of 325 knots, and you wait until 4000 feet to start your pullout, you would have to make a 6-g pullout; a 4-g pullout would not clear the terrain. See figure 4-6. Maneuvers should be planned so that if they terminate in a near vertical dive, the aircraft may be pulled on through to a shallower dive angle before the speed becomes excessive or too low an altitude is reached.

Note

It is a good idea to memorize a few specific conditions from the dive charts so that you have a basis for judgments on pullouts.

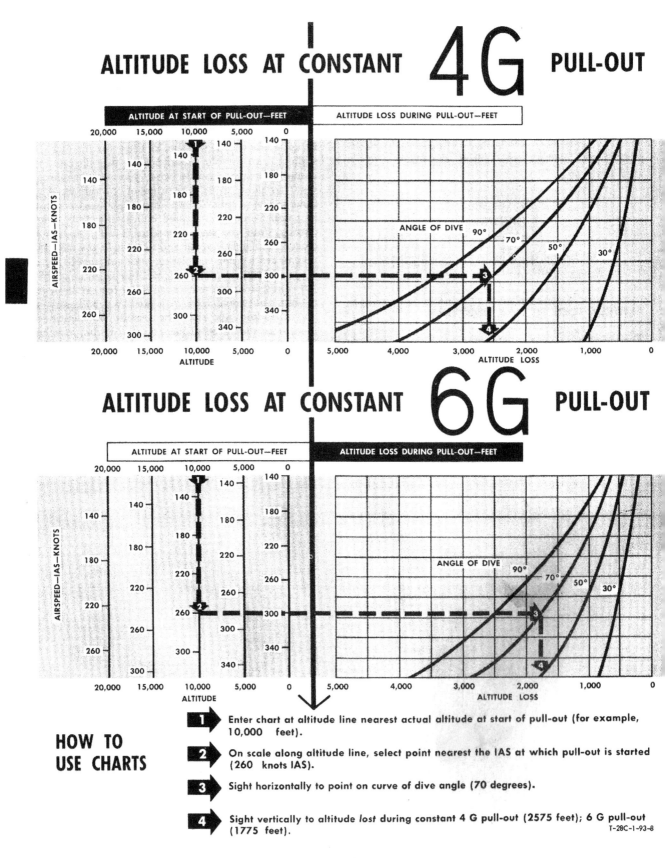

ALTITUDE LOSS AT CONSTANT 4G PULL-OUT

ALTITUDE LOSS AT CONSTANT 6G PULL-OUT

HOW TO
USE CHARTS

1 Enter chart at altitude line nearest actual altitude at start of pull-out (for example, 10,000 feet).

2 On scale along altitude line, select point nearest the IAS at which pull-out is started (260 knots IAS).

3 Sight horizontally to point on curve of dive angle (70 degrees).

4 Sight vertically to altitude *lost* during constant 4 G pull-out (2575 feet); 6 G pull-out (1775 feet).

T-28C-1-93-8

Figure 4-6

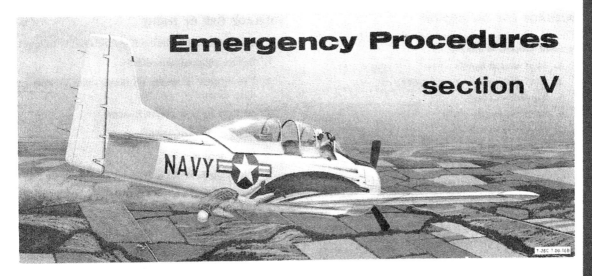

Emergency Procedures
section V

TABLE OF CONTENTS

GENERAL

The most commonly known emergencies, with their procedures, are covered in this section. All pilots will familiarize themselves with the contents of this section and maintain a thorough understanding of required procedures.

GROUND EMERGENCIES

ENGINE FIRE DURING START

If an engine fire occurs during start, proceed as follows:

1. Leave mixture control in IDLE CUTOFF position.

2. Do not prime engine again.

3. Continue cranking in an attempt to clear or start engine, as fire may be drawn through engine or blown out the exhaust stacks and extinguished.

4. If engine does not start, continue cranking.

5. FUEL shutoff handle—OFF.

6. IGNITION switch—OFF.

7. Carburetor air—DIRECT.

8. Throttle—OPEN.

9. If fire continues, stop cranking.

10. DC POWER switch—OFF.

Note

Signal ground crew to use portable fire extinguishing equipment when appropriate. Access to the engine accessory section is through an access door on the lower right side of the engine cowl.

11. ABANDON THE AIRCRAFT.

ENGINE FIRE AFTER START

If an engine fire occurs after the engine has started, proceed as follows:

1. FUEL shutoff handle—OFF.

2. Mixture control—IDLE CUTOFF.

3. Throttle—FULL OPEN.

4. IGNITION switch—OFF.

5. DC POWER switch—OFF.

Note

Signal ground crew to use portable fire extinguishing equipment when appropriate. Access to the engine accessory section is gained through an access door on the lower right side of the engine cowl.

6. ABANDON THE AIRCRAFT.

FUSELAGE FIRE ON GROUND

Should a fuselage fire occur while the aircraft is on the ground, proceed as follows:

1. FUEL shutoff handle—OFF.
2. MIXTURE control—IDLE CUTOFF.
3. Throttle—CLOSED.
4. IGNITION switch—OFF.
5. DC POWER switch—OFF.
6. Signal ground crew to use fire extinguisher.
7. ABANDON THE AIRCRAFT.

Note

Open baggage compartment to combat fire. The battery access door on the left side of the fuselage can also be opened for insertion of a fire extinguisher nozzle.

TAKE-OFF EMERGENCY

ENGINE FAILURE DURING TAKE-OFF

Should the engine fail during take-off, or if it becomes necessary to abort, proceed as follows:

1. Throttle—CLOSED.
2. Apply maximum braking.
3. Mixture control—IDLE CUTOFF.
4. Canopy handle—EMERG OPEN.
5. FLAP handle—UP.
6. DC POWER switch—OFF.

If anticipating going off runway into unprepared terrain in excess of 15 knots:

7. Landing gear handle—UP. (A very hard pull is necessary to override the gear handle downlock.)
8. Lower seat.

IN-FLIGHT EMERGENCIES

ENGINE FIRE IN FLIGHT

Depending upon seriousness of fire, either bail out immediately or attempt to extinguish fire as follows:

1. FUEL shutoff handle—OFF.
2. MIXTURE control—IDLE CUTOFF.
3. COWL & OIL COOLER FLAP switch—OPEN.
4. IGNITION switch—OFF.
5. DC POWER switch—OFF.

WARNING

Do not attempt to restart engine after fire goes out.

6. If a forced landing is elected, follow emergency landing pattern procedure.

FUSELAGE FIRE IN FLIGHT

If a fuselage fire occurs during flight, proceed as follows:

1. Reduce airspeed immediately.
2. Use oxygen if smoke or fumes enter cockpit or open canopy.
3. COCKPIT HEATER CONTROL—OFF.
4. DC POWER switch—OFF.

If fire persists,

5. Fuel shutoff handle—OFF.
6. MIXTURE control—IDLE CUTOFF.
7. IGNITION switch—OFF.
8. If fire is not extinguished immediately, BAIL OUT.
9. If a forced landing is elected, follow emergency landing pattern procedure.

WING FIRE IN FLIGHT

If a wing fire occurs, proceed as follows:

1. Landing light swiches—OFF.
2. Landing light circuit breakers—OUT.
3. EXT. MASTER lights switch—OFF.
4. Pitot heater switch—OFF.
5. Attempt to extinguish fire by sideslipping aircraft away from flame.
6. If fire is not extinguished immediately, BAIL OUT.

ELECTRICAL FIRE

Circuit breakers protect most electrical circuits and automatically interrupt power to prevent a fire when a short occurs. If necessary, however, turn DC POWER switch OFF to remove power from all electrical equipment, and land as soon as practicable. On aircraft having ASC 36 complied with, the DC POWER control switch in the aft cockpit may be positioned to EMERG OFF to remove power from all electrical equipment. If electrical power is essential, as during instrument flight, an attempt to identify and isolate the defective system may be possible. Proceed as follows:

1. DC POWER switch—OFF.
2. All electrical switches—OFF.
3. DC POWER switch—BAT. & GEN. If generator circuit is shorted, move switch to BAT. ONLY position.
4. Individually turn each system on again, allowing a short period of time before proceeding to the next, until the shorted circuit is identified.
5. Land as soon as practicable.

SMOKE/FUMES ELIMINATION

Should smoke or fumes enter the cockpit, proceed as follows:

1. Cockpit air control—open.
2. Air outlets—open.
3. Windshield and canopy defrost control handle—ON.

   If smoke or fumes persist:

4. If smoke enters cockpit from air outlets, cockpit air control handle—emergency OFF.
5. Oxygen—100 percent.
6. Canopy—OPEN.

ENGINE FAILURE IN FLIGHT

Engine failures fall into two main categories; those occurring instantly, and those giving ample warning. The instant failure is rare and usually occurs only if ignition or fuel flow completely fails. Most engine failures are gradual and afford the alert pilot ample indication that he may expect a failure.

PRECAUTIONARY EMERGENCY LANDING

When indications point to a possible engine failure or when reliability of the engine is questionable, a precautionary emergency landing will be made. An extremely rough running engine, loss of oil pressure, excessive cylinder head temperature under normal flight conditions, loss of manifold pressure, or fluctuating rpm are indications that a failure may occur. An additional engine failure warning device is the oil system sump plug warning light on the instrument panel. If any of these conditions occur, carry out the following procedure:

1. MIXTURE control—RICH.
2. Throttle—20 to 25 inches manifold pressure. (If possible, maintain 140 to 160 KIAS.)
3. PROP control lever—1900 to 2000 rpm.
4. COWL & OIL COOLER FLAPS—Adjust as necessary.
5. Cockpit—systematic check to determine possible cause.
6. Fly to the high key position over a hard surfaced runway and execute emergency landing pattern procedures.
7. At high key, close the throttle and advance the prop to full INCREASE RPM. As power is available, use power if necessary to control descent. DO NOT secure the engine.

ENGINE FAILURE (HIGH ALTITUDE)

In the event of an engine failure at altitude, a decision to make a landing or bailout must be made. For bailout, refer to BAILOUT in this section. If a landing is elected, establish a glide of 130 KIAS, landing gear, flaps, speed brake up and cowl flaps closed. Start toward the selected field, if not already doing so, and perform an air start, altitude permitting. Make a MAYDAY report. See figure 5-2 for emergency landing pattern.

During descent, vary turns to lose altitude to arrive at high key on airspeed and altitude. If high at 90-degree position, excess altitude can be lost by delaying final turn, slipping on final, lowering full flaps (if not previously done), extending speed brake, and/or advancing the propeller control lever to full increase rpm (to increase the drag of the propeller). The most effective way of losing altitude is the slip. In case of undershooting, sink rate can be decreased by placing propeller control lever to full decrease rpm (if not already there) raising flaps to one-half (above 600 feet), or raising landing gear. The landing gear is the highest drag item.

Note

- With the engine windmilling, the gear can be retracted in approximately 7 seconds and extended in approximately 4 seconds. It is possible to carry a gear-up approach to an altitude of 300 feet and still place the gear down for landing. Decreases in flap settings are not recommended below 600 feet.

- Flare for landing should be started approximately 200 feet above the runway.

WARNING

To prevent the normal tendency to undershoot, the high key must be established over the intended point of landing one-third distance down the runway; the low key must be one wing tip distance abeam the intended point of landing.

ENGINE FAILURE (LOW ALTITUDE)

If the engine fails at low altitude:

1. Immediately lower nose to maintain airspeed above stall.
2. Landing gear handle:
   UP if unprepared surface or water.
   DOWN for prepared surface.
3. Canopy handle—EMERG OPEN.
4. Shoulder harness—locked.
5. Fuel shutoff handle—OFF.
6. DC POWER switch—OFF.
7. Flap handle—DOWN.
8. Land straight ahead, changing direction only enough to miss obstacles.

WARNING

Do not try to turn back to the field. Making a crash landing straight ahead, with the aircraft under control, is much better than turning back and taking the chance of an uncontrolled crash.

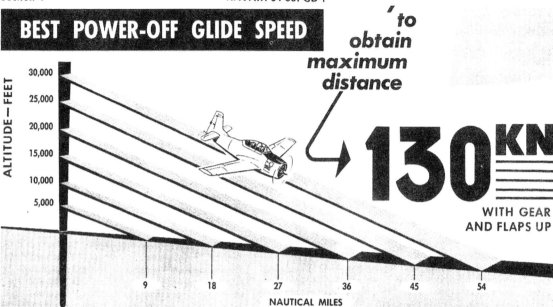

BEST POWER-OFF GLIDE SPEED 'to obtain maximum distance

130 KN

WITH GEAR
AND FLAPS UP

You will glide approximately 9 miles for each 5000 feet of altitude lost by holding 130 knots IAS. No wind condition.

T-28C-1-00-17

Figure 5-1

SIMULATED EMERGENCIES

For training purposes, the pilot initiating the simulated emergency will be referred to as the safety pilot.

SIMULATED ENGINE FAILURE (HIGH ALTITUDE)

When performing a simulated engine failure at altitude, conform to engine failure (high altitude) procedure except for the following:

The simulated engine failure (high altitude) will not be initiated above 5000 feet or below 2000 feet. The safety pilot will initiate the simulated engine failure by setting 16 inches MAP and 1600 rpm. As airspeed approaches 130 KIAS, the safety pilot will take electrical control, extend speed brake, and lower one-half flaps. The MAYDAY report will be simulated on ICS to the safety pilot. After the air start is simulated, check mixture rich. In the emergency landing pattern (figure 5-2), the safety pilot will place the propeller lever in full increase rpm at low key. Use of one-half flaps will be simulated by closing the throttle. Simulate CANOPY—EMERG OPEN; fuel shutoff handle—OFF; DC POWER switch—OFF.

At farmer's fields, the safety pilot will initiate the wave-off to remain at least 300 feet above the terrain.

SIMULATED ENGINE FAILURE (LOW ALTITUDE)

When performing a simulated engine failure at low altitude, conform to engine failure (low altitude) procedures except as indicated.

The simulated engine failure (low altitude) will not be given below 500 feet AGL or higher than 2000 feet AGL. The flaps must be up and the airspeed at least

120 knots. The safety pilot will initiate the procedure by closing the throttle, mixture rich, and propeller control lever full increase rpm. Simulate CANOPY—EMERG OPEN; fuel shutoff handle—OFF; DC POWER switch—OFF. The safety pilot will initiate the waveoff to remain at least 300 feet above the terrain.

PRACTICE PRECAUTIONARY EMERGENCY LANDING

The procedures for a practice precautionary emergency landing are basically the same as a precautionary emergency landing with the addition of clearing the engine at low key. See figure 5-2.

BEST GLIDE

If the engine fails during flight, maximum gliding distance can be obtained by maintaining a speed of 130 KIAS with gear, flaps, and speed brake retracted (figure 5-1), and the PROP control lever at full DECREASE RPM. Engine rpm will be approximately 1150, generator output will be normal, and the hydraulic system will maintain 1500 pounds pressure at this windmill rpm. Best engine-off glide speeds vary between 125 and 135 knots, depending upon gross weight. Glide ratio and rate of sink at best glide speed under varying configurations with windmilling engine are as follows:

LANDING GEAR	FLAPS	SPEED BRAKE	CANOPY	KIAS	GLIDE RATIO	RATE OF SINK (FPM)
Up	Up	Up	Closed	130	11.7 to 1	1120
Down	Up	Up	Closed	110	8.1 to 1	1370
Up	Down	Up	Closed	100	6.6 to 1	1525
Down	Down	Up	Closed	100	5.7 to 1	1780
Down	Down	Up	Open	100	5.2 to 1	1940

EMERGENCY LANDING PATTERN

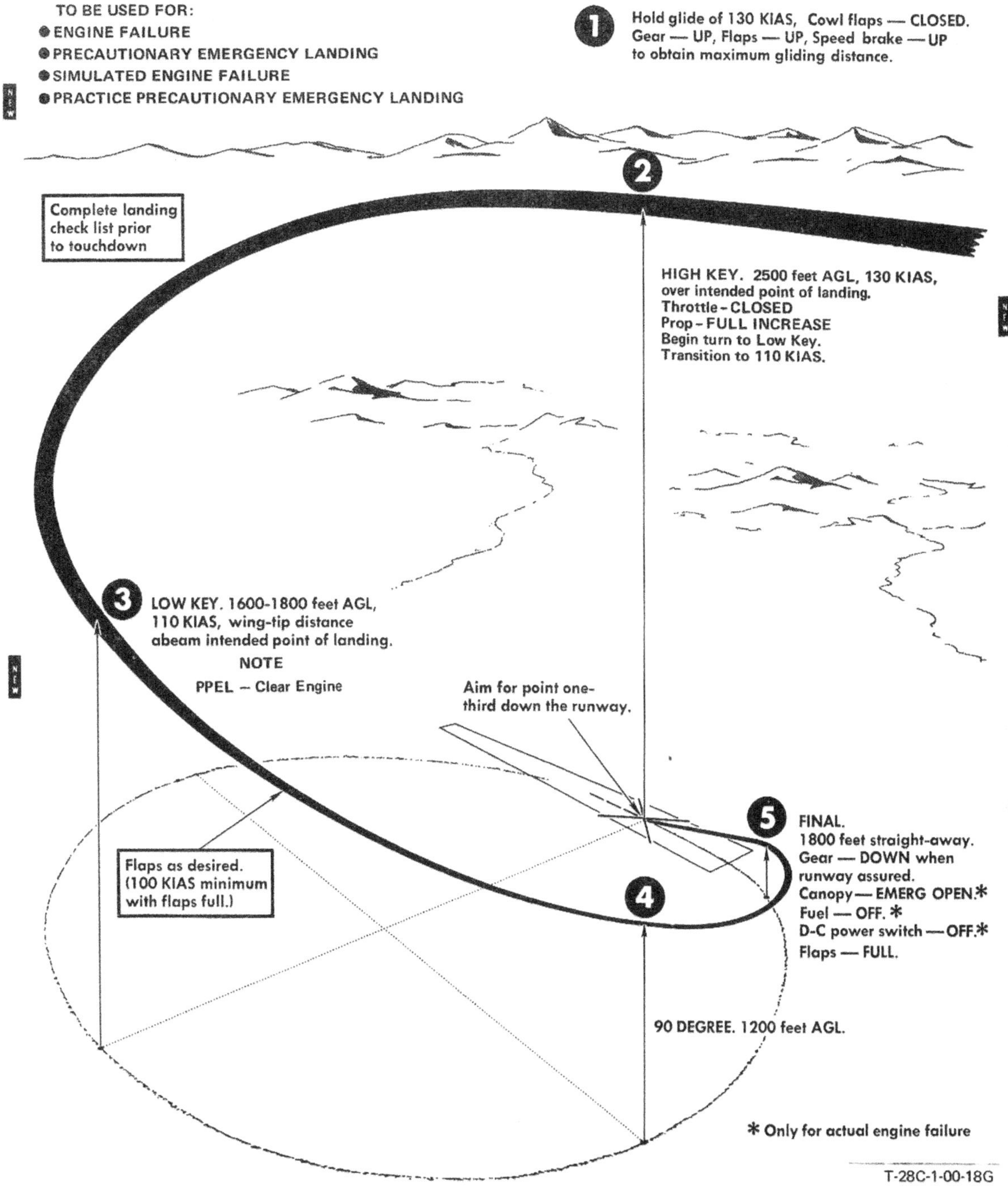

TO BE USED FOR:
- ENGINE FAILURE
- PRECAUTIONARY EMERGENCY LANDING
- SIMULATED ENGINE FAILURE
- NEW PRACTICE PRECAUTIONARY EMERGENCY LANDING

1 Hold glide of 130 KIAS, Cowl flaps — CLOSED.
Gear — UP, Flaps — UP, Speed brake — UP
to obtain maximum gliding distance.

2

Complete landing
check list prior
to touchdown

HIGH KEY. 2500 feet AGL, 130 KIAS,
over intended point of landing.
Throttle – CLOSED
Prop – FULL INCREASE
Begin turn to Low Key.
Transition to 110 KIAS.

3 LOW KEY. 1600-1800 feet AGL,
110 KIAS, wing-tip distance
abeam intended point of landing.
NOTE
PPEL — Clear Engine

Aim for point one-
third down the runway.

5 FINAL.
1800 feet straight-away.
Gear — DOWN when
runway assured.
Canopy — EMERG OPEN.*
Fuel — OFF. *
D-C power switch — OFF.*
Flaps — FULL.

Flaps as desired.
(100 KIAS minimum
with flaps full.)

4

90 DEGREE. 1200 feet AGL.

* Only for actual engine failure

T-28C-1-00-18G

Figure 5-2

AIR START

Should engine failure occur in flight, establish 130 KIAS glide and if the cause is determined to be fuel or electrical system failure or some minor malfunction and altitude is sufficient, an attempt to restart the engine may be made by using the following procedures:

1. Fuel shutoff handle—ON.
2. Throttle—cracked approximately ¾ inch.
3. PROP control lever—fuel increase rpm.
4. MIXTURE control—RICH.
5. IGNITION switch—BOTH.
6. DC POWER switch—BAT. & GEN. with generator operating.
    —BAT. ONLY—with generator failure and fuel pressure less than 19 psi.
7. Fuel pressure—check 19 to 25 psi.

Note

Low fuel pressure with generator failure indicates loss of both fuel boost pump and engine-driven fuel pump. To regain fuel boost pump, the DC POWER switch must be in the BAT. ONLY position.

If the engine fails to start:

8. MIXTURE control—IDLE CUTOFF.
9. Throttle—full open to clear engine.
10. Throttle—cracked approximately ¾ inch.
11. MIXTURE control—RICH.

Engine still fails to start:

12. Primer—Hold down for 1 to 2 seconds.

If the engine starts on primer, hold the primer down and adjust the throttle until the engine is running as smoothly as possible (approximately 20 to 22 inches MAP and 1400 to 1600 rpm):

BAILOUT

The decision to abandon the aircraft in flight is the responsibility of the pilot in command and should be made as soon as possible. If this decision is delayed, speed and g-forces may build to a point where bailing out is extremely difficult or impossible.

The following should be considered prior to bailout:

1. Although parachute deployment is accomplished during a descent of 200 feet at an escape airspeed between 100 to 125 KIAS, human reaction precludes marginal success if escape is made below 1200 feet AGL.
2. Because air velocity will hold the body against the aircraft, escape is marginal above 200 KIAS.

3. Recommended minimum bailout altitude for uncontrolled flight is 5000 feet.
4. Immediately on exit, make a *HARD, FIRM PULL* on the "D" ring.

All escapes from level flight should be made from the right side of the aircraft, taking advantage of the downward force of the propeller wash, greatly reducing the danger of striking the horizontal stabilizer. This is especially true for the pilot in the rear cockpit.

WARNING

The chances of striking the stabilizer are increased with higher airspeeds.

Within airspeed limitations, the use of flaps may be helpful; however, it should be noted that the increased drag created through use of flaps will proportionately increase rate of sink. The greatest advantage in using flaps is that approximately 2 feet of surface area will be removed, affording the pilots more area in which to clear the tail surface.

The first and foremost step in bailout procedure is to maintain level flight at the lowest airspeed possible. Secondly, in all cases of bailout, exert the maximum possible effort in your downward push away from the cockpit.

The following procedure should be used only when the aircraft is under control and the speed can be reduced to below 120 knots.

1. Pilot in command warns copilot that bailout is necessary.
2. Head toward uninhabited area.
3. Airspeed—Reduce.
4. Canopy control—EMERG OPEN.
5. Seat—raised.
6. Radio and oxygen—Disconnect.
7. Fuel shutoff handle—OFF.
8. IGNITION switch—OFF.
9. DC POWER switch—OFF.
10. Seat belt and shoulder harness—Release.
11. Pilot in command—signal copilot to bail out.
12. Pilot in command—bail out.

Note

Rear seat pilot dives forcibly toward trailing edge of wing. The front seat pilot should roll onto the wing.

13. When clear, pull "D" ring.

HIGH-SPEED BAILOUT

1. Radio and oxygen—Disconnect.
2. Seat belt and shoulder harness—locked.

3. Canopy handle—EMERG OPEN.

4. Elevator trim control—full nose down.

5. Aircraft roll inverted.

6. Seat belt—Release.

7. When clear, pull "D" ring.

BAILOUT FROM SPINS

If it is necessary to bail out during a spin, exit toward the outside of the spin. IF THE SPIN IS TO THE LEFT, EXIT OVER THE RIGHT SIDE AND VICE VERSA. Gravity, induced by aircraft rotation, will tend to hold you in the seat. However, as soon as you are free of the seat, you will probably be thrown out. Keep this in mind and make sure that your personal gear does not become fouled as you leave. To escape during an inverted spin, simply release your safety belt and you will fall out aided by the centrifugal force of the spin. For all bailouts, make all necessary preparation before the safety belt is released. For all high-speed bailouts, if altitude permits, delay pulling the "D" ring until your free-fall speed has decelerated to a constant rate.

AIRBORNE DAMAGED AIRCRAFT

1. Aircraft controllable—Climb to at least 5000 feet.

2. Communicate—State difficulty and request visual in-flight inspection.

3. Check flight characteristics in landing configuration, decreasing airspeed in increments of 10 knots to a minimum of 90 knots.

CAUTION

DO NOT STALL THE AIRCRAFT.

4. Fly a wide easy approach; if control problems exist, fly straight in, with airspeed at least 10 knots above minimum obtained during flight characteristics check.

DITCHING

T-28 aircraft have been successfully ditched a number of times in relatively calm waters. Bailouts have also generally been successful; therefore, no recommendation is made as to the preferred procedure. If a ditching is elected, or is unavoidable, proceed as follows:

1. Check that personal equipment will not foul when you leave the aircraft (PK-2 pararaft kit lanyard attached to Mae West).

2. Radio and oxygen—Disconnect.

3. Seat belt and shoulder harness—locked.

4. Landing gear handle—UP.

5. Speed brake switch—OFF.

6. Canopy handle—EMERG OPEN.

7. DC POWER switch—OFF.

8. Flap handle—DOWN.

9. Make normal approach with power, if possible, and flare to normal landing attitude, touching down with minimum sink rate.

Maintain airspeed above stall until contacting water.

Note

● Unless wind is high or sea is rough, plan approach heading parallel to any uniform swell pattern and try to touch down along wavecrest just after crest passes.

● If wind is as high as 25 knots or surface is irregular, the best procedure is to approach into the wind and touch down on the falling side of a wave.

PROPELLER GOVERNOR FAILURE

If the linkage to the propeller governor fails, a centering spring in the governor automatically sets rpm between 2000 and 2200, depending on throttle setting. Ample power is available in this range to maintain flight. Should a failure of the propeller governor occur, either of the following may result:

HIGH RPM (LOW PITCH)

The propeller may fail to the low pitch (high rpm) stop, resulting in a runaway propeller. Prompt corrective action is essential.

1. Throttle—Retard to maintain below 2700 rpm.

2. Climb to load propeller.

3. PROP control lever—Manipulate to restore governing.

4. Land as soon as practicable.

LOW RPM (HIGH PITCH)

The propeller may fail in high pitch (low rpm). This type of failure is rare. Sufficient power may be available at low altitudes to maintain flight or greatly extend glide.

1. Supercharger handle—LOW.

2. Throttle—lowest MAP to maintain flight.

3. MIXTURE control lever—RICH.

4. Land as soon as practicable.

FUEL SYSTEM MALFUNCTIONS

ENGINE-DRIVEN PUMP FAILURE

If the engine-driven fuel pump fails, the booster pump will supply fuel to the engine. Under most conditions, indicated fuel pressure will remain within the normal range, with no indication of failure.

BOOST PUMP FAILURE

Should the sump tank boost pump fail, the engine-driven pump will draw sufficient fuel for engine operation up to approximately 10,000 feet and only a slight drop in fuel pressure indication may be noted. Above that altitude, the low atmospheric pressures tend to vaporize the fuel in the lines. As a result, the pump must handle a combination of vapor and fuel which greatly reduces pumping capacity, and sufficient fuel may not be supplied to the engine. This condition is aggravated by high outside air temperatures. If loss of power or erratic engine operation is encountered at or above 10,000 feet, proceed as follows:

1. Descend to an altitude where normal operation is restored.

2. Land as soon as practicable.

HYDRAULIC SYSTEM FAILURE

Loss of hydraulic system pressure will be evidenced by a low or zero reading on the hydraulic pressure gage any time that a hydraulic system component is actuated. Loss of pressure is normally caused by failure of the engine-driven hydraulic pump or loss of hydraulic fluid.

To determine if the pressure loss was due to engine-driven pump failure, depress the canopy handle button with the handle in the CLOSE position while actuating the handpump. If hydraulic pressure is indicated, the engine-driven pump has failed and the components of the system can be operated by making normal selections and actuating the handpump to provide hydraulic pressure. If no pressure is indicated, the pressure loss was not due to failure of the engine-driven pump. In this situation, neither the flaps nor the speed brake can be extended but other components can be operated as follows:

LANDING GEAR EMERGENCY EXTENSION

1. Airspeed—115 KIAS or below.

2. Landing gear handle—DOWN.

3. Yaw if necessary to lock main gear down.

4. Check for safe gear indications.

CANOPY EMERGENCY OPENING

To open the canopy from inside the cockpit, move the canopy handle to the EMERG OPEN position. If the pneumatic system fails, the canopy can be operated manually.

SPEED BRAKE EMERGENCY RETRACTION

If hydraulic failure occurs with the speed brake extended, moving the speed brake switch to OFF will allow air loads to close the brake to a trail position.

WHEEL BRAKES

Wheel brakes will operate normally.

CANOPY EMERGENCY STOPPING

To stop hydraulically operated movement of the canopy, depress the canopy emergency stop button on the instrument panel shroud.

BOMB AND ROCKET EMERGENCY JETTISON

Bombs and rockets can be jettisoned in an emergency by pulling the EMERG JETTISON handle on the armament control panel. On the armament modified T-28C aircraft, stores may be jettisoned by depressing the STORES JETTISON button on the armament control panel.

ELECTRICAL SYSTEM FAILURES

GENERATOR FAILURE (ASC 36 NOT INCORPORATED)

Illumination of the GENERATOR-OFF warning light with the DC POWER switch at BAT. & GEN. indicates that the generator is inoperative and the battery is supplying all the current to the electrical system.

1. Instruments and radio essential.
   (a) DC POWER switch—BAT ONLY.
   (b) INST POWER switch—NO. 2 INV.

2. Instruments, but no radios, essential.
   (a) DC POWER switch—BAT. & GEN.
   (b) INST POWER switch—NO. 2 INV.

3. Instruments and radios not essential.
   (a) DC POWER switch—OFF.

Conserve power by turning off all nonessential equipment. Pull circuit breakers if necessary.

GENERATOR FAILURE (ASC 36 INCORPORATED)

The electrical system has been modified to remove the d-c power and a-c inverter circuit from the cockpit control transfer relay. The d-c power switch in the forward cockpit retains control of the battery and generator operation, while the d-c power switch in the aft cockpit can be operated in an emergency to disconnect all electrical power from the aircraft except the battery bus.

1. Instruments and radios essential.
   (a) DC POWER switch—BAT. ONLY.
   (b) INST POWER switch—NO. 1 INV.

2. Instruments, but no radios, essential.
   (a) DC POWER switch—BAT. & GEN.
   (b) INST POWER switch—NO. 1 INV.

3. Instruments and radios not essential.
   (a) DC POWER switch—OFF.

Conserve power by turning off all nonessential equipment. Pull circuit breakers if necessary.

INVERTER FAILURE

Failure of the selected a-c inverter is indicated by illumination of the FLT INST POWER FAILURE warning light. If the light illuminates with the INST POWER switch at NO. 1 INV., move the switch to NO. 2 INV. If the warning light does not go out, either power is interrupted to attitude gyro or both inverters have failed—check attitude gyro fuses.

In aircraft with ASC 36 incorporated, two instrument power failure relays are installed to provide separate instrument power failure indications which require individual inverter selection in each cockpit. When either switch is moved into the NO. 2 INV position, TACAN is inoperative.

Note

A circuit breaker for each inverter is provided to protect the d-c circuits to the inverters. Should either inverter fail, check that the appropriate circuit breaker has not popped because of a temporary overload. If transfer from one inverter to another is necessary, pull the circuit breaker for the inoperative inverter to prevent possible additional damage to the inverter, or an overload on the generator.

COMPLETE ELECTRICAL FAILURE

If complete electrical failure occurs, land as soon as practicable.

CAUTION

Instrument flying will be impossible, as all radio communications equipment and essential flight attitude instruments will be inoperative.

EMERGENCY COMMUNICATIONS

Any time a pilot is in urgent distress he will transmit on guard channel the following information, as time permits:

1. MAYDAY, MAYDAY, MAYDAY.
2. Identification.
3. Position (geographical or bearing and distance from a fixed point).
4. Altitude.
5. Nature of emergency.
6. Intended actions.

Remain on guard channel for assistance. If emergency situation is corrected, notify all stations on guard channel.

LOST AIRCRAFT PROCEDURES

The primary requirements when lost are as follows:

1. Confess.
2. Communicate.
3. Climb.
4. Conserve.
5. Conform.
6. Know any peculiar local area/ship procedures.

More detailed requirements are found in NWP 41(A), Flight Planning Document, and the FLIP Enroute Supplement.

LANDING EMERGENCIES

GEAR HANDLE CANNOT BE MOVED TO DOWN POSITION

1. Place all hydraulically actuated equipment in the CLOSED or CLEAN position.
2. Check hydraulic pressure for an abnormal (pressurized) indication.
3. If hydraulic system is pressurized, place canopy control handle to MANUAL position and depress and hold the canopy handle button.
4. When hydraulic pressure has dropped off to fullest extent, firmly move landing gear handle to DOWN position.
5. Check all indicators for safe gear indication and execute a normal landing.

LANDING GEAR UNSAFE INDICATION

In all cases, when landing with unsafe gear indications, roll out straight ahead and do not attempt to taxi until landing gear safety pins have been inserted.

LANDING WITH GEAR RETRACTED

If the gear fails to extend, a wheels-up landing can be made on either hard or soft ground as follows:

1. Establish a normal flaps-down approach.

2. Open canopy.

3. Lock shoulder harness.

4. Flare out as in a normal landing.

5. Shut down engine just before touchdown.

6. When aircraft stops, get out immediately.

ONE MAIN WHEEL RETRACTED

A wheels-up landing is preferable to a landing with one main wheel retracted. However, if such a landing cannot be avoided, proceed as follows.

1. Make a normal flaps-down approach with wing low on extended gear side.

2. Open canopy.

3. Touch down on extended main wheel. Use ailerons to hold up wing with retracted gear.

4. Shut down engine.

5. When wing tip strikes ground, apply maximum opposite brake pressure. (If landing area permits, a turn in the direction of the retracted gear will reduce ground speed before wing tip strikes the ground.)

NOSE WHEEL RETRACTED

If the nose wheel fails to extend, proceed as follows:

1. Make a normal landing.

2. Secure engine at touchdown.

3. Hold a nose-high attitude to allow speed and engine rpm to diminish.

NOSE GEAR TIRE FAILED

If nose wheel tire is flat, make normal landing and hold nose off as long as possible. Use brakes sparingly after nose wheel is on the ground.

MAIN GEAR TIRE FAILED

With main gear tire failed, proceed as follows.

1. If a main wheel tire is flat, land on the side of the runway nearest the inflated tire. Hold flat tire off as long as possible. If brakes are necessary, brake mainly with the wheel that has the inflated tire.

2. If both main tires are flat, make normal landing in center of runway.

EMERGENCY ENTRANCE

To open the canopy from the outside in an emergency, pull canopy external handle on left side of fuselage out and back to EMERG. If pneumatic system is ineffective,

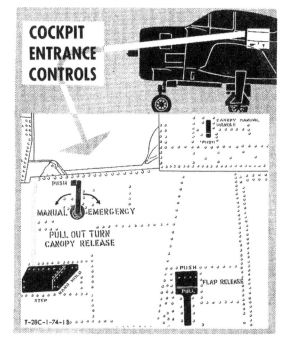

Figure 5-3

move canopy external handle forward to MANUAL and pull canopy open by means of manual handle on frame of rear section of canopy. See figure 5-3.

LANDING — USE OF EMERGENCY FIELD ARRESTING GEAR (T-28C only)

There are several types of field arresting gear. These types include the anchor chain cable, water squeezer, and Morest-type equipment. All of these types require engagement of the arresting hook in a cable pendant rigged across the runway. Location of the pendant in relation to the runway will classify the gear as follows:

1. Midfield gear-Located near the halfway point of the runway. Usually requires prior notification in order to rig for arrestment in the direction desired.

2. Abort gear-Located 1500 to 2500 feet short of the upwind end of the duty runway and usually will be rigged for immediate use.

3. Overrun gear-Located shortly past the upwind end of the duty runway. Usually will be rigged for immediate use.

Some fields will have all of these types of gear, others none. For this reason, it is imperative that all pilots be aware of the the type, location, and compatibility of the gear in use with the aircraft, and the policy of the local air station with regard to which gear is rigged for use and when.

The approximate maximum permissible engaging speed, gross weight, and off-center engagement distance for field arrestment of aircraft are listed in figure 5-4.

WARNING

- Under no circumstances should a pilot's decision to abort a take-off be delayed because of knowledge that an emergency arresting gear is available at the end of the runway. Decision to abort should be based on the usual parameters of remaining runway and distance required for stopping, using wheel brakes. The arresting gear will then serve as an assist to stop the aircraft from rolling off the runway onto unprepared surfaces.

- If off center, just prior to engaging the arresting gear, do not attempt to go for the center of the runway. Continue straight ahead parallel to the centerline.

As various modifications to the basic types of arresting gear are used, exact speeds will vary accordingly. Certain aircraft service changes may affect engaging speed and weight limitations. Severe damage to the aircraft is usually sustained if an engagement into the chain gear is made in the wrong direction.

Realizing that runway conditions, weather, time, fuel remaining and other considerations may make strict compliance impractical, the following recommendations are made.

In an emergency situation, first determine the extent of the emergency by whatever means are possible (instruments, other aircraft, LSO, RDO, tower or other ground personnel). Next, determine the most advantageous arresting gear available and the type of arrestment to be made under the existing conditions. Whenever deliberate field arrestment is intended, notify control tower personnel as much in advance as possible and state estimated landing time in minutes. If gear is not rigged, it will probably require 10 to 20 minutes to prepare it for use. If foaming of the runway or area of arrestment is required or desired, it should be requested by the pilot at this time.

In general, the arresting gear is engaged on the centerline at as slow a speed as possible. Burn down to 1500 pounds of fuel or less. While burning down, make practice passes to accurately locate the arresting gear. Engagement should be made with feet off the brakes, shoulder harness locked, and with the aircraft in a 3-point attitude. After engaging the

gear, good common sense and existing conditions now dictate whether to keep the engine running or to shut it down and abandon the aircraft.

SHORT FIELD ARRESTMENTS

If at any time prior to landing, it is known that a directional control problem exists or a minimum rollout is desired, a short field arrestment should be made and the assistance of an LSO requested. He should be stationed near the touchdown point and equipped with a radio. Inform the LSO of the desired touchdown point. A constant glide slope approach to touchdown is permitted (mirror or Fresnel Lens Landing Aid utilized) with touchdown on centerline at or just prior to the arresting wire with the hook extended. The hook should be lowered while airborne and a positive hook-down check should be made, if possible. If midfield gear or Morest type is available, it should be used. If neither are available, use abort gear. Use an approach speed commensurate with the emergency experienced. Landing approach power will be maintained until arrestment is assured or a wave-off is taken. Be prepared for a wave-off if the gear is missed. After engaging the gear, retard the throttle to IDLE or secure engine and abandon aircraft, depending on existing conditions.

LONG FIELD ARRESTMENTS

The long field arrestment is used when a stopping problem exists with insufficient runway remaining (i.e., aborted take-offs, icy or wet runways, loss of brakes after touchdown, etc.). Lower the hook, allowing sufficient time for it to extend fully prior to engagement. Do not lower the hook too early and weaken the hook point. Line up the aircraft on the runway centerline. Inform the control tower of your intentions to engage the arresting gear, so that aircraft landing behind you may be waved off. If no directional control problem exists (crosswind, brakes out, etc.), secure the engine.

ABORTED TAKE-OFF

Where an aircraft take-off must be aborted, a roll-in type engagement of all arresting gear is recommended to prevent overrun. The aircraft is cleared up to the maximum take-off gross weight specified in the Aborted Take-off column of figure 5-4. Additionally, the data provided in the Long Field Landing column may be used for light weight aborted take-off, where applicable.

Note

The taxi light may be of use in locating arresting/abort gear at night.

FIELD ARRESTMENT DATA — (T-28C ONLY)

ARRESTING GEAR	SHORT-FIELD LANDING (g)		LONG-FIELD LANDING		ABORTED TAKE-OFF		MAXIMUM OFF-CENTER ENGAGEMENT (FEET)
	AIRCRAFT GROSS WEIGHT (f)	MAXIMUM ENGAGING SPEED (KNOTS)	AIRCRAFT GROSS WEIGHT	MAXIMUM ENGAGING SPEED (KNOTS)	AIRCRAFT GROSS WEIGHT	MAXIMUM ENGAGING SPEED (KNOTS)	
M-2	8300	108 (a)	10,900	108 (a)	11,000	107 (a)	20
E-14-1	8300	113 (a)	10,900	108 (a)	11,000	108 (a)	35
E-27	8300	104 (a)	10,900	101 (a)	11,000	101 (a)	20
E-15 (200-foot span)	8300	82 (a)	10,900	80 (a)	11,000	80 (a)	20
E-15 (300-foot span)	8300	110 (a)	10,900	105 (a)	11,000	105 (a)	40
M-21	8300	90 (a)	10,900	90 (a)	11,000	90 (a)	10
E-28	8300	101 (a)	10,900	95 (a)	11,000	95 (a)	40
E-5 (standard chain)	8300	107 (b)	10,900	107 (b)	11,000	107 (b)	(e)
E-5-1 (standard chain)	8300	107 (b)	10,900	107 (b)	11,000	107 (b)	(e)
E-5 (heavy chain)	8300	103 (a,b)	10,900	103 (a,b)	11,000	103 (a,b)	(e)
E-5-1 (heavy chain)	8300	103 (a)	10,900	103 (a)	11,000	103 (a)	(e)
BAK-6	8300	150 (a)	10,900	150 (a)	11,000	150 (a)	15
BAK-9	8300	138 (d)	10,900	136 (a)	11,000	136 (a)	30
BAK-12	8300	128 (a)	10,900	126 (a)	11,000	126 (a)	50

Note

(a) Maximum engaging speed limited by aircraft arresting hook strength.

(b) Maximum engaging speed limited by aircraft limit horizontal drag load factor (mass item limit "G").

(c) Maximum engaging speed limited by aircraft landing gear strength.

(d) Maximum engaging speed limited by arresting gear.

(e) Off-center engagement may not exceed 25 percent of the runway span.

(f) Recommended approach airspeed for 8300 pounds is 80 KCAS.

(g) Degree glide slope setting.

Figure 5-4

All-Weather Operation

section VI

T-28B-1-00-37

TABLE OF CONTENTS

INTRODUCTION

Except where repetition is necessary for emphasis, clarity, or continuity of thought, this section contains only those procedures that differ from, or are in addition to, the normal operating procedures in Sections III and IV. Refer to Section I, Part 2, for engine operation.

TURBULENCE AND THUNDERSTORMS

Intentional flight through thunderstorms is not recommended.

If inadvertently entering turbulence or thunderstorms, power setting and attitude are the keys to proper flight technique. The power setting and pitch attitude required for desired penetration airspeed, and established before entering the storm, will, if maintained throughout the storm, result in a fairly constant airspeed, regardless of any false readings of the airspeed indicator. Following are specific recommendations for preparing to enter a storm or turbulent area and flying in it.

TURBULENCE PENETRATION

Before entering turbulence, prepare the aircraft as follows:

1. PROP control—2000 rpm.

2. MIXTURE control—NORMAL.

3. Pitot heater switch—ON.

4. Carburetor air control—as required.

5. Throttle—adjusted as necessary to obtain desired penetration speed (125 to 185 KIAS).

6. Gyro instruments—proper settings.

7. Tighten safety belt and shoulder harness.

8. To reduce static, turn off any radio equipment that is rendered useless by static.

Note

Do not rely on the automatic direction finding equipment in or near thunderstorms, as the radio compass may give false readings in the COMP. position.

9. If flight is at night, turn cockpit lights full bright to minimize the blinding effect of lightning.

Do not lower the landing gear or the flaps during flight in turbulent air as they decrease the aerodynamic efficiency of the aircraft and limit your airspeed.

IN THE STORM

While flying through the storm, observe the following precautions:

1. Maintain power settings and attitude (established before entering the storm) throughout the storm.

6-1

2. Use as little elevator control as possible to maintain your attitude in order to minimize the stresses imposed on the aircraft.

Note

● Normally, the least turbulent area in a thunderstorm will be at altitudes below 10,000 feet. Altitudes between 10,000 and 20,000 feet are usually the most turbulent.

● The altimeter may be unreliable in thunderstorms because of differential barometric pressure within the storm.

COLD WEATHER OPERATION

The normal operating procedures outlined in Section III should be followed during cold weather operation with the exceptions and additions as follows:

BEFORE ENTERING AIRCRAFT

1. Remove protective covers from aircraft. Leave engine cover on if it is necessary to preheat engine before starting.

Note

MIL-L-22851 oil shall be used at starting temperatures down to 25°F (−4°C). If MIL-L-22851 oil is not available, MIL-L-6082, Grade 1100 may be used as an alternate. When temperatures below 25°F are expected, MIL-L-22851 oil or MIL-L-6082, Grade 1100 oil shall be preheated or diluted, or MIL-L-6082, Grade 1065 oil shall be used. When using Grade 1065 oil, inlet temperatures should be maintained between 65° and 75°C during engine operation to obtain proper lubrication and to prevent the accumulation of moisture and volatile products of oxidation in the oil. Grade 1065 oil will require preheat for starting temperatures below 0°F (−18°C). A general rule which may be applied in the use of preheat is that 1 minute of preheat should be used for each 2 degrees of temperature below 0°F. If preheat is not available, use oil dilution in accordance with BuWeps Instruction 10350.1 and superseding instructions. Oil temperature limitations are as follows:

MIL-L-22851 OIL OR GRADE 1100 OIL

Minimum	40°C
Normal	75° - 90°C
Maximum	95°C

GRADE 1065 OIL

Minimum	40°C
Normal	65° - 75°C
Maximum	80°C

2. Check "Y" drain and oil tank sump drain and continue heating if flow is unsatisfactory.

3. Clean gear shock struts and arresting hook of dirt and ice.

4. Remove snow and ice from surfaces, control hinges, propeller, pitot tube, fuel and oil vents, and crankcase breather outlet.

5. Drain moisture from all fuel tank and fuel system drains.

6. Have external power source connected for starting.

7. Remove engine cover and ground heater.

BEFORE STARTING ENGINE

If engine cannot be readily turned over by starter, insufficient oil dilution is indicated and additional preheat should be applied. Before starting engine, depress starter button for a few seconds (with IGNITION switch OFF) and make sure engine will turn over at least 50 rpm. If an engine cranking speed of 50 rpm (three propeller blades each 2 seconds) cannot be maintained by the starter, insufficient oil dilution is indicated and additional preheat should be applied.

STARTING ENGINE

Use normal starting procedure, supplemented by the following:

1. If there is no indication of oil pressure after 30 seconds running, or if pressure drops after a few minutes ground operation, stop engine and investigate.

2. Use some carburetor alternate air after starting to assist vaporization and combustion and to reduce tendency to backfire.

CAUTION

Do not apply carburetor alternate air until after engine is started.

WARMUP AND GROUND CHECK

1. Warm up engine at 1500 rpm to prevent fouling of spark plugs.

2. Cowl and oil cooler flaps open.

3. Check all instruments for normal operation.

4. After oil temperature and pressure are up to normal, operate propeller control through three complete cycles, and check for drop of approximately 400 rpm.

5. Operate flaps and canopy through one complete cycle.

6. If oil has been diluted more than 15 percent, dilution fuel in excess of 15 percent should be boiled off by running engine at 1600 rpm at an oil temperature of at least 40°C. Run engine 2 minutes for each percentage of dilution above 15 percent. The engine must then be run for 2 minutes at take-off power and visual observation made that no oil is discharged from the engine breather. If discharge occurs, reduce power immediately and run engine at 1600 rpm for 5 minutes at an oil temperature of at least 40°C; then recheck for oil discharge at take-off power for 2 minutes. This procedure should be repeated until a 2-minute run at take-off power can be accomplished without oil discharge from the breather. Fuel and oil tanks should be refilled if extensive ground running is required.

TAXIING

Use only essential electrical equipment to preserve battery life while taxiing at low engine speeds.

WARNING

In cold weather, make sure all instruments have warmed up sufficiently to ensure normal operation. Check for sluggish instruments during taxiing.

BEFORE TAKE-OFF

1. Check controls very carefully for free and proper movement.

2. Hold brakes and run up engine to 2300 rpm (T-28C), field barometric pressure (T-28B), until spark plugs have burned clean and engine is operating smoothly. Then check magneto dropoff.

3. Normally, carburetor air control should be at DIRECT for take-off. However, if icing conditions exist, move handle to ALTERNATE, prior to take-off, to ensure elimination of ice from induction system. When outside air temperature is below −18°C (0°F), use sufficient carburetor heat to maintain carburetor air temperature near 15°C, during take-off, to ensure smooth engine operation.

4. Turn pitot heater ON just before rolling into position for take-off.

TAKE-OFF

1. At start of take-off run, advance throttle to take-off setting and check that full power is available. If full power is not obtained, immediately discontinue take-off.

Note

During take-off in cold weather, the cockpit combustion heater should be on to keep the windshield from frosting.

AFTER TAKE-OFF

After take-off from a wet snow or slush-covered field, operate the landing gear, flaps, and hook through several complete cycles to prevent their freezing in the retracted position. Expect considerably slower operation of the landing gear and flaps in cold weather.

DURING FLIGHT

1. Use alternate air as required to maintain carburetor air temperature outside the icing range (−10° to +5°C). If full alternate air will not maintain carburetor air temperature above the icing range, it is better to maintain a carburetor air temperature below −10°C than within the icing range. Do not exceed 38°C in low blower, 15°C in high blower.

2. If icing is encountered, occasionally increase rpm momentarily from 2400 to 2600 in an attempt to throw off ice that may have accumulated on the propeller.

WARNING

Flight should not be attempted through known or forecast icing conditions, as there is no means of removing ice from the aircraft. A reduction in cruising speed and cruising range, and an increase in stalling speed, will result from ice forming on the aircraft.

APPROACH TO PATTERN

1. Make sure ice is not jamming the carburetor venturi. Test by moving throttle back and forth several times.

2. Use carburetor heat during approach and landing. Be prepared to turn heat off if waveoff should be necessary.

3. Pump brake pedals several times on approach.

4. If ice has formed on the aircraft, increase approach speed to where you have good control over the rate of descent.

LANDING

Use normal landing procedure. Watch for ice on the runway and avoid braking in these spots if possible.

ENGINE SHUTDOWN

Use normal shutdown procedure unless engine oil is to be diluted. If temperatures below 25°F (−4°C) are expected prior to the next start when using MIL-L-22851 oil or Grade 1100 oil, or below 0°F (−18°C) when using Grade 1065 oil, and preheat is not available, use oil dilution as shown under OIL DILUTION.

OIL DILUTION

1. Allow oil to cool to 40°C or below.

2. Accomplish dilution at 1100 rpm.

3. Advance throttle to 1500 rpm and cycle propeller two or three times through its full governing range during the last portion of the dilution period.

4. Shut down engine 30 seconds after dilution is completed, in order to circulate diluted oil throughout engine.

Note

Oil dilution of MIL-L-22851 or Grade 1100 oil to 5 percent, suitable for anticipated starting, temperatures of −4° to −7°C (25°F to 20°F), can be accomplished in 45 seconds.

5. Dilution of MIL-L-22851 or Grade 1100 oil can be accomplished as follows:

ANTICIPATED TEMPERATURE		DILUTION REQUIRED (PERCENT)	DILUTION TIME (MINUTES)
°C	°F		
−7	20	5	0.75
−12	10	10	2.00
−20	−5	15	3.50
−33	−20	20	5.00

6. Dilution of Grade 1065 oil can be accomplished as follows:

ANTICIPATED TEMPERATURE		DILUTION REQUIRED (PERCENT)	DILUTION TIME (MINUTES)
°C	°F		
−12	10	0	
−21	−5	5	0.75
−29	−20	10	2.00
−37	−35	15	3.50
−46	−50	20	5.00

Note

Dilution exceeding 15 percent is not recommended, as excessive boiloff time will be required.

BEFORE LEAVING AIRCRAFT

1. Clean dirt and ice from shock struts.

2. Inspect fuel and oil tank vents and breathers and remove ice.

3. Leave canopy partially open to prevent cracking of canopy or windshield glass due to differential contraction. Air circulation also retards formation of frost.

4. Install protective covers.

5. Drain oil tank sumps, "Y" drain, and all fuel drains of condensate approximately 30 minutes after stopping engine. If aircraft is to be idle for several days, oil may be drained.

6. Check specific gravity of battery at least weekly. If it is less than 1.250, remove and service battery. If layover of several days is anticipated, or if temperature is below −29°C (−20°F) and aircraft will be idle more than 4 hours, remove battery.

HOT WEATHER OPERATION

Hot weather and desert procedures are the same as the normal procedures shown in Section III. In addition, the following steps should be observed:

Note

If aircraft has been parked in the sun, either wear gloves or use caution when making the exterior inspection.

1. If carburetor air intake has not been covered, see that any accumulation of sand or dust is removed.

2. Check tires for possible overinflation and signs of deterioration.

3. Check for fuel, oil, and hydraulic leaks.

4. Make engine run-up as short as possible to avoid overheating.

5. If run-up area is sandy or dusty, make run-up so propeller wash will be away from personnel, other aircraft, and ground installations.

6. Use caution, when taxiing, to avoid overheating the brakes.

7. If in desert or dusty country, do not take off in the wake of another aircraft.

8. Remember that ground roll will be increased in hot weather.

9. Expect gusts and turbulent air at low altitudes.

10. When flight is completed and aircraft is secured, install protective covers and, if blowing sand or dust is not a hazard, keep canopy open to allow the air to circulate.

Refer to NWP-41(A) for approved hand and light signals and the FLIP/Enroute Supplement for Lost Plane/Lost Communications procedures.

Weapons Systems

section VIII

TABLE OF CONTENTS

ARMAMENT SYSTEMS

ARMAMENT TRAINING PACKAGE, AERO 1A

For training purposes, the aircraft may be fitted with an armament training system, Aero 1A, incorporating a Mark 6, Mod 0 fire control system and utilizing various armament packages. The armament control panel (figure 8-4) mounts in the center of the floor directly beneath the instrument panel in the front cockpit. The armament package mounts externally under each wing inner panel (figure 8-1) and consists of two gun packages or two bomb racks. Each rack will accommodate one bomb, one Aero 4B practice container, or a launcher with three rockets. A gun camera is mounted in the leading edge of the left wing, when guns or rockets are installed. Mixed combinations of armament cannot be carried. Strakes are required on each side of the fuselage of T-28C aircraft while carrying external stores.

GUN PACKAGES

A detachable gun pod containing one Type M2 or M3, .50-caliber machine gun, 100 rounds of ammunition, and a pneumatic gun-charging system can be installed at each inboard wing station. The charging systems are controllable from the front cockpit, and each has sufficient capacity to charge its respective gun about 20 times. When the guns are fired, the charging systems are inoperative, preventing accidental simultaneous gun firing and charging. The gun pods cannot be jettisoned from the aircraft.

BOMBS AND ROCKETS

To deliver bombs or rockets, the aircraft is configured with a modified Mark 51 Mod 14 bomb rack at each of the two external stations. Each rack is capable of carrying an Aero 4B practice container, with either eight MK 23, eight MK 43, or six MK 5 practice bombs, one AN/M38A2 practice bomb, one AN/M2A2 practice cluster, or equipped with rocket launcher, three 2.25-inch SCAR rockets. Bomb and rocket selection, arming, release, and firing are accomplished electrically by controls in the front cockpit. Sighting is done with the Mark 8 Mod 5 sight and individual buttons on the stick grip release bombs or fire rockets.

CAMERA

A Type AN-N6 or -N6A camera can be installed in the leading edge of the left wing to photograph the target. The camera, powered by the armament bus, operates automatically when the gun trigger or rocket-firing button is depressed and, in addition, continues to photograph the target for a period of 1 to 5 seconds after the trigger or rocket-firing button is released. The time of operation after trigger or rocket-firing button is released can be varied by the ground crew. No camera adjustments can be made by the pilot during flight.

TOW TARGETS

Tow targets of the sleeve type or the banner type may be utilized by installation of the tow-target equipment. Refer to TOW-TARGET EQUIPMENT, in this section.

EXTERNAL STORES

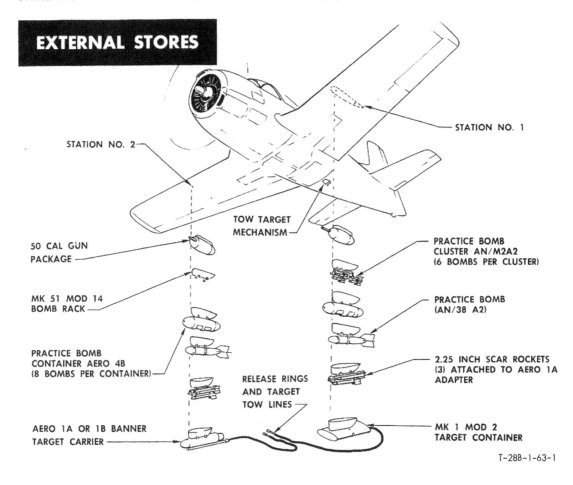

STATION NO. 1

STATION NO. 2

TOW TARGET
MECHANISM

50 CAL GUN
PACKAGE

PRACTICE BOMB
CLUSTER AN/M2A2
(6 BOMBS PER CLUSTER)

MK 51 MOD 14
BOMB RACK

PRACTICE BOMB
(AN/38 A2)

PRACTICE BOMB
CONTAINER AERO 4B
(8 BOMBS PER CONTAINER)

RELEASE RINGS
AND TARGET
TOW LINES

2.25 INCH SCAR ROCKETS
(3) ATTACHED TO AERO 1A
ADAPTER

AERO 1A OR 1B BANNER
TARGET CARRIER

MK 1 MOD 2
TARGET CONTAINER

T-28B-1-63-1

Figure 8-1

ARMAMENT (MODIFIED T-28C)

Some T-28C aircraft have been modified to accommodate a wide range of stores selection. Modifications include six store stations, three on the lower surface of each wing to accommodate various complements composed of fragmentation, general-purpose, napalm, and practice bombs; 2.75- and 5-inch rockets, and .50-caliber gun pods. A modified armament control panel (figure 8-5), utilized with the Mark 6 Mod 0 fire control system, supplies control of the armament system on the modified aircraft. Strakes must be installed when carrying external stores. See figure 8-2 for external stores loading capability.

WING STATIONS

The six wing stations mount armament packages that may consist of two M2 or M3 .50-caliber machine guns and pneumatic gun charger packages and four Aero 15C/15C-1 bomb rack/rocket launchers with adapters, or the gun packages may be removed and replaced by Aero

15C/15C-1 bomb rack/rocket launchers with adapters. Each station may be used for numerous stores within the station weight limitations, and mixed combinations of stores may be carried symmetrically.

BOMBING SYSTEM

The Aero 15C/15C-1 removable bomb rack has been adapted to the six store stations. The racks are capable of carrying stores of recommended type within the weight limitations of each store station. See figure 8-2. Six bomb select switches, one for each store station, are located on the aft side of the wheel wells. When the Aero 4B practice bomb container is carried, one of the wheel well bomb select switches must be placed in the DISABLE position, for each practice bomb container carried, to preclude inadvertent dropping of the container. The practice bomb containers may still be emergency jettisoned. Bomb selection, arming, and release are accomplished electrically by the controls in the front cockpit. Bomb sighting is done with the Mark 8 Mod 5 sight and bombs are

EXTERNAL STORES

MODIFIED T-28C

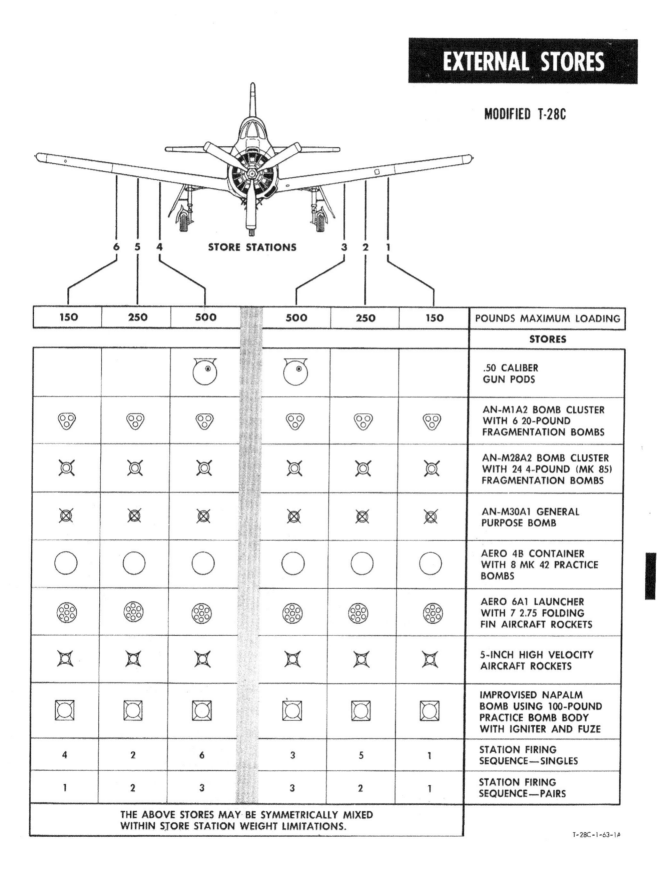

150	250	500		500	250	150	POUNDS MAXIMUM LOADING
							STORES
		⬭		⬭			.50 CALIBER GUN PODS
⬡	⬡	⬡		⬡	⬡	⬡	AN-M1A2 BOMB CLUSTER WITH 6 20-POUND FRAGMENTATION BOMBS
✳	✳	✳		✳	✳	✳	AN-M28A2 BOMB CLUSTER WITH 24 4-POUND (MK 85) FRAGMENTATION BOMBS
⊗	⊗	⊗		⊗	⊗	⊗	AN-M30A1 GENERAL PURPOSE BOMB
◯	◯	◯		◯	◯	◯	AERO 4B CONTAINER WITH 8 MK 42 PRACTICE BOMBS
◎	◎	◎		◎	◎	◎	AERO 6A1 LAUNCHER WITH 7 2.75 FOLDING FIN AIRCRAFT ROCKETS
✦	✦	✦		✦	✦	✦	5-INCH HIGH VELOCITY AIRCRAFT ROCKETS
▢	▢	▢		▢	▢	▢	IMPROVISED NAPALM BOMB USING 100-POUND PRACTICE BOMB BODY WITH IGNITER AND FUZE
4	2	6		3	5	1	STATION FIRING SEQUENCE—SINGLES
1	2	3		3	2	1	STATION FIRING SEQUENCE—PAIRS

THE ABOVE STORES MAY BE SYMMETRICALLY MIXED WITHIN STORE STATION WEIGHT LIMITATIONS.

released by the bomb release button on the control stick grip. All other bombing system controls are on the armament control panel.

ROCKET SYSTEM

Each of the six wing store stations can accommodate various rocket pods containing several 2.75-inch FFA rockets. The rockets and pods are mounted on an Aero 15C/15C-1 combination bomb rack and rocket launcher. Rocket selection and firing are accomplished electronically by controls in the front cockpit. Rocket stations are fired individually, in pairs, or in salvo, depending upon the setting of the station selector switch. Aiming is accomplished with the Mark 8 Mod 5 sight and the contents of a single pod or pairs of pods are ripple-fired with each depression of the rocket-firing button on the stick grip. The gun camera operates automatically during rocket firing.

FIRE CONTROL SYSTEM

The Mark 6 Mod 0 is a pilot-operated fire control system providing lead angle information for precision aiming of the fixed guns, bombs, or rockets.

SIGHT

The system uses the Mark 8 Mod 5 sight primarily as a combined lead-computing sight and also as a fixed sight. The target is viewed through a clear glass plate on which two reticle images, produced by two similar optical systems, are reflected. The reticle images are focused at infinity and appear to be projected or superimposed on the target. The cross of the fixed reticle image establishes a fixed sight line which indicates the direction in which the aircraft is pointing. The center pip of the lead-computing gyro reticle image establishes a sight line which is automatically offset from the fixed sight line at the proper angle for tracking the target. Using the image, the aiming and tracking problem is simplified to flying the aircraft so the gyro reticle image remains on the target, and following the sight line toward the target until the attack is completed. When the lead-computing system of the sight is used, the reticle image consists of a center dot and an outer circle formed by six, equally spaced, diamond-shaped dots with the center dot establishing a sight line. When the fixed reticle sight is used, the reticle consists of a ladder pattern below a center cross. The control settings of the sight system must be changed before initiating various types of attacks, to be in accordance with the specific settings necessary for firing or release of the respective armament being carried. Sight unit controls are located on the sight body, armament control panel, and in the throttle twist grip.

ARMAMENT CONTROLS AND INDICATORS

SIGHT UNIT

Target Span Lever

The target span lever (figure 8-3), on the sight, is used to vary the diameter of the reticle in proportion to the span of the target so that correct range values may be obtained by the target spanning process. Graduated markings (from 30 to 120) on the scale represent the span, in feet, of the target. The lever should be set before the attack to correspond to the span of the target.

Fixed-reticle Masking Lever

A fixed-reticle masking lever (figure 8-3) is on the left side of the sight. The fixed reticle is normal when the masking lever is in the aft position. When the lever is moved forward, all of the fixed-reticle image except the center cross is blanked out. The lever is provided to eliminate the confusion of using both the fixed and gyro images together and yet enable the fixed reticle cross to be used with the gyro reticle for indications of lead.

Sight Range Dial

The range dial (figure 8-3), visible through a window on the left side of the sight, indicates the target range in hundreds of feet as determined by sight range control. The dial is graduated from 600 to 2400 feet.

SIGHT RANGE CONTROL

A twist grip incorporated in the throttle provides range control for the computer circuits. Rotation of the twist grip varies the diameter of the sight reticle. Clockwise rotation of the grip increases the range (decreases the reticle size); counterclockwise movement decreases the range (increases reticle size). When the grip is turned to the extreme maximum range position, the sight gyro is caged to prevent tumbling of the gyro and blurring of the gyro image.

ARMAMENT CONTROL PANEL

EMERG JETTISON Handle

The EMERG JETTISON handle (figure 8-4) may be used to jettison bombs and rockets in an emergency. Placing the ARMAMENT MASTER switch to OFF prior to jettison will cause the stores to drop in a SAFE condition.

STORES JETTISON Button (Modified T-28C)

The STORES JETTISON button (figure 8-5) performs the same function as the EMERG JETTISON handle. The ARMAMENT MASTER switch position determines whether bombs drop SAFE or ARMED.

TARGET SPAN
LEVER

FIXED-RETICLE
MASKING LEVER

SIGHT RANGE
DIAL

NO HAND HOLD

MARK 8 SIGHT UNIT

T-28B-1-60-1B

Figure 8-3

ARMAMENT MASTER Switch

The ON-OFF ARMAMENT MASTER switch (figures 8-4 and 8-5) controls power to the armament bus. With this switch in the ON position, power is available for operation of the sight, guns, and bombs and rocket release systems.

ARMAMENT SELECTOR Switch

The rotary ARMAMENT SELECTOR switch (figure 8-4) on the armament control panel has six positions: OFF, GUNS, ROCKETS, BOMBS STA. 1, BOMBS STA. 2, and BOMBS SALVO. With the switch in the OFF position, the gun, rocket, and bomb systems are inoperative. To fire the guns or rockets, the switch must be turned to the respective position. When the switch is turned to BOMBS STA. 1, the left bomb is released when the bomb release button on the control stick grip is depressed. The right bomb is released when the selector switch is at BOMBS STA. 2 and both bombs are released simultaneously when the switch is at BOMBS SALVO. Practice bombs are released from the Aero 4B container with the selector switch set in the same position as for conventional bombs.

ARMAMENT SELECTOR Switch (Modified T-28C)

The rotary ARMAMENT SELECTOR switch (figure 8-5) on the armament control panel has four positions: OFF, GUNS, ROCKETS, and BOMBS. With the switch in the OFF position, the gun, rocket, and bomb systems are inoperative. To fire the guns, rockets, or drop the bombs,

the switch must be turned to the respective position. The armament selector switch must be used in conjunction with the station selector switch and the station select advance switch for proper armament (except guns) and station selection. After selections of armament and desired station, pressing the control stick switch for type of armament will fire or release the stores. Practice bombs are released from the Aero 4B container with the selector switch set in the same position as for conventional bombs.

ROCKETS Station Selector Switch

The setting of the ROCKETS station selector switch (figuse 8-4), located on the armament control panel, determines the rocket-firing order. With the switch set to SINGLES 1, rocket No. 1 is fired first and the switch automatically rotates to No. 2 position in preparation for the next firing. To fire rockets in pairs, the station selector is rotated to PAIRS 4. To ensure release of all rockets that are carried, the switch should not be moved to any intermediate position between SINGLES 1 and PAIRS 4 before initial firing.

Station Selector Switch (Modified T-28C)

The station selector switch (figure 8-5), located on the armament control panel, has seven positions: 1, 5, 3, 6-1, 2-5, 4-3, and ALL above a white blocked semicircle and SINGLES, PAIRS, and SALVO below the semicircle. With the switch placed on 1 above the SINGLES side of the

ARMAMENT
CONTROL PANEL

T-28C-1-54-48

Figure 8-4

semicircle, pressing the rocket firing or bomb release buttons on the control stick will fire or release station No. 1 and a station advance coil will move the station selector to the next station, and so on, until all stations are fired or released. The firing or release order is 1, 5, 3, 6, 2, and 4. To fire or release the stations in pairs, the station selector switch should be placed to the 6-1 figure on the white semicircle above PAIRS; then, pressing of the appropriate button on the control stick will release the stores in pairs with the station advance coil advancing the station selector to the next station pair until all stations are fired or released. Pairs firing or release sequence is 6-1, 2-5, and 4-3. The ALL position will salvo all stores, except gun packages, at once.

STA SELECT ADVANCE Switch (Modified T-28C)

The STA SELECT ADVANCE switch (figure 8-5), located on the armament control panel, has two positions: DISABLE and NORMAL. Placing the switch to the DISABLE position disconnects the station advance coil from the station selector switch and allows individual station selectivity. The station selector must then be rotated manually to desired stations as required.

Sight Reticle SELECTOR Switch

The sight reticle SELECTOR switch (figures 8-4 and 8-5) on the armament control panel is used to select the desired sight reticle image. Moving the switch from OFF to GYRO causes the gyro reticle image to appear on the reflector glass. With the switch at FIXED & GYRO, both the fixed and gyro images are visible. At the FIXED position, only the fixed image is visible, and the sight is suitable only as a fixed-reticle-type sight for estimating leads. The switch is powered by the armament bus.

Sight DIMMER Knob

The sight DIMMER knob (figures 8-4 and 8-5) on the armament control panel controls a rheostat that varies the brightness of the reticle image for proper contrast with background light conditions. The knob is powered by the armament bus and can be rotated from DIM to BRIGHT as desired.

GUN FIRING Switch

The armament bus-powered, three-position GUN FIRING switch on the armament control panel (figures 8-4 and 8-5) simultaneously controls the two gun-charging systems. Spring-loaded to the center OFF position, the switch is momentarily held at SAFE to retract the gun bolt and eject a shell from the breech. The bolt stays retracted when the switch is at SAFE and OFF, but moves forward to bring a new shell into the gun when the switch is moved to READY. The guns are fired when the trigger

ARMAMENT CONTROL PANEL

(MODIFIED AIRCRAFT)

T-28C-1-54-6A

Figure 8-5

is pressed and will recharge automatically as long as the trigger is held depressed and no jam or misfire occurs.

Note

If electrical power fails during gunnery operations, detachable gun package gun bolts will retract through action from the pneumatic gun charging system and the bolts will hold in the safe position with the chambers clear of rounds.

Fire Control Selector Switch

The fire control selector switch (figures 8-4 and 8-5), located on the armament control panel, has three positions: GUNS, ROCKETS, and BOMBS. Moving the switch to the position corresponding to the armament carried adjusts the sight reticle to the correct offset point for the particular armament. The switch is powered by the armament bus.

DIVE ANGLE Switch

The DIVE ANGLE switch (figures 8-4 and 8-5) on the armament control panel is used during bomb release and rocket firing. For attack angles between 0 and 35 degrees, the switch is set at 35° & UNDER and for attacks of 35 degrees or more, the switch is set at 35° & OVER. For a dive angle near 35 degrees, either setting gives satisfactory results, so that accurate estimation of dive angle by the pilot is unnecessary.

BOMB ARMING Switch

Arming of the bombs is controlled by the BOMB ARMING switch (figures 8-4 and 8-5) on the armament control panel. Bombs carried within the practice bomb container contain no explosive and, therefore, are not armed. With the arming switch at SAFE, the bombs are released unarmed. Setting the switch to NOSE & TAIL arms both nose and tail fuzes for instantaneous detonation of the bomb on contact. Bombs are released in a tail-fuze-armed condition when the switch is in the TAIL ONLY position, providing for delayed detonation.

ARM SAFETY DISABLING Switch

The guarded momentary ARM SAFETY DISABLING switch (figures 8-4 and 8-5), located on the armament control panel, is provided for use by the ground crew. Normally, the switch is OFF (guard down) and the armament electrical circuit is disconnected when the aircraft is on the ground. To energize the armament bus when the aircraft is on the ground, it is necessary to hold the ARM SAFETY DISABLING switch ON while the ARMAMENT MASTER switch is turned ON.

WARNING

To disconnect the armament electrical circuit, it is necessary to move the ARMAMENT MASTER switch to OFF.

PANEL LIGHT **Knob**

The PANEL LIGHT knob (figures 8-4 and 8-5), located on the armament control panel, controls the armament control panel floodlight intensity.

BOMB RELEASE BUTTON

This button, lettered "B," is located on the stick grip in the front cockpit. Armament bus power is supplied to the bomb release circuits through the bomb release button. With the associated switches properly positioned, bombs are released when the button is depressed.

ROCKET-FIRING BUTTON

This button, lettered "R," is located on the stick grip in the front cockpit. Armament bus power is supplied to the rocket-firing and camera circuits through the rocket-firing button. With the associated switches properly positioned, rockets are fired when the button is depressed.

GUN TRIGGER

The gun trigger is located on the stick grip in the forward cockpit. Armament bus power is supplied to the gun-firing and gun camera circuits through the gun trigger. With the associated switches properly positioned, the guns will fire when the trigger is depressed.

TOW-TARGET EQUIPMENT

The installation of the tow-target equipment consists of a target container or carrier mounted on each bomb rack, a target release mechanism mounted on the belly of the fuselage, and a target control panel mounted below the instrument panel in the front cockpit. The target container or carrier can be either the sleeve-type target container or the banner-type target carrier. If desired, a sleeve-type target container can be mounted on one bomb rack and a banner-type target carrier can be mounted on the other bomb rack. The two target tow ropes from the target containers or carriers are hooked to the target release mechanism. Approximately 900 feet of tow rope can be carried. The target control panel has two sets of momentary switches. The left set controls the target on the left wing and the right set controls the target on the right wing.

WARNING

Only *one* target at a time is to be launched. Drop first target before launching the second.

TARGET CONTAINERS AND CARRIERS

Either the Mark 1 Mod 2 sleeve target container or the Aero 1A banner target carrier can be installed on the bomb rack under each wing. Each target container or

carrier houses one target and tow rope. If desired, both types of targets can be carried at the same time, one mounted on each bomb rack. The launching of the target is accomplished by a momentary switch on the target control panel, marked LAUNCH TARGET.

RELEASE MECHANISM

The target release mechanism consists of two independently controlled hook mechanisms mounted in the bottom of the aircraft, just aft of the baggage compartment door. An external release adjacent to the hooks is provided for opening the hooks when on the ground. The tow ropes are attached to the hooks by inserting the rings on the tow ropes into their respective hook openings and pressing firmly against the upper face of the hook opening. The hooks are automatically self-locking. With the ring installed, a sharp pull on the tow rope will determine whether the hook is locked. The momentary switches on the target control panel marked DROP TARGET will electrically open the hook mechanism and allow the target to drop.

TARGET CONTROL PANEL

The target control panel is located below the instrument panel in the front cockpit only and has duplicate sets of momentary switches for the right side and left side. The three momentary switches for each side are LAUNCH TARGET, DROP TARGET, and DROP TARGET CONTAINER. An emergency jettison button is located in the center of the target control panel. The button is marked EMERGENCY JETTISON EXT. STORES. In case of emergency, the button electrically jettisons both target containers or carriers and both tow ropes simultaneously.

ARMAMENT SYSTEM OPERATION

ANGLE-OF-ATTACK RELATIONSHIP CHART

The angle-of-attack chart can be used to determine flight attitude of the aircraft for any gross weight and flight condition. Flight attitude, thus obtained, is used for computing lead angles for bombing, air-to-ground gunnery, and rocketry when the gun sight is caged. Flight attitude is not required for air-to-air gunnery, since the gyro computing sight automatically corrects for angle-of-attack effects. To determine the angle of attack in degrees or mils to be used in lead angle computations, see figure 8-6.

FIRING GUNS

1. ARMAMENT MASTER switch—ON.

2. ARMAMENT SELECTOR switch—GUNS.

3. Fire control selector switch—GUNS.

4. Charge guns by moving GUN FIRING switch to SAFE and then back to READY.

5. Sight reticle SELECTOR switch—as desired.

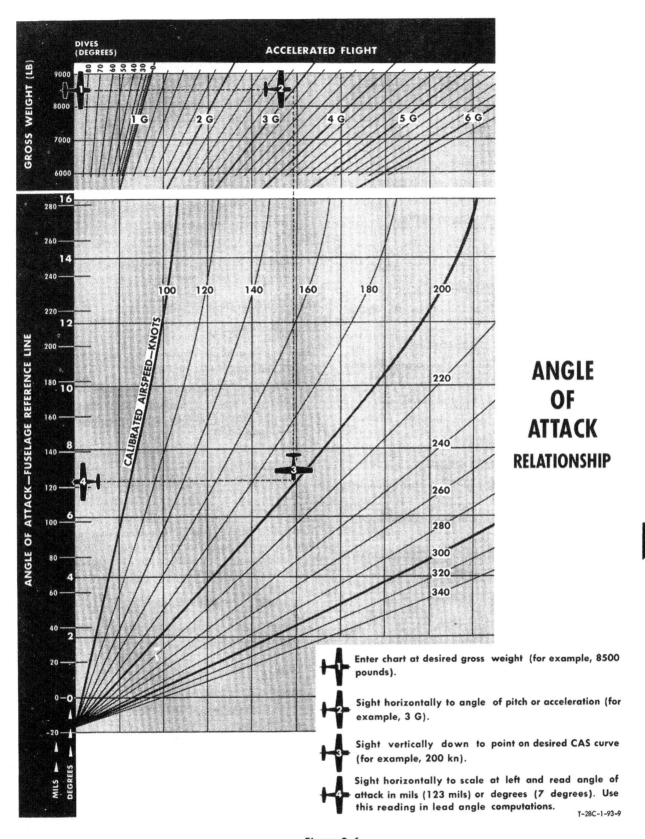

ANGLE OF ATTACK RELATIONSHIP

1. Enter chart at desired gross weight (for example, 8500 pounds).

2. Sight horizontally to angle of pitch or acceleration (for example, 3 G).

3. Sight vertically down to point on desired CAS curve (for example, 200 kn).

4. Sight horizontally to scale at left and read angle of attack in mils (123 mils) or degrees (7 degrees). Use this reading in lead angle computations.

T-28C-1-93-9

Figure 8-6

6. Sight DIMMER knob—adjusted as desired.

7. Fixed-reticle masking lever—positioned as desired.

8. Target span lever—set to span of target.

9. Twist sight range control (throttle grip) to extreme clockwise position to cage sight gyro.

10. Fly the aircraft so that the target is continuously centered in the reticle circle and rotate throttle twist grip for ranging control until diameter of the reticle circle corresponds to the size of the target.

11. Continue operating the range control, keeping target constantly framed within reticle circle.

12. Track target without slipping or skidding.

13. Depress trigger.

FIRING ROCKETS

1. ARMAMENT MASTER switch—ON.

2. Sight reticle SELECTOR switch—GYRO or FIXED & GYRO.

3. Fixed-reticle masking lever—as desired.

4. Sight range control twist grip rotated to full clockwise position.

5. Sight DIMMER knob—adjusted as desired.

6. ARMAMENT SELECTOR switch—ROCKETS.

7. Fire control switch—ROCKETS.

8. Station selector switch—as desired.

9. STA SELECT ADVANCE switch—as desired (modified T-28C).

10. DIVE ANGLE switch—35° & OVER or 35° & UNDER as desired.

11. Keep pipper on target and track target smoothly.

12. To fire—Press rocket-firing button.

RELEASING BOMBS

1. ARMAMENT MASTER switch—ON.

2. Sight reticle SELECTOR switch—GYRO or FIXED & GYRO.

3. Fixed-reticle masking lever—as desired.

4. Sight range control twist grip rotated to full clockwise position.

5. Sight DIMMER knob—adjusted as desired.

6. Fire control switch—BOMBS.

7. ARMAMENT SELECTOR switch—as desired.

8. BOMB ARMING switch—NOSE & TAIL or TAIL ONLY.

9. Release bombs by depressing bomb release button on top of control stick.

RELEASING BOMBS (MODIFIED T-28C)

1. ARMAMENT MASTER switch—ON.

2. Sight reticle selector switch—GYRO or FIXED & GYRO.

3. Fixed-reticle masking lever—as desired.

4. Sight range control twist grip rotated to full clockwise position.

5. Sight DIMMER knob—adjusted as desired.

6. Fire control switch—BOMBS.

7. ARMAMENT SELECTOR switch—BOMBS.

8. Station selector switch—as desired.

9. STA SELECT ADVANCE switch—as desired.

10. BOMB ARMING switch—NOSE & TAIL or TAIL ONLY.

11. Release bombs by depressing bomb release button on top of control stick grip.

TOW-TARGET OPERATION

EXTERIOR CHECK

Make normal exterior inspection as given in Section III, and, in addition, check the following:

1. Security of the tow-target containers or carriers.

2. Release latch on the tow-target container for proper locking cord or proper installation of banner-type target.

3. Tow ropes to see that they are hooked into the proper target release hook and that the target release mechanism is properly locked.

TAKE-OFF

Accomplish normal take-off procedure as given in Section III. In the event the target is released during take-off, release target immediately by holding down the momentary switch marked DROP TARGET.

Note

Be sure to hold down the correct switch for the launched target.

LAUNCH

Launching either the sleeve-type or banner-type target from its container or carrier should be accomplished as follows:

1. Reduce speed to 120 knots IAS or less.

2. Start a level, standard-rate turn toward the target container to be used.

3. Launch correct target by holding down the switch marked LAUNCH TARGET.

4. Maintain rate of turn and airspeed until target has streamed and is being towed.

5. If target hangs up out of its container or carrier and cannot be extended, jettison container and tow rope by depressing the switches marked DROP TARGET and DROP TARGET CONTAINER simultaneously. Only the switches on the fouled-target side are to be operated.

FLIGHT

After target is launched and in tow, aircraft may be maneuvered as necessary. Target towing speed can be from 200 to 260 knots IAS for the sleeve-type target and from 180 to 210 knots IAS for the banner-type target. The difference in maximum speeds depends on the model and design of the target.

RELEASE

Upon completion of gunnery exercise, fly over designated target recovery area at predetermined altitude and airspeed and drop target by depressing the switch marked DROP TARGET. Then listen for confirmation of release of the target from either the control tower or the guard aircraft flying with you.

If target is not dropped, and tow-aircraft pilot assumes target is dropped, serious injury to personnel and equipment on the ground may be caused by the tow rope.

EMERGENCIES

Bailout

Before bailout, be sure to jettison tow-target equipment by pushing the button marked EMERGENCY JETTISON EXT. STORES. Then bail out in normal manner.

Ditching

To prevent becoming tangled up in the tow rope after ditching, jettison tow-target equipment before ditching by pushing button marked EMERGENCY JETTISON EXT. STORES.

section IX

Flight Crew Coordination

This section is not applicable to T-28B/C aircraft.

NATOPS Evaluation
section X

T-28C-1-00-10A

TABLE OF CONTENTS

PART 1 — T-28 NATOPS EVALUATION PROGRAM

CONCEPT

The standard operating procedures prescribed in this manual represent the optimum method of operating T-28 aircraft. The NATOPS evaluation is intended to evaluate compliance with NATOPS procedures by observing and grading individuals and units. This evaluation is tailored for compatibility with various operational commitments and missions of both Navy and Marine Corps units. The prime objective of the NATOPS evaluation program is to assist the unit commanding officer in improving unit readiness and safety through constructive comment. Maximum benefit from the NATOPS program is achieved only through the vigorous support of the program by commanding officers as well as flight crewmembers.

DEFINITIONS

The following terms, used throughout this section, are defined as to their specific meaning within the NATOPS program.

NATOPS EVALUATION

A periodic evaluation of individual flight crewmember standardization consisting of an open book examination,

a closed book examination, an oral examination, and a flight evaluation.

NATOPS RE-EVALUATION

A partial NATOPS evaluation administered to a flight crewmember who has been placed in an Unqualified status by receiving an Unqualified grade for any of his ground examinations or the flight evaluation. Only those areas in which an unsatisfactory level was noted need be observed during a re-evaluation.

QUALIFIED

That degree of standardization demonstrated by a very reliable flight crewmember who has a good knowledge of standard operating procedures and a thorough understanding of aircraft capabilities and limitations.

CONDITIONALLY QUALIFIED

That degree of standardization demonstrated by a flight crewmember who meets the minimum acceptable standards. He is considered safe enough to fly as a pilot in command or to perform normal duties without supervision but more practice is needed to become qualified.

UNQUALIFIED

That degree of standardization demonstrated by a flight crewmember who fails to meet minimum acceptable criteria. He should receive supervised instruction until he has achieved a grade of Qualified or Conditionally Qualified.

AREA

A routine of preflight, flight, or postflight.

SUB-AREA

A performance subdivision within an area, which is observed and evaluated during an evaluation flight.

CRITICAL AREA

Any area or sub-area which covers items of significant importance to the overall mission requirements, the marginal performance of which would jeopardize safe conduct of the flight.

EMERGENCY

An aircraft component, system failure, or condition which requires instantaneous recognition, analysis, and proper action.

MALFUNCTION

An aircraft component or system failure or condition which requires recognition and analysis, but which permits more deliberate action than that required for an emergency.

IMPLEMENTATION

The NATOPS evaluation program shall be carried out in every unit operating naval aircraft. Pilots desiring to attain/retain qualification in the T-28 shall be evaluated initially in accordance with OPNAVINST 3510.9 series, and at least once during the 12 months following initial and subsequent evaluations. Individual and unit NATOPS evaluations will be conducted annually; however, instruction in and observation of adherence to NATOPS procedures must be on a daily basis within each unit to obtain maximum benefits from the program. The NATOPS coordinators, evaluators, and instructors shall administer the program as outlined in OPNAVINST 3510.9 series. Evaluees who receive a grade of Unqualified on a ground or flight evaluation shall be allowed 30 days in which to complete a re-evaluation. A maximum of 60 days may elapse between the date the ground evaluation was commenced and the date the flight evaluation is satisfactorily completed.

GROUND EVALUATION

Prior to commencing the flight evaluation, an evaluee must achieve a grade of Qualified on the open and closed book examinations. The oral examination is also part of the ground evaluation but may be conducted as part of the flight evaluation. To assure a degree of standardization between units, the NATOPS instructors may use the bank of questions contained in this section in preparing portions of the written examinations.

OPEN BOOK EXAMINATION

Up to 50 percent of the questions used may be taken from the question bank. The number of questions on the examination will not exceed 40 or be less than 20. The purpose of the open book examination portion of the written examination is to evaluate the pilot's knowledge of appropriate publications and the aircraft.

CLOSED BOOK EXAMINATION

Up to 50 percent of the closed book examination may be taken from the question bank and shall include questions concerning normal procedures and aircraft limitations. The number of questions on the examination will not exceed 40 or be less than 20. Questions designated critical will be so marked. An incorrect answer to any question in the critical category will result in a grade of Unqualified being assigned to the examination.

ORAL EXAMINATION

The questions may be taken from this manual and drawn from the experience of the instructor/evaluator. Such questions should be direct and positive and should in no way be opinionated.

GRADING INSTRUCTIONS

Examination grades shall be computed on a 4.0 scale and converted to an adjective grade of Qualified or Unqualified.

OPEN BOOK EXAMINATION

To obtain a grade of Qualified, an evaluee must obtain a minimum score of 3.5.

CLOSED BOOK EXAMINATION

To obtain a grade of Qualified, an evaluee must obtain a minimum score of 3.3.

ORAL EXAMINATION

A grade of Qualified or Unqualified shall be assigned by the instructor/evaluator.

FLIGHT EVALUATION

The number of flights required to complete the flight evaluation should be kept to a minimum, normally one flight. The areas and sub-areas to be observed and graded on an evaluation flight are outlined in the grading criteria with critical areas marked by an asterisk (*). Sub-area grades will be assigned in accordance with the grading criteria. These sub-areas shall be combined to arrive at the overall grade for the flight. Area grades, if desired, shall also be determined in this manner.

FLIGHT EVALUATION GRADE DETERMINATION

The following procedure shall be used in determining the flight evaluation grade: A grade of Unqualified in any critical area will result in an overall grade of Unqualified for the flight. Otherwise, flight evaluation (or area) grades shall be determined by assigning the following numerical equivalents to the adjective grade for each sub-area. Only the numeral 0, 2, or 4 will be assigned in sub-areas. No interpolation is allowed.

Unqualified 0.0
Conditionally Qualified 2.0
Qualified 4.0

To determine the numerical grade for each area and the overall grade for the flight, add all the points assigned to the sub-areas and divide this sum by the number of sub-areas graded. The adjective grade shall then be determined on the basis of the following scale:

0.0 to 2.19—Unqualified
2.2 to 2.99—Conditionally Qualified
3.0 to 4.0 —Qualified

EXAMPLE: (Add sub-area numerical equivalents)
$$\frac{4+2+4+2+4}{5} = \frac{16}{5} = 3.20 \text{ Qualified}$$

FINAL GRADE DETERMINATION

The final NATOPS evaluation grade shall be the same as the grade assigned to the evaluation flight. An evaluee who receives an Unqualified on any ground examination or the flight evaluation shall be placed in an Unqualified status until he achieves a grade of Conditionally Qualified or Qualified on a re-evaluation.

RECORDS AND REPORTS

A NATOPS evaluation report (OPNAV Form 3510-8) shall be completed for each evaluation and forwarded to the evaluee's commanding officer.

This report shall be filed in the individual flight training record and retained therein for 18 months. In addition, an entry shall be made in the pilot's flight logbook under "Qualifications and Achievements" as follows:

QUALIFICATION		DATE	SIGNATURE	
NATOPS EVAL.	T-28 Pilot	(Date)	(Authenticating Signature)	(Unit which Administered Eval.)

In addition to the NATOPS evaluation report, a NATOPS flight evaluation worksheet, OPNAV Form 3510/10, is provided for use by the evaluator/instructor during the evaluation flight. All of the flight areas and sub-areas are listed on the worksheet with space allowed for related notes. Copies of these forms are located in Part 2 of this section.

FLIGHT EVALUATION GRADING CRITERIA

Only those sub-areas provided or required will be graded. The grades assigned for a sub-area shall be determined by comparing the degree of adherence to standard operating procedures with adjectival ratings listed. Momentary deviations from standard operating procedures should not be considered as unqualifying provided such deviations do not jeopardize flight safety and the evaluee applies prompt corrective action.

MISSION PLANNING

PERSONAL FLYING EQUIPMENT

Qualified — Possessed all required flying clothing, dog tags, and survival equipment as listed in Section II of this manual and the current edition of OPNAVINST 3710.7, and had a good knowledge of its use.

Conditionally Qualified — Possessed the necessary equipment and checked presence, readiness, and security of all other required safety equipment, and had satisfactory knowledge of its use.

Unqualified — Lacked necessary equipment or was not familiar with use of equipment.

FLIGHT PREPARATION

Qualified — Sound working knowledge and use of flight publications, NOTAMS, weather, departure routes, and airport facilities available in the selection of route, altitude, destination, and alternate and/or emergency airports. Correctly completed flight plan log and DD-175.

Conditionally Qualified — Limited knowledge and use of flight publications, NOTAMS, weather, departure procedures, and airport facilities available in selection of route, altitude, destination, and alternate airports. Minor errors in flight plan log and DD-175.

Unqualified — Definite lack of knowledge and use of flight publications, NOTAMS, weather, departure procedures, and airport facilities available in the selection of route, altitude, destination, and alternate airports resulted in planning an *unsafe flight*.

CREW/PASSENGER BRIEFING*

Qualified — Conducted a thorough, detailed, and professional briefing for the dual pilot/passenger, covering route, altitude, destination, weather factors, use of personal and emergency equipment and emergency procedures, smoking privileges, etc, in accordance with current directives.

Unqualified — Conducted no briefing, or failed to cover emergency procedures to the extent necessary to assure effective action during emergencies.

AIRCRAFT TAKE-OFF DATA*

Not applicable to T-28 aircraft.

PREFLIGHT

AIRCRAFT INSPECTION

Qualified — Completed inspection thoroughly and effectively.

Conditionally Qualified — Completed inspection with omissions in minor areas which did not affect the safety of the proposed flight.

Unqualified — Failed to conduct inspection properly and omitted several important items.

CHECK LIST

Qualified — Used NATOPS Check List in an accurate manner with no omissions.

Conditionally Qualified — Made minor omissions to the check list or hurried through without making adequate inspection of each item.

Unqualified — Did not use check list or failed to make complete check.

PRETAKE-OFF

START

Qualified — Complete knowledge and proficiency in normal and emergency procedures during engine start, including proper operational sequence and limitations.

Conditionally Qualified — Knowledge and proficiency in normal and emergency procedures during engine start was limited. Unsure of operation sequence and limitations. Did not jeopardize crew and aircraft safety.

Unqualified — Lacked knowledge and proficiency in normal procedures and emergency procedures during engine start.

CHECK LIST

Qualified — Demonstrated thoroughness in completion of pretaxi check list. Completely checked and properly set the communication/navigation equipment that was required for the successful completion of the flight.

Conditionally Qualified — Omitted minor items in pretaxi check. Checked and set the minimal communication/navigation equipment required for successful completion of the flight. Limited knowledge of proper operation.

Unqualified — Omitted major items of the pretaxi check list. Failed to check or set the communication/navigation equipment.

TAXI

Qualified — Handled aircraft safely, with proper technique in the use of power, rudder, and brakes. Followed hand signals.

Conditionally Qualified — Handled aircraft roughly, with improper use of brakes. Did not follow hand signals. Taxied fast.

Unqualified — Taxied too fast, did not maintain proper lookout. Dangerous.

ENGINE RUNUP*

Qualified — Safely positioned aircraft for runup. Complete knowledge of runup procedures, limitations, and required checks. Completed engine runup and take-off check lists.

Conditionally Qualified — Careless positioning of aircraft for runup, i.e., nose wheel cocked, etc. Limited knowledge of runup procedures and limitations. Completed engine runup and take-off check lists.

Unqualified — Unsafe positioning of the aircraft for runup. Did not know runup procedures, limitations, or checks. Doubtful if malfunctions serious enough to abort aircraft flight would have been recognized. Failed to complete engine runup and take-off check lists.

TAKE-OFF

TAKE-OFF PROCEDURES*

Qualified — Properly aligned aircraft with runway. Applied power properly and maintained directional control with proper use of rudders. Assumed proper take-off attitude and flew aircraft smoothly into air.

Conditionally Qualified — Erratic directional control but able to correct with rudder. Rough rotational technique. Aircraft in unbalanced flight and drifted off runway track.

Unqualified — Had to use brakes to correct swerve. Dangerous rotational technique. Aircraft allowed to settle after lift-off, or aircraft assumed excessive nose-high attitude.

TRANSITION*

Qualified — Maintained the proper climbing attitude. Operated gear/flaps in accordance with NATOPS procedures.

Conditionally Qualified — Overcorrecting nose attitude with erratic airspeed control. Late with gear retraction.

Unqualified — Excessive nose-high attitude with resultant slow airspeed or nose-low attitude with loss of altitude. Forgot gear and would have exceeded limits.

BASIC AIRWORK

CLIMB

Qualified — Maintained airspeed within 10 knots and heading within 5 degrees.

Conditionally Qualified — Maintained airspeed within 15 knots and heading within 10 degrees.

Unqualified — Deviated greater than 10 degrees or 15 knots.

LEVEL FLIGHT

Qualified — Aircraft in balanced flight. Altitude held within 100 feet, heading within 10 degrees, and airspeed within 5 knots.

Conditionally Qualified — Altitude within 200 feet, heading within 15 degrees, and airspeed within 10 knots.

Unqualified — Aircraft not in balanced flight. Deviation from altitude in excess of 200 feet, heading in excess of 15 degrees, and airspeed in excess of 10 knots.

EMERGENCIES*

ENGINE FAILURE*

Qualified — Followed correct procedures as listed in Section V and NATOPS Pocket Check List. Demonstrated ability to effect a safe landing.

Conditionally Qualified — Did not follow correct procedures but demonstrated ability to effect safe landing.

Unqualified — Not able to effect safe landing.

FIRE IN FLIGHT*

Qualified — Followed correct emergency procedure as listed in Section V. Demonstrated complete knowledge of system.

Conditionally Qualified — Did not follow correct emergency procedure but covered all items.

Unqualified — Did not follow correct emergency procedure and would have jeopardized flight safety.

SYSTEMS FAILURE*

Qualified — Followed correct procedures as listed in Section V and NATOPS Pocket Check List.

Conditionally Qualified — Did not follow correct procedures but demonstrated ability to effect desired results.

Unqualified — Did not use correct procedures, did not effect desired results. Jeopardized crew or aircraft safety.

INSTRUMENT PROCEDURES

HOLDING

Qualified — Proper entry and holding procedures with slight deviation, and maintained airspeed within 5 knots, altitude within 100 feet. Met fix departure time within 20 seconds. Displayed adequate knowledge of wind corrections.

Conditionally Qualified — Knew procedures but displayed erratic tracking. Stayed within limits of holding pattern. Held altitude within 200 feet, airspeed within 10 knots, and met fix departure time within 30 seconds.

10-5

Unqualified — Unfamiliar with procedures, could not maintain aircraft within limits of holding pattern. Could not maintain altitude, airspeed, or timing within limits stated under Conditionally Qualified.

APPROACH/PENETRATION

Qualified — Followed procedures as published in appropriate terminal charts. Complied strictly with approach control instructions. Maintained airspeed within 10 knots, altitude within safe limits, and did not descend below published approach altitudes. Maintained field minimum altitude within plus 150 feet, and indicated that aircraft was over the field within 15 seconds of published time. Executed missed approach as published.

Conditionally Qualified — Deviated slightly from prescribed procedures. Did not jeopardize crew or aircraft. Maintained airspeed within 15 knots. Did not descend below minimum altitude and indicated that aircraft was over the field within 30 seconds of published time. Executed missed approach as published.

Unqualified — Unsafe procedures, failed to comply with approach control instructions, or failed to meet airspeed, altitude, and time criteria. Deviated from missed approach procedure to the extent that safety of crew and aircraft were jeopardized.

PRECISION RADAR APPROACH

Qualified — Complied strictly with instructions. Maintained airspeed within 10 knots. Altitude held within 100 feet when altitude assigned. Minor deviations in glide slope and alignment.

Conditionally Qualified — Complied with all instructions. Maintained airspeed within 15 knots. Assigned altitudes held within 200 feet. Erratic in glide slope and alignment, but did not jeopardize safety of aircraft or crew.

Unqualified — Lacked knowledge of procedures. Failure to comply with instructions made completion of safe landing impossible. Exceeded limitations.

LANDING

CHECK LIST*

Qualified — Landing check list completed.

Conditionally Qualified — Hurried through the check list without making adequate inspection of each item.

Unqualified — Did not use check list or failed to make complete check.

DESCENT*

Qualified — Planned and executed descent so as to arrive at the desired entry point at the proper altitude with only minor deviations that did not restrict the effectiveness of the procedure.

Conditionally Qualified — Slow to react to instructions and/or directives. Arrived at pattern entry point with incorrect altitude and/or airspeed.

Unqualified — Ignored instructions and/or directives. Arrived at pattern entry point with incorrect altitude and/or airspeed.

PATTERN*

Qualified — Conformed to field traffic pattern within 100 feet deviation in altitude, within 5 knots airspeed.

Conditionally Qualified — Deviation in pattern but not sufficient to interfere with safety of flight. Within 200 feet deviation in altitude, within 10 knots airspeed.

Unqualified — Serious deviations in pattern that interfered with normal traffic or other deviations jeopardized flight safety. Exceeded 200 feet deviation in altitude and 10 knots airspeed.

LANDING AND ROLLOUT*

Qualified — Aircraft aligned within runway limits throughout final approach. Slight variations in rate of descent and airspeed. Smooth flareout and touchdown in first third of runway. Maintained directional control through proper use of aileron and rudder. Reduced to safe speed prior to clearing runway.

Conditionally Qualified	Had difficulty aligning aircraft with runway, rough handling of aircraft, and used poor technique throughout final and touchdown. Landed on first third of runway. Erratic directional control but able to correct with rudder. Aircraft slightly fast on turnoff.
Unqualified	Did not align aircraft with runway, erratic rate of descent. Allowed airspeed to go below minimum safe approach speed. Touchdown dangerously short/long (past the one-third runway mark), or to the extreme side of runway. Erratic directional control through improper use of aileron, rudder, or brakes. Aircraft not slowed sufficiently prior to turnoff.

POSTFLIGHT

ENGINE SHUTDOWN

Qualified	Secured engine and aircraft in accordance with NATOPS procedure.
Unqualified	Failed to properly secure engine and aircraft.

CHECK LIST

Not applicable to T-28.

POSTFLIGHT INSPECTION

Qualified	Conducted inspection thoroughly and effectively.
Conditionally Qualified	Completed inspection with omissions in minor areas.
Unqualified	Failed to conduct inspection properly and omitted several important items.

MISSION DEBRIEF

Not applicable to T-28.

PART 2 — NATOPS FORMS

NATOPS EVALUATION REPORT
OPNAV FORM 3510-8 (8-65) 0107-723-0000

NAME (Last, first initial)		GRADE	SERVICE NUMBER
SQUADRON/UNIT	AIRCRAFT MODEL		CREW POSITION
TOTAL PILOT/FLIGHT HOURS	TOTAL HOURS IN MODEL		DATE OF LAST EVALUATION

NATOPS EVALUATION

REQUIREMENT	DATE COMPLETED	GRADE		
		Q	CQ	U
OPEN BOOK EXAMINATION			/////	
CLOSED BOOK EXAMINATION			/////	
ORAL EXAMINATION			/////	
*EVALUATION FLIGHT				
FLIGHT DURATION	AIRCRAFT BUNO	OVERALL FINAL GRADE		

REMARKS OF EVALUATOR/INSTRUCTOR

☐ CHECK IF CONTINUED ON REVERSE SIDE

GRADE, NAME OF EVALUATOR/INSTRUCTOR	SIGNATURE	DATE
GRADE, NAME OF EVALUEE	SIGNATURE	DATE

REMARKS OF UNIT COMMANDER

RANK, NAME OF UNIT COMMANDER	SIGNATURE	DATE

*WST, OFT, COT, or cockpit check in accordance with OPNAVINST 3510.9 (effective edition)

VT PILOT NATOPS EVALUATION WORKSHEET

OPNAV FORM 3510/10 (11/65)

Asterisk (*) denotes a critical area

NAME	GRADE	SERVICE NUMBER
SQUADRON/UNIT	AIRCRAFT MODEL	CREW POSITION PILOT
TOTAL PILOT/FLIGHT HOURS	TOTAL HOURS IN MODEL	DATE OF LAST EVALUATION

NATOPS EVALUATION

REQUIREMENT	DATE COMPLETED	GRADE		
		Q	CQ	U
OPEN BOOK EXAMINATION				
CLOSED BOOK EXAMINATION				
ORAL EXAMINATION				
FLIGHT EVALUATION				

FLIGHT DURATION	AIRCRAFT BUNO	OVERALL FINAL GRADE
GRADE, NAME OF EVALUATOR/INSTRUCTOR		DATE

REMARKS

S/N-0107-723-1500

A-20965

OPNAV FORM 3510/10 (11/65) *Asterisk (*) denotes a critical area*

1. MISSION PLANNING	ADJECTIVE AREA GRADE				REMARKS
SUB-AREAS	Q	CQ	U	POINTS	
A. PERSONAL FLYING EQUIP.					
B. FLIGHT PREPARATION					
*C. CREW/PASSENGER BRIEFING					
*D. AIRCRAFT TAKEOFF DATA					
NUMERICAL AREA GRADE		TOTAL POINTS			

2. PREFLIGHT	ADJECTIVE AREA GRADE			
SUB-AREAS	Q	CQ	U	POINTS
A. AIRCRAFT INSPECTION				
B. CHECKLISTS				
NUMERICAL AREA GRADE		TOTAL POINTS		

3. PRE-TAKEOFF	ADJECTIVE AREA GRADE			
SUB-AREAS	Q	CQ	U	POINTS
A. START				
B. CHECKLISTS				
C. TAXI				
*D. ENGINE RUNUP				
NUMERICAL AREA GRADE		TOTAL POINTS		

4. TAKEOFF	ADJECTIVE AREA GRADE			
SUB-AREAS	Q	CQ	U	POINTS
*A. TAKEOFF PROCEDURES				
*B. TRANSITION				
NUMERICAL AREA GRADE		TOTAL POINTS		

PAGE 2

OPNAV FORM 3510/10 (11/65)

Asterisk (*) denotes critical area

5. BASIC AIRWORK	ADJECTIVE AREA GRADE				REMARKS
SUB-AREAS	Q	CQ	U	POINTS	
A.					
B.					
C.					
D.					
NUMERICAL AREA GRADE		TOTAL POINTS			

*6. EMERGENCIES	ADJECTIVE AREA GRADE				
SUB-AREAS	Q	CQ	U	POINTS	
*A. ENGINE FAILURE					
*B. FIRE INFLIGHT					
*C. SYSTEM FAILURE					
NUMERICAL AREA GRADE		TOTAL POINTS			

7. INSTRUMENT PROCEDURES	ADJECTIVE AREA GRADE				
SUB-AREAS	Q	CQ	U	POINTS	
A. HOLDING					
B. APPROACH/PENETRATION					
C. PRECISION RADAR APPROACH					
NUMERICAL AREA GRADE		TOTAL POINTS			

8. LANDING	ADJECTIVE AREA GRADE				
SUB-AREAS	Q	CQ	U	POINTS	
*A. CHECKLISTS					
*B. DESCENT					
*C. PATTERN					
*D. LANDING AND ROLLOUT					
NUMERICAL AREA GRADE		TOTAL POINTS			

PAGE 3

OPNAV FORM 3510/10 (11/65)

Asterisk (*) denotes a critical area

9. POSTFLIGHT	ADJECTIVE AREA GRADE				REMARKS
SUB-AREAS	Q	CQ	U	POINTS	
A. ENGINE SHUTDOWN					
B. CHECKLIST (NA TO JETS)					
C. POSTFLIGHT INSPECTION					
D. MISSION DEBRIEF					
NUMERICAL AREA GRADE		TOTAL POINTS			

A. TOTAL ALL SUB-AREA POINTS		
B. TOTAL NO. SUB-AREAS GRADED		
C. FLT. EVAL. NUMERICAL GRADE	$\frac{A}{B}$	
**EVALUATION ADJECTIVE GRADE		

**See OPNAVINST 3510.9 Series.

PAGE 4

PART 3 — NATOPS EVALUATION QUESTION BANK

The following bank of questions is intended to assist the unit NATOPS Instructor/Evaluator in the preparation of ground examinations and to provide an abbreviated study guide. These questions cover material presented in this manual as well as material covered in T-28 Indoctrination courses. The questions from the bank should be combined with locally originated questions as well as questions obtained from the Model Manager in the preparation of ground examinations.

1. What is the purpose of the external flap handle?

2. What is the total capacity and total usable capacity of the engine oil tank?

3. What is the recommended oleo strut extension of the main gear?

4. Why will loss of the port cowling cause severe damage to the canopy in flight?

5. What is the optimum airspeed and altitude for bailout in a controllable flight situation?

6. Where is the engine-driven fuel pump drain?

7. Why is it necessary to check the baggage compartment door seal for wear and cracks?

8. Where is the emergency canopy air bottle located and what is the normal pressure range?

9. Does operation of the command control shift switch turn on the AN/ARC-27? Is it necessary to have control of the AN/ARC-27 in order to change frequencies?

10. To start the engine on prime, the mixture control lever should be in what position?

11. If oil pressure does not register in _____ seconds or rise to _____ psi in _____ seconds, secure the engine and investigate.

12. The engine will be cranked through _____ blades prior to turning the ignition switch to BOTH.

13. On normal or long field arrestments, the hook will be lowered after the aircraft is on the deck to prevent _____ .

14. At what airspeed will rudder control become effective?

15. Assume the take-off attitude when the _____ becomes effective and let the aircraft fly itself off the deck at _____ - _____ knots.

16. Which mixer switch(es) should be forward (on) to monitor signals from the AN/ARN-6 radio compass?

17. How is it possible to regain reception of radio signals when the ICS amplifier is lost?

18. During operation of the AN/ARA-25, is it necessary to change the position of the UHF radio mode select switch in order to transmit?

19. Is it necessary to have control of the NAV-GYRO COMP group in order to operate the AN/ARN-6?

20. How is the AN/ARN-12 marker beacon receiver turned on?

21. With both cockpit VHF NAV control panel power switches ON, is it possible to receive two stations simultaneously?

22. To set a course in the ID-249, it is necessary to have _____ of the AN/ARN-14 and have the set _____ _____ .

23. With loss of both inverters, is it possible to use the course selector in the ID-249?

24. What is the recommended power setting and airspeed for holding in the T-28?

25. Maintain _____ airspeed in a low approach (instrument) until completing procedure turn.

26. When inbound to the station on an instrument approach, with the gear and 1/2 flaps down, what airspeed should be maintained?

27. At low station on an instrument approach, reduce MAP to _____ inches and descend to field minimums at _____ knots.

28. The GCA final should be flown at _____ knots with _____ flaps.

29. When preflighting the radio equipment in the baggage compartment, why is it necessary to check the UHF control box COMM switch in the REMOTE position?

30. With hydraulic pump failure, which of the hydraulically operated systems can still be used?

31. With hydraulic failure caused by a break in the line, which of the hydraulically operated systems can still be used?

32. With complete loss of hydraulic fluid, is normal operation of the wheel brake system possible? Why?

33. Where is the engine-driven hydraulic pump drain?

34. What happens when the canopy handle is placed in the emergency position? Can canopy normal operation be resumed after selection of the emergency position?

35. Can the parking brake be set or released from the rear cockpit?

36. What precautions have been taken to prevent accidental gear retraction on the deck?

37. With complete electrical failure, which hydraulically operated systems can still be used?

38. Where is the flight control system hydraulic boost package located?

39. The fuel shutoff handle controls the _____ and the _____.

40. The fuel boost pump supplies fuel under a pressure of _____.

41. The engine-driven fuel pump supplies fuel at a pressure of _____.

42. What danger is inherent with loss of the electric boost pump above 10,000 feet?

43. Where is the sump tank and how does it receive fuel from the wing tanks?

44. Where are the fuel tank overboard vents located?

45. The fuel strainer is at the lowest point in the fuel system. If it should be leaking, where would you look for the drain?

46. Due to the type of fuel system in the T-28, it is possible to encounter uneven fuel flow due to _____.

47. The T-28 has a _____ volt d-c electrical system powered by a _____ ampere engine-driven generator and a _____ volt storage battery which serves as a standby power source.

48. In aircraft not having ASC 36 complied with, a _____ volt-ampere main inverter supplies alternating current for operation of the _____, _____, and the _____. A _____ volt-ampere spare inverter serves as standby.

49. In aircraft not having ASC 36 complied with and the generator operating, what four buses are receiving power?

50. With the DC POWER switch in the BAT. GEN. position and the aircraft in the clean configuration, what buses are lost with a generator failure?

51. What two methods are there of applying power to the bus(es) that are lost when the generator fails?

52. In aircraft having ASC 36 complied with, what bus(es) receive power when the DC POWER switch in the rear cockpit is placed in the EMER OFF position?

53. In aircraft not having ASC 36 complied with, is it necessary to switch inverters when the generator fails in order to conserve power? Why?

54. In aircraft having ASC 36 complied with, is it necessary to switch inverters when the generator fails in order to conserve power? Why?

55. In aircraft having ASC 36 complied with, is it possible to operate the AN/ARN-21 (TACAN) with one inverter inoperative? Why?

56. In aircraft having ASC 36 complied with, is it possible to select different inverters from each cockpit simultaneously?

57. Is it possible to change the a-c electrical system fuses in flight?

58. With generator failure, is it possible to use the heater-defroster system?

59. A minimum of _____ rpm is required to start the heater. Why?

60. What is the minimum rpm for heater operation once it has been started?

61. What two switches must be positioned before the gear position lights will come on?

62. What three switches must be positioned before the landing lights will function?

63. Two independent cylinder head temperature indication systems are provided, one for each cockpit. To which two cylinders are these temperature indicators connected and in which cockpit do they read?

64. One of the two cylinder head temperature indicators normally reads higher than the other. To which cylinder does the higher temperature relate?

65. In the shutdown procedures, why is it necessary to let the cylinder head temperatures stabilize at 150 degrees or less?

66. With a windmilling engine, what electrical and hydraulic systems will be inoperative?

67. The external flap handle performs its designed purpose by _____?

68. The nose wheel oleo strut should extend a minimum of _____ inches.

69. The electrical fuel boost pump drain is located in the _____.

70. MIL-L-6082, Grade 1100, may be used as an alternate oil. Recommended oil is _____.

71. Which instruments are operated by the pitot-static system?

72. An external canopy handle is provided on the _____ side of the fuselage. Is it possible to operate the canopy hydraulically with the external handle?

73. Each pilot is responsible for adequate personal flying equipment. An anti-exposure suit is required on overwater flights when the water temperature is _____ or the outside air temperature is_____ or the combined air/water temperature is_____.

74. In preparation for solo flight, what items must the pilot check in the rear cockpit?

75. To allow even fuel flow, the port and starboard fuel tank vent outlets should be _____ and _____.

76. The power plant cowling consists of how many sections? When properly secured, the end of the shear pin should protrude how far through the shear pin receptacle?

77. Where is the battery located in the T-28B and T-28C?

78. As the use of oxygen may be necessary during flight, minimum servicing pressure of _____ psi is recommended.

79. After the engine is running smoothly on prime, what is the procedure for selecting rich mixture?

80. What are the reasons for operating the engine at 1200 rpm when taxiing is delayed?

81. During blower shift from high to low ratio, a sudden decrease in manifold pressure indicates _____.

82. What is the minimum in-flight oil pressure and when do you check for this indication on the ground?

83. Waveoff from simulated high-altitude and low-altitude emergencies will be completed by _____ feet.

84. During a dead-engine landing, a decrease in flap setting is not recommended below _____ feet.

85. What access route is used to extinguish a fuselage fire on the ground?

86. During an in-flight restart, the DC POWER switch is placed in the BAT. ONLY position for what reason?

87. With the propeller at FULL DECREASE rpm and the speed brake up, engine rpm during a 130-knot dead-engine glide will be approximately _____ rpm. Generator output will be _____.

88. Caution should be used to avoid undershooting during a dead-engine landing; however, if undershooting is anticipated, what corrective actions can be applied?

89. If it is necessary to bail out, the decision to abandon the aircraft in flight should be made as soon as possible for what reason?

90. What is the procedure for a high-speed bailout?

91. When ditching in a high wind or irregular sea state, the best procedure is to approach into the wind and touch on _____.

92. Total usable fuel is _____ gallons.

93. List the items that are transferred on operation of the intercockpit control shift switch.

94. On a Standard Day, with 52.5 inches manifold pressure and 2700 rpm, how much horsepower does the R-1820-86A engine develop?

95. Engine rpm in excess of _____ requires an engine change.

96. Fast throttle bursts should be made only while governing at _____ rpm or less.

97. Why is it necessary to scavenge the engine at 1200 rpm for 60 seconds prior to shutting down?

98. What is maximum allowable manifold pressure at 7000 feet when operating at 1800 rpm in low blower?

99. What is maximum allowable carburetor air temperature? For each _____ degrees above the desired maximum, it is necessary to reduce MAP _____ inches.

100. In a T-28, clean configuration, gross weight 7500 pounds, what is the power-off stall speed in a 30-degree bank? What is power-off stall speed with gear and flaps down in a 30-degree bank?

101. Maximum continuous operating rpm is:
    (a) 2700
    (b) 2500
    (c) 2780
    (d) 2650

102. Best power-off glide speed to obtain maximum distance with gear and flaps retracted is:
    (a) 100 knots
    (b) 110 knots
    (c) 120 knots
    (d) 130 knots

103. The control lock not only locks the surface controls but also locks the:
    (a) Throttle in the closed position
    (b) Mixture control in the idle cutoff position
    (c) Fuel shutoff handle in the off position
    (d) Parking brakes

104. During warmup, the cowl and oil cooler flaps should be in the:
    (a) Closed position
    (b) 1/4 open position
    (c) 1/2 open position
    (d) Full open position

105. In the event of engine-driven hydraulic pump failure in flight:
    (a) It is possible to lower the flaps to the full down position, but not an intermediate position
    (b) It is necessary to move the canopy handle to the EMERGENCY position in order to open the canopy
    (c) The brakes, gear, and speed brake can be operated
    (d) All of the preceding are correct

106. In the event of complete electrical failure in flight, the flaps may be extended by:
    (a) Placing the flap handle in the emergency down position
    (b) Using the handpump
    (c) Placing the flap handle in the desired position
    (d) By all of the preceding methods

107. In flight with gear and flaps retracted, a hydraulic pressure indication of 0 to 100 psi:
    (a) Is normal
    (b) Indicates impending failure of the hydraulic system
    (c) Indicates a complete loss of hydraulic fluid
    (d) Should be reported after the flight

108. The landing gear will not be lowered at speeds in excess of:
    (a) 140 mph
    (b) 125 knots
    (c) 130 knots
    (d) 140 knots

109. In the event of complete electrical failure in flight, the speed brake:
    (a) Cannot be extended
    (b) Can be fully retracted
    (c) Will automatically go to trail position
    (d) All of the preceding

110. The wing flaps will not be lowered at speeds in excess of:
    (a) 115 knots
    (b) 120 knots
    (c) 130 knots
    (d) 140 knots

111. Which of the following statements is false?
    (a) Landing lights may be controlled from either cockpit.
    (b) The engine may be started from either cockpit.
    (c) Solo flight is permitted from the front cockpit only.
    (d) The parking brake may be released from either cockpit.

112. The voltmeter is graduated in d-c volts. Normal indication is approximately:
    (a) 24.9
    (b) 28.2
    (c) 36.9
    (d) 27.7

113. The minimum fuel pressure for start is:
    (a) 21 psi
    (b) 13 psi
    (c) 21 to 25 psi
    (d) 17 psi

114. Which of the following would be lost in the event of a-c power failure:
    (a) Turn-and-bank indicator
    (b) Tachometer
    (c) Attitude gyro
    (d) Cylinder head temperature

115. Which instruments would be lost with failure of the 28-volt d-c electrical system:
    (a) Oil temperature, cylinder head temperature, and tachometer
    (b) Oil temperature, carburetor air temperature, and tachometer
    (c) Cylinder head temperature, fuel pressure, and free air temperature
    (d) Oil temperature, cylinder head temperature, and carburetor air temperature

116. When starting the engine utilizing an APU, the DC POWER switch should be in the:
    (a) BAT. & GEN. position
    (b) OFF position
    (c) BAT. ONLY position
    (d) APU position

117. All exterior lights may be controlled:
    (a) From both cockpits simultaneously
    (b) From the front cockpit only
    (c) From the rear cockpit only
    (d) By the pilot who last operated his control shift switch

118. The recommended fuel pressure range for continuous operation is:
    (a) 21—25 psi
    (b) 22—25 psi
    (c) 20—25 psi
    (d) 20—23 psi

119. The fuel low-level warning light will illuminate if fuel quantity falls below approximately:
    (a) 100 pounds
    (b) 200 pounds
    (c) 100 gallons
    (d) 200 gallons

120. During engine start, oil pressure must rise to at least 40 psi within:
    (a) 5 seconds
    (b) 10 seconds
    (c) 15 seconds
    (d) 20 seconds

121. Inverted flight in the T-28:
    (a) Is not permitted
    (b) Is permitted for 10 seconds
    (c) Is permitted for 20 seconds
    (d) Is permitted for 30 seconds

122. Minimum and maximum oil pressure for flight is:
    (a) 65—90 psi
    (b) 40—90 psi
    (c) 65—75 psi
    (d) 40—75 psi

123. The carburetor air temperature and cylinder head temperature indicators are dc powered.
    (a) True
    (b) False

124. Maximum continuous rpm for operation in high blower is:
    (a) 2400
    (b) 2500
    (c) 2600
    (d) 2700

125. Minimum rpm recommended in flight is:
    (a) 1200
    (b) 1300
    (c) 1400
    (d) 1500

126. Maximum allowable rpm that can be used in high blower is:
    (a) 2700
    (b) 2600
    (c) 2500
    (d) 2400

127. For starting and runup, the supercharger should:
    (a) Be in high blower for checking operation
    (b) Be in low blower for de-sludging
    (c) Be in high blower
    (d) Be in low blower

128. Because of additional stresses imposed on the T-28, maximum permissible acceleration in a rolling pull-out is:
    (a) Plus 6 g's
    (b) One-half the maximum permissible acceleration for a normal pullout
    (c) Two-thirds the maximum permissible acceleration for a normal pullout
    (d) Three g's less than normal for a given air-speed and altitude

129. Recommended indicated airspeed in severe turbulence is:
    (a) Below 210 knots
    (b) 135—195 knots
    (c) 125—185 knots
    (d) 160—200 knots

130. In the event it is necessary to override the canopy handle (and button) and stop movement of the canopy when it is being operated hydraulically, press the canopy emergency stop button.
    (a) True
    (b) False

131. If taxiing is delayed for any reason and you are required to stop, maintain 1200 rpm.
    (a) True
    (b) False

132. When attempting an air start with the generator operating, the DC POWER switch should be placed in the_____position.
    (a) BAT. & GEN.
    (b) BAT. ONLY
    (c) OFF
    (d) Any of the preceding

133. Minimum oil pressure for continuous flight is 65 psi.
    (a) True
    (b) False

134. After securing the engine and extinguishing the flames following an engine fire in flight, an engine restart will be attempted.
    (a) True
    (b) False

135. After adjusting the throttle to obtain manifold pressure equal to field barometric pressure, an acceptable power check will be (select two):
    (a) 2150 (±50) T-28C
    (b) 2250 (±50) T-28C
    (c) 2150 (±50) T-28B
    (d) 2250 (±50) T-28B

136. It is possible to maintain flight by use of the primer.
    (a) True
    (b) False

137. To bail out during a spin:
    (a) Bail out to the inside of the spin
    (b) Bail out to the outside of the spin

138. If complete electrical and hydraulic failure is experienced, the nose gear will not extend.
    (a) True
    (b) False

139. Idle speed is approximately 750 to 850 rpm.
    (a) True
    (b) False

140. Maximum recommended gross weight for landing is 8600 pounds (T-28B).
    (a) True
    (b) False

141. In an engine failure emergency, the PROP lever will be placed in FULL INCREASE rpm position for increased glide range.
    (a) True
    (b) False

142. If it is necessary to bail out during level flight, the _____ side should be used to take advantage of the downward force of the propeller wash.
    (a) Right
    (b) Left

143. Accessory section fires can be extinguished by inserting the extinguisher nozzle through the spring-loaded access door in the lower left side of the engine cowl.
    (a) True
    (b) False

144. The loadmeter indicates the percent of the generator output being used. The normal range is 0.3 to 0.5.
    (a) True
    (b) False

145. With the engine windmilling, the landing gear cannot be retracted.
    (a) True
    (b) False

146. With the engine windmilling, the landing gear can be extended in approximately 4 seconds.
    (a) True
    (b) False

147. All _____ circuits are protected from overloads by push-to-reset circuit breakers.
    (a) AC
    (b) DC

148. _____ circuits are protected by fuses.
    (a) AC
    (b) DC

149. If the engine fails to start after 30 seconds continuous cranking, allow starter cooling for 5 minutes before repeating the start procedure.
    (a) True
    (b) False

150. Oil pressure for continuous operation is 65—75 psi.
    (a) True
    (b) False

151. The minimum indicated voltage for start is 20 volts.
    (a) True
    (b) False

152. During ground operation of the T-28C, rpm between _____ should be avoided.
    (a) 1900—2100
    (b) 2000—2300
    (c) 1900—2200
    (d) 2000—2400

153. The minimum and maximum oil temperature range is 40° to 95°C (MIL-L-22851).
    (a) True
    (b) False

154. RPM in excess of 2800 requires an engine inspection.
    (a) True
    (b) False

155. Normal hydraulic pressure (system pressurized) is 1250—1650 psi.
    (a) True
    (b) False

156. If hydraulic failure occurs in flight with the speed brake open, positioning the speed brake switch to OFF allows air loads to close the brake to a trail position.
    (a) True
    (b) False

157. Following an aborted take-off, if it is seen that the aircraft will run off the end onto an unprepared surface at a speed in excess of 15 knots, the landing gear should be retracted before leaving the runway.
    (a) True
    (b) False

158. To conserve electrical power following generator failure, the small inverter should be selected and the circuit breaker for the large inverter should be pulled out. On aircraft not having ASC 36 incorporated, the small inverter is the number one inverter.
    (a) True
    (b) False

159. Maximum continuous cylinder head temperature in flight is 260°C.
    (a) True
    (b) False

160. Holding 130 KIAS, gear up, flaps up, and no wind. The glide distance is _____ miles for each 5000 feet.
    (a) 9
    (b) 5
    (c) 12
    (d) 7

161. If the engine fails shortly after take-off:
    (a) Turn back toward field
    (b) In any event, land into wind
    (c) Maintain flying speed and land straight ahead
    (d) None of the preceding

162. Loss of propeller control and subsequent stabilization between 2000 and 2200 rpm indicates:
    (a) Prop governor failure
    (b) Prop governor linkage failure
    (c) Prop governor counterweight failure
    (d) An oil leak in the propeller dome

163. In the event of propeller overspeed, you should:
    (a) Retard the throttle
    (b) Manipulate the PROP control lever in an attempt to restore governing
    (c) Raise the nose to increase the load on the propeller
    (d) All of the preceding

164. In the event of propeller surge, best corrective action is:
    (a) Placing the mixture control in normal and reducing speed to 140 knots
    (b) Placing the mixture control in rich and accelerating to 190 knots to expedite return
    (c) Reducing rpm to 1600
    (d) Placing mixture control in rich and checking carburetor air temperature

165. In the emergency landing pattern, the desired straight-away should be:

(a) 1400—1600 feet
(b) 1600—1800 feet
(c) 1800—2000 feet
(d) 2000—2200 feet

166. Recommended rpm with a sump plug warning light is 1900—2000 rpm.

(a) True
(b) False

167. When performing the propeller check, a drop of approximately 400 rpm should be noted.

(a) True
(b) False

168. Brake pucks should be no thinner than 1/16 of an inch.

(a) True
(b) False

169. The sump fuel tank is located in the starboard wheel well.

(a) True
(b) False

170. The mixture control is in the_____position while starting the engine.

(a) Rich
(b) Normal
(c) Idle cutoff

171. Recommended emergency landing gear extension airspeed is 115 knots.

(a) True
(b) False

172. To scavenge the engine,_____rpm will be maintained for 1 minute.

(a) 1300
(b) 1000
(c) 1200

173. Maximum acceptable rpm drop during the ignition system check is_____.

(a) 50
(b) 75
(c) 85
(d) 100

174. The proper trim tab setting for take-off is aileron —0 degrees; elevator—5 degrees nose-down; rudder—0 degrees.

(a) True
(b) False

175. When performing the exterior inspection, make certain the dipstick retaining wire is properly seated after replacing the dipstick and that the oil filter cap is properly secured. Oil quantity should be a minimum of_____gallons for flight.

(a) 8.8
(b) 9.0
(c) 8.0
(d) 7.5

176. To prevent possible seizure of the brake pucks and brake disks, the parking brake should not be set if the brakes are overheated.

(a) True
(b) False

177. MAP used for take-off is 52.5 inches Hg. Maximum allowable MAP at sea level is 52.5 inches.

(a) True
(b) False

178. To prevent excessive engine cooling, a simulated engine failure emergency will not be initiated above_____feet.

(a) 2500
(b) 10,000
(c) 5000
(d) 3500

179. As the aircraft will settle on retraction of the flaps, the flaps will not be raised below 200 feet.

(a) True
(b) False

180. If an engine fire occurs during start, correct procedure is:

(a) Mixture idle cutoff, continue priming, continue cranking in an attempt to start the engine
(b) Mixture idle cutoff, stop priming, continue cranking in an attempt to start the engine
(c) Mixture idle cutoff, stop priming, continue cranking in an attempt to clear or to start the engine

181. In the emergency landing pattern, the most effective way to lose altitude is:

(a) Delaying the final turn
(b) Slipping on final
(c) Advancing propeller to full increase rpm
(d) Extending speed brake

182. To prevent the tendency to undershoot in the emergency landing pattern, set up for a point one-third down the runway.

(a) True
(b) False

183. In order to perform the recommended procedure for bailout, airspeed must be reduced below 140 knots.

(a) True
(b) False

184. In the event of complete electrical failure, instrument flying will be impossible.

(a) True
(b) False

185. Which statement is true?

    (a) The gear should be left down when landing on an unprepared surface

    (b) If the nose wheel fails to extend, raise the main gear and make a gear-up landing

    (c) A wheels-up landing is preferred to a landing with one main wheel extended

186. If smoke enters the cockpit from the air outlets, open the canopy for proper smoke elimination.

    (a) True

    (b) False

187. In the event of generator failure:

    (a) Circuit breakers for nonessential equipment should be pulled

    (b) Instrument flight can be maintained by placing the DC POWER switch in the appropriate position

    (c) Radio communication is possible with the DC POWER switch in appropriate position

    (d) All the preceding are correct

188. Maximum airspeed with the landing lights extended is:

    (a) 140 knots

    (b) 120 knots

    (c) 115 knots

189. If an engine fire occurs after the engine starts, you should proceed as follows:

    (a) Fuel shutoff handle off

    (b) Mixture idle cutoff

    (c) Ignition and DC POWER switches off

    (d) All the preceding

190. Proper fuel(s) specification for the T-28 is (are):

    (a) 115/145

    (b) 115/145 and 100/130 alternate

    (c) 115/145 and 100/130 emergency

    (d) 115/145 and 100/130

191. To prevent overheating of the supercharger clutch, shifts from high to low ratio will not be initiated at less than 5-minute intervals.

    (a) True

    (b) False

192. When carrying out the precautionary emergency landing procedure, propeller control lever should be set:

    (a) 1900 to 2200 rpm

    (b) 1900 to 2000 rpm

    (c) 2000 to 2200 rpm

193. If the aircraft is damaged in flight, climb to at least 2500 feet prior to testing aircraft slow flight characteristics.

    (a) True

    (b) False

194. Desired continuous cylinder head temperature is 150° to 230°C.

    (a) True

    (b) False

195. Most engine failures are gradual and afford the pilot ample indication of impending failure. An instant failure is rare and usually occurs only if ignition or fuel flow completely fails.

    (a) True

    (b) False

196. When complying with the precautionary emergency landing procedure, retard throttle to maintain straight-and-level flight between:

    (a) 140—150 knots

    (b) 140 knots

    (c) 120—140 knots

    (d) 140—160 knots

197. You would shift to low blower and retard the throttle to the lowest possible manifold pressure to sustain flight if the prop:

    (a) Went to full high pitch

    (b) Went to full increase rpm

    (c) Linkage broke

    (d) Went to full low pitch

198. Carburetor icing critical temperature range is −10° to +5°C.

    (a) True

    (b) False

199. For ditching, the landing gear may be positioned at the pilot's discretion.

    (a) True

    (b) False

200. To ensure proper canopy emergency operation, the emergency air bottle should be serviced to a minimum of:

    (a) 1250 psi

    (b) 1300 psi

    (c) 1650 psi

TABLE OF CONTENTS

PART 1 — STANDARD CHARTS, TAKE-OFF, LANDING, AND STOPPING DATA

INTRODUCTION

The purpose of this section is to provide aircraft performance data which will facilitate mission planning in the most efficient manner possible. The performance data are based on an NASA Standard Day (+59°F at sea level, and decreasing uniformly to −67°F at 35,332 feet) unless other temperatures are stated. By using the charts most nearly applicable to the configuration of your aircraft, you will be assured of maximum performance, safety, and efficiency. Frequent reference to the charts cannot be overemphasized. Learning to get top performance from your aircraft by knowing the recommended airspeeds and power settings will give you a distinct advantage over the pilot who neglects this part of his training.

WEIGHT SUMMARY

T-28B, Clean, Full Fuel, Two Crewmembers	8250
T-28C, Clean, Full Fuel, Two Crewmembers	8400
Armament Kit, Aero 1A	100
Gun Pod, .50-caliber, 100 Rounds (two)	308
Bomb Rack, MK 51 Mod 14 (two)	40
Bomb Container, Aero 4B	40
Six MK 5 Practice Bombs	18
Eight MK 23 Practice Bombs	24
Eight MK 43 Practice Bombs	34
Practice Bomb, AN/M38A2	100
2.25-inch SCAR (three), Supports/Launcher	67
Practice Bomb Cluster, AN/M2A2	
Banner Target Carrier, Aero 1B	
Target Container, MK 1 Mod 2	
T-28C (modified), Clean, Full Fuel, Two Crewmembers	8550
Gun Pod, .50-caliber, 100 Rounds (two)	308
Pylon, Aero 15C-1	27
Rocket Launcher, Aero 6A	148
Rocket Launcher, LAU-3/A	429
Rocket Launcher, LAU-32/A	173
Rocket, 5-inch HVA with Adapter	215
Bomb Cluster, Practice, AN/M2A2	
Bomb Cluster, AN/M1A2	120

Bomb Cluster, AN/M28A2	119
GP Bomb, AN/M30A1	137
GP Bomb, AN/M57A1 (conic fins)	290
Napalm Bomb, BLU-1/A	250
Napalm Bomb, BLU-11/B	500
Practice Bomb Container, Aero 4B	40
Practice Multiple Bomb Rack, A/A37B-3	87
Six MK 76 Mod 0 Practice Bombs	143
Six MK 76 Mod 5 Practice Bombs	153

STANDARD CHARTS

AIRSPEED POSITION ERROR CORRECTION

These charts (figures 11-1 and 11-2) show airspeed position error (correction to be added or subtracted) versus indicated airspeed (corrected for instrument error) for the clean configuration and the landing configuration. Adding the correction to the indicated airspeed gives the calibrated airspeed (CAS). With this value of CAS and the corrected free air temperature at a given pressure altitude, the true airspeed (TAS) can be found by using the Airspeed—Mach Number Curves chart (figure 11-3) or a dead-reckoning computer.

AIRSPEED CORRECTIONS

IAS—Indicated airspeed is the reading taken from the airspeed indicator.

CAS—Calibrated airspeed is indicated airspeed corrected for installation effects.

EAS—Equivalent airspeed is calibrated airspeed corrected for compressibility effects.

TAS—True airspeed is equivalent airspeed corrected for atmospheric density.

GS—Ground speed is true airspeed corrected for wind.

AIRSPEED — MACH NUMBER CURVES

With the value for calibrated airspeed established, true airspeed can be found through use of the Airspeed—Mach Number Curves chart (figure 11-3). For atmospheric conditions other than standard, the chart may also be used as long as the temperature correction is applied.

EXAMPLE:
  CAS: 160 knots
  Altitude: 15,000 feet
  TAS: 190 knots (standard atmosphere −14.7°C) or about 195 knots at −40°C

TEMPERATURE CORRECTION CHART

Calibrated airspeed (CAS) may be corrected for compressibility by using the chart presented in figure 11-4. The compressibility chart is used in conjunction with Airspeed—Mach Number Curves (figure 11-3) for correcting calibrated airspeed to true airspeed. To correct temperature for compressibility, enter the chart at calibrated airspeed. Advance to the flight altitude and follow this line to the intersection of the flight Mach number. The indicated air temperature correction is then read directly from the plotted intersection point. The free air temperature in degrees centigrade for a given flight speed and altitude is determined by subtracting the temperature correction from the indicated air temperature.

STANDARD ATMOSPHERE TABLE

The Standard Atmosphere Table (figure 11-5) is a tabular form chart which provides the Standard Day conditions at various altitudes for density ratio, $\frac{1}{\sqrt{\sigma}}$ temperature, speed of sound in knots, and pressure in inches of mercury and pressure ratio. To find the value of any item on a Standard Day, read the figure to the right of the altitude in the appropriate column.

DENSITY ALTITUDE CHART

The Density Altitude Chart (figure 11-6) provides $\frac{1}{\sqrt{\sigma}}$ and density altitude when the pressure altitude and the ambient temperature are known. The chart can also be used for operations during other than Standard Day conditions.

The Standard Day temperature-altitude relationship is shown by the line from 27 degrees at the bottom of the chart to −55 degrees at the pressure altitude of 36,000 feet and then vertically to the top of the chart. To use the chart, enter at the known temperature and project this line vertically to the intersection of the pressure altitude curve. From the intersection point, a horizontal line permits the density altitude to be read from the left scale and the $\frac{1}{\sqrt{\sigma}}$ factor from the right scale. The true airspeed at the density altitude may then be calculated by multiplying the equivalent airspeed by the $\frac{1}{\sqrt{\sigma}}$ factor.

EXAMPLE:
  Temperature: −15°C
  Pressure altitude: 10,000 feet
  Density altitude: 8700 feet
  $\frac{1}{\sqrt{\sigma}}$ factor: 1.14

ENGINE OPERATING LIMITS

Primarily this chart (figure 11-7) defines the operating limits of the engine under no ram conditions, in standard atmosphere. The solid lines show the rpm and the dotted lines give the unrammed manifold pressure required for a given brake horsepower and altitude. Note that one chart is for low blower operation and the other is for high blower.

An unrammed power setting can be obtained from the charts, for a desired brake horsepower, at a given standard altitude. Enter the chart (at proper blower setting) from the left at the desired bhp and proceed to the altitude at which the bhp is to be obtained. By interpolation, the recommended rpm and manifold pressure can be obtained. Desired bhp's falling to the left of the propeller load and bmep lines (dashed) are in the part-throttle region of the chart. Note that in this region, any desired bhp has a given rpm, with altitude determining the manifold pressure required. Full throttle power settings occur to the right of the propeller load and bmep lines, and for a desired bhp, it can be seen that rpm increases and manifold pressure decreases as altitude is increased. Putting it quite simply, to maintain a desired bhp at full throttle, increase the rpm as altitude is increased.

The effect of ram (the increase in pressure at the carburetor intake due to aircraft speed) increases the power output of the engine. This effect will not show up as a change in manifold absolute pressure or rpm as obtained in the chart, but as a change in the position of the throttle. This change in throttle position is dependent on the ram airspeed. The higher the ram, the lower the throttle setting required to maintain a given manifold absolute pressure. Basically, ram effect increases the full throttle critical altitude above the value shown. Therefore, when using power settings selected from the chart, for a desired bhp and altitude, keep this fact in mind. A comparison of power settings with and without ram can be made by comparing figure 1-26 with figure 11-7. The increase in full throttle altitude (engine critical altitude) in figure 1-26 as compared with figure 11-7 is due to ram at a cruise power airspeed.

Since figure 11-7 is based on standard altitude, it becomes evident that additional corrections for air temperature and humidity are necessary because of their effect on bhp. Air at temperatures above standard is less dense and, therefore, will cause a drop in horsepower at a given power setting. Likewise, humid air contains water vapor which causes richer mixture and a resultant decrease in horsepower. The decrease in horsepower due to humidity effects is negligible at altitude for this engine and can, therefore, be ignored.

To obtain full throttle power settings on a hot day for a desired bhp, add 1 percent to the desired bhp for each 10°F (6°C) above Standard Day conditions, and enter the chart with the resulting hot-day bhp. The power settings obtained will give the desired power at the increased temperature for the altitude selected. For part throttle, maintain the Standard Day rpm and increase the chart manifold pressure by approximately ½ in. Hg for each 10°F rise over standard. This correction is to be made provided that the carburetor air temperature does not exceed 38°C in low blower or 15°C in high blower. For each 6°C increase in carburetor air temperature above 38°C in low blower, or 15°C in high blower, the manifold pressure should be reduced 1 in. Hg.

GROUND PERFORMANCE CHARTS

TAKE-OFF DISTANCES

The take-off graph (figure 11-8) as given in this section is a composite plot of take-off data for a hard-surface runway, using a take-off horsepower of 1425 bhp (52.5 in. Hg manifold pressure and 2700 rpm at sea level) with the flaps in the one-half down position and the cowl flaps full open. The graph consists of an altitude-temperature curve, a ground roll distance curve, and parameters of gross weight. A correction plot for various head winds and a conversion graph from ground roll distance to total take-off distance over a 50-foot obstacle are included. The final plot gives the decrease in total take-off distance due to head wind. From this graph it is possible to predict the required ground roll and total distance over a 50-foot obstacle if the runway altitude, temperature, aircraft gross weight, and head wind are known.

LANDING DISTANCES

The landing distance graph (figure 11-9) gives the lengths of a landing roll on a runway with a hard, dry surface at various altitudes, temperatures, and head winds. The engine is idling and the flaps are full down. The total landing distance required to clear a 50-foot obstacle is given as 140 percent of the ground roll distance under the same conditions.

STOPPING DISTANCES

The stopping distance graph (figure 11-10) presents the distance to stop on a hard, dry runway as a function of airspeed for several altitudes. The data are based on flaps half down, hard braking, and idle power.

TAKE-OFF AND LANDING CROSS-WIND CHART

The Take-off and Landing Cross-wind Chart (figure 11-11) is used to obtain the head-wind component under all cross-wind conditions. This component can be used in determining take-off or landing distance. For cross-wind operation, the minimum nose wheel lift-off and touch-down speeds are tabulated at the top of the chart.

When cross-wind conditions exist, enter the Take-off and Landing Cross-wind Chart at the vector point of the cross-wind velocity and direction. Read horizontally from this point to determine the head-wind component. Read downward perpendicularly from this point to find the 90-degree cross-wind component. Read upward vertically to obtain the minimum nose wheel lift-off and touch-down speed.

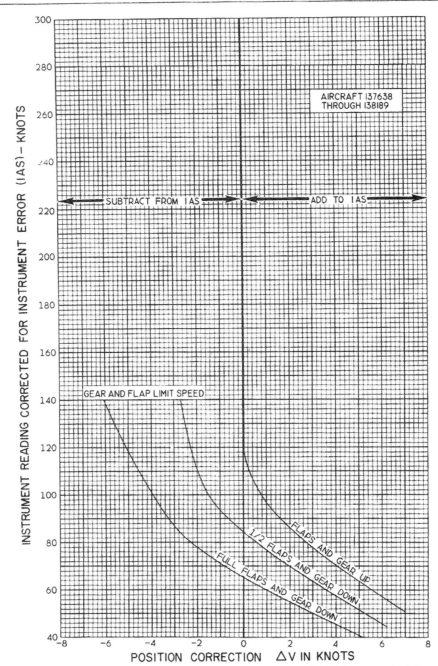

AIRSPEED POSITION ERROR CORRECTION
STANDARD DAY
WITH OR WITHOUT EXTERNAL STORES

MODEL: T-28B

AIRCRAFT 137638
THROUGH 138189

SUBTRACT FROM IAS — ADD TO IAS

GEAR AND FLAP LIMIT SPEED

FLAPS AND GEAR UP
1/2 FLAPS AND GEAR DOWN
FULL FLAPS AND GEAR DOWN

INSTRUMENT READING CORRECTED FOR INSTRUMENT ERROR (IAS) — KNOTS

POSITION CORRECTION   ΔV IN KNOTS

NOTE: 1. Apply correction to indicated airspeed (IAS), corrected for
          instrument error, to obtain calibrated airspeed (CAS).

DATA AS OF: 9-17-53
DATA BASED ON FLIGHT TEST DATA, NAA REPORT NA-53-34-10

T-28B-1-93-58

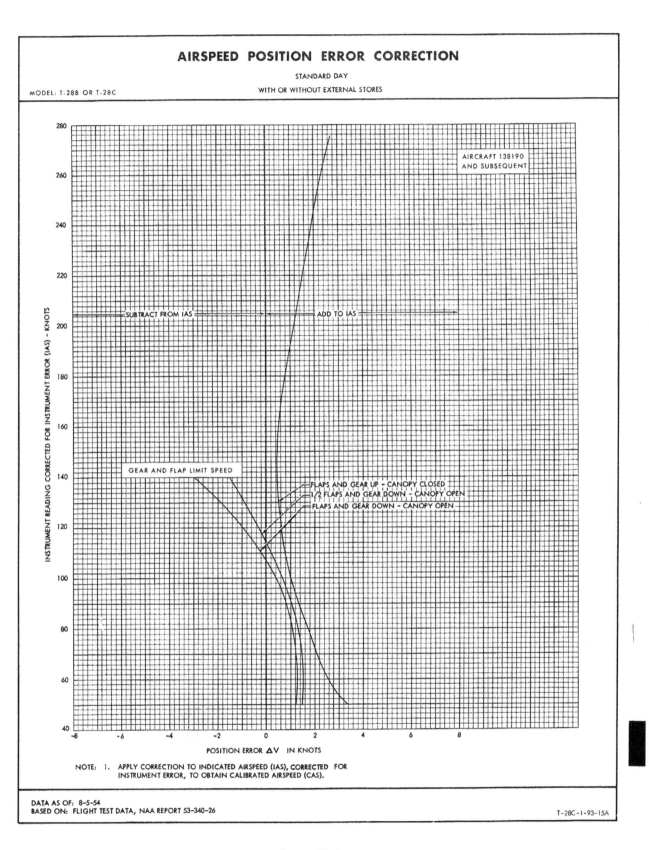

AIRSPEED POSITION ERROR CORRECTION

STANDARD DAY

WITH OR WITHOUT EXTERNAL STORES

MODEL: T-28B OR T-28C

AIRCRAFT 138190 AND SUBSEQUENT

SUBTRACT FROM IAS — ADD TO IAS

GEAR AND FLAP LIMIT SPEED

FLAPS AND GEAR UP - CANOPY CLOSED
1/2 FLAPS AND GEAR DOWN - CANOPY OPEN
FLAPS AND GEAR DOWN - CANOPY OPEN

INSTRUMENT READING CORRECTED FOR INSTRUMENT ERROR (IAS) - KNOTS

POSITION ERROR ΔV IN KNOTS

NOTE: 1. APPLY CORRECTION TO INDICATED AIRSPEED (IAS), CORRECTED FOR INSTRUMENT ERROR, TO OBTAIN CALIBRATED AIRSPEED (CAS).

DATA AS OF: 8-5-54
BASED ON: FLIGHT TEST DATA, NAA REPORT 53-340-26

T-28C-1-93-15A

Figure 11-2

AIRSPEED — MACH NUMBER CURVES

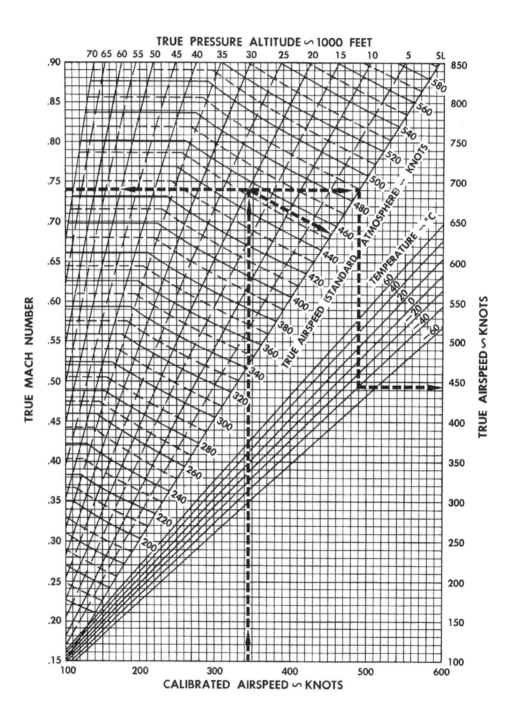

Figure 11-3

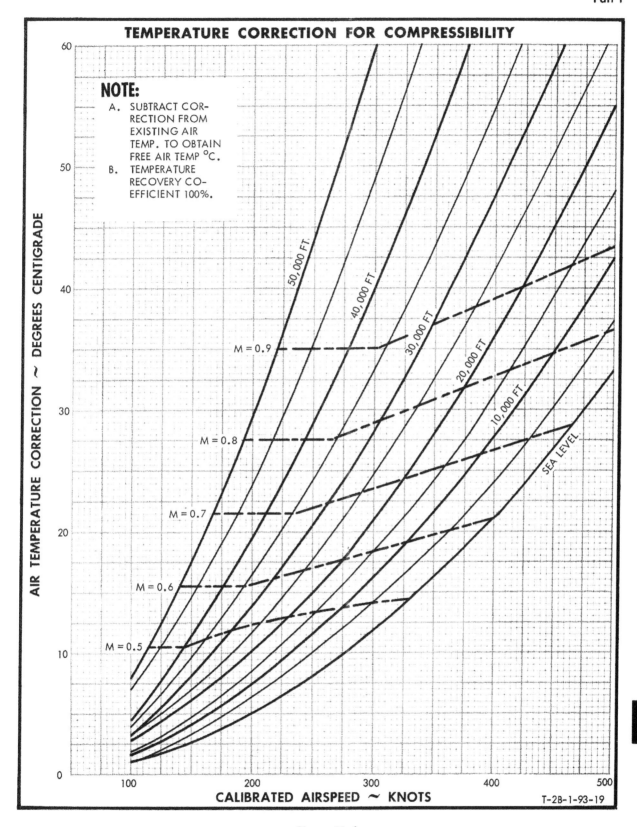

Figure 11-4

STANDARD ATMOSPHERE TABLE

STANDARD S L CONDITIONS:

TEMPERATURE 15°C (59°F)
PRESSURE 29-921 IN. Hg 2116.216 LB/SQ FT
DENSITY .0023769 SLUGS/CU FT
SPEED OF SOUND 1116.89 FT/SEC 661.7 KNOTS

CONVERSION FACTORS:

1 IN. Hg 70.727 LB/SQ FT
1 IN. Hg 0.49116 LB/SQ IN.
1 KNOT 1.151 M.P.H.
1 KNOT 1.688 FT/SEC

ALTITUDE FEET	DENSITY RATIO σ	$\dfrac{1}{\sqrt{\sigma}}$	TEMPERATURE		SPEED OF SOUND (KNOTS)	PRESSURE	
			DEG. C	DEG F		IN. OF Hg	RATIO P/PO
0	1.0000	1.000	15.0	59.0	661.7	29.92	1.0000
1000	.9711	1.015	13.0	55.4	659.5	28.86	.9644
2000	.9428	1.030	11.0	51.9	657.2	27.82	.9298
3000	.9151	1.045	9.0	48.3	654.9	26.82	.8963
4000	.8881	1.061	7.1	44.7	652.6	25.84	.8637
5000	.8617	1.077	5.1	41.2	650.3	24.90	.8321
6000	.8359	1.094	3.1	37.6	648.7	23.98	.8014
7000	.8107	1.111	1.1	34.1	645.6	23.09	.7717
8000	.7860	1.128	-0.8	30.5	643.3	22.23	.7429
9000	.7620	1.146	-2.8	26.9	640.9	21.39	.7149
10000	.7385	1.164	-4.8	23.4	638.6	20.58	.6878
11000	.7156	1.182	-6.8	19.8	636.2	19.80	.6616
12000	.6933	1.201	-8.8	16.3	633.9	19.04	.6362
13000	.6715	1.220	-10.8	12.7	631.5	18.30	.6115
14000	.6502	1.240	-12.7	9.1	629.0	17.58	.5877
15000	.6294	1.260	-14.7	5.6	626.6	16.89	.5646
16000	.6092	1.281	-16.7	2.0	624.2	16.23	.5423
17000	.5894	1.303	-18.6	-1.5	621.8	15.58	.5206
18000	.5702	1.324	-20.6	-5.1	619.4	14.95	.4997
19000	.5514	1.347	-22.6	-8.7	617.0	14.35	.4795
20000	.5331	1.370	-24.6	-12.2	614.6	13.76	.4599
21000	.5153	1.393	-26.6	-15.8	612.1	13.20	.4410
22000	.4980	1.417	-28.5	-19.3	609.6	12.65	.4228
23000	.4811	1.442	-30.5	-22.9	607.1	12.12	.4051
24000	.4646	1.467	-32.5	-26.5	604.6	11.61	.3881
25000	.4486	1.493	-34.5	-30.0	602.1	11.12	.3716
26000	.4330	1.520	-36.5	-33.6	599.6	10.64	.3557
27000	.4178	1.547	-38.4	-37.1	597.1	10.18	.3404
28000	.4031	1.575	-40.4	-40.7	594.6	9.742	.3256
29000	.3887	1.604	-42.4	-44.3	592.1	9.315	.3113
30000	.3747	1.634	-44.4	-47.8	589.5	8.904	.2976
31000	.3612	1.664	-46.4	-51.4	586.9	8.507	.2843
32000	.3480	1.695	-48.3	-54.9	584.4	8.125	.2715
33000	.3351	1.727	-50.3	-58.5	581.8	7.757	.2592
34000	.3227	1.760	-52.4	-62.1	579.2	7.402	.2474
35000	.3106	1.794	-54.3	-65.6	576.6	7.061	.2360
36000	.2989	1.829	-56.2	-69.2	574.0	6.733	.2250
37000	.2853	1.872	-56.5	-69.7	573.7	6.418	.2145
38000	.2719	1.918	-56.5	-69.7	573.7	6.118	.2045
39000	.2592	1.964	-56.5	-69.7	573.7	5.832	.1949
40000	.2471	2.012	-56.5	-69.7	573.7	5.559	.1858
41000	.2356	2.019	-56.5	-69.7	573.7	5.299	.1771
42000	.2245	2.110	-56.5	-69.7	573.7	5.051	.1681
43000	.2140	2.161	-56.5	-69.7	573.7	4.815	.1609
44000	.2040	2.214	-56.5	-69.7	573.7	4.590	.1534
45000	.1945	2.267	-56.5	-69.7	573.7	4.376	.1462
46000	.1854	2.322	-56.5	-69.7	573.7	4.171	.1394
47000	.1768	2.379	-56.5	-69.7	573.7	3.976	.1329
48000	.1685	2.436	-56.5	-69.7	573.7	3.791	.1267
49000	.1606	2.495	-56.5	-69.7	573.7	3.614	.1208
50000	.1531	2.556	-56.5	-69.7	573.7	3.445	.1151
51000	.1460	2.617	-56.5	-69.7	573.7	3.284	.1098
52000	.1392	2.681	-56.5	-69.7	573.7	3.131	.1046
53000	.1327	2.746	-56.5	-69.7	573.7	2.984	.0997
54000	.1265	2.812	-56.5	-69.7	573.7	2.845	.0951
55000	.1206	2.880	-56.5	-69.7	573.7	2.712	.0906
56000	.1149	2.950	-56.5	-69.7	573.7	2.586	.0864
57000	.1096	3.021	-56.5	-69.7	573.7	2.465	.0824
58000	.1044	3.094	-56.5	-69.7	573.7	2.350	.0785
59000	.0996	3.169	-56.5	-69.7	573.7	2.240	.0749
60000	.0949	3.246	-56.5	-69.7	573.7	2.136	.0714
61000	.0905	3.324	-56.5	-69.7	573.7	2.036	.0680
62000	.0863	3.405	-56.5	-69.7	573.7	1.941	.0649
63000	.0823	3.487	-56.5	-69.7	573.7	1.850	.0618
64000	.0784	3.571	-56.5	-69.7	573.7	1.764	.0590
65000	.0748	3.657	-56.5	-69.7	573.7	1.682	.0536
66000	.0713	3.746	-56.5	-69.7	573.7	1.603	
67000	.0680	3.836	-56.5	-69.7	573.7	1.529	.0511
68000	.0648	3.929	-56.5	-69.7	573.7	1.457	.0487
69000	.0618	4.024	-56.5	-69.7	573.7	1.389	.0464
70000	.0589	4.121	-56.5	-69.7	573.7	1.325	.0443

T2J-1-1-93-26A

Figure 11-5

DENSITY ALTITUDE CHART
ICAO

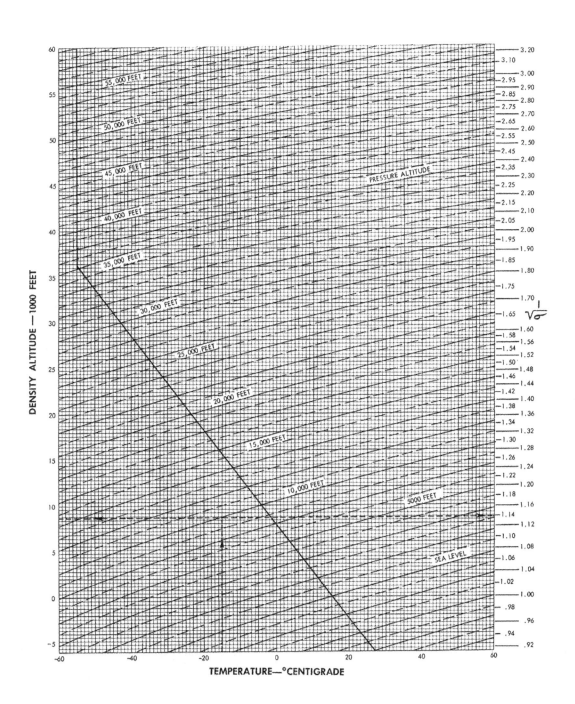

Figure 11-6

T2J-1-1-93-278

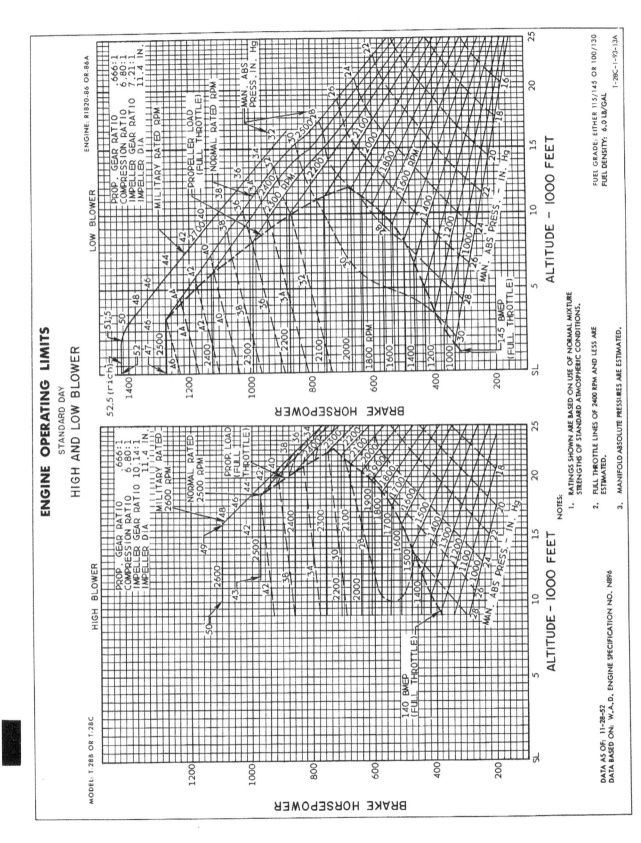

Figure 11-7

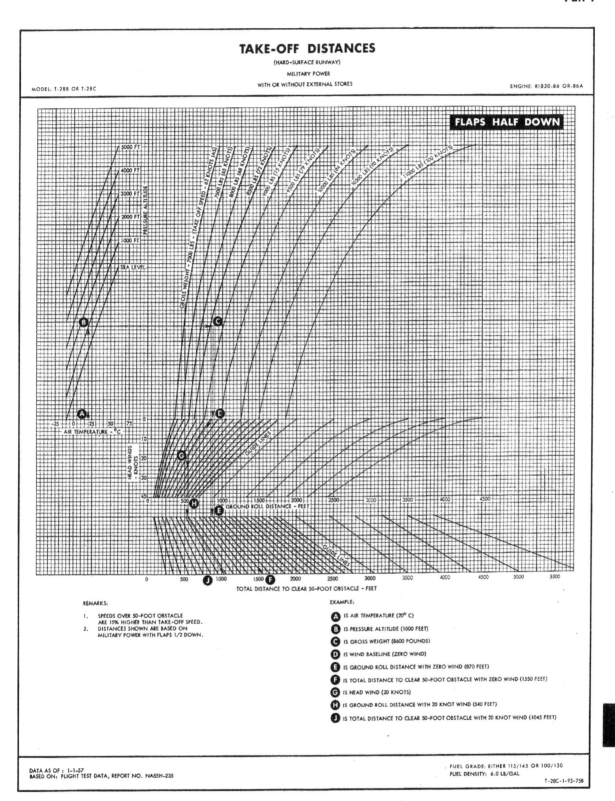

TAKE-OFF DISTANCES
(HARD-SURFACE RUNWAY)

MILITARY POWER

WITH OR WITHOUT EXTERNAL STORES

MODEL: T-28B OR T-28C

ENGINE: R1820-86 OR -86A

FLAPS HALF DOWN

REMARKS:

1. SPEEDS OVER 50-FOOT OBSTACLE ARE 15% HIGHER THAN TAKE-OFF SPEED.
2. DISTANCES SHOWN ARE BASED ON MILITARY POWER WITH FLAPS 1/2 DOWN.

EXAMPLE:

Ⓐ IS AIR TEMPERATURE (20° C)

Ⓑ IS PRESSURE ALTITUDE (1000 FEET)

Ⓒ IS GROSS WEIGHT (8600 POUNDS)

Ⓓ IS WIND BASELINE (ZERO WIND)

Ⓔ IS GROUND ROLL DISTANCE WITH ZERO WIND (870 FEET)

Ⓕ IS TOTAL DISTANCE TO CLEAR 50-FOOT OBSTACLE WITH ZERO WIND (1550 FEET)

Ⓖ IS HEAD WIND (20 KNOTS)

Ⓗ IS GROUND ROLL DISTANCE WITH 20 KNOT WIND (540 FEET)

Ⓙ IS TOTAL DISTANCE TO CLEAR 50-FOOT OBSTACLE WITH 20 KNOT WIND (1045 FEET)

DATA AS OF : 1-1-57
BASED ON: FLIGHT TEST DATA, REPORT NO. NA55H-235

FUEL GRADE: EITHER 115/145 OR 100/130
FUEL DENSITY: 6.0 LB/GAL

T-28C-1-93-75B

Figure 11-8

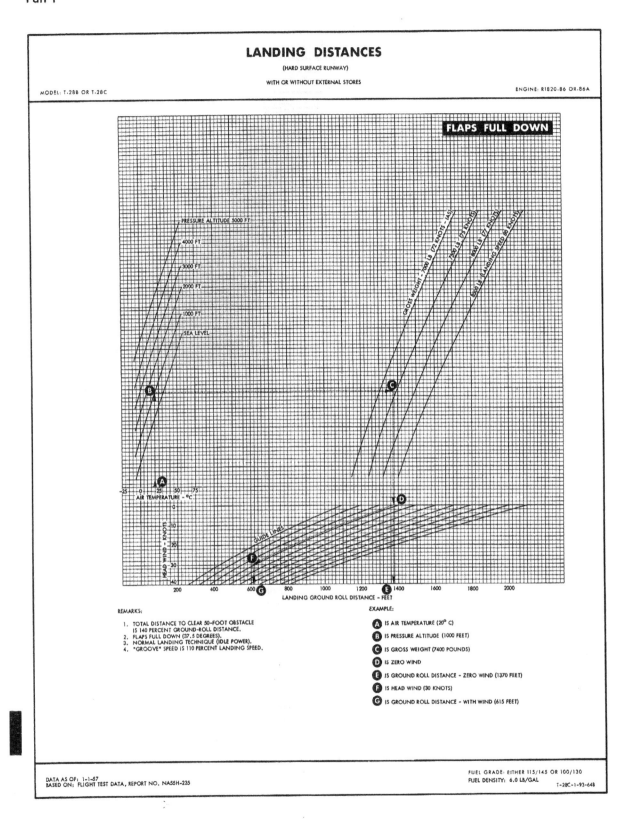

LANDING DISTANCES

(HARD SURFACE RUNWAY)

WITH OR WITHOUT EXTERNAL STORES

MODEL: T-28B OR T-28C

ENGINE: R1820-86 OR-86A

FLAPS FULL DOWN

REMARKS:

1. TOTAL DISTANCE TO CLEAR 50-FOOT OBSTACLE IS 140 PERCENT GROUND-ROLL DISTANCE.
2. FLAPS FULL DOWN (37.5 DEGREES).
3. NORMAL LANDING TECHNIQUE (IDLE POWER).
4. "GROOVE" SPEED IS 110 PERCENT LANDING SPEED.

EXAMPLE:

Ⓐ IS AIR TEMPERATURE (20° C)
Ⓑ IS PRESSURE ALTITUDE (1000 FEET)
Ⓒ IS GROSS WEIGHT (7400 POUNDS)
Ⓓ IS ZERO WIND
Ⓔ IS GROUND ROLL DISTANCE - ZERO WIND (1370 FEET)
Ⓕ IS HEAD WIND (30 KNOTS)
Ⓖ IS GROUND ROLL DISTANCE - WITH WIND (615 FEET)

DATA AS OF: 1-1-57
BASED ON: FLIGHT TEST DATA, REPORT NO. NA55H-235

FUEL GRADE: EITHER 115/145 OR 100/130
FUEL DENSITY: 6.0 LB/GAL

T-28C-1-93-64B

Figure 11-9

STOPPING DISTANCE

(HARD-SURFACE RUNWAY)
STANDARD DAY
WITH OR WITHOUT EXTERNAL STORES

MODEL: T-28B OR T-28C

ENGINE: R1820-86 OR-86A

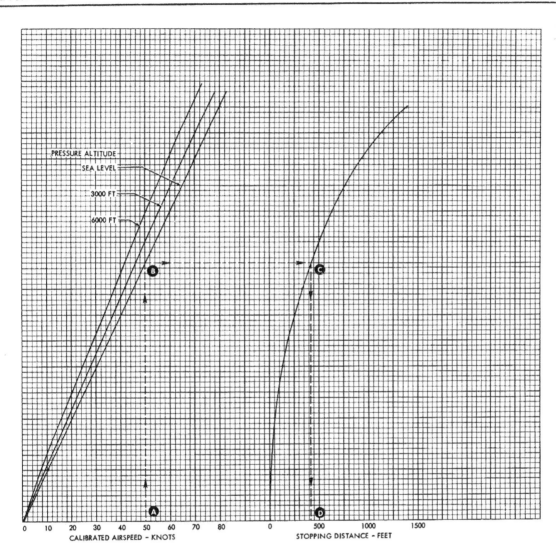

REMARKS:

1. FLAPS HALF DOWN.

2. STOPPING DISTANCE IS PREDICTED
    ON HARD BRAKING, NO POWER.

3. NO WIND.

4. DISTANCES SHOWN MAY BE USED WITH ALL
    GROSS WEIGHTS AND CONFIGURATIONS.

EXAMPLE:

Ⓐ IS CALIBRATED AIRSPEED (50 KNOTS).

Ⓑ IS PRESSURE ALTITUDE (SEA LEVEL).

Ⓒ IS BASE LINE.

Ⓓ IS STOPPING DISTANCE (413 FEET).

DATA AS OF: 1-1-57
BASED ON: FLIGHT TEST DATA, REPORT NO. NA55H-235

FUEL GRADE: EITHER 115/145 OR 100/130
FUEL DENSITY: 6.0 LB/GAL

T-28C-1-93-68C

TAKE-OFF AND LANDING CROSSWIND CHART

MODEL: T-28B/C

ENGINE: R-1820-86 OR 86A

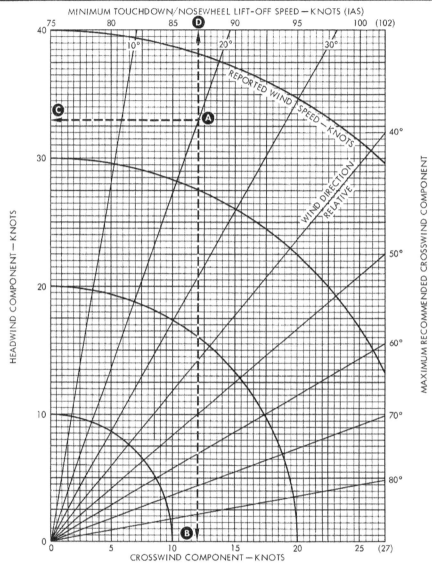

TO DETERMINE CROSSWIND COMPONENT:
(1) LOCATE REPORTED WINDSPEED ON RELATIVE BEARING LINE.
(2) FROM INTERSECTION OF WINDSPEED AND BEARING, DROP VERTICALLY TO BASELINE TO FIND CROSSWIND COMPONENT.
(3) FROM INTERSECTION, PROJECT A LINE HORIZONTALLY TO FIND HEADWIND COMPONENT.
(4) PROJECT VERTICALLY TO FIND MINIMUM TOUCHDOWN/ NOSEWHEEL LIFT-OFF SPEED.

EXAMPLE:
Ⓐ REPORTED WIND OF 35 KNOTS, 20 DEGREES OFF RUNWAY
Ⓑ CROSSWIND COMPONENT = 12 KNOTS
Ⓒ HEADWIND COMPONENT = 33 KNOTS
Ⓓ MINIMUM TOUCHDOWN/NOSEWHEEL LIFT-OFF SPEED = 87 KNOTS

DATA AS OF: 4-1-66
BASED ON: FLIGHT TEST DATA

FUEL GRADE: EITHER 115/145 OR 100/130
FUEL DENSITY: 6.0 LB/GAL

T-28B-1-93-69

Figure 11-11

PART 2 — MISSION PLANNING

The following mission planning sample problems use the T-28B performance data charts in Part 3 of this section.

SAMPLE PROBLEM NO. 1

A bombing run is to be made on a target 88 nautical miles from the home field. Normal rated power will be used going into the target at 5000 feet. Military power will be used during the runs in the target area at sea level plus 50 feet for an estimated 5 minutes.

Return to the home field is to be made by way of a checkpoint 90 nautical miles distant from the target, and 71 nautical miles from the home field. After completion of mission over target, a climb from sea level to 10,000 feet is to be made on course to the checkpoint. This altitude will be maintained for the remainder of the flight, using 2200 rpm and 32 inches Hg manifold pressure. A 20-knot tail wind is expected during the target-to-checkpoint leg, and a 20-knot head wind is expected on the checkpoint-to-home-base leg.

List the conditions of the problem and find the fuel and time required for the entire flight.

Total distance	249 nautical miles
Weather	
First leg	Clear
Target area	Clear
Second leg	Scattered cumulus
Third leg	Scattered cumulonimbus
Winds aloft	
First leg (5000 feet)	Light variable
Target area (SL)	Light variable
Second leg (10,000 feet)	20-knot tail wind
Third leg (10,000 feet)	20-knot head wind
Flight plan	VFR
Field elevation	1000 feet
Basic weight, empty (including trapped fuel, oil, and miscellaneous equipment)	6725 pounds
Crew weight (two)	400 pounds
Maximum fuel (177 U.S. gallons)	1062 pounds
Oil (8.8 U.S. gallons)	66 pounds
Armament (two 100-pound bombs)	200 pounds
Total gross weight	8453 pounds
Minimum weight (empty including crew and oil)	7191 pounds

Now that the conditions of the flight are determined, it is necessary to establish the fuel and time required for each leg of the mission. In the statement of the problem, no mention was made of the required allowances

and reserves that will be required for warmup, take-off, and unexpected difficulties. The following shows how the charts in this section can be utilized to plan an efficient mission:

Reserve for
unexpected difficulties............174 pounds (1 hour)

A 1-hour fuel reserve at 5000 feet is considered sufficient for this mission. The Long-range Prediction—Time chart (figure 11-57) for clean aircraft will be used, since this reserve is desired at the end of the flight. Enter the chart at the minimum weight, empty (7191 pounds), at 5000 feet (desired altitude for flight to alternate airfield); the corresponding time is 8.05 hours. The 1-hour desired reserve, subtracted from this time gives the gross weight with reserve fuel aboard. The difference in gross weights is the weight of fuel required for 1-hour reserve flight at maximum range, 5000 feet altitude.

$$7191 \text{ pounds} = 8.05 \text{ hours} \quad (5000 \text{ feet})$$
$$7365 \text{ pounds} = 1.00 \text{ hour} \quad (\text{reserve})$$
$$7365 - 7191 = 7.05 \text{ hours} \quad (5000 \text{ feet})$$
$$= 174 \text{ pounds}$$

Warmup and take-off............157 pounds (10 minutes)

There is no exact method for calculating the fuel used for engine warmup, taxi, and take-off. Therefore, an approximation is made using 10 minutes at normal rated power. Turn to the Military and Normal Rated Power Fuel Flow chart (figure 11-59) and obtain the fuel flow at field elevation (1000 feet) = 15.7 pounds per minute.

Fuel required = 15.7 pounds per minute × 10 minutes
= 157 pounds.

Climb (cruise power) after take-off (1000 feet to 5000 feet) 16 pounds............(4 minutes)

Using the weight at start of climb (total gross weight minus take-off allowance, 8453 − 157 = 8296 pounds), enter the Maximum Cruise Power Climb chart (figure 11-20) at 8296 pounds and 1000 feet. Follow the guide lines to 5000 feet to obtain fuel required.

Fuel required = 8296 − 8280 = 16 pounds
Distance traveled = 9.0 − 1.5 = 8 nautical miles
Time required = 4.5 minutes − 0.5 minute = 4 minutes

Cruise to target (80 nautical
miles)............296 pounds (18 minutes)

Normal rated power is to be used on the first leg, cruising into the target area. Use figure 11-32 which gives the specific range for 5000 feet, with bombs and a gross weight of 8280 pounds (weight at end of climb to 5000 feet). The specific range is 0.27 nautical mile per pound, at a calibrated airspeed of 244 knots (TAS = 262 knots).

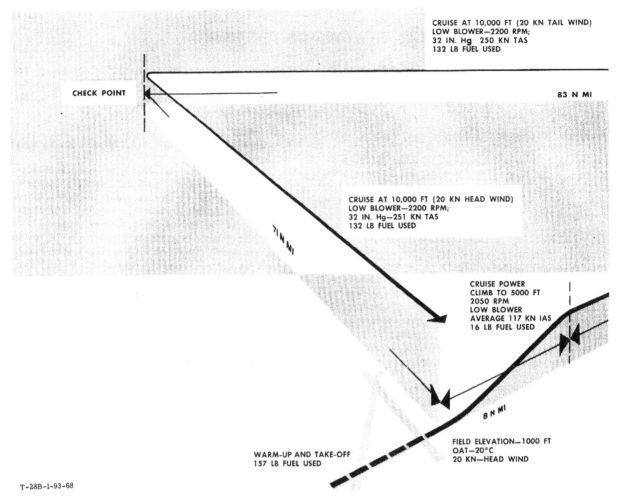

CRUISE AT 10,000 FT (20 KN TAIL WIND)
LOW BLOWER—2200 RPM;
32 IN. Hg 250 KN TAS
132 LB FUEL USED

CHECK POINT

83 N MI

CRUISE AT 10,000 FT (20 KN HEAD WIND)
LOW BLOWER—2200 RPM;
32 IN. Hg—251 KN TAS
132 LB FUEL USED

7 N MI

CRUISE POWER
CLIMB TO 5000 FT
2050 RPM
LOW BLOWER
AVERAGE 117 KN IAS
16 LB FUEL USED

8 N MI

FIELD ELEVATION—1000 FT
OAT—20°C
20 KN—HEAD WIND

WARM-UP AND TAKE-OFF
157 LB FUEL USED

T-28B-1-93-68

Figure 11-12 (Sheet 1)

To obtain the fuel required, divide the distance traveled by the specific range:

Fuel required = 80 nautical miles ÷ 0.27 nautical mile per pound = 296 pounds

The time required is simply the distance divided by the ground speed. Since there is no wind on the first leg, TAS = ground speed. Time required = 80 nautical miles ÷ 262 knots (TAS) = 0.306 hour or 18 minutes. Initial weight at end of cruise = 8280 −296 = 7984 pounds.

Military power allowance (target area)........90 pounds (5 minutes)

This figure includes the descent to bombing altitude and necessary reconnaissance of the target area at sea level. From the Military and Normal Rated Power Fuel Flow chart (figure 11-59), obtain the sea level fuel flow (17.9 pounds per minute).

Time required = 5 minutes

Fuel required = 17.9 pounds per minute × 5 minutes = 90 pounds

Weight reduction due to bomb drop = 200 pounds

Weight at end of target occupation = 7984 − 90 − 200 = 7694 pounds

Climb (military power) from sea level to 10,000 feet...54 pounds (3 minutes)

Upon leaving the target area, a military power climb to 10,000 feet, on course, is made, to utilize a tail wind available at that altitude. Find the time, fuel, and distance required from figure 11-13, using a gross weight of 7694 pounds at start of climb. Since the bombs were dropped over the target, complete the calculations using clean configuration chart.

Fuel required = 7694 − 7640 = 54 pounds

Time required = 3.2 minutes

Distance traveled = 7.4 nautical miles (7 nautical miles)

Gross weight at end of climb = 7694 − 54 = 7640 pounds

Cruise to checkpoint (83 nautical miles)
10,000 feet..........................132 pounds (18.5 minutes)

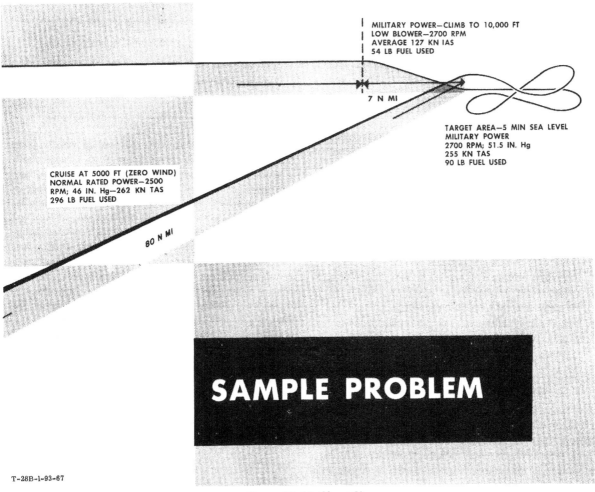

MILITARY POWER—CLIMB TO 10,000 FT
LOW BLOWER—2700 RPM
AVERAGE 127 KN IAS
54 LB FUEL USED

7 N MI

TARGET AREA—5 MIN SEA LEVEL
MILITARY POWER
2700 RPM; 51.5 IN. Hg
255 KN TAS
90 LB FUEL USED

CRUISE AT 5000 FT (ZERO WIND)
NORMAL RATED POWER—2500
RPM; 46 IN. Hg—262 KN TAS
296 LB FUEL USED

80 N MI

SAMPLE PROBLEM

T-28B-1-93-67

Figure 11-12 (Sheet 2)

A preselected power setting of 2200 rpm and 32 inches Hg manifold pressure is to be used for the remainder of the mission. Turn to figure 11-25, which gives specific range at 10,000 feet, zero wind. Note that the specific range for the desired power setting is 0.584 nautical mile per pound of fuel at zero wind. The calibrated airspeed is 216 knots and true airspeed is 250 knots. (Use 7640-pound gross weight.) The ground speed is true airspeed plus tail wind. To obtain the specific range for the wind condition, multiply the specific range for zero wind by the ratio of ground speed divided by true airspeed. The specific range with wind can also be found by entering figure 11-25 at the ground speed (using true airspeed scale) and tracing up to the desired power setting. The intersection is the specific range with wind at the desired power setting.

Ground speed = 250 knots + 20 knots = 270 knots

Specific range (with wind)
$$= \frac{0.584 \times 270}{250} = 0.630 \text{ nautical mile per pound}$$

Fuel required = 83 nautical miles ÷ 0.630 nautical mile per pound = 132 pounds

Time required = 83 nautical miles ÷ 270 knots = 0.308 hour or 18.5 minutes

Gross weight at end of cruise = 7640 − 132 = 7508 pounds

Cruise to home base (71 nautical miles)
10,000 feet......................132 pounds (18.5 minutes)

The last leg of the flight is calculated the same as the previous leg, using figure 11-25, with the exception of the 20-knot head wind and a new gross weight of 7508 pounds.

Specific range (zero wind, 7508 pounds)
= 0.585 nautical mile per pound

True airspeed = 251 knots

Ground speed = 251 − 20 = 231 knots

Specific range (20-knot head wind)
$$= \frac{0.585 \times 231}{251} = 0.538 \text{ nautical mile per pound}$$

Fuel required

    = 71 nautical miles ÷ 0.538 nautical mile per pound = 132 pounds

Time required

    = 71 nautical miles ÷ 231 knots = 0.307 hour or 18.5 minutes

Gross weight at end of cruise

        = 7508 − 132 = 7376 pounds

Collecting all the fuel quantities for each leg, including the allowances for take-off, reserve, and time on target, solve for total fuel used and total time required.

ITEM	FUEL REQUIRED (pounds)	TIME REQUIRED (minutes)
Reserve	174	*60
Take-off and warmup	157	*10
Climb (1000 to 5000 feet)	16	4
Cruise to target	296	18
Military power allowance	90	5
Climb (sea level to 10,000 feet)	54	3
Cruise to checkpoint	132	18.5
Cruise to home base	132	18.5
Totals	1051	67

                                    1 hour 7 minutes

*Not considered as time in flight

The mission, as planned, leaves 11 pounds of fuel (1062 − 1051 = 11 pounds) as an additional reserve upon arrival over the home base. This extra 11-pound reserve may be considered as an added safety margin, or the mission may be replanned to include the use of the additional 11 pounds.

Note that no allowance is made for descent from 10,000 feet to land. Since the fuel quantity is negligible, it is not considered in the mission requirements. However, the extra 11 pounds would be more than adequate for such a descent, leaving the 174-pound reserve still on board at landing.

SAMPLE PROBLEM NO. 2

Suppose that upon arrival over the checkpoint used in problem No. 1, the local weather station is reporting extreme thunderstorm activity between the checkpoint and the home field, with a recommendation of 30,000 feet as a cruising altitude to clear severe turbulence. Zero wind at 30,000 feet is also reported.

These conditions dictate an immediate change in flight plan for last leg of the mission. This change can be effected quite easily, using two charts. First, determine the fuel, time, and distance required to climb from the present altitude (10,000 feet) to the recommended altitude of 30,000 feet. Use the gross weight at the end of

the second leg of the mission (7508 pounds) to enter the Normal Rated Power Climb chart (figure 11-15).

Fuel required   = 7508 − 7405 = 103 pounds

Time required   = 14.7 − 3.2 = 12 minutes

Distance traveled =   39 − 7.8 = 31 nautical miles

Gross weight at
end of climb   = 7508 − 103 = 7405 pounds

Since 31 nautical miles were covered in climb, there remain but 40 nautical miles (71 − 31 = 40), at which to cruise at 30,000 feet. A reduction in power to recommended maximum range power at 30,000 feet is selected to ensure minimum fuel consumption for cruise. To determine whether the home base can be reached safely under the new flight plan, turn to the Long-range Prediction—Distance chart (figure 11-53) and with the gross weight at start of 30,000-foot cruise (7405 pounds), enter the chart and find a corresponding distance at 30,000 feet, 600 nautical miles. Add to this the required 40 nautical miles left to cruise, and re-enter the chart at 640 miles (600 + 40 = 640). Proceed to the 30,000-foot altitude curve and read directly below the gross weight at end of cruise, 7365 pounds. Since 7365 pounds are greater than the minimum empty weight (7191 pounds), it is quite evident that the base can be reached. In fact, arrival over the home base leaves 174 pounds reserve (7365 − 7191 = 174 pounds) which is the same as the 1-hour reserve at 5000 feet, originally allowed for in Problem No. 1.

The reserve of 174 pounds was originally obtained in Problem No. 1 as a 1-hour fuel reserve at 5000 feet using maximum range power settings. These power settings can be obtained from the Maximum Range Power Conditions chart (figure 11-47).

If the reserve is to be used for holding procedure or orbiting, then maximum time in the air is more important than maximum range, and the Maximum Endurance chart (figure 11-50) should be used to obtain power settings and time available at 5000 feet for the 174 pounds.

Fuel flow at 5000 feet (7365 pounds) = 125 pounds per hour

Time available = 174 pounds ÷ 125 pounds per hour = 1.39 hours or 1 hour 23 minutes

Additional information from the performance charts can be obtained and listed on the flight card. Although this information is not important from a range standpoint, the information listed will assist the student pilot in realizing all the capabilities of the aircraft.

Take-off distance over a 50-foot obstacle..........980 feet

The distance to take-off may be found from the Take-off Distances chart (figure 11-8). The field altitude is 1000 feet with the outside air temperature at 20°C (68°F) and a 20-knot wind down the runway. Enter the chart at this temperature and altitude and move horizontally to the 8600-pound weight line (take-off gross weight = 8575 pounds). Note that take-off should be at approximately 74 knots calibrated airspeed. To obtain the ground run distance required, drop down from the weight line to the head wind line and follow the wind guide lines to 20 knots. Read a ground-roll distance of 480 feet. Following through the remainder of the chart, determine the total distance to take-off over a 50-foot obstacle, to be 980 feet.

It is quite likely that the runway available is more than adequate for these distances, but for simulated carrier take-offs, or emergency field procedure, the take-off distance chart should be used.

Landing distance over a 50-foot obstacle...........842 feet

Using the same field conditions as for take-off with a 30-knot wind and a return gross weight of 7300 pounds, enter the Landing Distance chart (figure 11-9) at temperature (20°C) and altitude (1000 feet), and move horizontally to the weight at 7300 pounds. Follow down to the zero wind line and then down the wind guide lines to 30-knot head wind. Read a ground-roll distance of 602 feet. From note No. 1, obtain the total distance over the obstacle of:

Total distance = 602 feet × 140 percent = 842 feet

Stopping distance at sea level and 50 knots....413 feet

The use of the Stopping Distance chart (figure 11-10) is for the purpose of determining whether or not a safe stop can be made using the remaining runway. For example: Suppose that an engine failure is experienced during the take-off run and the speed at the time of engine failure is 50 knots. From the Stopping Distance chart (figure 11-10), obtain the distance required to stop, of 413 feet.

PART 3 — T-28B PERFORMANCE DATA

PERFORMANCE CHARTS (T-28B)

CLIMB CHARTS

Curves are given for time, fuel, and distance to climb at military power, normal rated power, and maximum cruise power for all gross weights and configurations. See figures 11-13 through 11-21. The data shown are based on the climbing speed schedule shown in the climbing speed chart, which gives a maximum rate of climb at the altitude and speed shown. The examples given on the climb graphs show how time, fuel, and distance to climb can be determined both for climbs from sea level and climbs in flight.

CLIMBING SPEEDS

As mentioned in the discussion on the climb charts, the climbing speeds chart (figure 11-21) gives a plot of best climbing speed (CAS) versus altitude. By following this speed schedule, it is possible to realize the most efficient rate of climb for the aircraft throughout the entire altitude range.

NAUTICAL MILES PER POUND OF FUEL

The graphs showing nautical miles per pound of fuel, from sea level through 35,000 feet in 5000-foot increments, form the nucleus of the cruise data and, therefore, some amount of skill should be developed in their use to ensure that the aircraft is operated under the best conditions possible toward the fulfillment of any mission. These graphs (figures 11-23 through 11-46) give the nautical miles per pound of fuel that may be obtained under various power conditions (i.e., rpm and manifold pressure) and at various weights and configurations. It can be noted that all the nautical miles per pound of fuel graphs are plotted with calibrated airspeed (CAS) with a subscale giving true airspeed (TAS). The superimposed curve of recommended airspeed on the aforementioned graphs is based on the highest speed possible which gives maximum nautical miles per pound for the instantaneous weights and altitudes of flight given on the graphs. All the cruise data shown are based on Standard Day conditions with the engine mixture control in the NORMAL position and the supercharger control handle in LOW blower position below 20,000 feet and in HIGH blower position above 20,000 feet. Operation in rich mixture will result in a decrease in nautical miles per pound of fuel from that shown on the charts. Refer to Section I, Part 2, for rich mixture operation under surging.

MAXIMUM RANGE

In these graphs (figures 11-47 through 11-49), the data given are representative of the cruise performance given in the nautical miles per pound of fuel graphs if the recommended CAS for maximum range is flown throughout the altitude and weight range. These graphs are helpful when maximum range cruising is anticipated, since all the power settings, airspeeds, and nautical miles per pound of fuel shown will give maximum range at the altitudes given.

MAXIMUM ENDURANCE

These graphs (figures 11-50 through 11-52), like those for maximum range, are a completion of data taken from the nautical miles per pound of fuel chart at the point of minimum fuel flow. On these graphs, maximum *time* that can be obtained in flight, not maximum range, is the primary concern. This maximum endurance condition is extremely important under such conditions as holding and orbiting, and during all operations that contain requirements of *time* in the air rather than distance to travel. Power settings, airspeeds, and minimum fuel flows are given for gross weight and altitude, using the same mixture and blower setting as given on the nautical miles per pound of fuel graphs.

LONG-RANGE PREDICTION—DISTANCE

These graphs of nautical miles versus gross weight at various altitudes (figures 11-53 through 11-55) present a picture of maximum aircraft range when the aircraft is flown at the recommended calibrated airspeed (CAS).

LONG-RANGE PREDICTION—TIME

These graphs of time versus gross weight at various altitudes (figures 11-56 through 11-58) present a picture of time required to cruise (at recommended CAS) for a given amount of fuel used at a constant altitude.

MILITARY AND NORMAL RATED POWER FUEL FLOW

The curves on figure 11-59 give fuel flow in pounds per minute for both normal rated power and military power.

EMERGENCY CLIMB

The purpose of the emergency climb graphs (figures 11-60 through 11-62) is to give an indication of the change in rate of climb due to change in configuration (flaps, gear, canopy, etc). Climbs are based on military power.

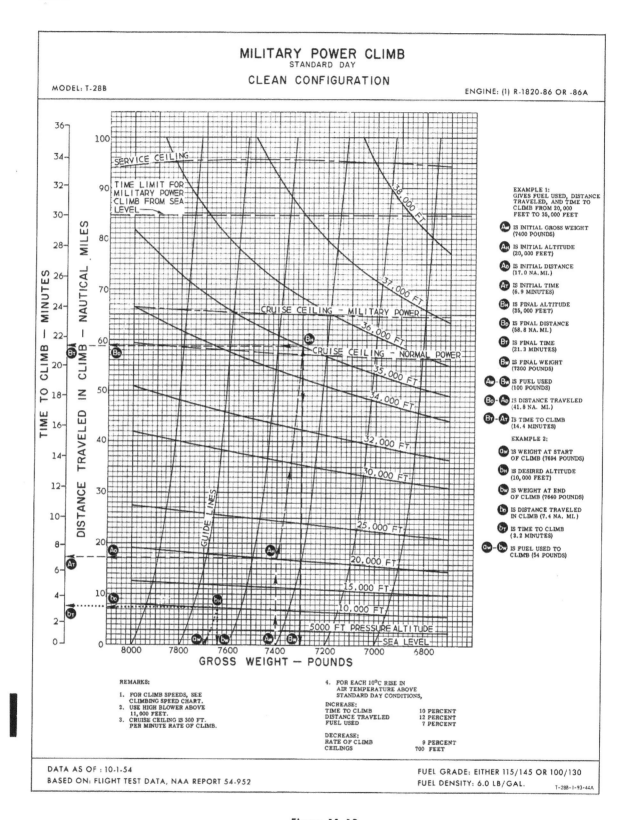

MILITARY POWER CLIMB
STANDARD DAY
CLEAN CONFIGURATION

MODEL: T-28B

ENGINE: (1) R-1820-86 OR -86A

EXAMPLE 1:
GIVES FUEL USED, DISTANCE TRAVELED, AND TIME TO CLIMB FROM 20,000 FEET TO 35,000 FEET

A_W IS INITIAL GROSS WEIGHT (7400 POUNDS)

A_H IS INITIAL ALTITUDE (20,000 FEET)

A_D IS INITIAL DISTANCE (17.0 NA. MI.)

A_T IS INITIAL TIME (6.9 MINUTES)

B_H IS FINAL ALTITUDE (35,000 FEET)

B_D IS FINAL DISTANCE (58.8 NA. MI.)

B_T IS FINAL TIME (21.3 MINUTES)

B_W IS FINAL WEIGHT (7300 POUNDS)

A_W - B_W IS FUEL USED (100 POUNDS)

B_D - A_D IS DISTANCE TRAVELED (41.8 NA. MI.)

B_T - A_T IS TIME TO CLIMB (14.4 MINUTES)

EXAMPLE 2:

a_W IS WEIGHT AT START OF CLIMB (7694 POUNDS)

b_H IS DESIRED ALTITUDE (10,000 FEET)

b_W IS WEIGHT AT END OF CLIMB (7640 POUNDS)

b_D IS DISTANCE TRAVELED IN CLIMB (7.4 NA. MI.)

b_T IS TIME TO CLIMB (3.2 MINUTES)

a_W - b_W IS FUEL USED TO CLIMB (54 POUNDS)

REMARKS:

1. FOR CLIMB SPEEDS, SEE CLIMBING SPEED CHART.
2. USE HIGH BLOWER ABOVE 11,000 FEET.
3. CRUISE CEILING IS 300 FT. PER MINUTE RATE OF CLIMB.

4. FOR EACH 10°C RISE IN AIR TEMPERATURE ABOVE STANDARD DAY CONDITIONS,

INCREASE:
TIME TO CLIMB   10 PERCENT
DISTANCE TRAVELED   12 PERCENT
FUEL USED   7 PERCENT

DECREASE:
RATE OF CLIMB   9 PERCENT
CEILINGS   700 FEET

DATA AS OF : 10-1-54
BASED ON: FLIGHT TEST DATA, NAA REPORT 54-952

FUEL GRADE: EITHER 115/145 OR 100/130
FUEL DENSITY: 6.0 LB/GAL.

T-28B-1-93-44A

Figure 11-13

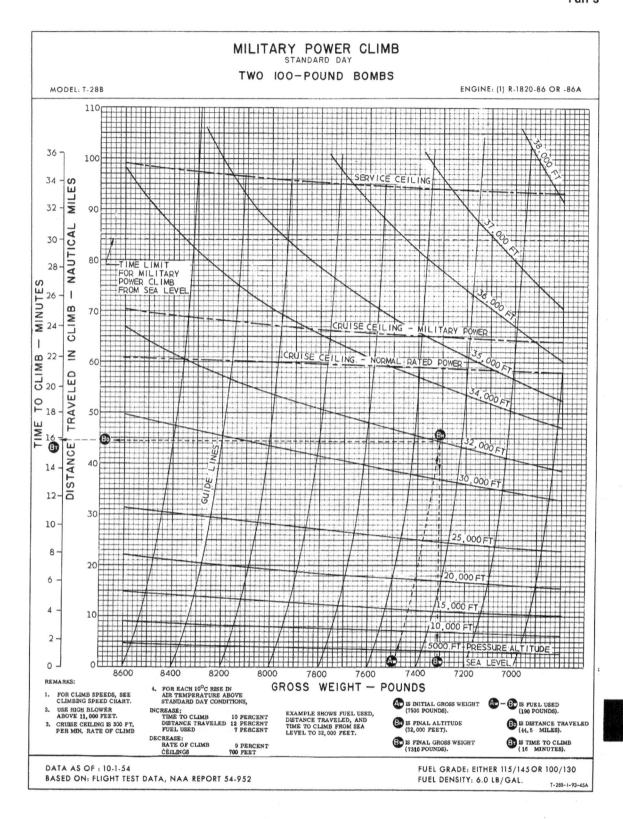

MILITARY POWER CLIMB
STANDARD DAY
TWO 100–POUND BOMBS

MODEL: T-28B

ENGINE: (1) R-1820-86 OR -86A

REMARKS:

1. FOR CLIMB SPEEDS, SEE CLIMBING SPEED CHART.
2. USE HIGH BLOWER ABOVE 11,000 FEET.
3. CRUISE CEILING IS 300 FT. PER MIN. RATE OF CLIMB.
4. FOR EACH 10°C RISE IN AIR TEMPERATURE ABOVE STANDARD DAY CONDITIONS,

INCREASE:
TIME TO CLIMB   10 PERCENT
DISTANCE TRAVELED   12 PERCENT
FUEL USED   7 PERCENT

DECREASE:
RATE OF CLIMB   9 PERCENT
CEILINGS   700 FEET

EXAMPLE SHOWS FUEL USED, DISTANCE TRAVELED, AND TIME TO CLIMB FROM SEA LEVEL TO 32,000 FEET.

Aᴡ IS INITIAL GROSS WEIGHT (7500 POUNDS).

Bₕ IS FINAL ALTITUDE (32,000 FEET).

Bᴡ IS FINAL GROSS WEIGHT (7310 POUNDS).

Aᴡ – Bᴡ IS FUEL USED (190 POUNDS).

Bᴅ IS DISTANCE TRAVELED (44.5 MILES).

Bₜ IS TIME TO CLIMB (16 MINUTES).

DATA AS OF : 10-1-54
BASED ON: FLIGHT TEST DATA, NAA REPORT 54-952

FUEL GRADE: EITHER 115/145 OR 100/130
FUEL DENSITY: 6.0 LB/GAL.

T-28B-1-93-45A

Figure 11-14

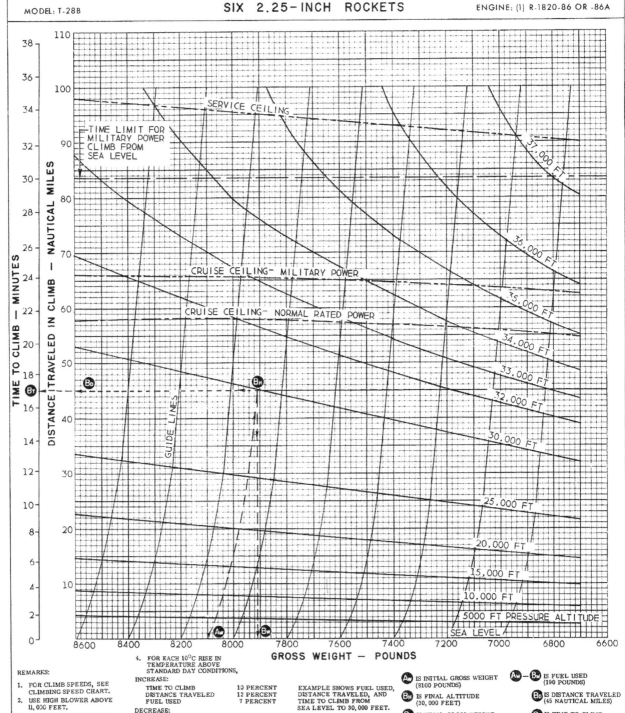

MILITARY POWER CLIMB
STANDARD DAY
TWO .50-CALIBER GUN PACKAGES OR
SIX 2.25-INCH ROCKETS

MODEL: T-28B

ENGINE: (1) R-1820-86 OR -86A

SERVICE CEILING

TIME LIMIT FOR MILITARY POWER CLIMB FROM SEA LEVEL

CRUISE CEILING- MILITARY POWER

CRUISE CEILING- NORMAL RATED POWER

37,000 FT
36,000 FT
35,000 FT
34,000 FT
33,000 FT
32,000 FT
30,000 FT
25,000 FT
20,000 FT
15,000 FT
10,000 FT
5000 FT PRESSURE ALTITUDE
SEA LEVEL

GUIDE LINES

TIME TO CLIMB — MINUTES

DISTANCE TRAVELED IN CLIMB — NAUTICAL MILES

GROSS WEIGHT — POUNDS

REMARKS:

1. FOR CLIMB SPEEDS, SEE CLIMBING SPEED CHART.
2. USE HIGH BLOWER ABOVE 11,000 FEET.
3. CRUISE CEILING IS 300 FT. PER MINUTE RATE OF CLIMB.

4. FOR EACH 10°C RISE IN TEMPERATURE ABOVE STANDARD DAY CONDITIONS,

INCREASE:

TIME TO CLIMB	10 PERCENT
DISTANCE TRAVELED	12 PERCENT
FUEL USED	7 PERCENT

DECREASE:

RATE OF CLIMB	9 PERCENT
CEILINGS	700 FEET

EXAMPLE SHOWS FUEL USED, DISTANCE TRAVELED, AND TIME TO CLIMB FROM SEA LEVEL TO 30,000 FEET.

Aw IS INITIAL GROSS WEIGHT (8100 POUNDS)

Bw IS FINAL ALTITUDE (30,000 FEET)

Bw IS FINAL GROSS WEIGHT (7910 POUNDS)

Aw — Bw IS FUEL USED (190 POUNDS)

Bo IS DISTANCE TRAVELED (45 NAUTICAL MILES)

Bт IS TIME TO CLIMB (17 MINUTES)

DATA AS OF: 10-1-54
BASED ON: FLIGHT TEST DATA, NAA REPORT 54-952

FUEL GRADE: EITHER 115/145 OR 100/130
FUEL DENSITY: 6.0 LB/GAL.

T-28B-1-93-62A

NORMAL RATED POWER CLIMB
STANDARD DAY
CLEAN CONFIGURATION

MODEL: T-28B

ENGINE: (1) R-1820-86 OR -86A

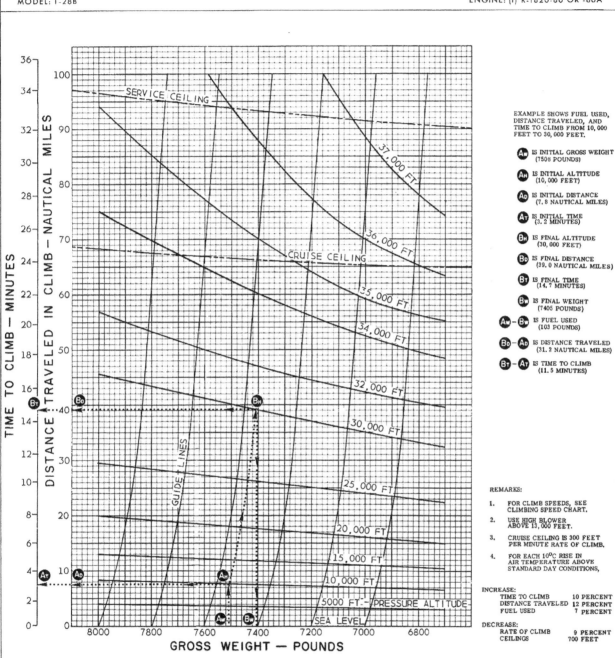

EXAMPLE SHOWS FUEL USED, DISTANCE TRAVELED, AND TIME TO CLIMB FROM 10,000 FEET TO 30,000 FEET.

Aw IS INITIAL GROSS WEIGHT (7508 POUNDS)

AH IS INITIAL ALTITUDE (10,000 FEET)

AD IS INITIAL DISTANCE (7.8 NAUTICAL MILES)

AT IS INITIAL TIME (3.2 MINUTES)

BH IS FINAL ALTITUDE (30,000 FEET)

BD IS FINAL DISTANCE (39.0 NAUTICAL MILES)

BT IS FINAL TIME (14.7 MINUTES)

BW IS FINAL WEIGHT (7405 POUNDS)

Aw – Bw IS FUEL USED (103 POUNDS)

BD – AD IS DISTANCE TRAVELED (31.2 NAUTICAL MILES)

BT – AT IS TIME TO CLIMB (11.5 MINUTES)

REMARKS:

1. FOR CLIMB SPEEDS, SEE CLIMBING SPEED CHART.
2. USE HIGH BLOWER ABOVE 13,000 FEET.
3. CRUISE CEILING IS 300 FEET PER MINUTE RATE OF CLIMB.
4. FOR EACH 10°C RISE IN AIR TEMPERATURE ABOVE STANDARD DAY CONDITIONS,

INCREASE:
TIME TO CLIMB	10 PERCENT
DISTANCE TRAVELED	12 PERCENT
FUEL USED	7 PERCENT

DECREASE:
RATE OF CLIMB	9 PERCENT
CEILINGS	700 FEET

DATA AS OF: 10-1-54
BASED ON: FLIGHT TEST DATA, NAA REPORT 54-952

FUEL GRADE: EITHER 115/145 OR 100/130
FUEL DENSITY: 6.0 LB/GAL.

T-28B-1-93-42A

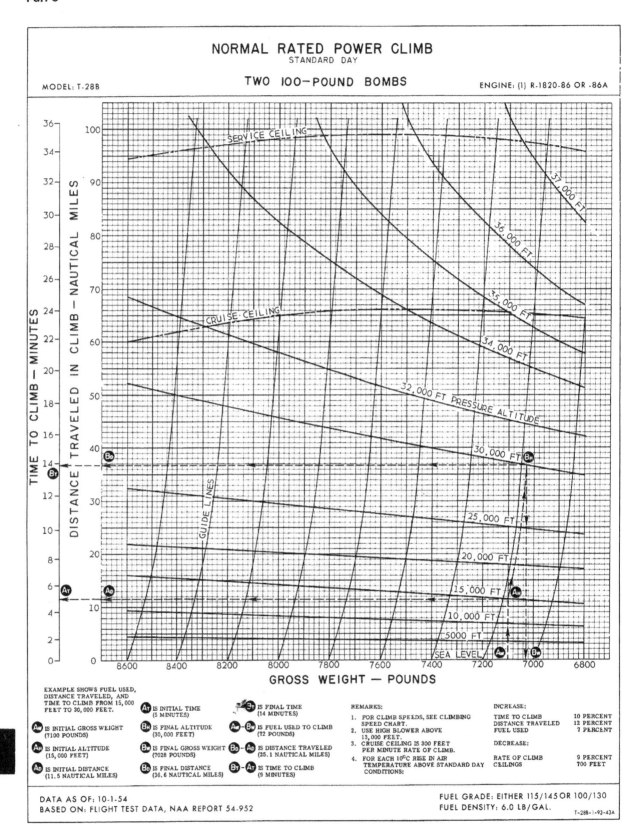

NORMAL RATED POWER CLIMB
STANDARD DAY

TWO 100-POUND BOMBS

MODEL: T-28B

ENGINE: (1) R-1820-86 OR -86A

EXAMPLE SHOWS FUEL USED, DISTANCE TRAVELED, AND TIME TO CLIMB FROM 15,000 FEET TO 30,000 FEET.

Aw IS INITIAL GROSS WEIGHT (7100 POUNDS)

Ah IS INITIAL ALTITUDE (15,000 FEET)

Ad IS INITIAL DISTANCE (11.5 NAUTICAL MILES)

At IS INITIAL TIME (5 MINUTES)

Bh IS FINAL ALTITUDE (30,000 FEET)

Bw IS FINAL GROSS WEIGHT (7028 POUNDS)

Bd IS FINAL DISTANCE (36.6 NAUTICAL MILES)

Bt IS FINAL TIME (14 MINUTES)

Aw—Bw IS FUEL USED TO CLIMB (72 POUNDS)

Bd—Ad IS DISTANCE TRAVELED (25.1 NAUTICAL MILES)

Bt—At IS TIME TO CLIMB (9 MINUTES)

REMARKS:
1. FOR CLIMB SPEEDS, SEE CLIMBING SPEED CHART.
2. USE HIGH BLOWER ABOVE 13,000 FEET.
3. CRUISE CEILING IS 300 FEET PER MINUTE RATE OF CLIMB.
4. FOR EACH 10°C RISE IN AIR TEMPERATURE ABOVE STANDARD DAY CONDITIONS:

INCREASE:

TIME TO CLIMB	10 PERCENT
DISTANCE TRAVELED	12 PERCENT
FUEL USED	7 PERCENT

DECREASE:

| RATE OF CLIMB | 9 PERCENT |
| CEILINGS | 700 FEET |

DATA AS OF: 10-1-54
BASED ON: FLIGHT TEST DATA, NAA REPORT 54-952

FUEL GRADE: EITHER 115/145 OR 100/130
FUEL DENSITY: 6.0 LB/GAL.

T-28B-1-93-43A

Figure 11-17

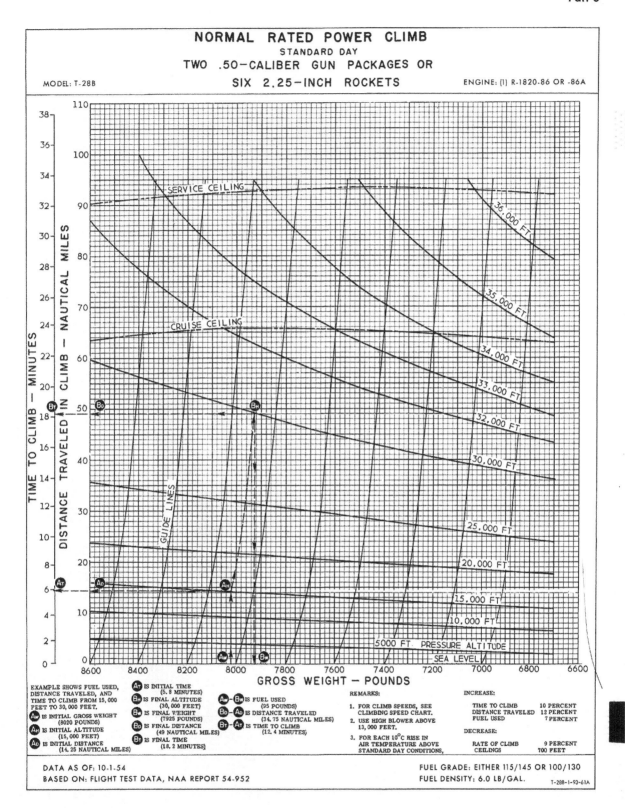

NORMAL RATED POWER CLIMB
STANDARD DAY
TWO .50—CALIBER GUN PACKAGES OR
SIX 2.25—INCH ROCKETS

MODEL: T-28B

ENGINE: (1) R-1820-86 OR -86A

Figure 11-18

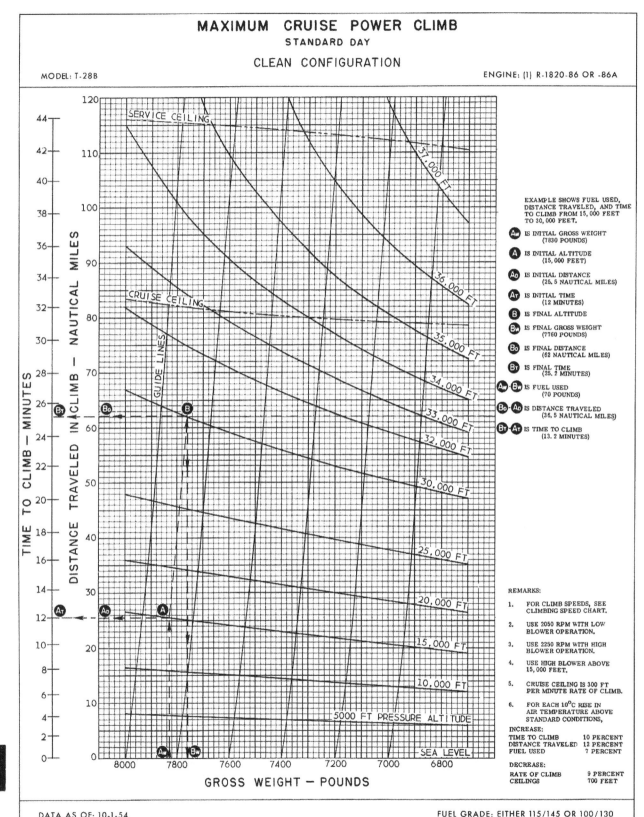

MAXIMUM CRUISE POWER CLIMB
STANDARD DAY
CLEAN CONFIGURATION

MODEL: T-28B

ENGINE: (1) R-1820-86 OR -86A

EXAMPLE SHOWS FUEL USED, DISTANCE TRAVELED, AND TIME TO CLIMB FROM 15,000 FEET TO 30,000 FEET.

Aw IS INITIAL GROSS WEIGHT (7830 POUNDS)

A IS INITIAL ALTITUDE (15,000 FEET)

AD IS INITIAL DISTANCE (25.5 NAUTICAL MILES)

AT IS INITIAL TIME (12 MINUTES)

B IS FINAL ALTITUDE

Bw IS FINAL GROSS WEIGHT (7760 POUNDS)

BD IS FINAL DISTANCE (62 NAUTICAL MILES)

BT IS FINAL TIME (25.2 MINUTES)

Aw-Bw IS FUEL USED (70 POUNDS)

BD-AD IS DISTANCE TRAVELED (36.5 NAUTICAL MILES)

BT-AT IS TIME TO CLIMB (13.2 MINUTES)

REMARKS:

1. FOR CLIMB SPEEDS, SEE CLIMBING SPEED CHART.

2. USE 2050 RPM WITH LOW BLOWER OPERATION.

3. USE 2250 RPM WITH HIGH BLOWER OPERATION.

4. USE HIGH BLOWER ABOVE 15,000 FEET.

5. CRUISE CEILING IS 300 FT PER MINUTE RATE OF CLIMB.

6. FOR EACH 10°C RISE IN AIR TEMPERATURE ABOVE STANDARD CONDITIONS,

INCREASE:

TIME TO CLIMB	10 PERCENT
DISTANCE TRAVELED	12 PERCENT
FUEL USED	7 PERCENT

DECREASE:

RATE OF CLIMB	9 PERCENT
CEILINGS	700 FEET

DATA AS OF: 10-1-54
BASED ON: FLIGHT TEST DATA , NAA REPORT 54-952

FUEL GRADE: EITHER 115/145 OR 100/130
FUEL DENSITY: 6.0 LB/GAL.

T-28B-1-93-40A

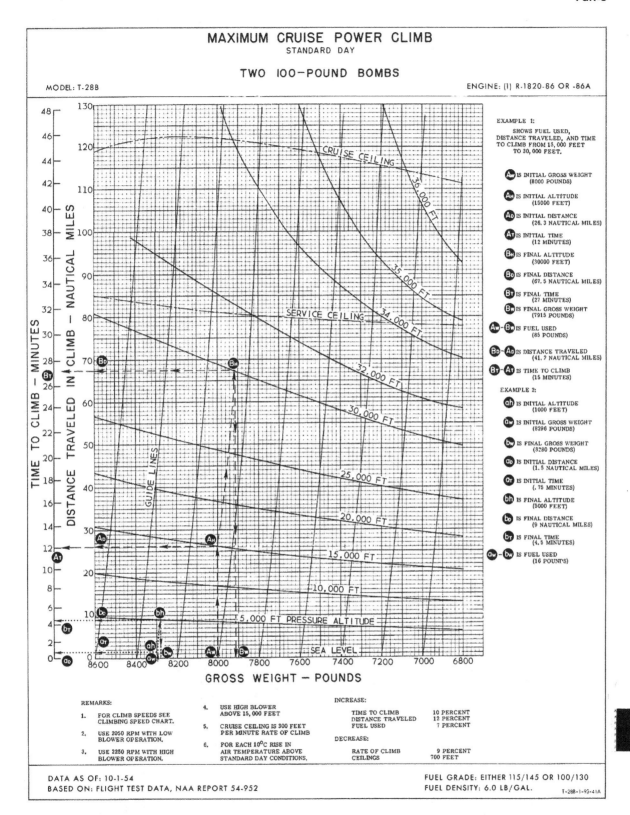

MAXIMUM CRUISE POWER CLIMB
STANDARD DAY

TWO 100-POUND BOMBS

MODEL: T-28B

ENGINE: (1) R-1820-86 OR -86A

EXAMPLE 1:

SHOWS FUEL USED, DISTANCE TRAVELED, AND TIME TO CLIMB FROM 15,000 FEET TO 30,000 FEET.

A_W IS INITIAL GROSS WEIGHT (8000 POUNDS)

A_H IS INITIAL ALTITUDE (15000 FEET)

A_D IS INITIAL DISTANCE (26.3 NAUTICAL MILES)

A_T IS INITIAL TIME (12 MINUTES)

B_H IS FINAL ALTITUDE (30000 FEET)

B_D IS FINAL DISTANCE (67.5 NAUTICAL MILES)

B_T IS FINAL TIME (27 MINUTES)

B_W IS FINAL GROSS WEIGHT (7915 POUNDS)

$A_W - B_W$ IS FUEL USED (85 POUNDS)

$B_D - A_D$ IS DISTANCE TRAVELED (41.2 NAUTICAL MILES)

$B_T - A_T$ IS TIME TO CLIMB (15 MINUTES)

EXAMPLE 2:

a_h IS INITIAL ALTITUDE (1000 FEET)

a_w IS INITIAL GROSS WEIGHT (8296 POUNDS)

b_w IS FINAL GROSS WEIGHT (8280 POUNDS)

a_D IS INITIAL DISTANCE (1.5 NAUTICAL MILES)

a_T IS INITIAL TIME (.75 MINUTES)

b_h IS FINAL ALTITUDE (5000 FEET)

b_D IS FINAL DISTANCE (9 NAUTICAL MILES)

b_T IS FINAL TIME (4.5 MINUTES)

$a_w - b_w$ IS FUEL USED (16 POUNDS)

REMARKS:

1. FOR CLIMB SPEEDS SEE CLIMBING SPEED CHART.

2. USE 2050 RPM WITH LOW BLOWER OPERATION.

3. USE 2250 RPM WITH HIGH BLOWER OPERATION.

4. USE HIGH BLOWER ABOVE 15,000 FEET

5. CRUISE CEILING IS 300 FEET PER MINUTE RATE OF CLIMB

6. FOR EACH 10°C RISE IN AIR TEMPERATURE ABOVE STANDARD DAY CONDITIONS,

INCREASE:

TIME TO CLIMB	10 PERCENT
DISTANCE TRAVELED	12 PERCENT
FUEL USED	7 PERCENT

DECREASE:

RATE OF CLIMB	9 PERCENT
CEILINGS	700 FEET

DATA AS OF: 10-1-54
BASED ON: FLIGHT TEST DATA, NAA REPORT 54-952

FUEL GRADE: EITHER 115/145 OR 100/130
FUEL DENSITY: 6.0 LB/GAL.

T-28B-1-93-41A

Figure 11-20

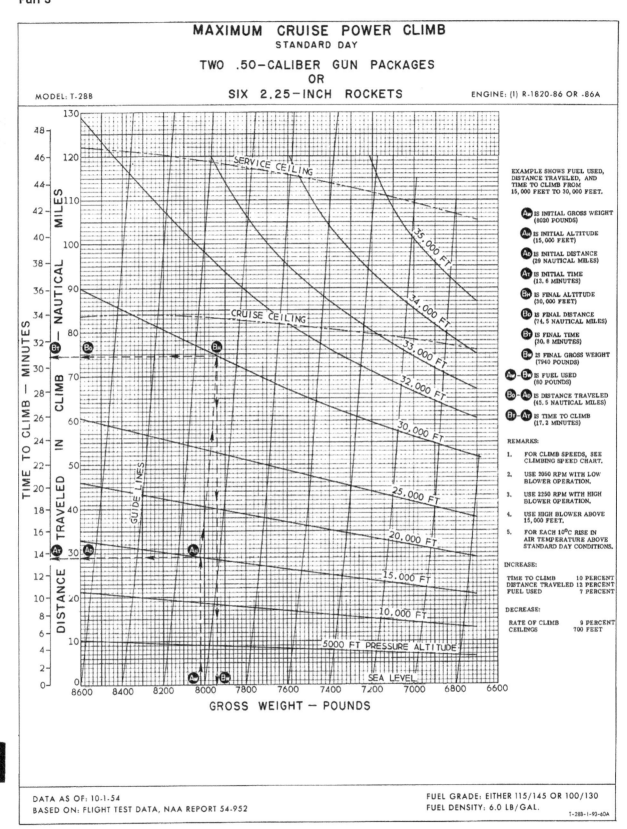

MAXIMUM CRUISE POWER CLIMB
STANDARD DAY
TWO .50-CALIBER GUN PACKAGES
OR
SIX 2.25-INCH ROCKETS

MODEL: T-28B

ENGINE: (1) R-1820-86 OR -86A

EXAMPLE SHOWS FUEL USED, DISTANCE TRAVELED, AND TIME TO CLIMB FROM 15,000 FEET TO 30,000 FEET.

Aw IS INITIAL GROSS WEIGHT (8020 POUNDS)

AH IS INITIAL ALTITUDE (15,000 FEET)

AD IS INITIAL DISTANCE (29 NAUTICAL MILES)

AT IS INITIAL TIME (13.6 MINUTES)

BH IS FINAL ALTITUDE (30,000 FEET)

BD IS FINAL DISTANCE (74.5 NAUTICAL MILES)

BT IS FINAL TIME (30.8 MINUTES)

BW IS FINAL GROSS WEIGHT (7940 POUNDS)

Aw-Bw IS FUEL USED (80 POUNDS)

BD-AD IS DISTANCE TRAVELED (45.5 NAUTICAL MILES)

BT-AT IS TIME TO CLIMB (17.2 MINUTES)

REMARKS:

1. FOR CLIMB SPEEDS, SEE CLIMBING SPEED CHART.

2. USE 2050 RPM WITH LOW BLOWER OPERATION.

3. USE 2250 RPM WITH HIGH BLOWER OPERATION.

4. USE HIGH BLOWER ABOVE 15,000 FEET.

5. FOR EACH 10°C RISE IN AIR TEMPERATURE ABOVE STANDARD DAY CONDITIONS.

INCREASE:

TIME TO CLIMB	10 PERCENT
DISTANCE TRAVELED	12 PERCENT
FUEL USED	7 PERCENT

DECREASE:

RATE OF CLIMB	9 PERCENT
CEILINGS	700 FEET

DATA AS OF: 10-1-54
BASED ON: FLIGHT TEST DATA, NAA REPORT 54-952

FUEL GRADE: EITHER 115/145 OR 100/130
FUEL DENSITY: 6.0 LB/GAL.

T-28-1-93-60A

Figure 11-21

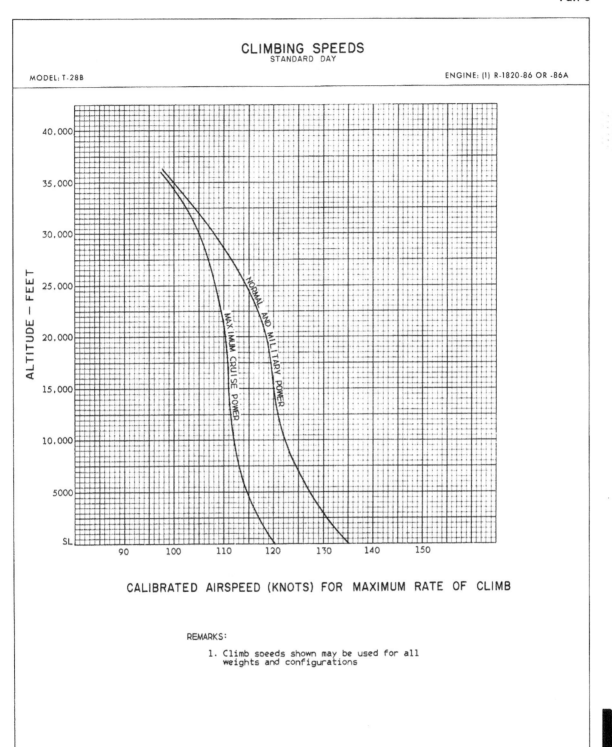

CLIMBING SPEEDS
STANDARD DAY

MODEL: T-28B

ENGINE: (1) R-1820-86 OR -86A

CALIBRATED AIRSPEED (KNOTS) FOR MAXIMUM RATE OF CLIMB

REMARKS:

1. Climb speeds shown may be used for all
weights and configurations

BASED ON: FLIGHT TEST DATA, NAA REPORT 54-952
DATA AS OF : 10-1-54

FUEL GRADE: EITHER 115/145 OR 100/130
FUEL DENSITY: 6.0 LB/GAL.

T-28B-1-93-46A

Figure 11-22

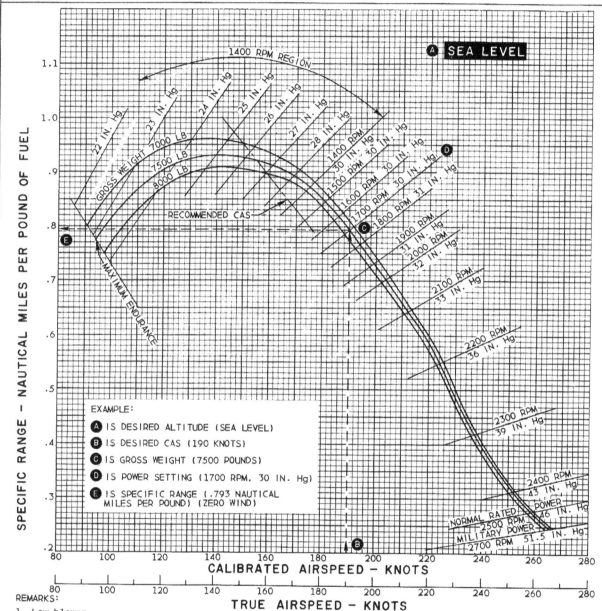

NAUTICAL MILES PER POUND OF FUEL
STANDARD DAY
CLEAN CONFIGURATION

MODEL: T-28B

ENGINE: (1) R-1820-86 OR -86A

Ⓐ SEA LEVEL

1400 RPM REGION

22 IN. Hg
23 IN. Hg
24 IN. Hg
25 IN. Hg
26 IN. Hg
27 IN. Hg
28 IN. Hg

GROSS WEIGHT 7000 LB
7500 LB
8000 LB

1400 RPM
1500 RPM 30 IN. Hg
1600 RPM 30 IN. Hg
1700 RPM 30 IN. Hg
1800 RPM 31 IN. Hg

30 IN. Hg
30 IN. Hg

Ⓓ

RECOMMENDED CAS

1900 RPM
31 IN. Hg
2000 RPM
32 IN. Hg

Ⓒ

2100 RPM
33 IN. Hg

MAXIMUM ENDURANCE

Ⓔ

2200 RPM
36 IN. Hg

2300 RPM
39 IN. Hg

EXAMPLE:

Ⓐ IS DESIRED ALTITUDE (SEA LEVEL)
Ⓑ IS DESIRED CAS (190 KNOTS)
Ⓒ IS GROSS WEIGHT (7500 POUNDS)
Ⓓ IS POWER SETTING (1700 RPM, 30 IN. Hg)
Ⓔ IS SPECIFIC RANGE (.793 NAUTICAL MILES PER POUND) (ZERO WIND)

2400 RPM
43 IN. Hg

NORMAL RATED POWER 2500 RPM 46 IN. Hg
MILITARY POWER
2700 RPM 51.5 IN. Hg

Ⓑ

SPECIFIC RANGE – NAUTICAL MILES PER POUND OF FUEL

1.1
1.0
.9
.8
.7
.6
.5
.4
.3
.2

CALIBRATED AIRSPEED – KNOTS
80 100 120 140 160 180 200 220 240 260 280

TRUE AIRSPEED – KNOTS
80 100 120 140 160 180 200 220 240 260 280

REMARKS:

1. Low blower.

2. For each 10°C above Standard Day conditions, hold Cas constant, increase true airspeed 1.8% and:

   • Part-throttle conditions-
      a. Hold rpm constant.
      b. Increase manifold pressure 1/2 IN. Hg.
      c. Do not change nautical miles per pound of fuel.

   • Full-throttle conditions-
      a. Increase rpm 1.5%.
      b. Decrease nautical miles per pound of fuel by one percent.

3. For each 10°C below Standard Day conditions, apply corrections in Remark 2, in the opposite direction.

DATA AS OF : 10-1-54
BASED ON: FLIGHT TEST DATA , NAA REPORT 54-952

FUEL GRADE: EITHER 115/145 OR 100/130
FUEL DENSITY: 6.0 LB/GAL.

T-28B-1-93-28A

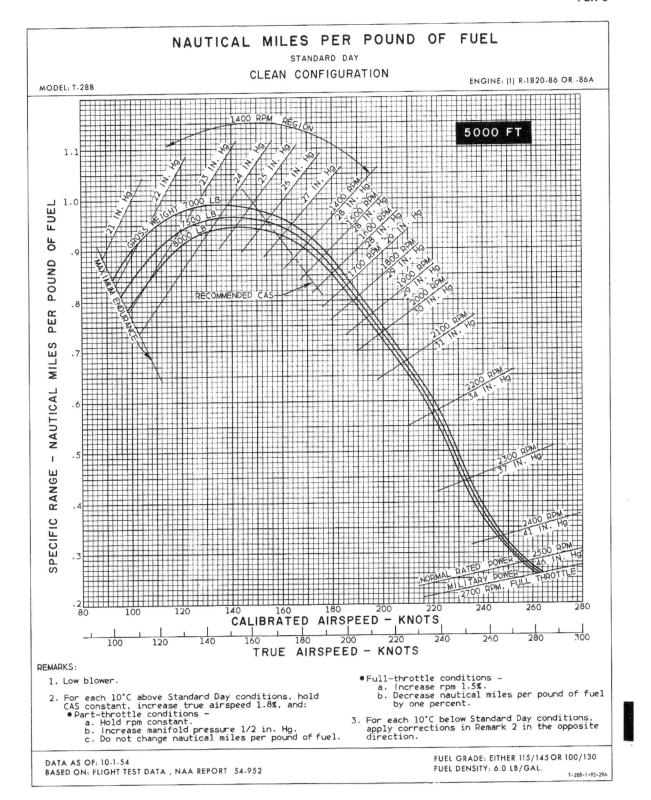

NAUTICAL MILES PER POUND OF FUEL
STANDARD DAY
CLEAN CONFIGURATION

MODEL: T-28B

ENGINE: (1) R-1820-86 OR -86A

5000 FT

REMARKS:

1. Low blower.

2. For each 10°C above Standard Day conditions, hold CAS constant, increase true airspeed 1.8%, and:
   - Part-throttle conditions –
     a. Hold rpm constant.
     b. Increase manifold pressure 1/2 in. Hg.
     c. Do not change nautical miles per pound of fuel.

   - Full-throttle conditions –
     a. Increase rpm 1.5%.
     b. Decrease nautical miles per pound of fuel by one percent.

3. For each 10°C below Standard Day conditions, apply corrections in Remark 2 in the opposite direction.

DATA AS OF: 10-1-54
BASED ON: FLIGHT TEST DATA , NAA REPORT 54-952

FUEL GRADE: EITHER 115/145 OR 100/130
FUEL DENSITY: 6.0 LB/GAL.

T-28B-1-93-29A

Figure 11-24

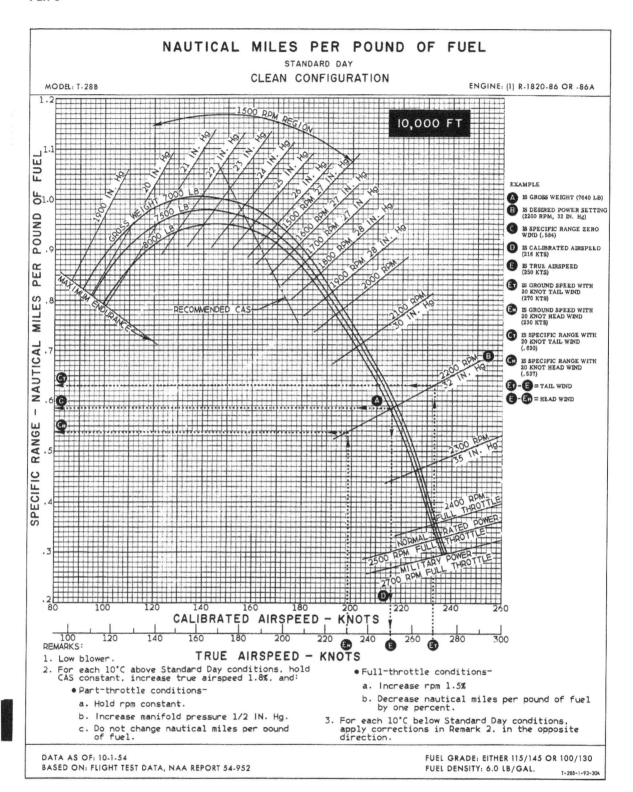

NAUTICAL MILES PER POUND OF FUEL
STANDARD DAY
CLEAN CONFIGURATION

MODEL: T-28B   ENGINE: (1) R-1820-86 OR -86A

10,000 FT

EXAMPLE

A IS GROSS WEIGHT (7640 LB)

B IS DESIRED POWER SETTING (2200 RPM, 32 IN. Hg)

C IS SPECIFIC RANGE ZERO WIND (.584)

D IS CALIBRATED AIRSPEED (216 KTS)

E IS TRUE AIRSPEED (250 KTS)

E_T IS GROUND SPEED WITH 20 KNOT TAIL WIND (270 KTS)

E_H IS GROUND SPEED WITH 20 KNOT HEAD WIND (230 KTS)

C_T IS SPECIFIC RANGE WITH 20 KNOT TAIL WIND (.630)

C_H IS SPECIFIC RANGE WITH 20 KNOT HEAD WIND (.537)

E_T − E = TAIL WIND

E − E_H = HEAD WIND

REMARKS:
1. Low blower.
2. For each 10°C above Standard Day conditions, hold CAS constant, increase true airspeed 1.8%, and:
   - Part-throttle conditions—
     a. Hold rpm constant.
     b. Increase manifold pressure 1/2 IN. Hg.
     c. Do not change nautical miles per pound of fuel.
   - Full-throttle conditions—
     a. Increase rpm 1.5%.
     b. Decrease nautical miles per pound of fuel by one percent.
3. For each 10°C below Standard Day conditions, apply corrections in Remark 2, in the opposite direction.

DATA AS OF: 10-1-54
BASED ON: FLIGHT TEST DATA, NAA REPORT 54-952

FUEL GRADE: EITHER 115/145 OR 100/130
FUEL DENSITY: 6.0 LB/GAL.

T-28B-1-93-30A

Figure 11-25

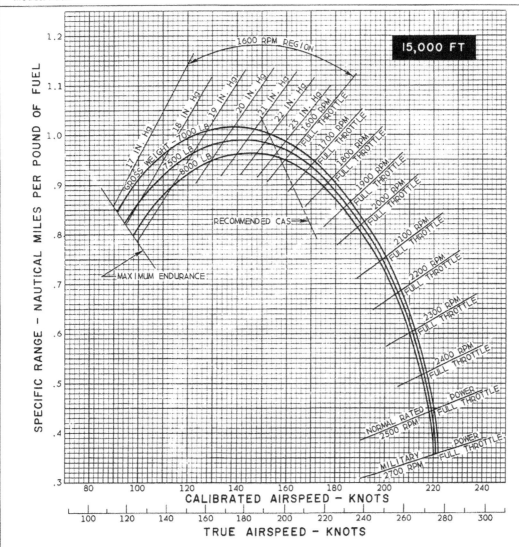

NAUTICAL MILES PER POUND OF FUEL
STANDARD DAY
CLEAN CONFIGURATION

MODEL: T-28B

ENGINE: (1) R-1820-86 OR -86A

REMARKS:

1. Low blower

2. For each 10°C above Standard Day conditions, hold CAS constant, increase true airspeed 1.8%, and:
   ● Part-throttle conditions –
      a. Hold rpm constant.
      b. Increase manifold pressure 1/2 in. Hg.
      c. Do not change nautical miles per pound of fuel.

   ● Full-throttle conditions –
      a. Increase rpm 1.5%.
      b. Decrease nautical miles per pound of fuel by one percent.

3. For each 10°C below Standard Day conditions, apply corrections in Remark 2 in the opposite direction.

DATA AS OF: 10-1-54
BASED ON: FLIGHT TEST DATA, NAA REPORT 54-952

FUEL GRADE: EITHER 115/145 OR 100/130
FUEL DENSITY: 6.0 LB/GAL.

T-28B-1-93-31A

Figure 11-26

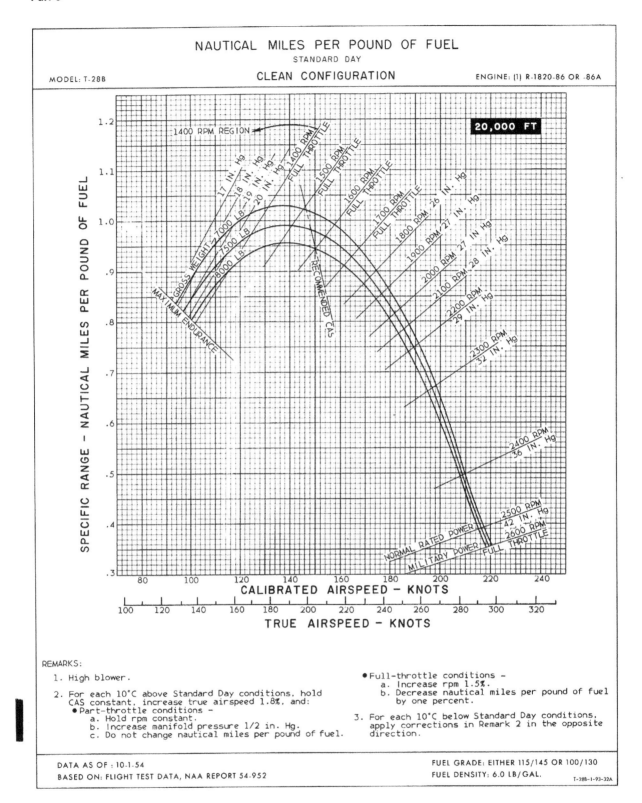

NAUTICAL MILES PER POUND OF FUEL
STANDARD DAY
CLEAN CONFIGURATION

MODEL: T-28B

ENGINE: (1) R-1820-86 OR -86A

20,000 FT

REMARKS:

1. High blower.

2. For each 10°C above Standard Day conditions, hold CAS constant, increase true airspeed 1.8%, and:
   • Part-throttle conditions –
      a. Hold rpm constant.
      b. Increase manifold pressure 1/2 in. Hg.
      c. Do not change nautical miles per pound of fuel.

   • Full-throttle conditions –
      a. Increase rpm 1.5%.
      b. Decrease nautical miles per pound of fuel by one percent.

3. For each 10°C below Standard Day conditions, apply corrections in Remark 2 in the opposite direction.

DATA AS OF : 10-1-54
BASED ON: FLIGHT TEST DATA, NAA REPORT 54-952

FUEL GRADE: EITHER 115/145 OR 100/130
FUEL DENSITY: 6.0 LB/GAL.

T-28B-1-93-32A

Figure 11-27

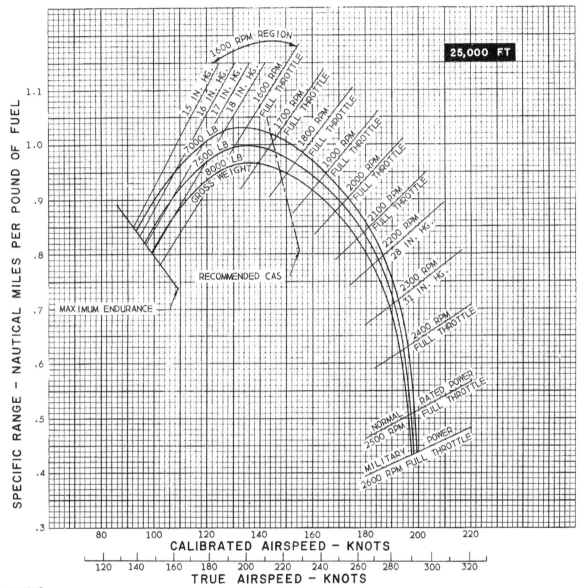

NAUTICAL MILES PER POUND OF FUEL
STANDARD DAY
CLEAN CONFIGURATION

MODEL: T-28B

ENGINE: (1) R-1820-86 OR -86A

25,000 FT

Chart labels: 1600 RPM REGION; 15 IN. HG.; 16 IN. HG.; 17 IN. HG.; 18 IN. HG.; 1600 RPM FULL THROTTLE; 1700 RPM FULL THROTTLE; 1800 RPM FULL THROTTLE; 1900 RPM FULL THROTTLE; 2000 RPM FULL THROTTLE; 2100 RPM FULL THROTTLE; 2200 RPM; 28 IN. HG.; 2300 RPM; 31 IN. HG.; 2400 RPM FULL THROTTLE; NORMAL RATED POWER 2500 RPM FULL THROTTLE; MILITARY POWER 2600 RPM FULL THROTTLE; 7000 LB; 7500 LB; 8000 LB GROSS WEIGHT; RECOMMENDED CAS; MAXIMUM ENDURANCE

Y-axis: SPECIFIC RANGE – NAUTICAL MILES PER POUND OF FUEL

X-axis: CALIBRATED AIRSPEED – KNOTS (80, 100, 120, 140, 160, 180, 200, 220)

TRUE AIRSPEED – KNOTS (120, 140, 160, 180, 200, 220, 240, 260, 280, 300, 320)

REMARKS:

1. High blower.

2. For each 10°C above Standard Day conditions, hold
   CAS constant, increase true airspeed 1.8%, and:
   • Part-throttle conditions –
     a. Hold rpm constant.
     b. Increase manifold pressure 1/2 in. Hg.
     c. Do not change nautical miles per pound of fuel.

• Full-throttle conditions –
   a. Increase rpm 1.5%.
   b. Decrease nautical miles per pound of fuel
      by one percent.

3. For each 10°C below Standard Day conditions,
   apply corrections in Remark 2 in the opposite
   direction.

DATA AS OF: 10-1-54
BASED ON: FLIGHT TEST DATA, NAA REPORT 54-952

FUEL GRADE: EITHER 115/145 OR 100/130
FUEL DENSITY: 6.0 LB/GAL.

T-28B-1-93-33A

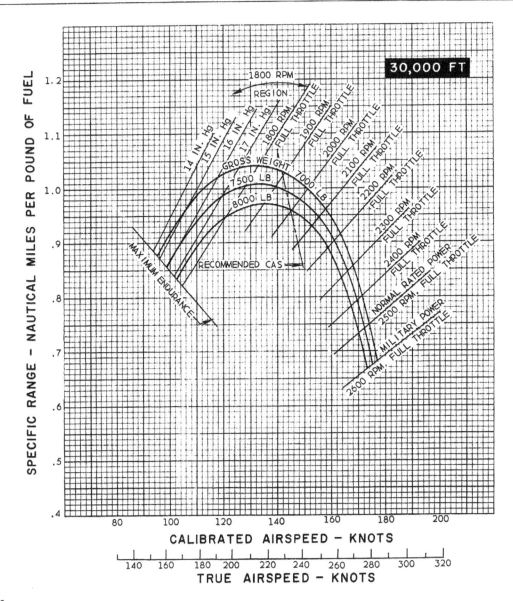

NAUTICAL MILES PER POUND OF FUEL
STANDARD DAY
CLEAN CONFIGURATION

MODEL: T-28B

ENGINE: (1) R-1820-86 OR -86A

30,000 FT

SPECIFIC RANGE — NAUTICAL MILES PER POUND OF FUEL

CALIBRATED AIRSPEED — KNOTS

TRUE AIRSPEED — KNOTS

REMARKS:

1. High blower.

2. For each 10°C above Standard Day conditions, hold
   CAS constant, increase true airspeed 1.8%, and:
   • Part-throttle conditions –
     a. Hold rpm constant.
     b. Increase manifold pressure 1/2 in. Hg.
     c. Do not change nautical miles per pound of fuel.

• Full-throttle conditions –
   a. Increase rpm 1.5%.
   b. Decrease nautical miles per pound of fuel
      by one percent.

3. For each 10°C below Standard Day conditions,
   apply corrections in Remark 2 in the opposite
   direction.

DATA AS OF : 10-1-54

BASED ON: FLIGHT TEST DATA, NAA REPORT 54-952

FUEL GRADE: EITHER 115/145 OR 100/130

FUEL DENSITY: 6.0 LB/GAL.

T-28B-1-93-34A

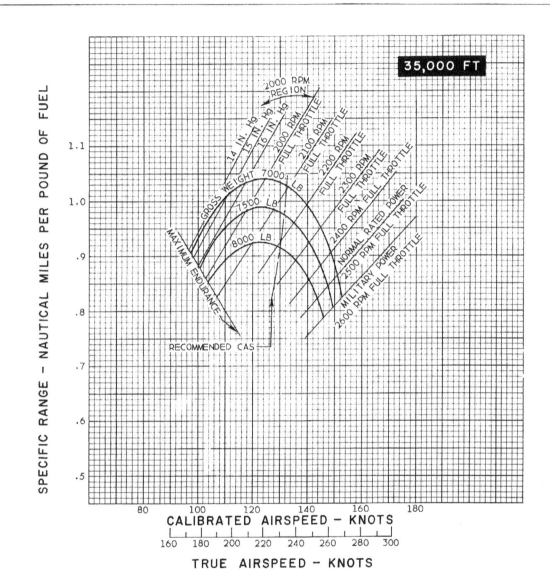

NAUTICAL MILES PER POUND OF FUEL
STANDARD DAY

CLEAN CONFIGURATION

MODEL: T-28B

ENGINE: (1) R-1820-86 OR -86A

35,000 FT

T-28B-1-93-35A

REMARKS:

1. High blower.

2. For each 10°C above Standard Day conditions, hold CAS constant, increase true airspeed 1.8%, and:
   - Part-throttle conditions –
     a. Hold rpm constant.
     b. Increase manifold pressure 1/2 in. Hg.
     c. Do not change nautical miles per pound of fuel.

   - Full-throttle conditions –
     a. Increase rpm 1.5%.
     b. Decrease nautical miles per pound of fuel by one percent.

3. For each 10°C below Standard Day conditions, apply corrections in Remark 2 in the opposite direction.

DATA AS OF : 10-1-54
BASED ON: FLIGHT TEST DATA, NAA REPORT 54-952

FUEL GRADE: EITHER 115/145 OR 100/130
FUEL DENSITY: 6.0 LB/GAL.

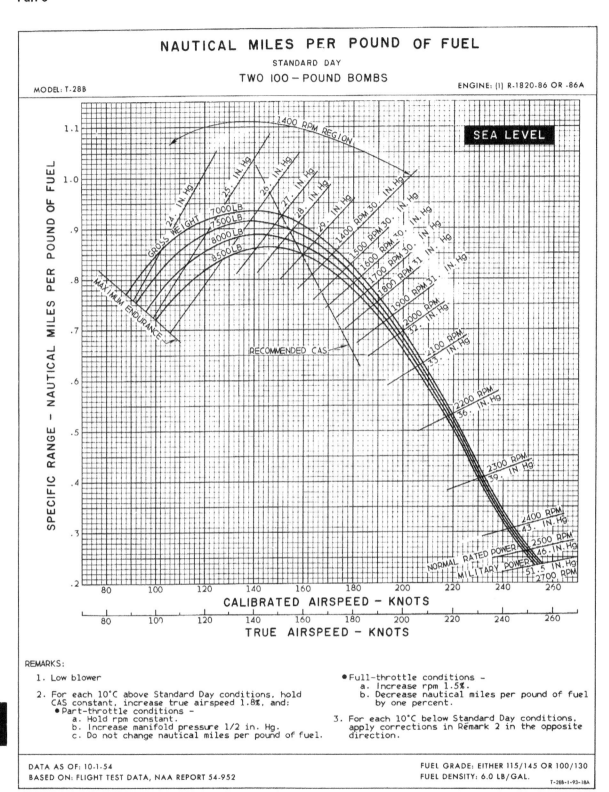

NAUTICAL MILES PER POUND OF FUEL
STANDARD DAY
TWO 100 – POUND BOMBS

MODEL: T-28B

ENGINE: (1) R-1820-86 OR -86A

SEA LEVEL

REMARKS:

1. Low blower

2. For each 10°C above Standard Day conditions, hold CAS constant, increase true airspeed 1.8%, and:
   • Part-throttle conditions –
      a. Hold rpm constant.
      b. Increase manifold pressure 1/2 in. Hg.
      c. Do not change nautical miles per pound of fuel.

• Full-throttle conditions –
   a. Increase rpm 1.5%.
   b. Decrease nautical miles per pound of fuel by one percent.

3. For each 10°C below Standard Day conditions, apply corrections in Remark 2 in the opposite direction.

DATA AS OF: 10-1-54
BASED ON: FLIGHT TEST DATA, NAA REPORT 54-952

FUEL GRADE: EITHER 115/145 OR 100/130
FUEL DENSITY: 6.0 LB/GAL.

T-28B-1-93-18A

Figure 11-31

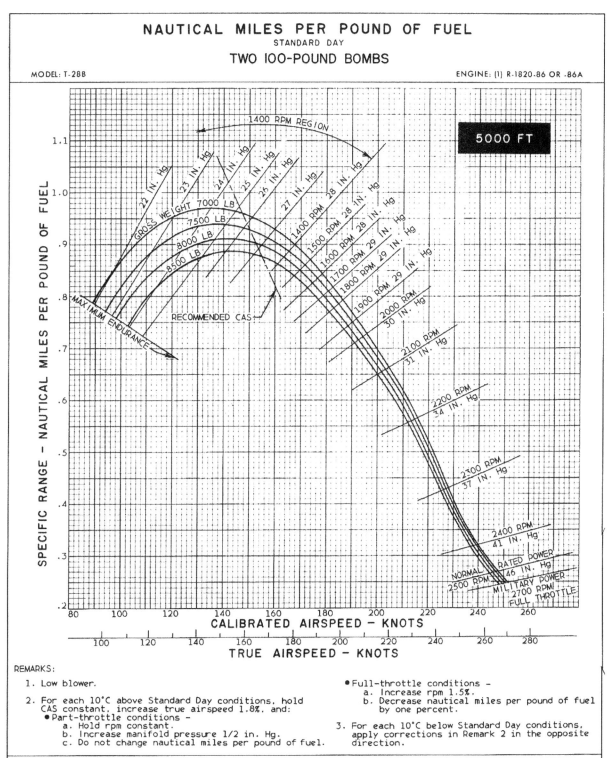

NAUTICAL MILES PER POUND OF FUEL
STANDARD DAY
TWO 100-POUND BOMBS

MODEL: T-28B

ENGINE: (1) R-1820-86 OR -86A

5000 FT

REMARKS:

1. Low blower.

2. For each 10°C above Standard Day conditions, hold CAS constant, increase true airspeed 1.8%, and:
   • Part-throttle conditions –
   a. Hold rpm constant.
   b. Increase manifold pressure 1/2 in. Hg.
   c. Do not change nautical miles per pound of fuel.

• Full-throttle conditions –
   a. Increase rpm 1.5%.
   b. Decrease nautical miles per pound of fuel by one percent.

3. For each 10°C below Standard Day conditions, apply corrections in Remark 2 in the opposite direction.

DATA AS OF: 10-1-54
BASED ON: FLIGHT TEST DATA, NAA REPORT 54-952

FUEL GRADE: EITHER 115/145 OR 100/130
FUEL DENSITY: 6.0 LB/GAL.

T-28B-1-93-19A

Figure 11-32

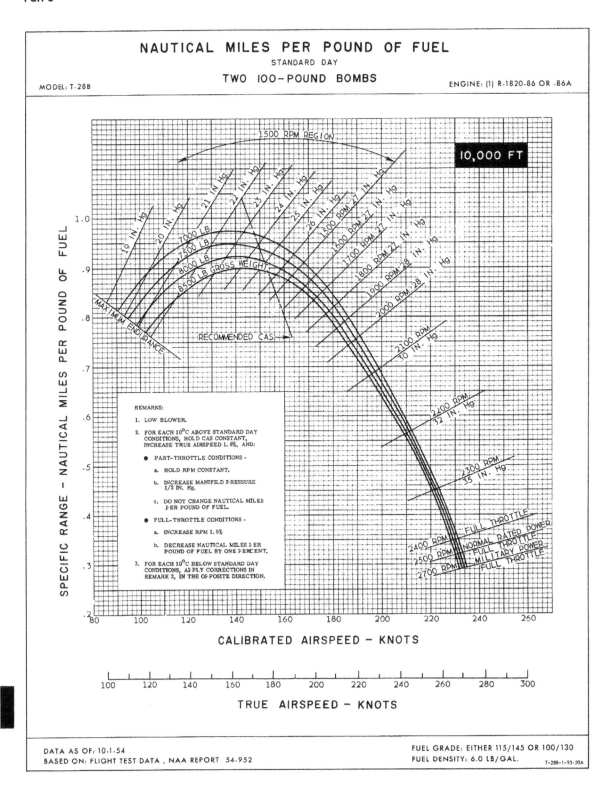

Figure 11-33

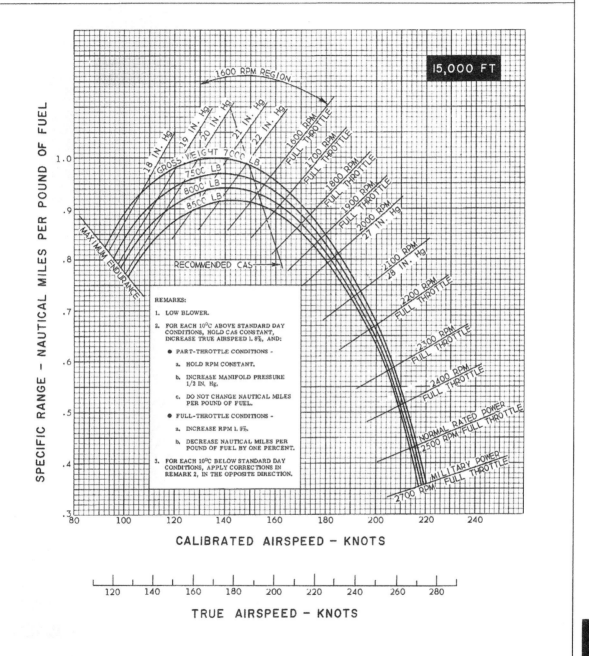

Figure 11-34

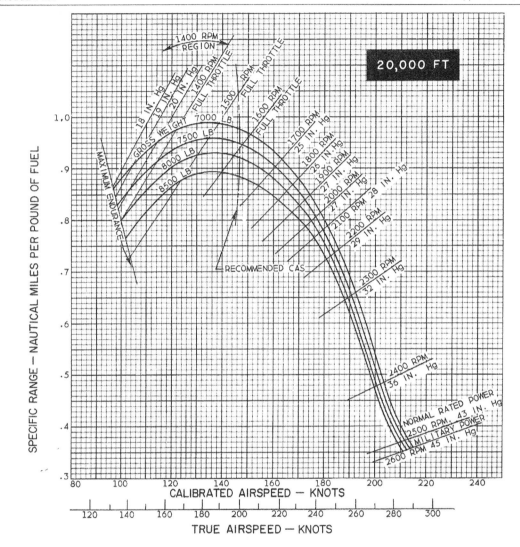

NAUTICAL MILES PER POUND OF FUEL
STANDARD DAY
TWO 100-POUND BOMBS

MODEL: T-28B

ENGINE: (1) R-1820-86 OR -86A

20,000 FT

REMARKS:

1. High blower.

2. For each 10°C above Standard Day conditions, hold CAS constant, increase true airspeed 1.8%, and:
   • Part-throttle conditions –
      a. Hold rpm constant.
      b. Increase manifold pressure 1/2 in. Hg.
      c. Do not change nautical miles per pound of fuel.

• Full-throttle conditions –
   a. Increase rpm 1.5%.
   b. Decrease nautical miles per pound of fuel by one percent.

3. For each 10°C below Standard Day conditions, apply corrections in Remark 2 in the opposite direction.

DATA AS OF : 10-1-54
BASED ON: FLIGHT TEST DATA, NAA REPORT 54-952

FUEL GRADE: EITHER 115/145 OR 100/130
FUEL DENSITY: 6.0 LB/GAL.

T-28B-1-93-22A

Figure 11-35

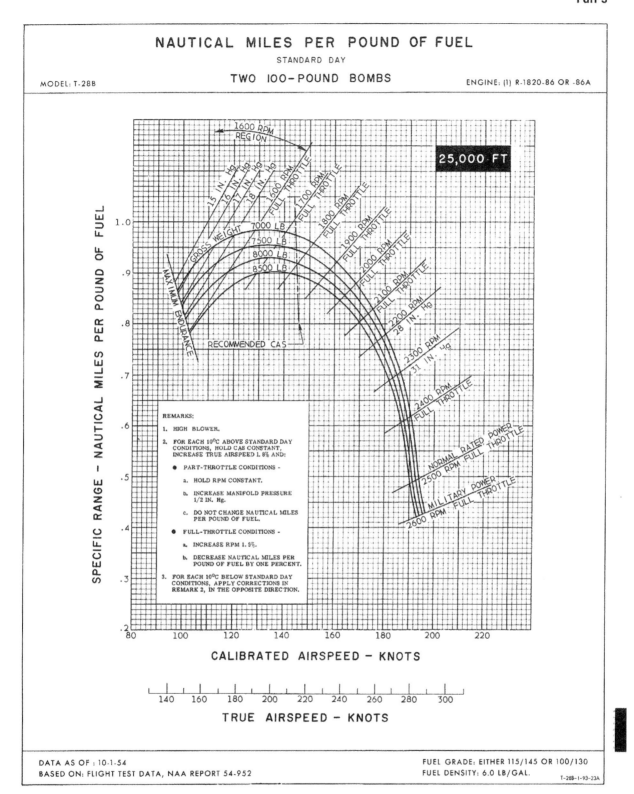

NAUTICAL MILES PER POUND OF FUEL

STANDARD DAY

TWO 100-POUND BOMBS

MODEL: T-28B

ENGINE: (1) R-1820-86 OR -86A

25,000 FT

REMARKS:

1. HIGH BLOWER.

2. FOR EACH 10°C ABOVE STANDARD DAY CONDITIONS, HOLD CAS CONSTANT, INCREASE TRUE AIRSPEED 1.8% AND:
   - PART-THROTTLE CONDITIONS -
     a. HOLD RPM CONSTANT.
     b. INCREASE MANIFOLD PRESSURE 1/2 IN. Hg.
     c. DO NOT CHANGE NAUTICAL MILES PER POUND OF FUEL.
   - FULL-THROTTLE CONDITIONS -
     a. INCREASE RPM 1.5%.
     b. DECREASE NAUTICAL MILES PER POUND OF FUEL BY ONE PERCENT.

3. FOR EACH 10°C BELOW STANDARD DAY CONDITIONS, APPLY CORRECTIONS IN REMARK 2, IN THE OPPOSITE DIRECTION.

DATA AS OF : 10-1-54
BASED ON: FLIGHT TEST DATA, NAA REPORT 54-952

FUEL GRADE: EITHER 115/145 OR 100/130
FUEL DENSITY: 6.0 LB/GAL.

T-28B-1-93-23A

Figure 11-36

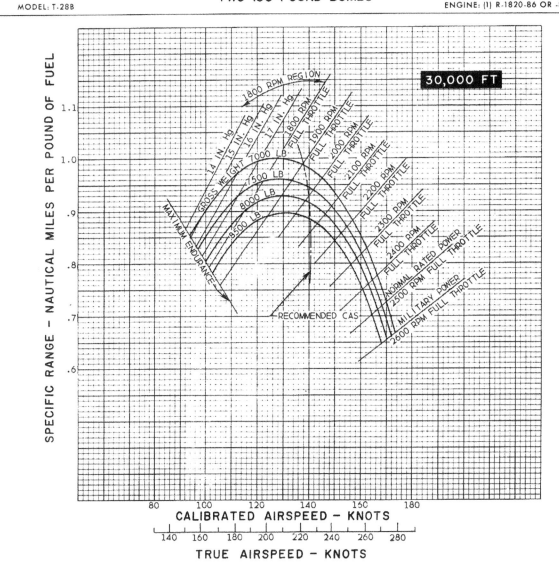

NAUTICAL MILES PER POUND OF FUEL
STANDARD DAY
TWO 100-POUND BOMBS

MODEL: T-28B

ENGINE: (1) R-1820-86 OR -86A

30,000 FT

REMARKS:

1. High blower.

2. For each 10°C above Standard Day conditions, hold CAS constant, increase true airspeed 1.8%, and:

   • Part-throttle conditions -
   a. Hold rpm constant.
   b. Increase manifold pressure 1/2 in. Hg.
   c. Do not change nautical miles per pound of fuel.

• Full-throttle conditions -
a. Increase rpm 1.5%.
b. Decrease nautical miles per pound of fuel by one percent.

3. For each 10°C below Standard Day conditions, apply corrections in Remark 2 in the opposite direction.

DATA AS OF: 10-1-54
BASED ON: FLIGHT TEST DATA, NAA REPORT 54-952

FUEL GRADE: EITHER 115/145 OR 100/130
FUEL DENSITY: 6.0 LB/GAL.

T-28B-1-93-24A

Figure 11-37

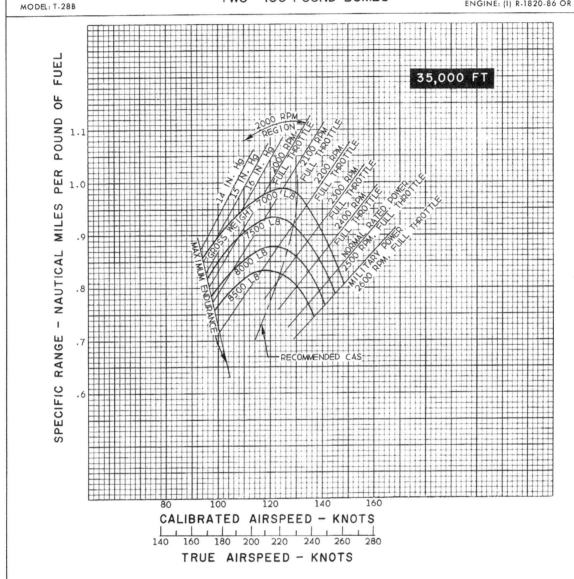

NAUTICAL MILES PER POUND OF FUEL
STANDARD DAY
TWO 100-POUND BOMBS

MODEL: T-28B

ENGINE: (1) R-1820-86 OR -86A

35,000 FT

REMARKS:

1. High blower.

2. For each 10°C above Standard Day conditions, hold CAS constant, increase true airspeed 1.8%, and:
   • Part-throttle conditions –
     a. Hold rpm constant.
     b. Increase manifold pressure 1/2 in. Hg.
     c. Do not change nautical miles per pound of fuel.

• Full-throttle conditions –
   a. Increase rpm 1.5%.
   b. Decrease nautical miles per pound of fuel by one percent.

3. For each 10°C below Standard Day conditions, apply corrections in Remark 2 in the opposite direction.

DATA AS OF: 10-1-54
BASED ON: FLIGHT TEST DATA , NAA REPORT 54-952

FUEL GRADE: EITHER 115/145 OR 100/130
FUEL DENSITY: 6.0 LB/GAL.

T-28B-1-93-25A

Figure 11-38

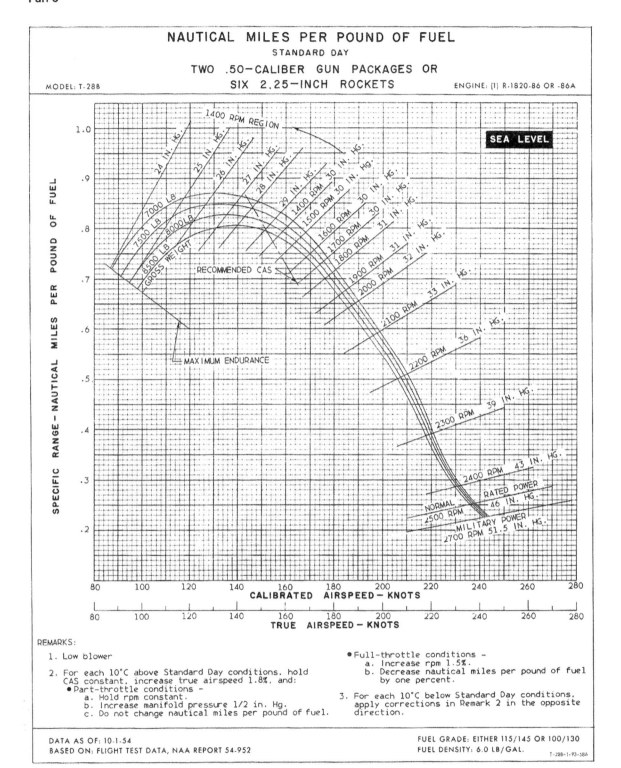

NAUTICAL MILES PER POUND OF FUEL
STANDARD DAY
TWO .50—CALIBER GUN PACKAGES OR
SIX 2.25—INCH ROCKETS

MODEL: T-28B

ENGINE: (1) R-1820-86 OR -86A

REMARKS:

1. Low blower

2. For each 10°C above Standard Day conditions, hold
CAS constant, increase true airspeed 1.8%, and:
 • Part-throttle conditions –
   a. Hold rpm constant.
   b. Increase manifold pressure 1/2 in. Hg.
   c. Do not change nautical miles per pound of fuel.

 • Full-throttle conditions –
   a. Increase rpm 1.5%.
   b. Decrease nautical miles per pound of fuel
      by one percent.

3. For each 10°C below Standard Day conditions,
apply corrections in Remark 2 in the opposite
direction.

DATA AS OF: 10-1-54
BASED ON: FLIGHT TEST DATA, NAA REPORT 54-952

FUEL GRADE: EITHER 115/145 OR 100/130
FUEL DENSITY: 6.0 LB/GAL.

T-28B-1-93-58A

Figure 11-39

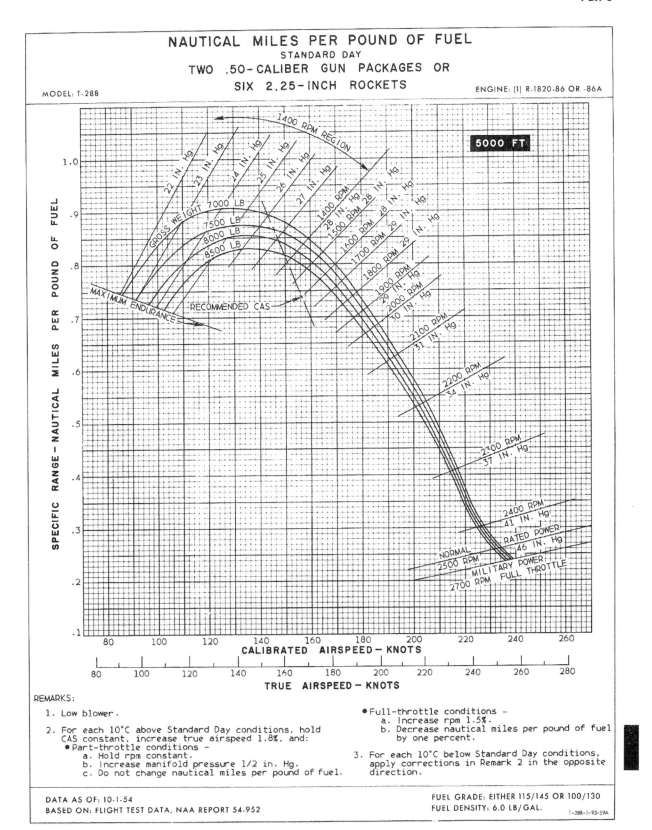

NAUTICAL MILES PER POUND OF FUEL
STANDARD DAY
TWO .50-CALIBER GUN PACKAGES OR
SIX 2.25-INCH ROCKETS

MODEL: T-28B

ENGINE: (1) R-1820-86 OR -86A

REMARKS:

1. Low blower.

2. For each 10°C above Standard Day conditions, hold CAS constant, increase true airspeed 1.8%, and:
   - Part-throttle conditions –
     a. Hold rpm constant.
     b. Increase manifold pressure 1/2 in. Hg.
     c. Do not change nautical miles per pound of fuel.

- Full-throttle conditions –
  a. Increase rpm 1.5%.
  b. Decrease nautical miles per pound of fuel by one percent.

3. For each 10°C below Standard Day conditions, apply corrections in Remark 2 in the opposite direction.

DATA AS OF: 10-1-54
BASED ON: FLIGHT TEST DATA, NAA REPORT 54-952

FUEL GRADE: EITHER 115/145 OR 100/130
FUEL DENSITY: 6.0 LB/GAL.

T-28B-1-93-59A

Figure 11-40

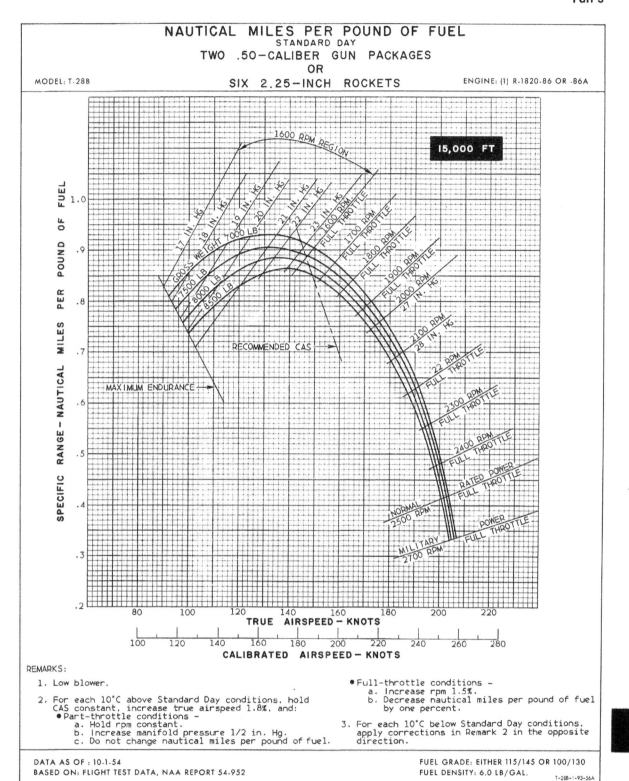

NAUTICAL MILES PER POUND OF FUEL
STANDARD DAY
TWO .50–CALIBER GUN PACKAGES
OR
SIX 2.25–INCH ROCKETS

MODEL: T-28B

ENGINE: (1) R-1820-86 OR -86A

REMARKS:

1. Low blower.

2. For each 10°C above Standard Day conditions, hold CAS constant, increase true airspeed 1.8%, and:
   - Part-throttle conditions –
     a. Hold rpm constant.
     b. Increase manifold pressure 1/2 in. Hg.
     c. Do not change nautical miles per pound of fuel.

- Full-throttle conditions –
  a. Increase rpm 1.5%.
  b. Decrease nautical miles per pound of fuel by one percent.

3. For each 10°C below Standard Day conditions, apply corrections in Remark 2 in the opposite direction.

DATA AS OF : 10-1-54
BASED ON: FLIGHT TEST DATA, NAA REPORT 54-952

FUEL GRADE: EITHER 115/145 OR 100/130
FUEL DENSITY: 6.0 LB/GAL.

T-28B-1-93-56A

Figure 11-42

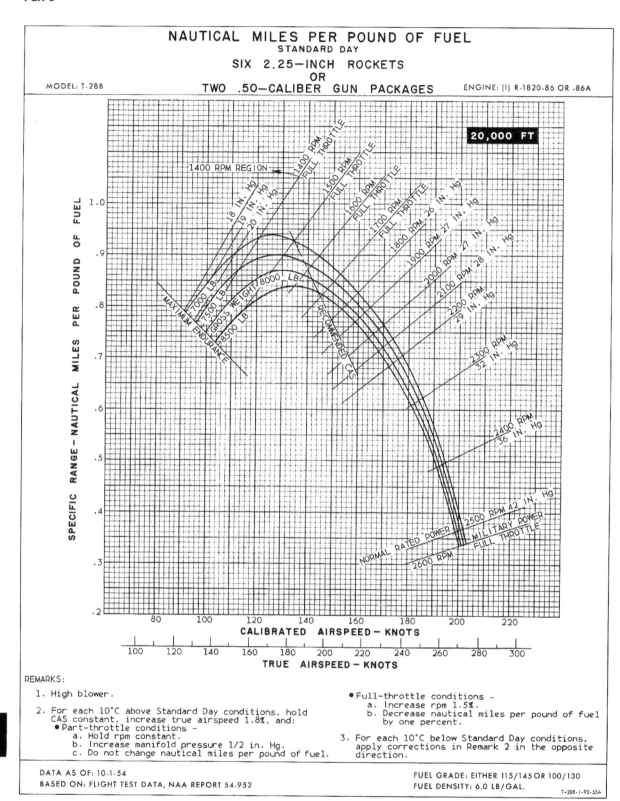

NAUTICAL MILES PER POUND OF FUEL
STANDARD DAY
SIX 2.25—INCH ROCKETS
OR
TWO .50—CALIBER GUN PACKAGES

MODEL: T-28B

ENGINE: (1) R-1820-86 OR .86A

REMARKS:

1. High blower.

2. For each 10°C above Standard Day conditions. hold
   CAS constant, increase true airspeed 1.8%, and:
   • Part-throttle conditions –
     a. Hold rpm constant.
     b. Increase manifold pressure 1/2 in. Hg.
     c. Do not change nautical miles per pound of fuel.

• Full-throttle conditions –
   a. Increase rpm 1.5%.
   b. Decrease nautical miles per pound of fuel
      by one percent.

3. For each 10°C below Standard Day conditions.
   apply corrections in Remark 2 in the opposite
   direction.

DATA AS OF: 10-1-54
BASED ON: FLIGHT TEST DATA, NAA REPORT 54-952

FUEL GRADE: EITHER 115/145 OR 100/130
FUEL DENSITY: 6.0 LB/GAL.

T-28B-1-93-55A

Figure 11-43

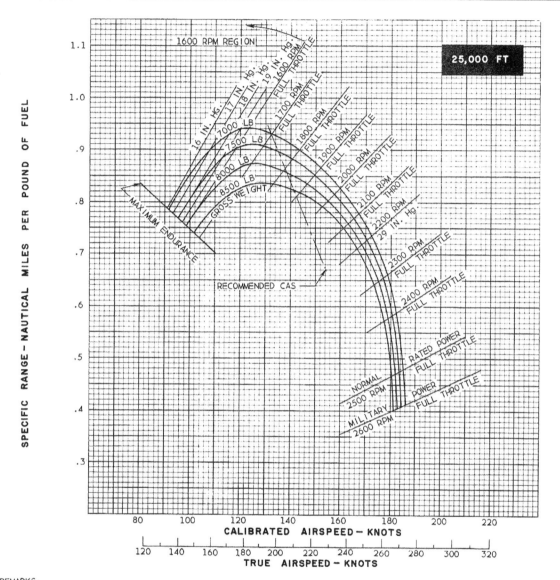

REMARKS:

1. High blower.

2. For each 10°C above Standard Day conditions, hold
   CAS constant, increase true airspeed 1.8%, and:
   • Part-throttle conditions –
     a. Hold rpm constant.
     b. Increase manifold pressure 1/2 in. Hg.
     c. Do not change nautical miles per pound of fuel.

• Full-throttle conditions –
   a. Increase rpm 1.5%.
   b. Decrease nautical miles per pound of fuel
      by one percent.

3. For each 10°C below Standard Day conditions,
   apply corrections in Remark 2 in the opposite
   direction.

BASED ON: FLIGHT TEST DATA, NAA REPORT 54-952
DATA AS OF: 10-1-54

FUEL GRADE: EITHER 115/145 OR 100/130
FUEL DENSITY: 6.0 LB/GAL.

T-28B-1-93-54A

Figure 11-44

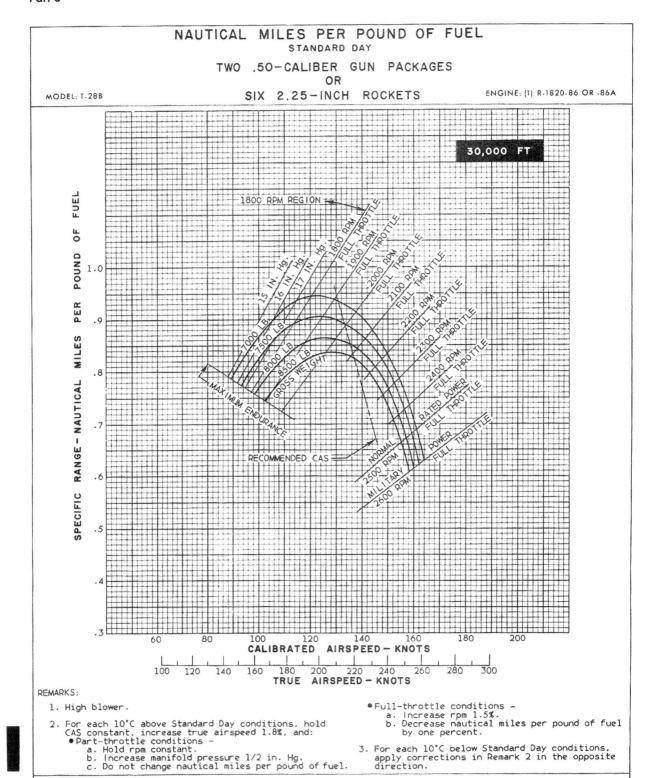

Figure 11-45

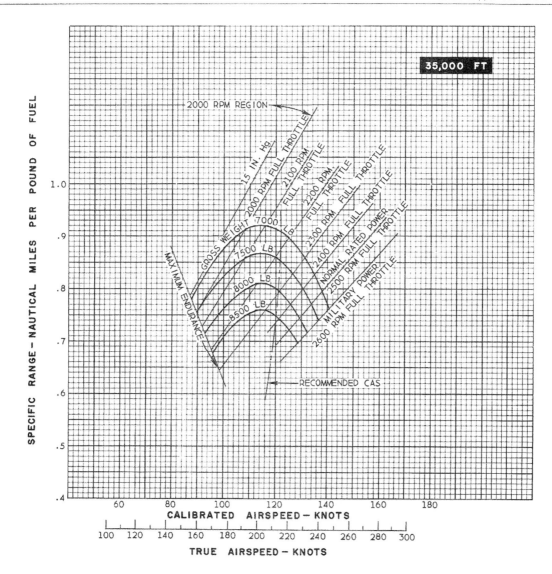

NAUTICAL MILES PER POUND OF FUEL
STANDARD DAY
TWO .50-CALIBER GUN PACKAGES OR
SIX 2.25-INCH ROCKETS

MODEL: T-28B

ENGINE: (1) R-1820-86 OR .86A

REMARKS:

1. High blower.

2. For each 10°C above Standard Day conditions, hold CAS constant, increase true airspeed 1.8%, and:
 • Part-throttle conditions –
  a. Hold rpm constant.
  b. Increase manifold pressure 1/2 in. Hg.
  c. Do not change nautical miles per pound of fuel.

• Full-throttle conditions –
 a. Increase rpm 1.5%.
 b. Decrease nautical miles per pound of fuel by one percent.

3. For each 10°C below Standard Day conditions, apply corrections in Remark 2 in the opposite direction.

DATA AS OF : 10-1-54
BASED ON: FLIGHT TEST DATA, NAA REPORT 54-952

FUEL GRADE: EITHER 115/145 OR 100/130
FUEL DENSITY: 6.0 LB/GAL.

T-28B-1-93-52A

Figure 11-46

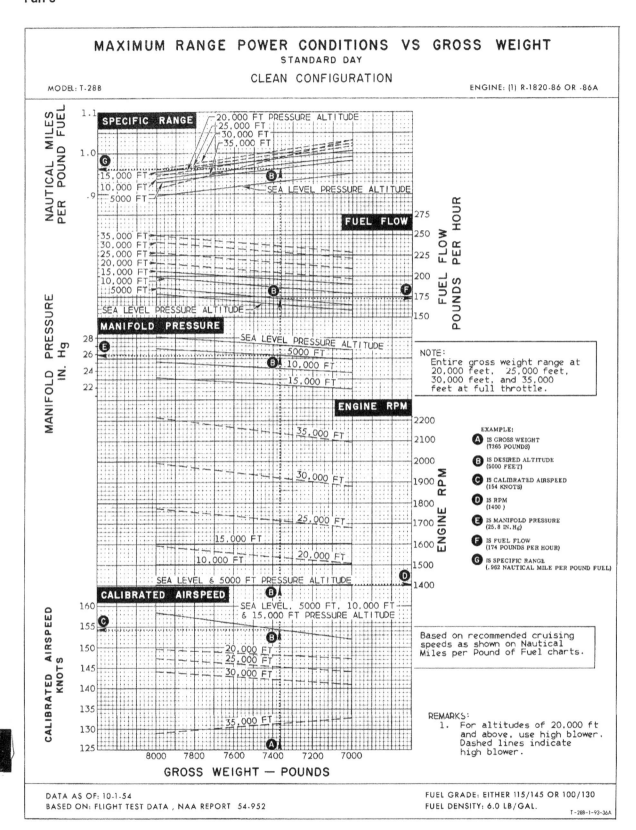

MAXIMUM RANGE POWER CONDITIONS VS GROSS WEIGHT

STANDARD DAY

CLEAN CONFIGURATION

MODEL: T-28B

ENGINE: (1) R-1820-86 OR -86A

Figure 11-47

DATA AS OF: 10-1-54
BASED ON: FLIGHT TEST DATA , NAA REPORT 54-952

FUEL GRADE: EITHER 115/145 OR 100/130
FUEL DENSITY: 6.0 LB/GAL.

T-28B-1-93-36A

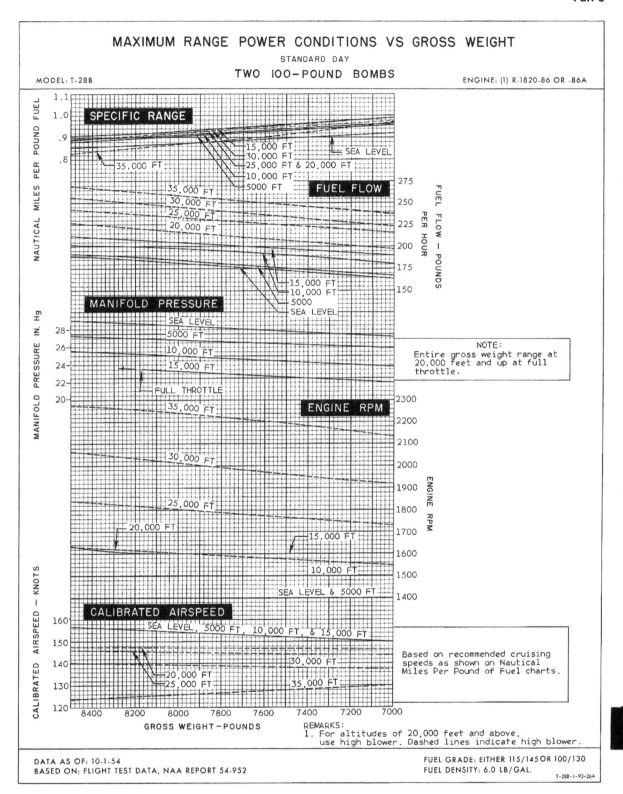

MAXIMUM RANGE POWER CONDITIONS VS GROSS WEIGHT
STANDARD DAY
TWO 100-POUND BOMBS

MODEL: T-28B

ENGINE: (1) R-1820-86 OR .86A

Figure 11-48

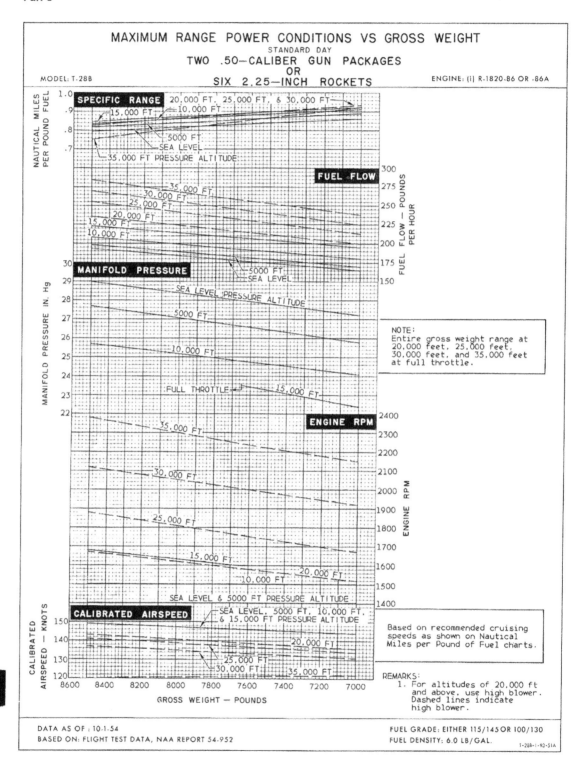

MAXIMUM RANGE POWER CONDITIONS VS GROSS WEIGHT

STANDARD DAY

TWO .50—CALIBER GUN PACKAGES
OR
SIX 2.25—INCH ROCKETS

MODEL: T-28B

ENGINE: (1) R-1820-86 OR -86A

NOTE:
Entire gross weight range at 20,000 feet, 25,000 feet, 30,000 feet, and 35,000 feet at full throttle.

Based on recommended cruising speeds as shown on Nautical Miles per Pound of Fuel charts.

REMARKS:
1. For altitudes of 20,000 ft and above, use high blower. Dashed lines indicate high blower.

DATA AS OF : 10-1-54
BASED ON: FLIGHT TEST DATA, NAA REPORT 54-952

FUEL GRADE: EITHER 115/145 OR 100/130
FUEL DENSITY: 6.0 LB/GAL.

T-28B-1-93-51A

Figure 11-49

Full page figure.

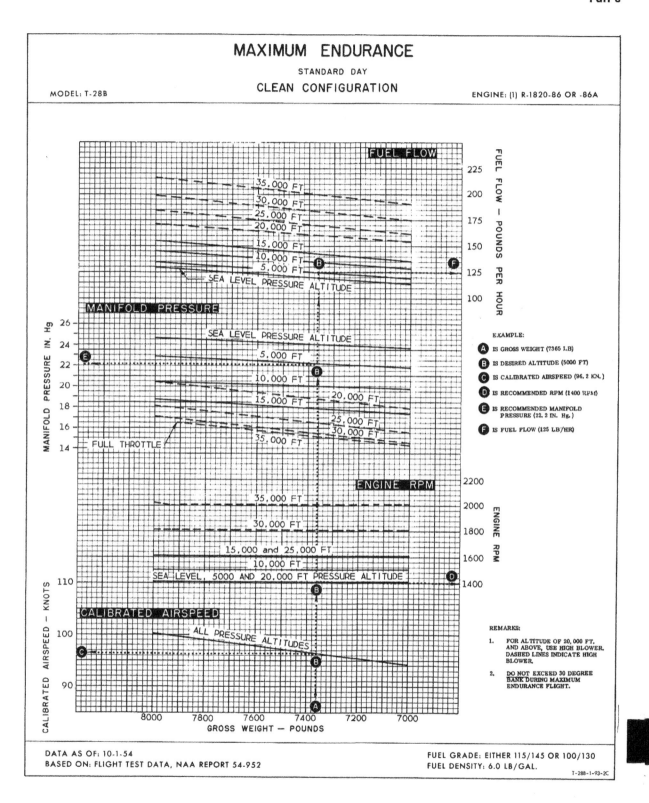

Figure 11-50

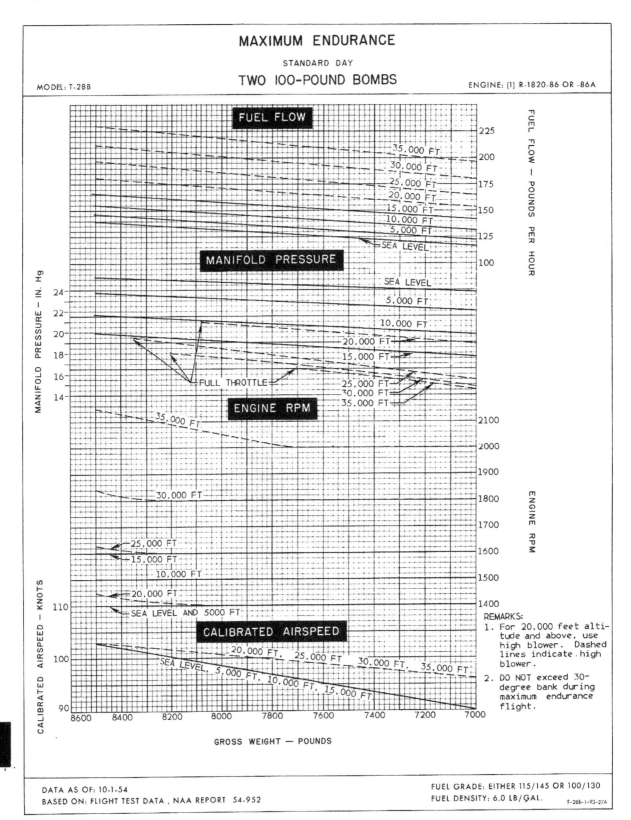

Figure 11-51

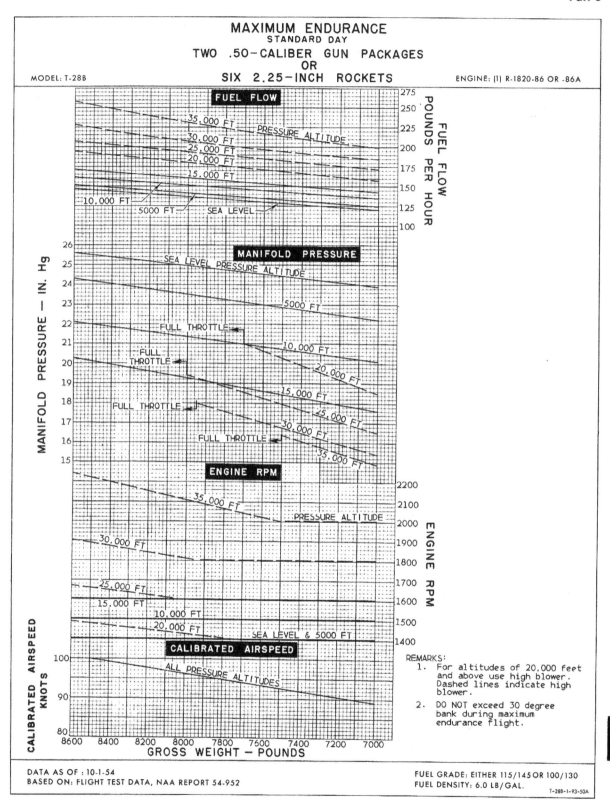

MAXIMUM ENDURANCE
STANDARD DAY
TWO .50-CALIBER GUN PACKAGES
OR
SIX 2.25-INCH ROCKETS

MODEL: T-28B

ENGINE: (1) R-1820-86 OR -86A

REMARKS:
1. For altitudes of 20,000 feet and above use high blower. Dashed lines indicate high blower.
2. DO NOT exceed 30 degree bank during maximum endurance flight.

DATA AS OF : 10-1-54
BASED ON: FLIGHT TEST DATA, NAA REPORT 54-952

FUEL GRADE: EITHER 115/145 OR 100/130
FUEL DENSITY: 6.0 LB/GAL.

T-28B-1-93-50A

Figure 11-52

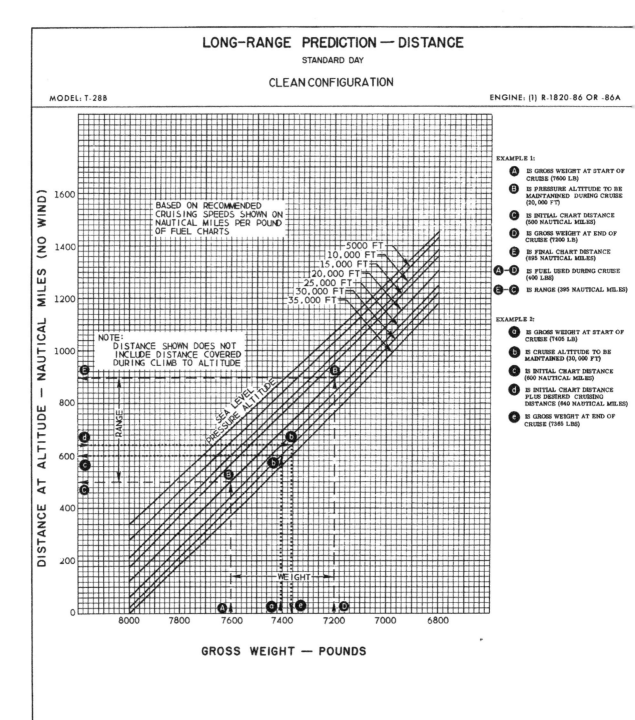

LONG–RANGE PREDICTION — DISTANCE

STANDARD DAY

CLEAN CONFIGURATION

MODEL: T-28B

ENGINE: (1) R-1820-86 OR -86A

EXAMPLE 1:

Ⓐ IS GROSS WEIGHT AT START OF CRUISE (7600 LB)

Ⓑ IS PRESSURE ALTITUDE TO BE MAINTAINED DURING CRUISE (20,000 FT)

Ⓒ IS INITIAL CHART DISTANCE (500 NAUTICAL MILES)

Ⓓ IS GROSS WEIGHT AT END OF CRUISE (7200 LB)

Ⓔ IS FINAL CHART DISTANCE (895 NAUTICAL MILES)

Ⓐ–Ⓓ IS FUEL USED DURING CRUISE (400 LBS)

Ⓔ–Ⓒ IS RANGE (395 NAUTICAL MILES)

EXAMPLE 2:

ⓐ IS GROSS WEIGHT AT START OF CRUISE (7405 LB)

ⓑ IS CRUISE ALTITUDE TO BE MAINTAINED (30,000 FT)

ⓒ IS INITIAL CHART DISTANCE (600 NAUTICAL MILES)

ⓓ IS INITIAL CHART DISTANCE PLUS DESIRED CRUISING DISTANCE (640 NAUTICAL MILES)

ⓔ IS GROSS WEIGHT AT END OF CRUISE (7365 LBS)

BASED ON RECOMMENDED CRUISING SPEEDS SHOWN ON NAUTICAL MILES PER POUND OF FUEL CHARTS

NOTE: DISTANCE SHOWN DOES NOT INCLUDE DISTANCE COVERED DURING CLIMB TO ALTITUDE

5000 FT
10,000 FT
15,000 FT
20,000 FT
25,000 FT
30,000 FT
35,000 FT

SEA LEVEL PRESSURE ALTITUDE

DISTANCE AT ALTITUDE — NAUTICAL MILES (NO WIND)

GROSS WEIGHT — POUNDS

DATA AS OF: 10-1-54
BASED ON: FLIGHT TEST DATA, NAA REPORT 54-952

FUEL GRADE: EITHER 115/145 OR 100/130
FUEL DENSITY: 6.0 LB/GAL.

T-28B-1-93-37A

Figure 11-53

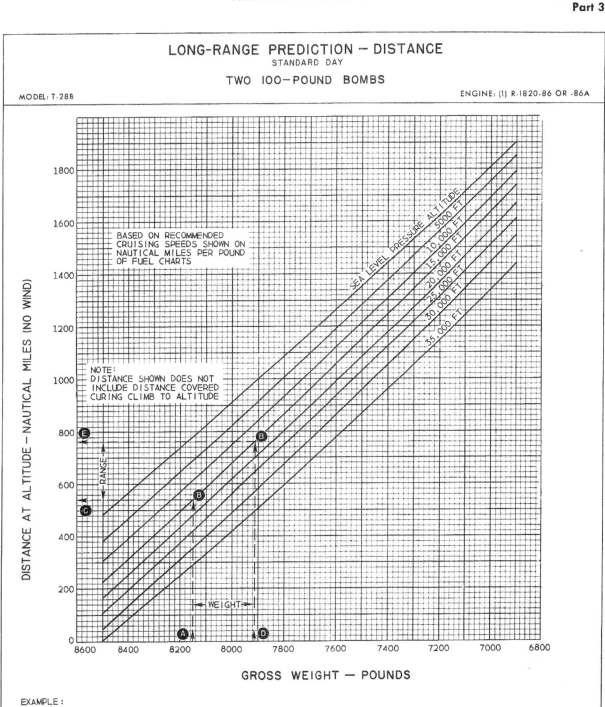

LONG-RANGE PREDICTION – DISTANCE
STANDARD DAY
TWO 100–POUND BOMBS

MODEL: T-28B
ENGINE: (1) R-1820-86 OR -86A

BASED ON RECOMMENDED CRUISING SPEEDS SHOWN ON NAUTICAL MILES PER POUND OF FUEL CHARTS

NOTE:
DISTANCE SHOWN DOES NOT INCLUDE DISTANCE COVERED DURING CLIMB TO ALTITUDE

EXAMPLE:

(A) IS GROSS WEIGHT AT START OF CRUISE (8150 LB)
(B) IS PRESSURE ALTITUDE TO BE MAINTAINED DURING FLIGHT (15,000 FT)
(C) IS INITIAL CHART DISTANCE (540 NAUTICAL MILES)
(D) IS GROSS WEIGHT AT END OF CRUISE (7915 LB)
(E) IS FINAL CHART DISTANCE (760 NAUTICAL MILES)
(A)–(D) IS FUEL USED DURING CRUISE (235 LB)
(E)–(C) IS RANGE (220 NAUTICAL MILES)

DATA AS OF: 10-1-54
BASED ON: FLIGHT TEST DATA, NAA REPORT 54-952
FUEL GRADE: EITHER 115/145 OR 100/130
FUEL DENSITY: 6.0 LB/GAL.
T-28B-1-93-47A

Figure 11-54

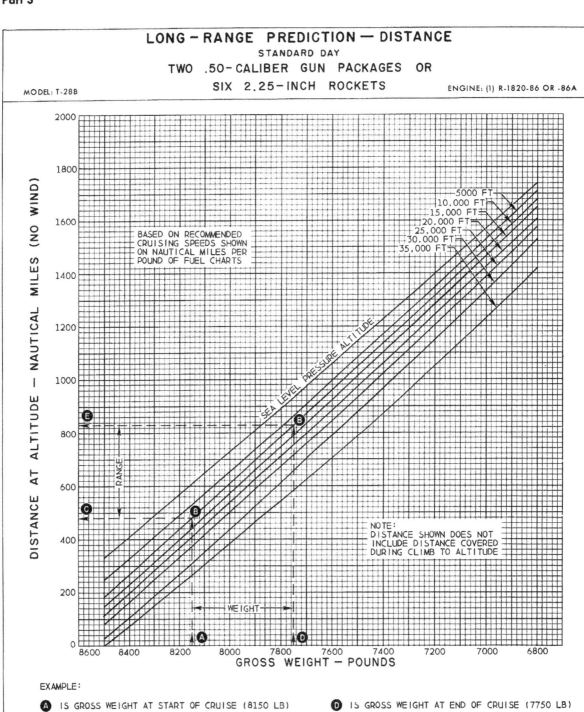

LONG – RANGE PREDICTION – DISTANCE
STANDARD DAY
TWO .50-CALIBER GUN PACKAGES OR
SIX 2.25-INCH ROCKETS

MODEL: T-28B

ENGINE: (1) R-1820-86 OR -86A

EXAMPLE:

Ⓐ IS GROSS WEIGHT AT START OF CRUISE (8150 LB)

Ⓑ IS PRESSURE ALTITUDE TO BE MAINTAINED DURING CRUISE (10,000 FT)

Ⓒ IS INITIAL CHART DISTANCE (480 NAUTICAL MILES)

Ⓓ IS GROSS WEIGHT AT END OF CRUISE (7750 LB)

Ⓔ IS FINAL CHART DISTANCE (830 NAUTICAL MILES)

Ⓐ-Ⓓ IS FUEL USED DURING CRUISE (400 LB)

Ⓔ-Ⓒ IS RANGE (350 NAUTICAL MILES)

DATA AS OF: 10-1-54
BASED ON: FLIGHT TEST DATA, NAA REPORT 54-952

FUEL GRADE: EITHER 115/145 OR 100/130
FUEL DENSITY: 6.0 LB/GAL.

T-28B-1-93-65A

Figure 11-55

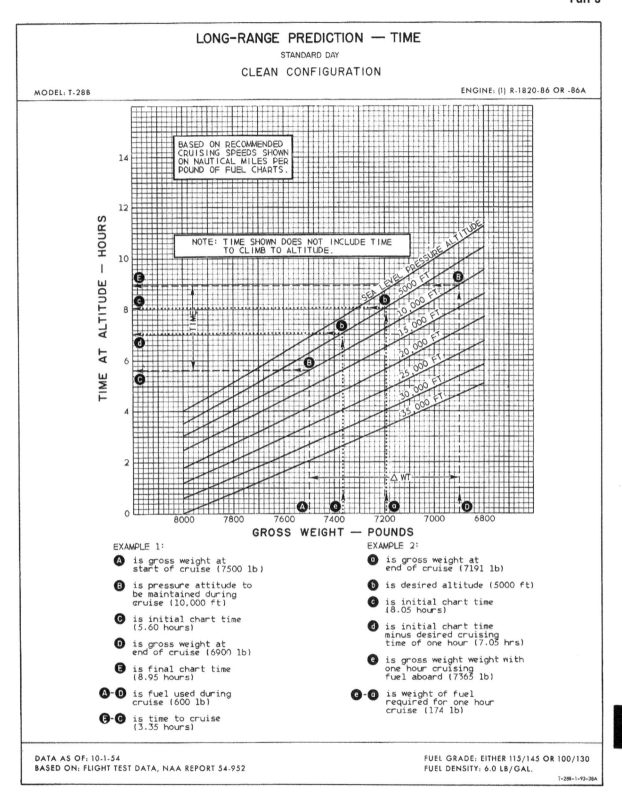

LONG-RANGE PREDICTION — TIME
STANDARD DAY
CLEAN CONFIGURATION

MODEL: T-28B

ENGINE: (1) R-1820-86 OR -86A

BASED ON RECOMMENDED
CRUISING SPEEDS SHOWN
ON NAUTICAL MILES PER
POUND OF FUEL CHARTS.

NOTE: TIME SHOWN DOES NOT INCLUDE TIME
TO CLIMB TO ALTITUDE.

EXAMPLE 1:

Ⓐ is gross weight at
start of cruise (7500 lb)

Ⓑ is pressure attitude to
be maintained during
cruise (10,000 ft)

Ⓒ is initial chart time
(5.60 hours)

Ⓓ is gross weight at
end of cruise (6900 lb)

Ⓔ is final chart time
(8.95 hours)

Ⓐ-Ⓓ is fuel used during
cruise (600 lb)

Ⓔ-Ⓒ is time to cruise
(3.35 hours)

EXAMPLE 2:

ⓐ is gross weight at
end of cruise (7191 lb)

ⓑ is desired altitude (5000 ft)

ⓒ is initial chart time
(8.05 hours)

ⓓ is initial chart time
minus desired cruising
time of one hour (7.05 hrs)

ⓔ is gross weight weight with
one hour cruising
fuel aboard (7365 lb)

ⓔ-ⓐ is weight of fuel
required for one hour
cruise (174 lb)

DATA AS OF: 10-1-54
BASED ON: FLIGHT TEST DATA, NAA REPORT 54-952

FUEL GRADE: EITHER 115/145 OR 100/130
FUEL DENSITY: 6.0 LB/GAL.

T-28B-1-93-38A

Figure 11-56

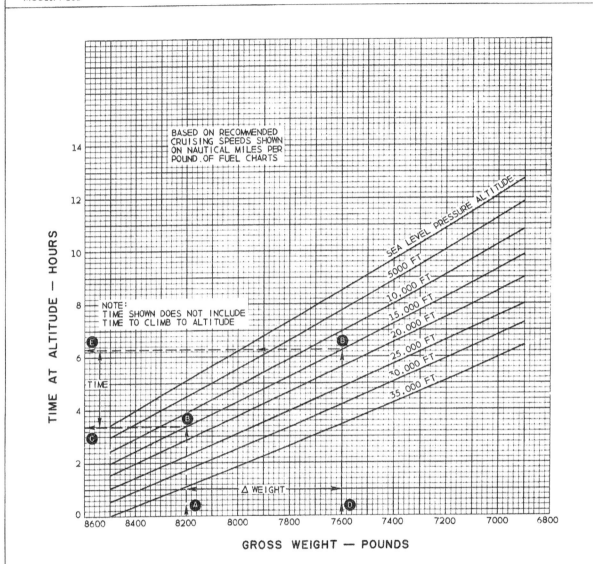

LONG-RANGE PREDICTION — TIME
STANDARD DAY
TWO 100-POUND BOMBS

MODEL: T-28B

ENGINE: (1) R-1820-86 OR -86A

EXAMPLE:

Ⓐ IS GROSS WEIGHT AT START OF CRUISE (8200 LB)

Ⓑ IS PRESSURE ALTITUDE TO BE MAINTAINED DURING FLIGHT (15,000 FT)

Ⓒ IS INITIAL CHART TIME (3.35 HOURS)

Ⓓ IS GROSS WEIGHT AT END OF CRUISE (7600 LB)

Ⓔ IS FINAL CHART TIME (6.25 HOURS)

Ⓐ–Ⓓ IS FUEL USED DURING CRUISE (600 LB)

Ⓔ–Ⓒ IS TIME TO CRUISE (2.90 HOURS)

DATA AS OF : 10-1-54
BASED ON: FLIGHT TEST DATA , NAA REPORT 54-952

FUEL GRADE: EITHER 115/145 OR 100/130
FUEL DENSITY: 6.0 LB/GAL.

T-28B-1-93-48A

Figure 11-57

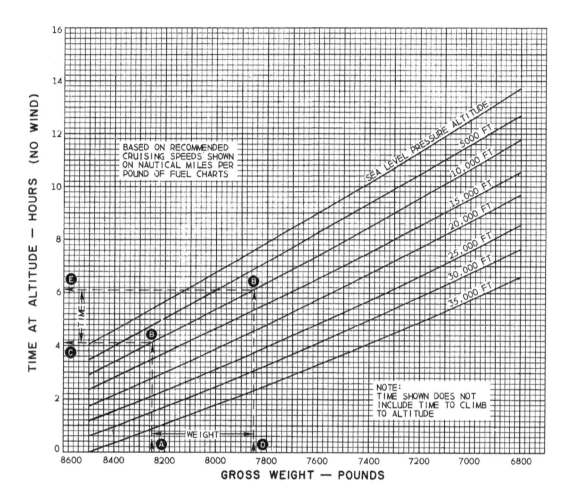

LONG – RANGE PREDICTION — TIME
STANDARD DAY
TWO .50-CALIBER GUN PACKAGES OR
SIX 2.25-INCH ROCKETS

MODEL: T-28B

ENGINE: (1) R-1820-86 OR -86A

Figure 11-58

EXAMPLE:

A IS GROSS WEIGHT AT START OF CRUISE (8250 LBS)

B IS PRESSURE ALTITUDE TO BE MAINTAINED DURING CRUISE (10,000 FT)

C IS INITIAL CHART TIME (4.10 HOURS)

D IS GROSS WEIGHT AT END OF CRUISE (7850)

E IS FINAL CHART TIME (6.10 HOURS)

A – D IS FUEL USED DURING CRUISE (400 LBS)

E – C IS TIME TO CRUISE (2.0 HOURS)

DATA AS OF : 10-1-54
BASED ON: FLIGHT TEST DATA, NAA REPORT 54-952

FUEL GRADE: EITHER 115/145 OR 100/130
FUEL DENSITY: 6.0 LB/GAL.

T-28B-1-93-64A

MILITARY AND NORMAL RATED
POWER FUEL FLOW

MODEL: T-28B

ENGINE: (1) R-1820-86 OR -86A

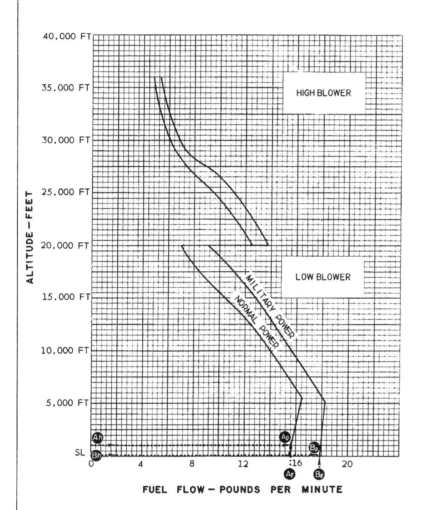

EXAMPLE 1:

(Ah) IS DESIRED ALTITUDE (1000 FT)

(Ap) IS DESIRED POWER (NORMAL POWER)

(Af) IS FUEL FLOW (15.7 LB./ HR.)

EXAMPLE 2:

(Bh) IS DESIRED ALTITUDE (SEA LEVEL)

(Bp) IS DESIRED POWER (MILITARY POWER)

(Bf) IS FUEL FLOW (17.9 LB./ HR.)

REMARKS:
1. BASED ON LEVEL FLIGHT SPEEDS SHOWN ON NAUTICAL MILES PER POUND OF FUEL CURVES.

2. USE HIGH BLOWER AT 20,000 FT. AND ABOVE.

DATA AS OF: 10-1-54
BASED ON: FLIGHT TEST DATA, NAA REPORT 54-952

FUEL GRADE: EITHER 115/145 OR 100/130
FUEL DENSITY: 6.0 LB/GAL.

T-28B-1-93-66A

Figure 11-59

EMERGENCY CLIMB

SEA LEVEL
STANDARD DAY
CLEAN CONFIGURATION

MODEL: T-28B

ENGINE: (1) R-1820-86 OR -86A

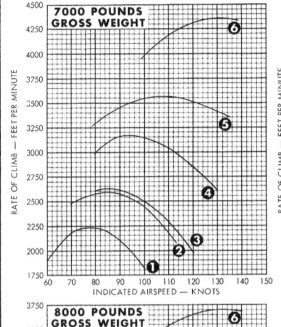

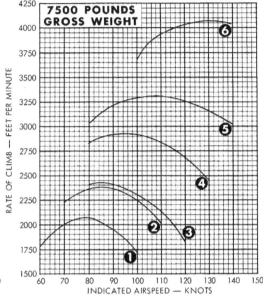

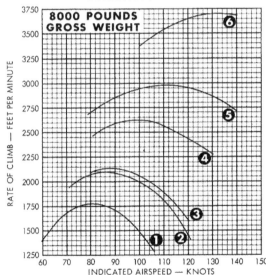

LEGEND:

1 WING FLAPS FULL DOWN, GEAR DOWN, COWL FLAPS OPEN, CANOPY OPEN, SPEED BRAKE CLOSED.

2 WING FLAPS FULL DOWN, GEAR UP, COWL FLAPS OPEN, CANOPY OPEN, SPEED BRAKE CLOSED.

3 WING FLAPS HALF DOWN, GEAR DOWN, COWL FLAPS OPEN, CANOPY OPEN, SPEED BRAKE CLOSED.

4 WING FLAPS HALF DOWN, GEAR UP, COWL FLAPS OPEN, CANOPY OPEN, SPEED BRAKE CLOSED.

5 WING FLAPS UP, GEAR UP, COWL FLAPS OPEN, CANOPY OPEN, SPEED BRAKE CLOSED.

6 WING FLAPS UP, GEAR UP, COWL FLAPS OPEN CANOPY CLOSED, SPEED BRAKE CLOSED.

REMARKS:

1. USE MILITARY POWER.

2. FOR EACH 10°C RISE IN AIR TEMPERATURE ABOVE STANDARD DAY CONDITIONS, DECREASE RATE OF CLIMB 9 PERCENT.

3. MAXIMUM FLAPS AND GEAR DOWN SPEED IS 140 KNOTS IAS.

DATA AS OF: 11-15-55
BASED ON: FLIGHT TEST DATA, NA55H-365

FUEL GRADE: EITHER 115/145 OR 100/130
FUEL DENSITY: 6.0 LB/GAL.
T-28B-1-93-4D

Figure 11-60

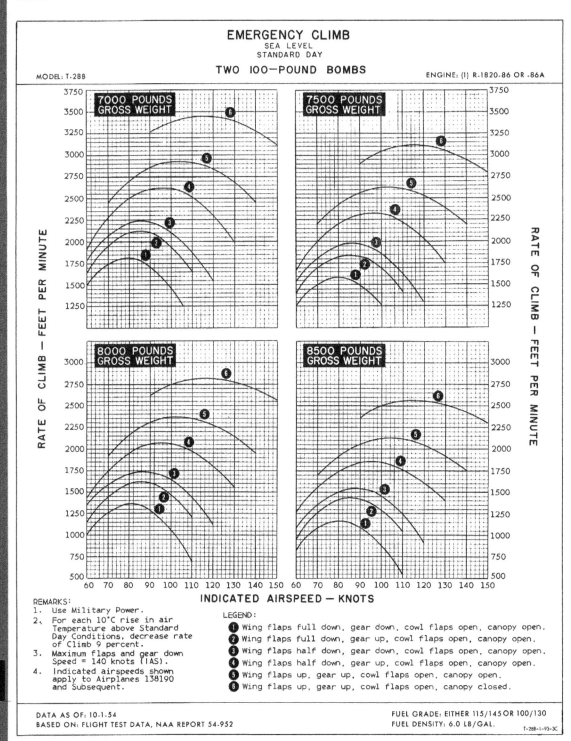

EMERGENCY CLIMB
SEA LEVEL
STANDARD DAY

TWO 100—POUND BOMBS

MODEL: T-28B

ENGINE: (1) R-1820-86 OR -86A

REMARKS:
1. Use Military Power.
2. For each 10°C rise in air Temperature above Standard Day Conditions, decrease rate of Climb 9 percent.
3. Maximum flaps and gear down Speed = 140 knots (IAS).
4. Indicated airspeeds shown apply to Airplanes 138190 and Subsequent.

LEGEND:
❶ Wing flaps full down, gear down, cowl flaps open, canopy open.
❷ Wing flaps full down, gear up, cowl flaps open, canopy open.
❸ Wing flaps half down, gear down, cowl flaps open, canopy open.
❹ Wing flaps half down, gear up, cowl flaps open, canopy open.
❺ Wing flaps up, gear up, cowl flaps open, canopy open.
❻ Wing flaps up, gear up, cowl flaps open, canopy closed.

DATA AS OF: 10-1-54
BASED ON: FLIGHT TEST DATA, NAA REPORT 54-952

FUEL GRADE: EITHER 115/145 OR 100/130
FUEL DENSITY: 6.0 LB/GAL.

T-28B-1-93-3C

Figure 11-61

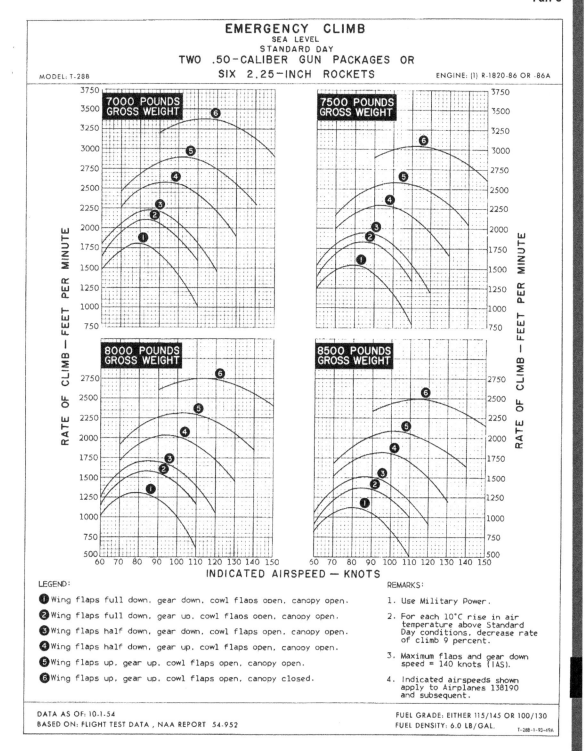

EMERGENCY CLIMB
SEA LEVEL
STANDARD DAY
TWO .50-CALIBER GUN PACKAGES OR
SIX 2.25-INCH ROCKETS

MODEL: T-28B

ENGINE: (1) R-1820-86 OR -86A

RATE OF CLIMB — FEET PER MINUTE

INDICATED AIRSPEED — KNOTS

LEGEND:

① Wing flaps full down, gear down, cowl flaps open, canopy open.
② Wing flaps full down, gear up, cowl flaps open, canopy open.
③ Wing flaps half down, gear down, cowl flaps open, canopy open.
④ Wing flaps half down, gear up, cowl flaps open, canopy open.
⑤ Wing flaps up, gear up, cowl flaps open, canopy open.
⑥ Wing flaps up, gear up, cowl flaps open, canopy closed.

REMARKS:

1. Use Military Power.

2. For each 10°C rise in air temperature above Standard Day conditions, decrease rate of climb 9 percent.

3. Maximum flaps and gear down speed = 140 knots (IAS).

4. Indicated airspeeds shown apply to Airplanes 138190 and subsequent.

DATA AS OF: 10-1-54
BASED ON: FLIGHT TEST DATA , NAA REPORT 54-952

FUEL GRADE: EITHER 115/145 OR 100/130
FUEL DENSITY: 6.0 LB/GAL.

T-28B-1-93-49A

Figure 11-62

PART 4 — T-28C PERFORMANCE DATA

PERFORMANCE CHARTS (T-28C)

The performance data charts in Section XI, Part 4, present data for the T-28C. Some reduction in performance results from the reduced diameter propeller and slight increase in gross weight over the T-28B. Layout and order of presentation of the T-28C charts is identical to that of Section XI, Part 3.

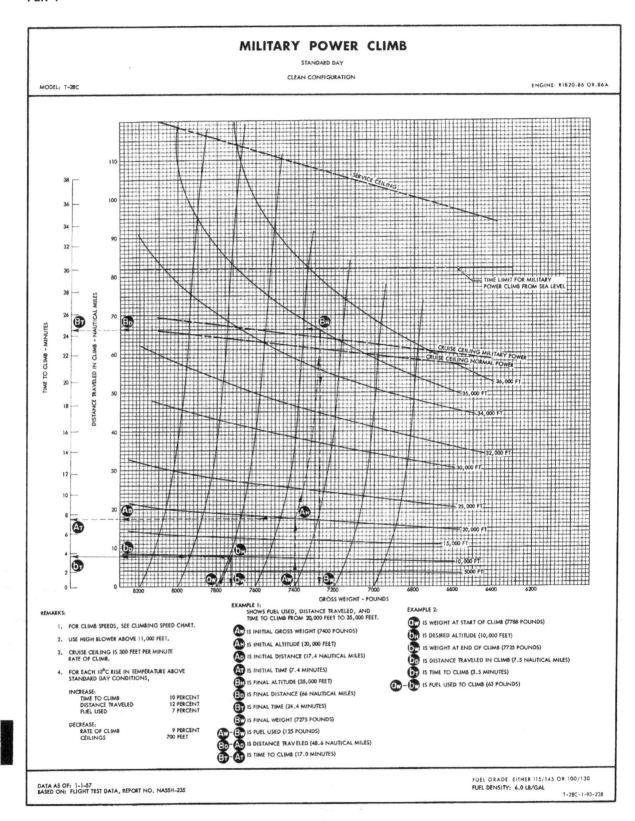

MILITARY POWER CLIMB

STANDARD DAY

CLEAN CONFIGURATION

MODEL: T-28C

ENGINE: R1820-86 OR.86A

REMARKS:

1. FOR CLIMB SPEEDS, SEE CLIMBING SPEED CHART.

2. USE HIGH BLOWER ABOVE 11,000 FEET.

3. CRUISE CEILING IS 300 FEET PER MINUTE RATE OF CLIMB.

4. FOR EACH 10°C RISE IN TEMPERATURE ABOVE STANDARD DAY CONDITIONS,

    INCREASE:
TIME TO CLIMB	10 PERCENT
DISTANCE TRAVELED	12 PERCENT
FUEL USED	7 PERCENT

    DECREASE:
RATE OF CLIMB	9 PERCENT
CEILINGS	700 FEET

EXAMPLE 1:

SHOWS FUEL USED, DISTANCE TRAVELED, AND TIME TO CLIMB FROM 20,000 FEET TO 35,000 FEET.

(Aw) IS INITIAL GROSS WEIGHT (7400 POUNDS)

(Ah) IS INITIAL ALTITUDE (20,000 FEET)

(Ad) IS INITIAL DISTANCE (17.4 NAUTICAL MILES)

(At) IS INITIAL TIME (7.4 MINUTES)

(Bh) IS FINAL ALTITUDE (35,000 FEET)

(Bd) IS FINAL DISTANCE (66 NAUTICAL MILES)

(Bt) IS FINAL TIME (24.4 MINUTES)

(Bw) IS FINAL WEIGHT (7275 POUNDS)

(Aw)-(Bw) IS FUEL USED (125 POUNDS)

(Bd)-(Ad) IS DISTANCE TRAVELED (48.6 NAUTICAL MILES)

(Bt)-(At) IS TIME TO CLIMB (17.0 MINUTES)

EXAMPLE 2:

(aw) IS WEIGHT AT START OF CLIMB (7788 POUNDS)

(ah) IS DESIRED ALTITUDE (10,000 FEET)

(bw) IS WEIGHT AT END OF CLIMB (7725 POUNDS)

(Dd) IS DISTANCE TRAVELED IN CLIMB (7.5 NAUTICAL MILES)

(Dt) IS TIME TO CLIMB (3.5 MINUTES)

(aw)-(bw) IS FUEL USED TO CLIMB (63 POUNDS)

DATA AS OF: 1-1-57
BASED ON: FLIGHT TEST DATA, REPORT NO. NA55H-235

FUEL GRADE: EITHER 115/145 OR 100/130
FUEL DENSITY: 6.0 LB/GAL

T-28C-1-93-238

Figure 11-63

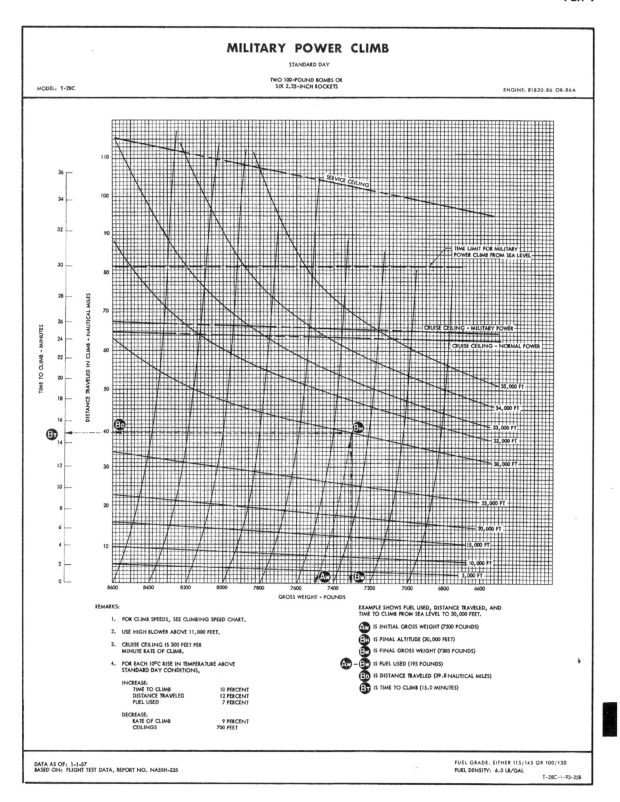

MILITARY POWER CLIMB

STANDARD DAY

TWO 100-POUND BOMBS OR
SIX 2.25-INCH ROCKETS

MODEL: T-28C

ENGINE: R1820.86 OR.86A

REMARKS:

1. FOR CLIMB SPEEDS, SEE CLIMBING SPEED CHART.

2. USE HIGH BLOWER ABOVE 11,000 FEET.

3. CRUISE CEILING IS 300 FEET PER MINUTE RATE OF CLIMB.

4. FOR EACH 10°C RISE IN TEMPERATURE ABOVE STANDARD DAY CONDITIONS,

INCREASE:
TIME TO CLIMB	10 PERCENT
DISTANCE TRAVELED	12 PERCENT
FUEL USED	7 PERCENT

DECREASE:
RATE OF CLIMB	9 PERCENT
CEILINGS	700 FEET

EXAMPLE SHOWS FUEL USED, DISTANCE TRAVELED, AND TIME TO CLIMB FROM SEA LEVEL TO 30,000 FEET.

Aw IS INITIAL GROSS WEIGHT (7500 POUNDS)

Bн IS FINAL ALTITUDE (30,000 FEET)

Bw IS FINAL GROSS WEIGHT (7305 POUNDS)

Aw — Bw IS FUEL USED (195 POUNDS)

Bd IS DISTANCE TRAVELED (39.8 NAUTICAL MILES)

Bт IS TIME TO CLIMB (15.0 MINUTES)

DATA AS OF: 1-1-57
BASED ON: FLIGHT TEST DATA, REPORT NO. NA55H-235

FUEL GRADE: EITHER 115/145 OR 100/130
FUEL DENSITY: 6.0 LB/GAL

T-28C-1-93-25B

Figure 11-64

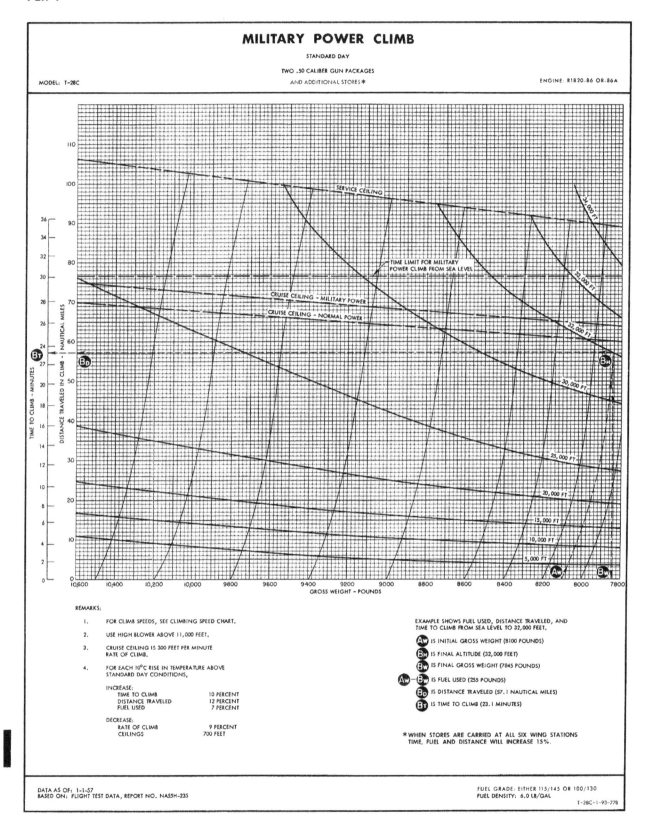

Figure 11-65

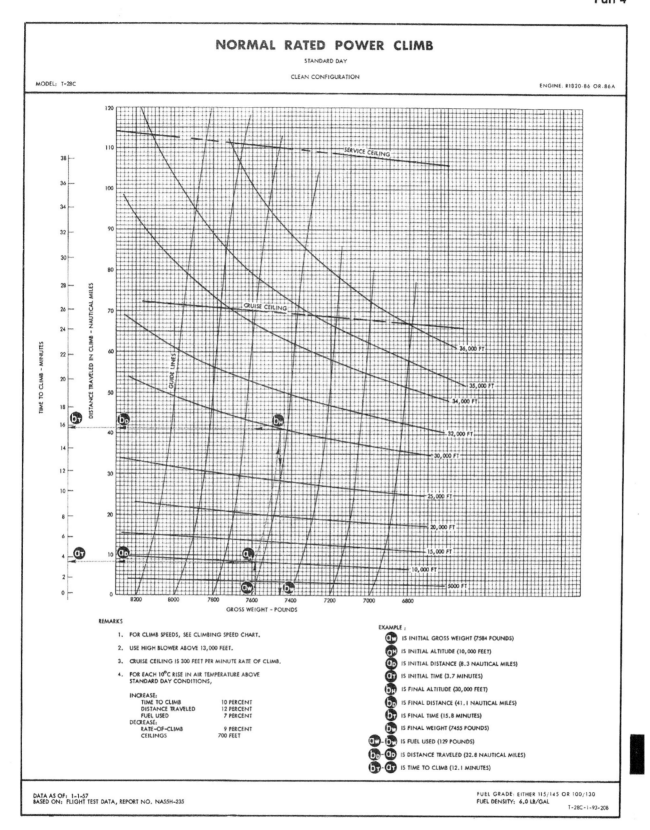

NORMAL RATED POWER CLIMB

STANDARD DAY

CLEAN CONFIGURATION

MODEL: T-28C

ENGINE: R1820-86 OR-86A

REMARKS

1. FOR CLIMB SPEEDS, SEE CLIMBING SPEED CHART.

2. USE HIGH BLOWER ABOVE 13,000 FEET.

3. CRUISE CEILING IS 300 FEET PER MINUTE RATE OF CLIMB.

4. FOR EACH 10°C RISE IN AIR TEMPERATURE ABOVE STANDARD DAY CONDITIONS,

INCREASE:
TIME TO CLIMB	10 PERCENT
DISTANCE TRAVELED	12 PERCENT
FUEL USED	7 PERCENT

DECREASE:
RATE-OF-CLIMB	9 PERCENT
CEILINGS	700 FEET

EXAMPLE :

aw IS INITIAL GROSS WEIGHT (7584 POUNDS)

aH IS INITIAL ALTITUDE (10,000 FEET)

aD IS INITIAL DISTANCE (8.3 NAUTICAL MILES)

aT IS INITIAL TIME (3.7 MINUTES)

bH IS FINAL ALTITUDE (30,000 FEET)

bD IS FINAL DISTANCE (41.1 NAUTICAL MILES)

bT IS FINAL TIME (15.8 MINUTES)

bW IS FINAL WEIGHT (7455 POUNDS)

aw-bw IS FUEL USED (129 POUNDS)

bD-aD IS DISTANCE TRAVELED (32.8 NAUTICAL MILES)

bT-aT IS TIME TO CLIMB (12.1 MINUTES)

DATA AS OF: 1-1-57
BASED ON: FLIGHT TEST DATA, REPORT NO. NA55H-235

FUEL GRADE: EITHER 115/145 OR 100/130
FUEL DENSITY: 6.0 LB/GAL

T-28C-1-93-208

Figure 11-66

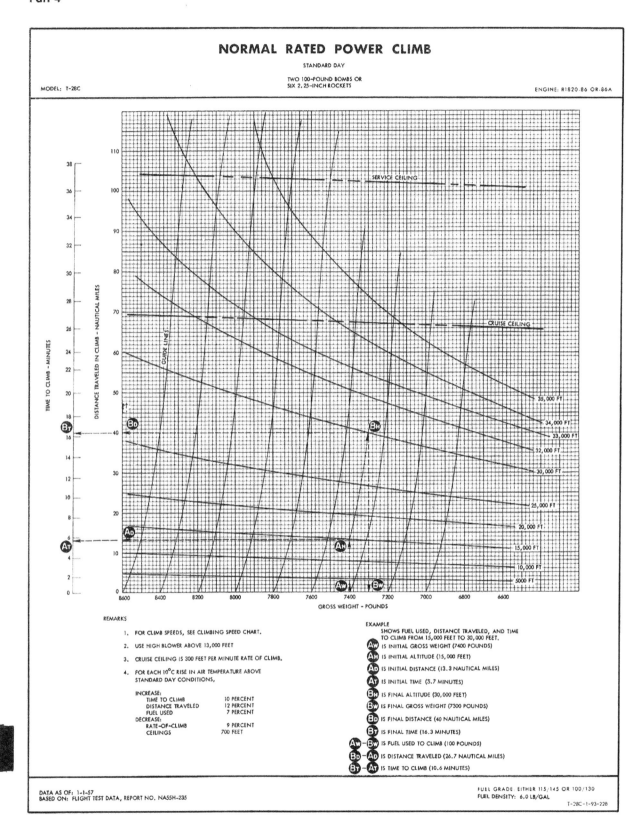

NORMAL RATED POWER CLIMB

STANDARD DAY

TWO 100-POUND BOMBS OR
SIX 2.25-INCH ROCKETS

MODEL: T-28C

ENGINE: R1820-86 OR-86A

REMARKS

1. FOR CLIMB SPEEDS, SEE CLIMBING SPEED CHART.

2. USE HIGH BLOWER ABOVE 13,000 FEET.

3. CRUISE CEILING IS 300 FEET PER MINUTE RATE OF CLIMB.

4. FOR EACH 10°C RISE IN AIR TEMPERATURE ABOVE
STANDARD DAY CONDITIONS,

INCREASE:
TIME TO CLIMB   10 PERCENT
DISTANCE TRAVELED   12 PERCENT
FUEL USED   7 PERCENT
DECREASE:
RATE-OF-CLIMB   9 PERCENT
CEILINGS   700 FEET

EXAMPLE
SHOWS FUEL USED, DISTANCE TRAVELED, AND TIME
TO CLIMB FROM 15,000 FEET TO 30,000 FEET.
(Aw) IS INITIAL GROSS WEIGHT (7400 POUNDS)
(Ah) IS INITIAL ALTITUDE (15,000 FEET)
(Ad) IS INITIAL DISTANCE (13.3 NAUTICAL MILES)
(At) IS INITIAL TIME (3.7 MINUTES)
(Bh) IS FINAL ALTITUDE (30,000 FEET)
(Bw) IS FINAL GROSS WEIGHT (7300 POUNDS)
(Bd) IS FINAL DISTANCE (40 NAUTICAL MILES)
(Bt) IS FINAL TIME (16.3 MINUTES)
(Aw)—(Bw) IS FUEL USED TO CLIMB (100 POUNDS)
(Bd)—(Ad) IS DISTANCE TRAVELED (26.7 NAUTICAL MILES)
(Bt)—(At) IS TIME TO CLIMB (10.6 MINUTES)

DATA AS OF: 1-1-57
BASED ON: FLIGHT TEST DATA, REPORT NO. NA55H-235

FUEL GRADE: EITHER 115/145 OR 100/130
FUEL DENSITY: 6.0 LB/GAL

T-28C-1-93-22B

Figure 11-67

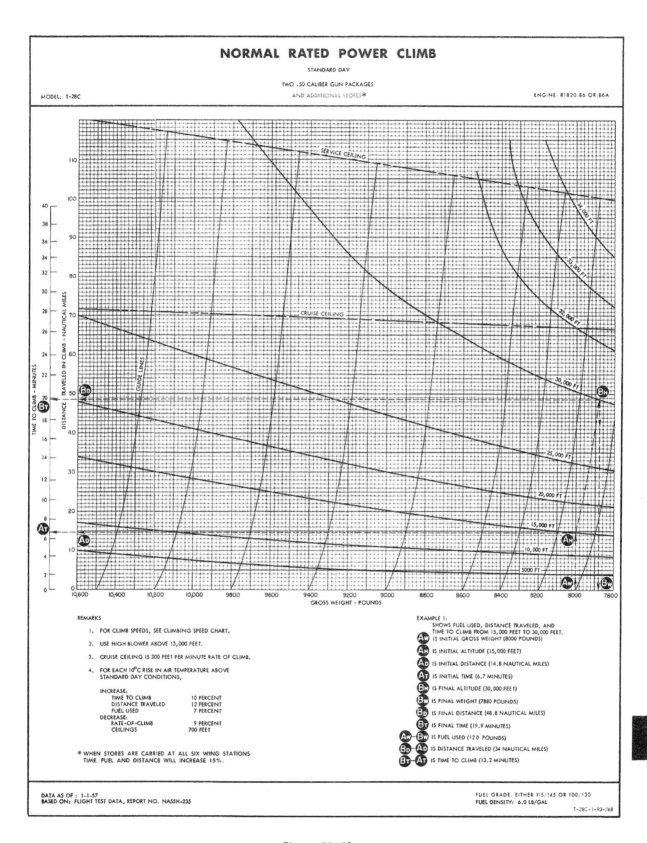

NORMAL RATED POWER CLIMB

STANDARD DAY

TWO .50 CALIBER GUN PACKAGES

AND ADDITIONAL STORES*

MODEL: T-28C

ENGINE: R1820-86 OR-86A

REMARKS

1. FOR CLIMB SPEEDS, SEE CLIMBING SPEED CHART.

2. USE HIGH BLOWER ABOVE 13,000 FEET.

3. CRUISE CEILING IS 300 FEET PER MINUTE RATE OF CLIMB.

4. FOR EACH 10°C RISE IN AIR TEMPERATURE ABOVE STANDARD DAY CONDITIONS,

INCREASE:	
TIME TO CLIMB	10 PERCENT
DISTANCE TRAVELED	12 PERCENT
FUEL USED	7 PERCENT
DECREASE:	
RATE-OF-CLIMB	9 PERCENT
CEILINGS	700 FEET

* WHEN STORES ARE CARRIED AT ALL SIX WING STATIONS TIME, FUEL AND DISTANCE WILL INCREASE 15%.

EXAMPLE 1:

SHOWS FUEL USED, DISTANCE TRAVELED, AND TIME TO CLIMB FROM 15,000 FEET TO 30,000 FEET.

Aw IS INITIAL GROSS WEIGHT (8000 POUNDS)

Ah IS INITIAL ALTITUDE (15,000 FEET)

Ad IS INITIAL DISTANCE (14.8 NAUTICAL MILES)

At IS INITIAL TIME (6.7 MINUTES)

Bh IS FINAL ALTITUDE (30,000 FEET)

Bw IS FINAL WEIGHT (7880 POUNDS)

Bd IS FINAL DISTANCE (48.8 NAUTICAL MILES)

Bt IS FINAL TIME (19.9 MINUTES)

Aw—Bw IS FUEL USED (120 POUNDS)

Bd—Ad IS DISTANCE TRAVELED (34 NAUTICAL MILES)

Bt—At IS TIME TO CLIMB (13.2 MINUTES)

DATA AS OF : 1-1-57
BASED ON: FLIGHT TEST DATA, REPORT NO. NA55H-235

FUEL GRADE: EITHER 115/145 OR 100/130
FUEL DENSITY: 6.0 LB/GAL

T-28C-1-93-768

Figure 11-68

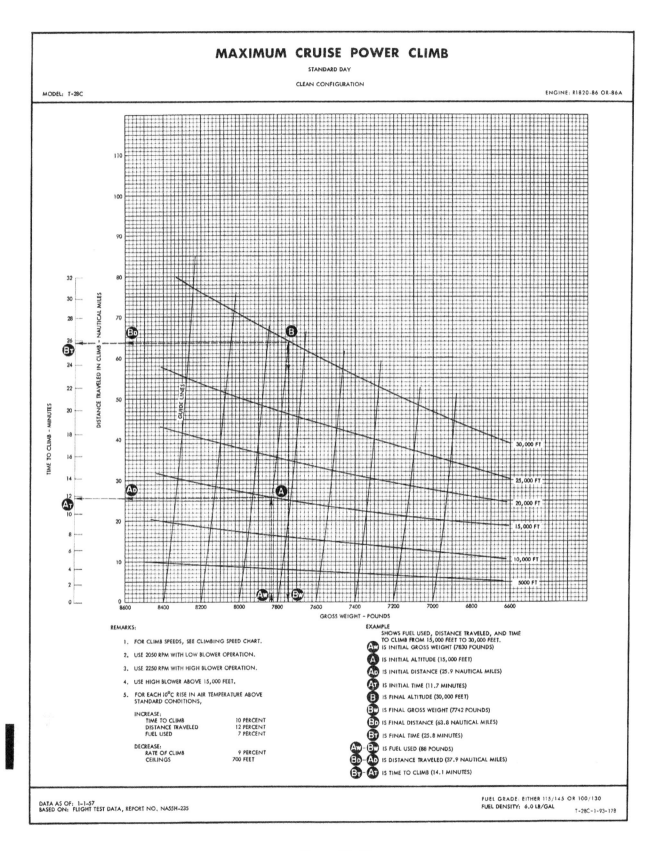

MAXIMUM CRUISE POWER CLIMB

STANDARD DAY

CLEAN CONFIGURATION

MODEL: T-28C

ENGINE: R1820-86 OR-86A

REMARKS:

1. FOR CLIMB SPEEDS, SEE CLIMBING SPEED CHART.

2. USE 2050 RPM WITH LOW BLOWER OPERATION.

3. USE 2250 RPM WITH HIGH BLOWER OPERATION.

4. USE HIGH BLOWER ABOVE 15,000 FEET.

5. FOR EACH 10°C RISE IN AIR TEMPERATURE ABOVE STANDARD CONDITIONS,

    INCREASE:
    TIME TO CLIMB .... 10 PERCENT
    DISTANCE TRAVELED .... 12 PERCENT
    FUEL USED .... 7 PERCENT

    DECREASE:
    RATE OF CLIMB .... 9 PERCENT
    CEILINGS .... 700 FEET

EXAMPLE

SHOWS FUEL USED, DISTANCE TRAVELED, AND TIME TO CLIMB FROM 15,000 FEET TO 30,000 FEET.

Aw IS INITIAL GROSS WEIGHT (7830 POUNDS)

A IS INITIAL ALTITUDE (15,000 FEET)

Ad IS INITIAL DISTANCE (25.9 NAUTICAL MILES)

At IS INITIAL TIME (11.7 MINUTES)

B IS FINAL ALTITUDE (30,000 FEET)

Bw IS FINAL GROSS WEIGHT (7742 POUNDS)

Bd IS FINAL DISTANCE (63.8 NAUTICAL MILES)

Bt IS FINAL TIME (25.8 MINUTES)

Aw - Bw IS FUEL USED (88 POUNDS)

Bd - Ad IS DISTANCE TRAVELED (37.9 NAUTICAL MILES)

Bt - At IS TIME TO CLIMB (14.1 MINUTES)

DATA AS OF: 1-1-57
BASED ON: FLIGHT TEST DATA, REPORT NO. NA55H-235

FUEL GRADE: EITHER 115/145 OR 100/130
FUEL DENSITY: 6.0 LB/GAL

T-28C-1-93-17B

Figure 11-69

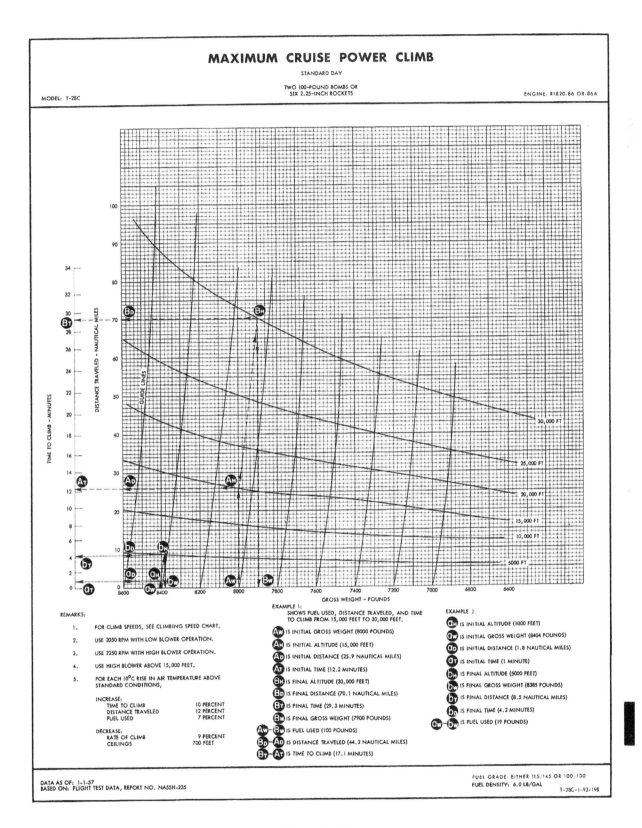

MAXIMUM CRUISE POWER CLIMB

STANDARD DAY

TWO 100-POUND BOMBS OR
SIX 2.25-INCH ROCKETS

MODEL: T-28C

ENGINE: R1820-86 OR-86A

REMARKS:

1. FOR CLIMB SPEEDS, SEE CLIMBING SPEED CHART.

2. USE 2050 RPM WITH LOW BLOWER OPERATION.

3. USE 2250 RPM WITH HIGH BLOWER OPERATION.

4. USE HIGH BLOWER ABOVE 15,000 FEET.

5. FOR EACH 10°C RISE IN AIR TEMPERATURE ABOVE STANDARD CONDITIONS,

INCREASE:	
TIME TO CLIMB	10 PERCENT
DISTANCE TRAVELED	12 PERCENT
FUEL USED	7 PERCENT
DECREASE:	
RATE OF CLIMB	9 PERCENT
CEILINGS	700 FEET

EXAMPLE 1:
SHOWS FUEL USED, DISTANCE TRAVELED, AND TIME TO CLIMB FROM 15,000 FEET TO 30,000 FEET.

Aw IS INITIAL GROSS WEIGHT (8000 POUNDS)

AH IS INITIAL ALTITUDE (15,000 FEET)

AD IS INITIAL DISTANCE (25.9 NAUTICAL MILES)

AT IS INITIAL TIME (12.2 MINUTES)

BH IS FINAL ALTITUDE (30,000 FEET)

BD IS FINAL DISTANCE (70.1 NAUTICAL MILES)

BT IS FINAL TIME (29.3 MINUTES)

BW IS FINAL GROSS WEIGHT (7900 POUNDS)

Aw−Bw IS FUEL USED (100 POUNDS)

BD−AD IS DISTANCE TRAVELED (44.2 NAUTICAL MILES)

BT−AT IS TIME TO CLIMB (17.1 MINUTES)

EXAMPLE 2:

aH IS INITIAL ALTITUDE (1000 FEET)

aw IS INITIAL GROSS WEIGHT (8404 POUNDS)

aD IS INITIAL DISTANCE (1.8 NAUTICAL MILES)

aT IS INITIAL TIME (1 MINUTE)

bH IS FINAL ALTITUDE (5000 FEET)

bw IS FINAL GROSS WEIGHT (8385 POUNDS)

bT IS FINAL DISTANCE (8.5 NAUTICAL MILES)

bD IS FINAL TIME (4.2 MINUTES)

aw−bw IS FUEL USED (19 POUNDS)

DATA AS OF: 1-1-57
BASED ON: FLIGHT TEST DATA, REPORT NO. NA55H-235

FUEL GRADE: EITHER 115/145 OR 100/130
FUEL DENSITY: 6.0 LB/GAL

1-28C-1-93-19B

Figure 11-70

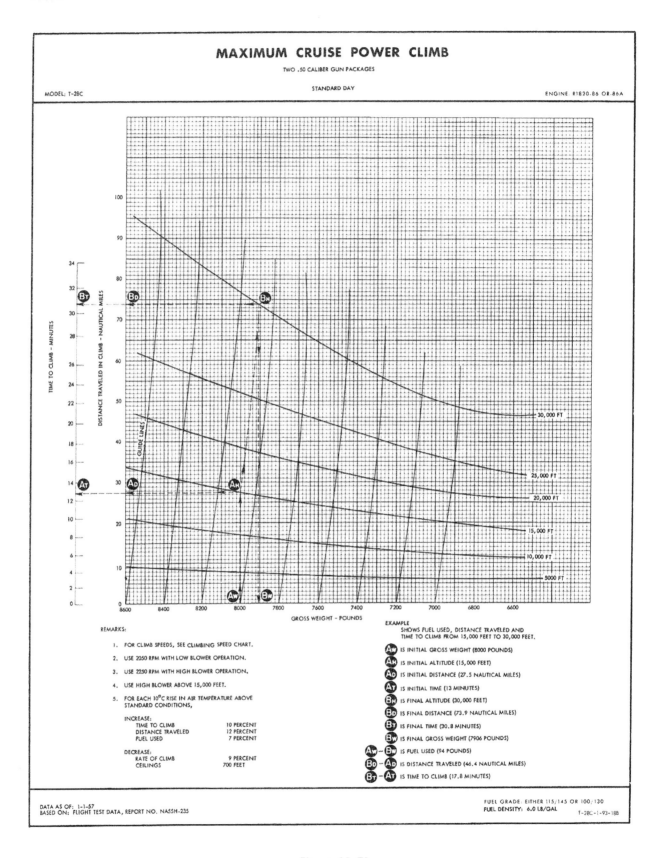

MAXIMUM CRUISE POWER CLIMB

TWO .50 CALIBER GUN PACKAGES

STANDARD DAY

MODEL: T-28C

ENGINE: R1820-86 OR-86A

REMARKS:

1. FOR CLIMB SPEEDS, SEE CLIMBING SPEED CHART.

2. USE 2050 RPM WITH LOW BLOWER OPERATION.

3. USE 2250 RPM WITH HIGH BLOWER OPERATION.

4. USE HIGH BLOWER ABOVE 15,000 FEET.

5. FOR EACH 10°C RISE IN AIR TEMPERATURE ABOVE STANDARD CONDITIONS,

INCREASE:
TIME TO CLIMB   10 PERCENT
DISTANCE TRAVELED   12 PERCENT
FUEL USED   7 PERCENT

DECREASE:
RATE OF CLIMB   9 PERCENT
CEILINGS   700 FEET

EXAMPLE

SHOWS FUEL USED, DISTANCE TRAVELED AND TIME TO CLIMB FROM 15,000 FEET TO 30,000 FEET.

Aw IS INITIAL GROSS WEIGHT (8000 POUNDS)

Ah IS INITIAL ALTITUDE (15,000 FEET)

Ad IS INITIAL DISTANCE (27.5 NAUTICAL MILES)

At IS INITIAL TIME (13 MINUTES)

Bh IS FINAL ALTITUDE (30,000 FEET)

Bd IS FINAL DISTANCE (73.9 NAUTICAL MILES)

Bt IS FINAL TIME (30.8 MINUTES)

Bw IS FINAL GROSS WEIGHT (7906 POUNDS)

Aw — Bw IS FUEL USED (94 POUNDS)

Bd — Ad IS DISTANCE TRAVELED (46.4 NAUTICAL MILES)

Bt — At IS TIME TO CLIMB (17.8 MINUTES)

DATA AS OF: 1-1-57
BASED ON: FLIGHT TEST DATA, REPORT NO. NA55H-235

FUEL GRADE: EITHER 115/145 OR 100/130
FUEL DENSITY: 6.0 LB/GAL

T-28C-1-93-18B

Figure 11-71

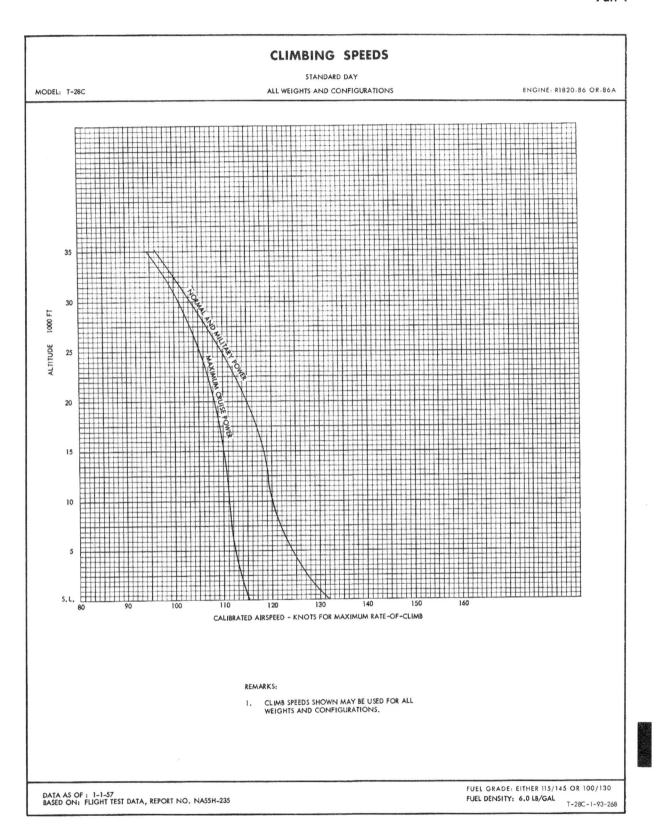

CLIMBING SPEEDS

STANDARD DAY

MODEL: T-28C

ALL WEIGHTS AND CONFIGURATIONS

ENGINE: R1820-86 OR-86A

REMARKS:

1. CLIMB SPEEDS SHOWN MAY BE USED FOR ALL WEIGHTS AND CONFIGURATIONS.

DATA AS OF : 1-1-57
BASED ON: FLIGHT TEST DATA, REPORT NO. NA55H-235

FUEL GRADE: EITHER 115/145 OR 100/130
FUEL DENSITY: 6.0 LB/GAL
T-28C-1-93-26B

Figure 11-72

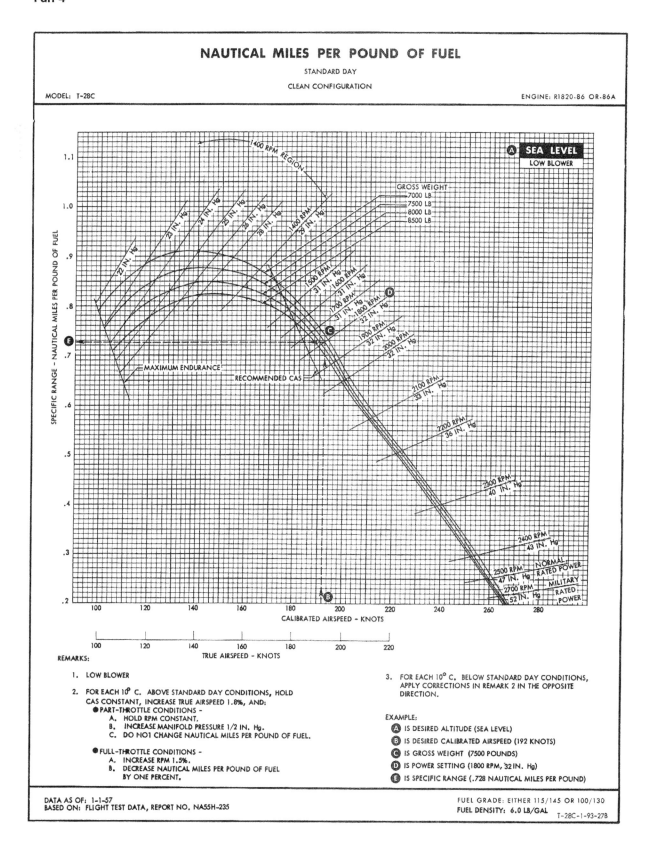

NAUTICAL MILES PER POUND OF FUEL

STANDARD DAY

CLEAN CONFIGURATION

MODEL: T-28C

ENGINE: R1820-86 OR-86A

REMARKS:

1. LOW BLOWER

2. FOR EACH 10° C. ABOVE STANDARD DAY CONDITIONS, HOLD
   CAS CONSTANT, INCREASE TRUE AIRSPEED 1.8%, AND:
   • PART-THROTTLE CONDITIONS -
     A. HOLD RPM CONSTANT.
     B. INCREASE MANIFOLD PRESSURE 1/2 IN. Hg.
     C. DO NOT CHANGE NAUTICAL MILES PER POUND OF FUEL.

   • FULL-THROTTLE CONDITIONS -
     A. INCREASE RPM 1.5%.
     B. DECREASE NAUTICAL MILES PER POUND OF FUEL
        BY ONE PERCENT.

3. FOR EACH 10° C. BELOW STANDARD DAY CONDITIONS,
   APPLY CORRECTIONS IN REMARK 2 IN THE OPPOSITE
   DIRECTION.

EXAMPLE:

Ⓐ IS DESIRED ALTITUDE (SEA LEVEL)
Ⓑ IS DESIRED CALIBRATED AIRSPEED (192 KNOTS)
Ⓒ IS GROSS WEIGHT (7500 POUNDS)
Ⓓ IS POWER SETTING (1800 RPM, 32 IN. Hg)
Ⓔ IS SPECIFIC RANGE (.728 NAUTICAL MILES PER POUND)

DATA AS OF: 1-1-57
BASED ON: FLIGHT TEST DATA, REPORT NO. NA55H-235

FUEL GRADE: EITHER 115/145 OR 100/130
FUEL DENSITY: 6.0 LB/GAL

T-28C-1-93-27B

Figure 11-73

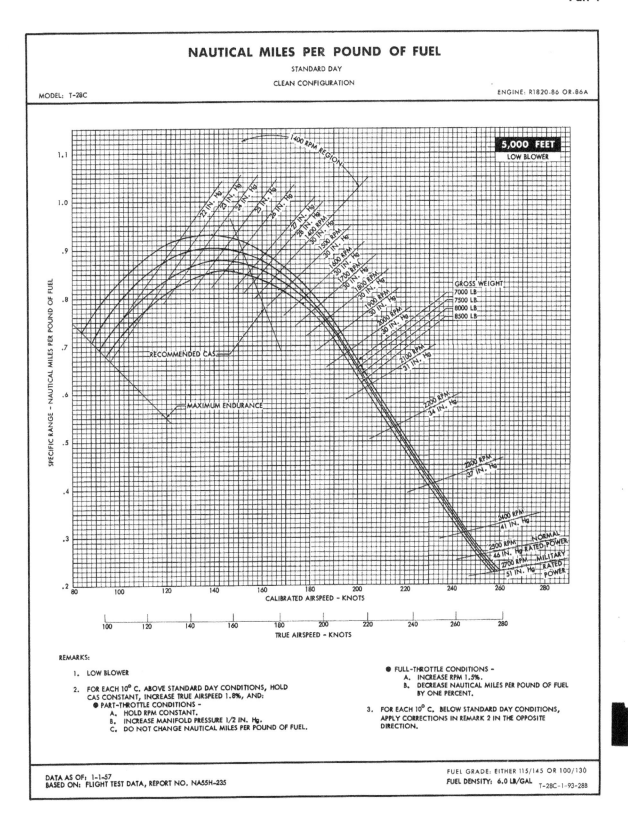

NAUTICAL MILES PER POUND OF FUEL

STANDARD DAY

CLEAN CONFIGURATION

MODEL: T-28C

ENGINE: R1820-86 OR-86A

5,000 FEET
LOW BLOWER

REMARKS:

1. LOW BLOWER

2. FOR EACH 10° C. ABOVE STANDARD DAY CONDITIONS, HOLD CAS CONSTANT, INCREASE TRUE AIRSPEED 1.8%, AND:
   ● PART-THROTTLE CONDITIONS -
   A. HOLD RPM CONSTANT.
   B. INCREASE MANIFOLD PRESSURE 1/2 IN. Hg.
   C. DO NOT CHANGE NAUTICAL MILES PER POUND OF FUEL.

● FULL-THROTTLE CONDITIONS -
   A. INCREASE RPM 1.5%.
   B. DECREASE NAUTICAL MILES PER POUND OF FUEL BY ONE PERCENT.

3. FOR EACH 10° C. BELOW STANDARD DAY CONDITIONS, APPLY CORRECTIONS IN REMARK 2 IN THE OPPOSITE DIRECTION.

DATA AS OF: 1-1-57
BASED ON: FLIGHT TEST DATA, REPORT NO. NA55H-235

FUEL GRADE: EITHER 115/145 OR 100/130
FUEL DENSITY: 6.0 LB/GAL

T-28C-1-93-28B

Figure 11-74

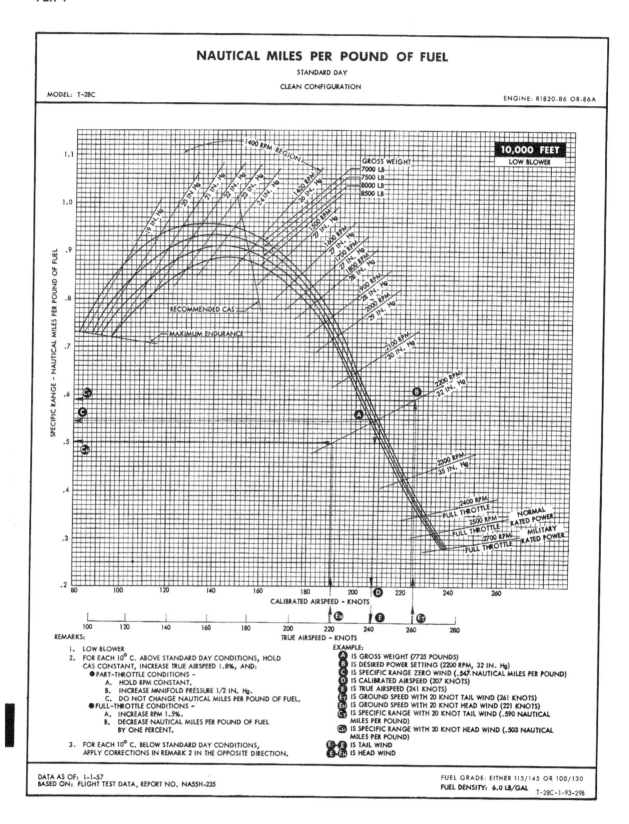

NAUTICAL MILES PER POUND OF FUEL

STANDARD DAY

CLEAN CONFIGURATION

MODEL: T-28C

ENGINE: R1820.86 OR.86A

REMARKS:

1. LOW BLOWER
2. FOR EACH 10° C. ABOVE STANDARD DAY CONDITIONS, HOLD CAS CONSTANT, INCREASE TRUE AIRSPEED 1.8%, AND:
   - PART-THROTTLE CONDITIONS –
     A. HOLD RPM CONSTANT.
     B. INCREASE MANIFOLD PRESSURE 1/2 IN. Hg.
     C. DO NOT CHANGE NAUTICAL MILES PER POUND OF FUEL.
   - FULL-THROTTLE CONDITIONS –
     A. INCREASE RPM 1.5%.
     B. DECREASE NAUTICAL MILES PER POUND OF FUEL BY ONE PERCENT.
3. FOR EACH 10° C. BELOW STANDARD DAY CONDITIONS, APPLY CORRECTIONS IN REMARK 2 IN THE OPPOSITE DIRECTION.

EXAMPLE:

Ⓐ IS GROSS WEIGHT (7725 POUNDS)
Ⓑ IS DESIRED POWER SETTING (2200 RPM, 32 IN. Hg)
Ⓒ IS SPECIFIC RANGE ZERO WIND (.547 NAUTICAL MILES PER POUND)
Ⓓ IS CALIBRATED AIRSPEED (207 KNOTS)
Ⓔ IS TRUE AIRSPEED (241 KNOTS)
Ⓔᵀ IS GROUND SPEED WITH 20 KNOT TAIL WIND (261 KNOTS)
Ⓔᴴ IS GROUND SPEED WITH 20 KNOT HEAD WIND (221 KNOTS)
Ⓒᵀ IS SPECIFIC RANGE WITH 20 KNOT TAIL WIND (.590 NAUTICAL MILES PER POUND)
Ⓒᴴ IS SPECIFIC RANGE WITH 20 KNOT HEAD WIND (.503 NAUTICAL MILES PER POUND)
Ⓔᵀ Ⓔ IS TAIL WIND
Ⓔ Ⓔᴴ IS HEAD WIND

DATA AS OF: 1-1-57
BASED ON: FLIGHT TEST DATA, REPORT NO. NA55H-235

FUEL GRADE: EITHER 115/145 OR 100/130
FUEL DENSITY: 6.0 LB/GAL

T-28C-1-93-29B

Figure 11-75

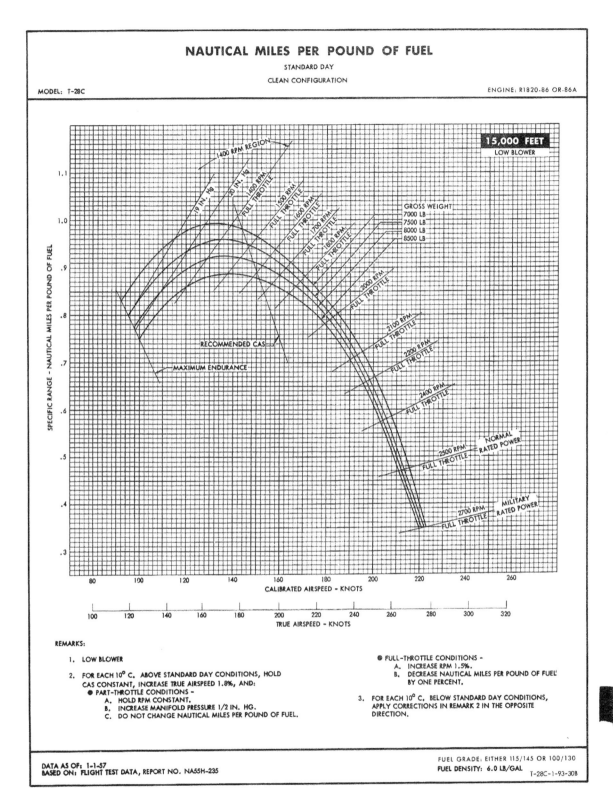

Figure 11-76

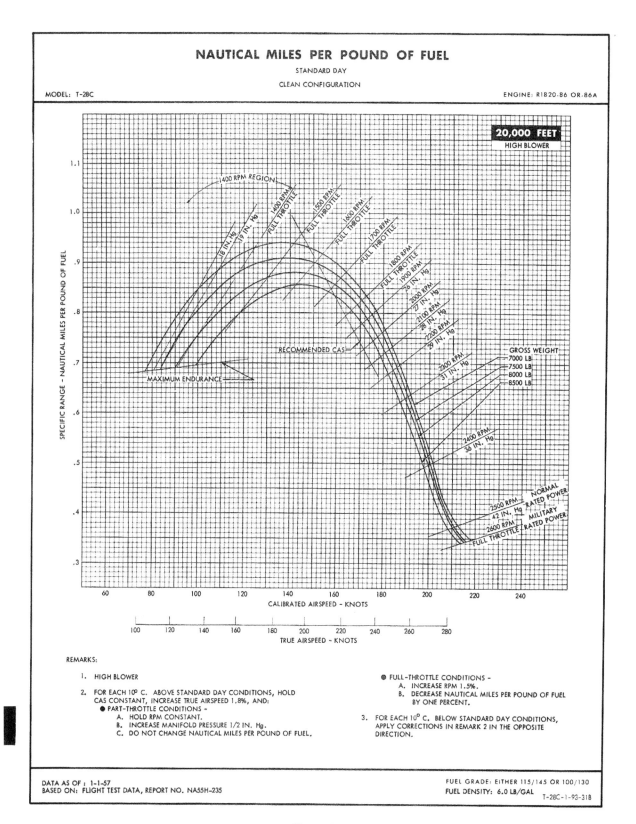

NAUTICAL MILES PER POUND OF FUEL

STANDARD DAY

CLEAN CONFIGURATION

MODEL: T-28C

ENGINE: R1820-86 OR-86A

20,000 FEET
HIGH BLOWER

REMARKS:

1. HIGH BLOWER

2. FOR EACH 10° C. ABOVE STANDARD DAY CONDITIONS, HOLD
   CAS CONSTANT, INCREASE TRUE AIRSPEED 1.8%, AND:
   ● PART-THROTTLE CONDITIONS -
      A. HOLD RPM CONSTANT.
      B. INCREASE MANIFOLD PRESSURE 1/2 IN. Hg.
      C. DO NOT CHANGE NAUTICAL MILES PER POUND OF FUEL.

● FULL-THROTTLE CONDITIONS -
   A. INCREASE RPM 1.5%.
   B. DECREASE NAUTICAL MILES PER POUND OF FUEL
      BY ONE PERCENT.

3. FOR EACH 10° C. BELOW STANDARD DAY CONDITIONS,
   APPLY CORRECTIONS IN REMARK 2 IN THE OPPOSITE
   DIRECTION.

DATA AS OF : 1-1-57
BASED ON: FLIGHT TEST DATA, REPORT NO. NA55H-235

FUEL GRADE: EITHER 115/145 OR 100/130
FUEL DENSITY: 6.0 LB/GAL

T-28C-1-93-31B

Figure 11-77

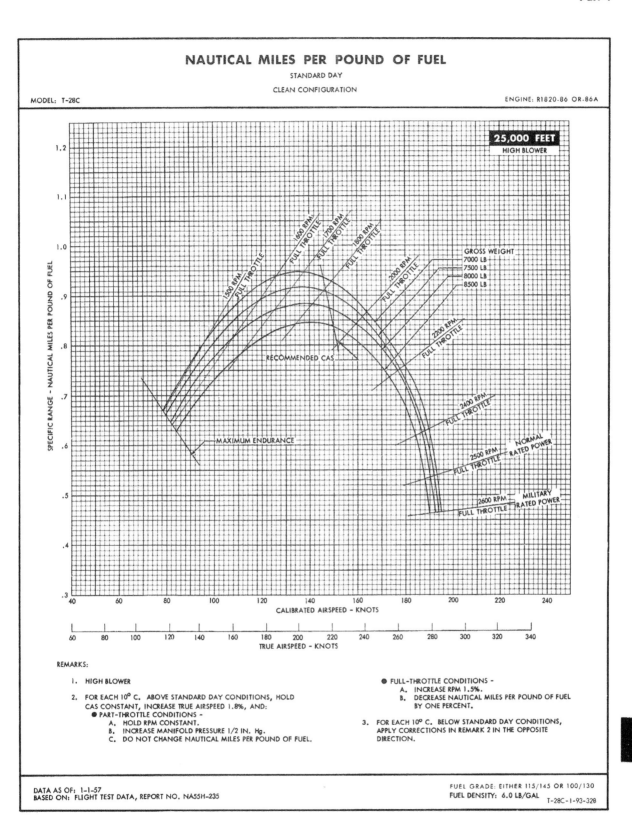

NAUTICAL MILES PER POUND OF FUEL

STANDARD DAY

CLEAN CONFIGURATION

MODEL: T-28C

ENGINE: R1820-86 OR-86A

25,000 FEET
HIGH BLOWER

REMARKS:

1. HIGH BLOWER

2. FOR EACH 10° C. ABOVE STANDARD DAY CONDITIONS, HOLD CAS CONSTANT, INCREASE TRUE AIRSPEED 1.8%, AND:
   - PART-THROTTLE CONDITIONS -
     A. HOLD RPM CONSTANT.
     B. INCREASE MANIFOLD PRESSURE 1/2 IN. Hg.
     C. DO NOT CHANGE NAUTICAL MILES PER POUND OF FUEL.

- FULL-THROTTLE CONDITIONS -
  A. INCREASE RPM 1.5%.
  B. DECREASE NAUTICAL MILES PER POUND OF FUEL BY ONE PERCENT.

3. FOR EACH 10° C. BELOW STANDARD DAY CONDITIONS, APPLY CORRECTIONS IN REMARK 2 IN THE OPPOSITE DIRECTION.

DATA AS OF: 1-1-57
BASED ON: FLIGHT TEST DATA, REPORT NO. NA55H-235

FUEL GRADE: EITHER 115/145 OR 100/130
FUEL DENSITY: 6.0 LB/GAL

T-28C-1-93-32B

Figure 11-78

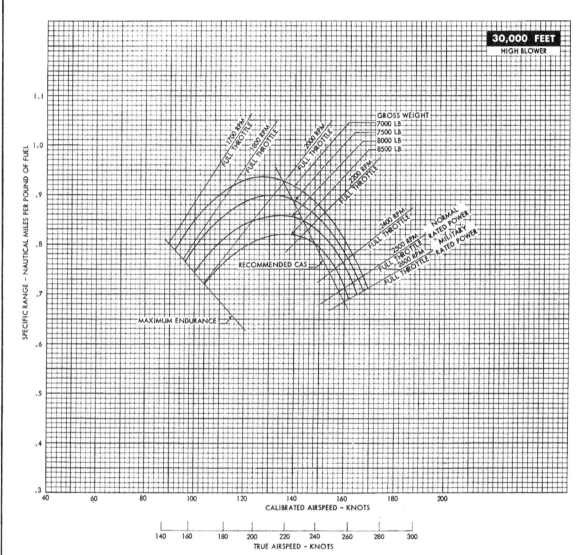

NAUTICAL MILES PER POUND OF FUEL
STANDARD DAY
CLEAN CONFIGURATION

MODEL: T-28C

ENGINE: R1820-86 OR-86A

REMARKS:

1. HIGH BLOWER

2. FOR EACH 10° C. ABOVE STANDARD DAY CONDITIONS, HOLD
CAS CONSTANT, INCREASE TRUE AIRSPEED 1.8%, AND:
● PART-THROTTLE CONDITIONS -
   A. HOLD RPM CONSTANT.
   B. INCREASE MANIFOLD PRESSURE 1/2 IN. Hg.
   C. DO NOT CHANGE NAUTICAL MILES PER POUND OF FUEL.

● FULL-THROTTLE CONDITIONS -
   A. INCREASE RPM 1.5%.
   B. DECREASE NAUTICAL MILES PER POUND OF FUEL
      BY ONE PERCENT.

3. FOR EACH 10° C. BELOW STANDARD DAY CONDITIONS,
APPLY CORRECTIONS IN REMARK 2 IN THE OPPOSITE
DIRECTION.

DATA AS OF: 1-1-57
BASED ON: FLIGHT TEST DATA, REPORT NO. NA55H-235

FUEL GRADE: EITHER 115/145 OR 100/130
FUEL DENSITY: 6.0 LB/GAL

T-28C-1-93-33B

Figure 11-79

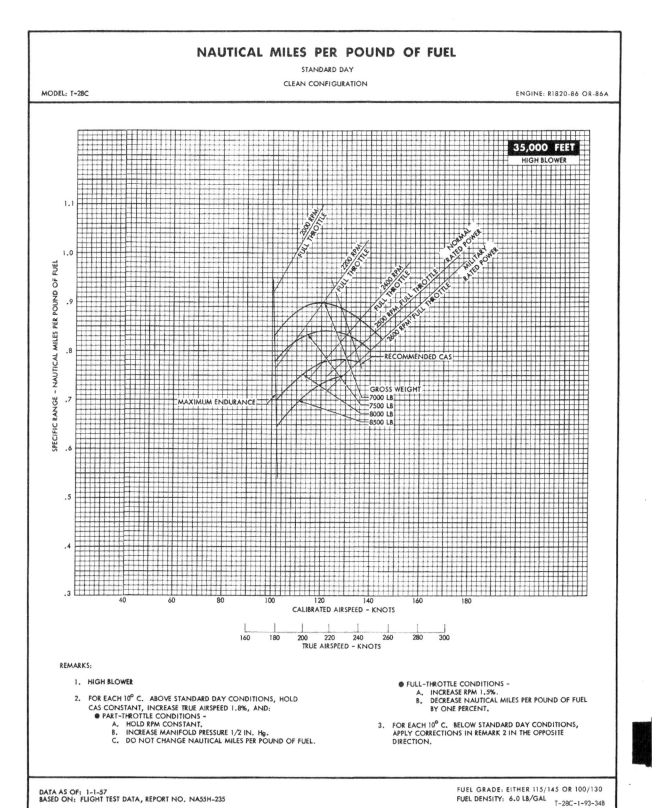

NAUTICAL MILES PER POUND OF FUEL

STANDARD DAY

CLEAN CONFIGURATION

MODEL: T-28C

ENGINE: R1820-86 OR-86A

35,000 FEET
HIGH BLOWER

REMARKS:

1. HIGH BLOWER

2. FOR EACH 10° C. ABOVE STANDARD DAY CONDITIONS, HOLD CAS CONSTANT, INCREASE TRUE AIRSPEED 1.8%, AND:
   ● PART-THROTTLE CONDITIONS -
      A. HOLD RPM CONSTANT.
      B. INCREASE MANIFOLD PRESSURE 1/2 IN. Hg.
      C. DO NOT CHANGE NAUTICAL MILES PER POUND OF FUEL.

● FULL-THROTTLE CONDITIONS -
   A. INCREASE RPM 1.5%.
   B. DECREASE NAUTICAL MILES PER POUND OF FUEL BY ONE PERCENT.

3. FOR EACH 10° C. BELOW STANDARD DAY CONDITIONS, APPLY CORRECTIONS IN REMARK 2 IN THE OPPOSITE DIRECTION.

DATA AS OF: 1-1-57
BASED ON: FLIGHT TEST DATA, REPORT NO. NA55H-235

FUEL GRADE: EITHER 115/145 OR 100/130
FUEL DENSITY: 6.0 LB/GAL

T-28C-1-93-34B

Figure 11-80

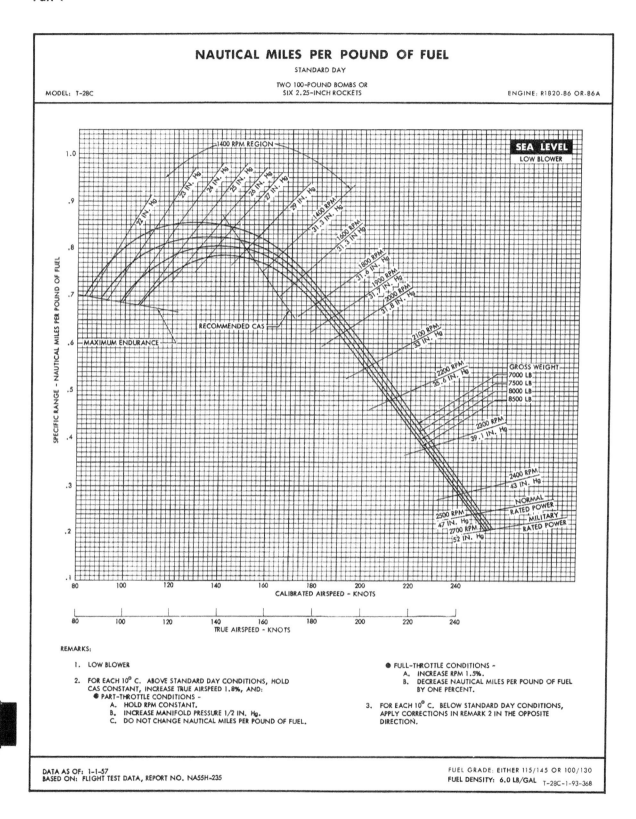

NAUTICAL MILES PER POUND OF FUEL

STANDARD DAY

TWO 100-POUND BOMBS OR
SIX 2.25-INCH ROCKETS

MODEL: T-28C

ENGINE: R1820-86 OR-86A

REMARKS:

1. LOW BLOWER

2. FOR EACH 10° C. ABOVE STANDARD DAY CONDITIONS, HOLD CAS CONSTANT, INCREASE TRUE AIRSPEED 1.8%, AND:
   ● PART-THROTTLE CONDITIONS -
   A. HOLD RPM CONSTANT.
   B. INCREASE MANIFOLD PRESSURE 1/2 IN. Hg.
   C. DO NOT CHANGE NAUTICAL MILES PER POUND OF FUEL.

● FULL-THROTTLE CONDITIONS -
A. INCREASE RPM 1.5%.
B. DECREASE NAUTICAL MILES PER POUND OF FUEL BY ONE PERCENT.

3. FOR EACH 10° C. BELOW STANDARD DAY CONDITIONS, APPLY CORRECTIONS IN REMARK 2 IN THE OPPOSITE DIRECTION.

DATA AS OF: 1-1-57
BASED ON: FLIGHT TEST DATA, REPORT NO. NA55H-235

FUEL GRADE: EITHER 115/145 OR 100/130
FUEL DENSITY: 6.0 LB/GAL   T-28C-1-93-36B

Figure 11-81

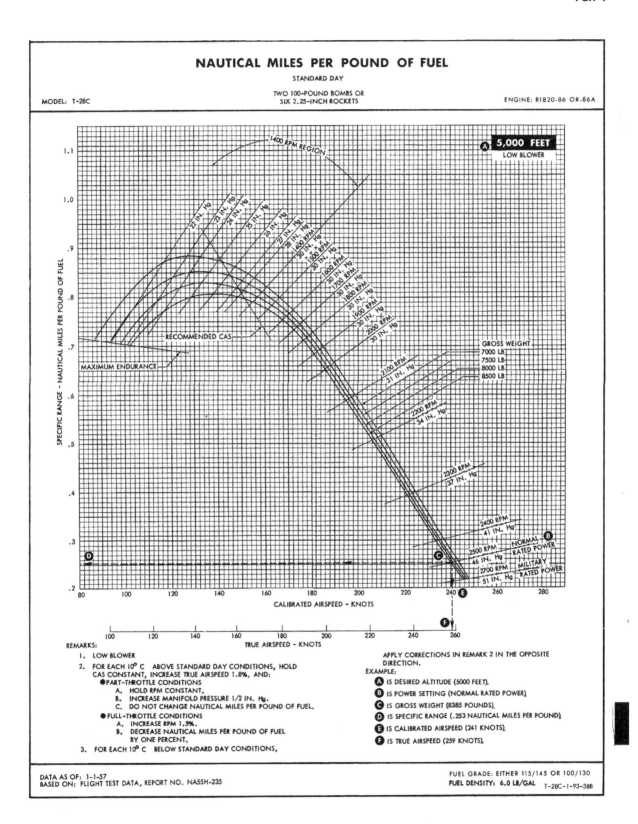

NAUTICAL MILES PER POUND OF FUEL

STANDARD DAY

TWO 100-POUND BOMBS OR
SIX 2.25-INCH ROCKETS

MODEL: T-28C

ENGINE: R1820-86 OR-86A

REMARKS:

1. LOW BLOWER
2. FOR EACH 10° C ABOVE STANDARD DAY CONDITIONS, HOLD CAS CONSTANT, INCREASE TRUE AIRSPEED 1.8%, AND:
   ● PART-THROTTLE CONDITIONS
     A. HOLD RPM CONSTANT.
     B. INCREASE MANIFOLD PRESSURE 1/2 IN. Hg.
     C. DO NOT CHANGE NAUTICAL MILES PER POUND OF FUEL.
   ● FULL-THROTTLE CONDITIONS
     A. INCREASE RPM 1.5%.
     B. DECREASE NAUTICAL MILES PER POUND OF FUEL BY ONE PERCENT.
3. FOR EACH 10° C BELOW STANDARD DAY CONDITIONS,

APPLY CORRECTIONS IN REMARK 2 IN THE OPPOSITE DIRECTION.

EXAMPLE:

Ⓐ IS DESIRED ALTITUDE (5000 FEET).
Ⓑ IS POWER SETTING (NORMAL RATED POWER).
Ⓒ IS GROSS WEIGHT (8385 POUNDS).
Ⓓ IS SPECIFIC RANGE (.253 NAUTICAL MILES PER POUND).
Ⓔ IS CALIBRATED AIRSPEED (241 KNOTS).
Ⓕ IS TRUE AIRSPEED (259 KNOTS).

DATA AS OF: 1-1-57
BASED ON: FLIGHT TEST DATA, REPORT NO. NA55H-235

FUEL GRADE: EITHER 115/145 OR 100/130
FUEL DENSITY: 6.0 LB/GAL

T-28C-1-93-38B

Figure 11-82

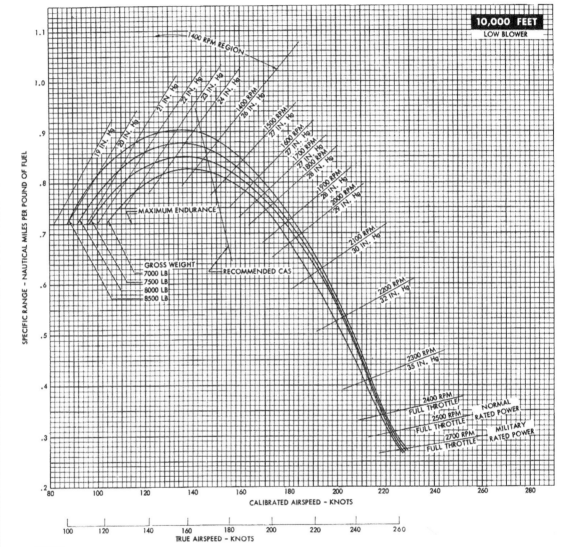

NAUTICAL MILES PER POUND OF FUEL

STANDARD DAY

TWO 100-POUND BOMBS OR
SIX 2.25-INCH ROCKETS

MODEL: T-28C

ENGINE: R1820-86 OR-86A

10,000 FEET
LOW BLOWER

REMARKS:

1. LOW BLOWER

2. FOR EACH 10° C. ABOVE STANDARD DAY CONDITIONS, HOLD
   CAS CONSTANT, INCREASE TRUE AIRSPEED 1.8%, AND:
   • PART-THROTTLE CONDITIONS
   A. HOLD RPM CONSTANT.
   B. INCREASE MANIFOLD PRESSURE 1/2 IN. Hg.
   C. DO NOT CHANGE NAUTICAL MILES PER POUND OF FUEL.

• FULL-THROTTLE CONDITIONS
   A. INCREASE RPM 1.5%.
   B. DECREASE NAUTICAL MILES PER POUND OF FUEL
       BY ONE PERCENT.

3. FOR EACH 10° C BELOW STANDARD DAY CONDITIONS,
   APPLY CORRECTIONS IN REMARK 2 IN THE OPPOSITE
   DIRECTION.

DATA AS OF : 1-1-57
BASED ON: FLIGHT TEST DATA, REPORT NO. NA55H-235

FUEL GRADE: EITHER 115/145 OR 100/130
FUEL DENSITY: 6.0 LB/GAL

T-28C-1-93-40B

Figure 11-83

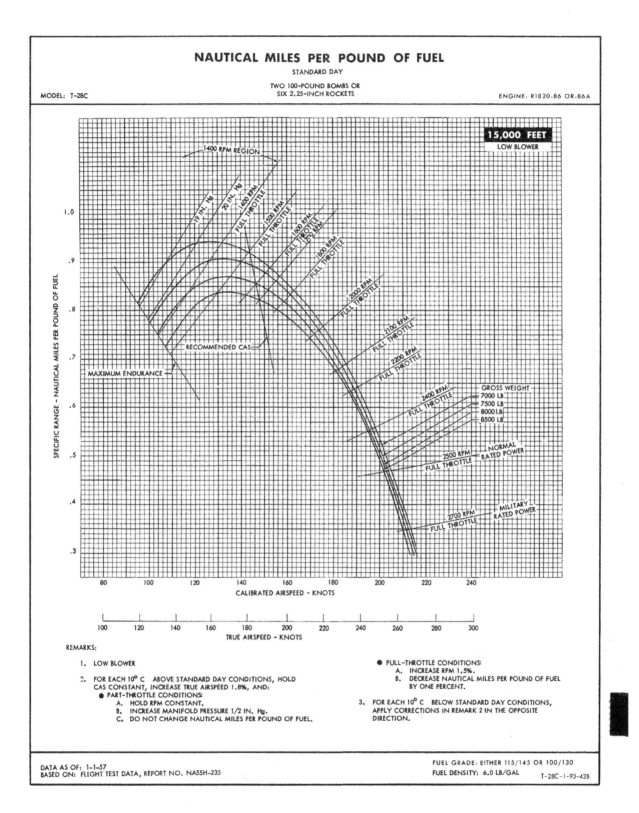

NAUTICAL MILES PER POUND OF FUEL
STANDARD DAY

TWO 100-POUND BOMBS OR
SIX 2.25-INCH ROCKETS

MODEL: T-28C

ENGINE: R1820-86 OR -86A

15,000 FEET
LOW BLOWER

REMARKS:

1. LOW BLOWER

2. FOR EACH 10° C ABOVE STANDARD DAY CONDITIONS, HOLD
CAS CONSTANT, INCREASE TRUE AIRSPEED 1.8%, AND:
   ● PART-THROTTLE CONDITIONS:
   A. HOLD RPM CONSTANT.
   B. INCREASE MANIFOLD PRESSURE 1/2 IN. Hg.
   C. DO NOT CHANGE NAUTICAL MILES PER POUND OF FUEL.

● FULL-THROTTLE CONDITIONS:
   A. INCREASE RPM 1.5%.
   B. DECREASE NAUTICAL MILES PER POUND OF FUEL
      BY ONE PERCENT.

3. FOR EACH 10° C BELOW STANDARD DAY CONDITIONS,
APPLY CORRECTIONS IN REMARK 2 IN THE OPPOSITE
DIRECTION.

DATA AS OF: 1-1-57
BASED ON: FLIGHT TEST DATA, REPORT NO. NA55H-235

FUEL GRADE: EITHER 115/145 OR 100/130
FUEL DENSITY: 6.0 LB/GAL

T-28C-1-93-42B

Figure 11-84

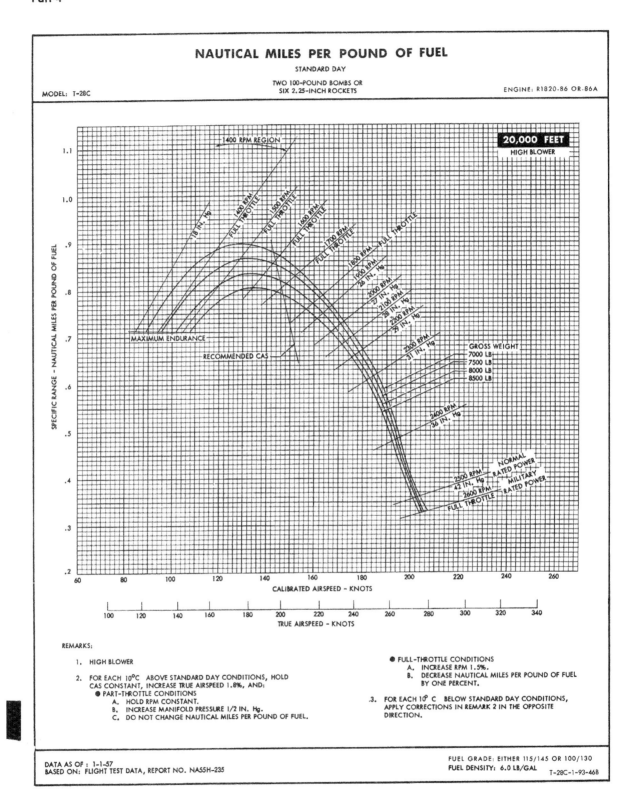

NAUTICAL MILES PER POUND OF FUEL
STANDARD DAY

TWO 100-POUND BOMBS OR
SIX 2.25-INCH ROCKETS

MODEL: T-28C

ENGINE: R1820-86 OR-86A

REMARKS:

1. HIGH BLOWER

2. FOR EACH 10°C ABOVE STANDARD DAY CONDITIONS, HOLD
   CAS CONSTANT, INCREASE TRUE AIRSPEED 1.8%, AND:
   ● PART-THROTTLE CONDITIONS
      A. HOLD RPM CONSTANT.
      B. INCREASE MANIFOLD PRESSURE 1/2 IN. Hg.
      C. DO NOT CHANGE NAUTICAL MILES PER POUND OF FUEL.

● FULL-THROTTLE CONDITIONS
   A. INCREASE RPM 1.5%.
   B. DECREASE NAUTICAL MILES PER POUND OF FUEL
      BY ONE PERCENT.

3. FOR EACH 10° C BELOW STANDARD DAY CONDITIONS,
   APPLY CORRECTIONS IN REMARK 2 IN THE OPPOSITE
   DIRECTION.

DATA AS OF : 1-1-57
BASED ON: FLIGHT TEST DATA, REPORT NO. NA55H-235

FUEL GRADE: EITHER 115/145 OR 100/130
FUEL DENSITY: 6.0 LB/GAL

T-28C-1-93-46B

Figure 11-85

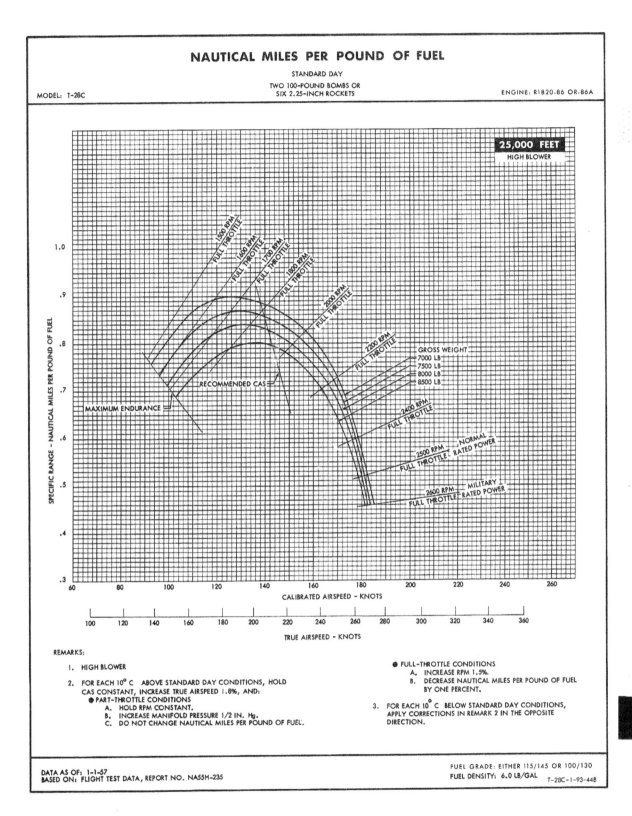

NAUTICAL MILES PER POUND OF FUEL

STANDARD DAY

TWO 100-POUND BOMBS OR
SIX 2.25-INCH ROCKETS

MODEL: T-28C

ENGINE: R1820-86 OR-86A

REMARKS:

1. HIGH BLOWER

2. FOR EACH 10° C ABOVE STANDARD DAY CONDITIONS, HOLD
   CAS CONSTANT, INCREASE TRUE AIRSPEED 1.8%, AND:
   ● PART-THROTTLE CONDITIONS
     A. HOLD RPM CONSTANT.
     B. INCREASE MANIFOLD PRESSURE 1/2 IN. Hg.
     C. DO NOT CHANGE NAUTICAL MILES PER POUND OF FUEL.

● FULL-THROTTLE CONDITIONS
   A. INCREASE RPM 1.5%.
   B. DECREASE NAUTICAL MILES PER POUND OF FUEL
      BY ONE PERCENT.

3. FOR EACH 10° C BELOW STANDARD DAY CONDITIONS,
   APPLY CORRECTIONS IN REMARK 2 IN THE OPPOSITE
   DIRECTION.

DATA AS OF: 1-1-57
BASED ON: FLIGHT TEST DATA, REPORT NO. NA55H-235

FUEL GRADE: EITHER 115/145 OR 100/130
FUEL DENSITY: 6.0 LB/GAL

T-28C-1-93-44B

Figure 11-86

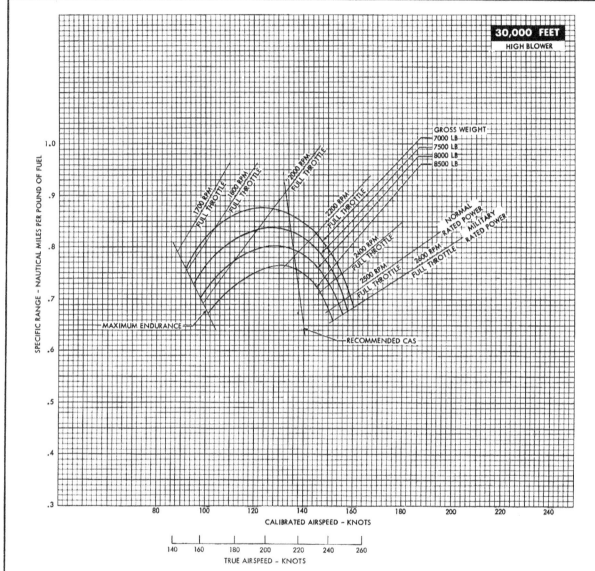

NAUTICAL MILES PER POUND OF FUEL

STANDARD DAY

TWO 100-POUND BOMBS OR
SIX 2.25-INCH ROCKETS

MODEL: T-28C

ENGINE: R1820-86 OR-86A

30,000 FEET
HIGH BLOWER

REMARKS:

1. HIGH BLOWER

2. FOR EACH 10° C ABOVE STANDARD DAY CONDITIONS, HOLD
   CAS CONSTANT, INCREASE TRUE AIRSPEED 1.8%, AND:
   ● PART-THROTTLE CONDITIONS
      A. HOLD RPM CONSTANT.
      B. INCREASE MANIFOLD PRESSURE 1/2 IN. Hg.
      C. DO NOT CHANGE NAUTICAL MILES PER POUND OF FUEL.

● FULL-THROTTLE CONDITIONS
   A. INCREASE RPM 1.5%.
   B. DECREASE NAUTICAL MILES PER POUND OF FUEL
      BY ONE PERCENT.

3. FOR EACH 10° C BELOW STANDARD DAY CONDITIONS,
   APPLY CORRECTIONS IN REMARK 2 IN THE OPPOSITE
   DIRECTION.

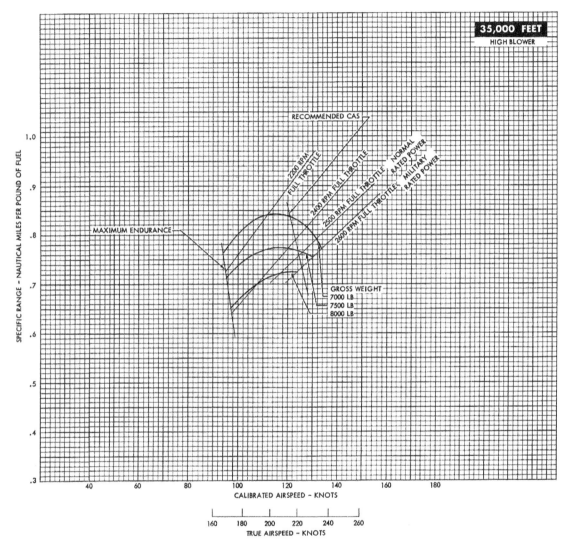

NAUTICAL MILES PER POUND OF FUEL

STANDARD DAY

TWO 100-POUND BOMBS OR
SIX 2.25-INCH ROCKETS

MODEL: T-28C

ENGINE: R1820-86 OR-86A

REMARKS:

1. HIGH BLOWER

2. FOR EACH 10° C ABOVE STANDARD DAY CONDITIONS, HOLD
   CAS CONSTANT, INCREASE TRUE AIRSPEED 1.8%, AND:
   ● PART-THROTTLE CONDITIONS
      A. HOLD RPM CONSTANT.
      B. INCREASE MANIFOLD PRESSURE 1/2 IN. Hg.
      C. DO NOT CHANGE NAUTICAL MILES PER POUND OF FUEL.

● FULL-THROTTLE CONDITIONS
   A. INCREASE RPM 1.5%.
   B. DECREASE NAUTICAL MILES PER POUND OF FUEL
      BY ONE PERCENT.

3. FOR EACH 10° C BELOW STANDARD DAY CONDITIONS,
   APPLY CORRECTIONS IN REMARK 2 IN THE OPPOSITE
   DIRECTION.

DATA AS OF: 1-1-57
BASED ON: FLIGHT TEST DATA, REPORT NO. NA55H-235

FUEL GRADE: EITHER 115/145 OR 100/130
FUEL DENSITY: 6.0 LB/GAL

T-28C-1-93-50B

Figure 11-88

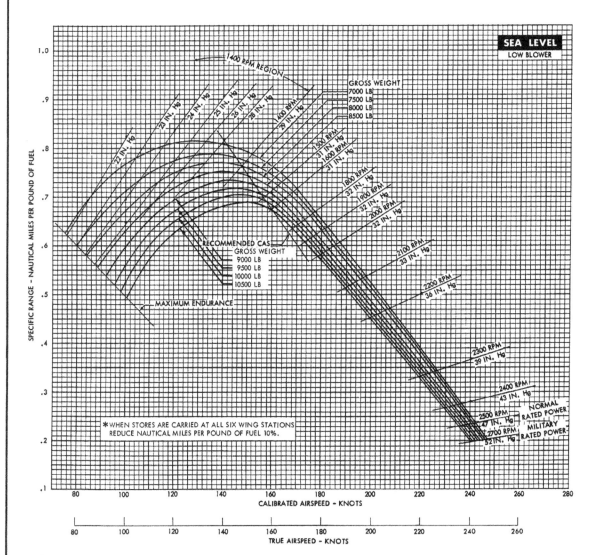

NAUTICAL MILES PER POUND OF FUEL

STANDARD DAY

TWO .50 CALIBER GUN PACKAGES
AND ADDITIONAL STORES *

MODEL: T-28C

ENGINE: R1820-86 OR-86A

SEA LEVEL
LOW BLOWER

1400 RPM REGION

GROSS WEIGHT
7000 LB
7500 LB
8000 LB
8500 LB

23 IN. Hg
24 IN. Hg
25 IN. Hg
26 IN. Hg
28 IN. Hg
22 IN. Hg

1400 RPM
29 IN. Hg

1500 RPM
31 IN. Hg
1600 RPM
31 IN. Hg

1800 RPM
32 IN. Hg
1900 RPM
32 IN. Hg
2000 RPM
32 IN. Hg

RECOMMENDED CAS
GROSS WEIGHT
9000 LB
9500 LB
10000 LB
10500 LB

2100 RPM
33 IN. Hg

2200 RPM
36 IN. Hg

MAXIMUM ENDURANCE

2300 RPM
39 IN. Hg

2400 RPM
43 IN. Hg

2500 RPM
47 IN. Hg

NORMAL
RATED POWER

2700 RPM
52 IN. Hg

MILITARY
RATED POWER

* WHEN STORES ARE CARRIED AT ALL SIX WING STATIONS
REDUCE NAUTICAL MILES PER POUND OF FUEL 10%.

SPECIFIC RANGE - NAUTICAL MILES PER POUND OF FUEL

CALIBRATED AIRSPEED - KNOTS

TRUE AIRSPEED - KNOTS

REMARKS:

1. LOW BLOWER

2. FOR EACH 10° C. ABOVE STANDARD DAY CONDITIONS, HOLD
CAS CONSTANT, INCREASE TRUE AIRSPEED 1.8%, AND:
● PART-THROTTLE CONDITIONS -
    A. HOLD RPM CONSTANT.
    B. INCREASE MANIFOLD PRESSURE 1/2 IN. Hg.
    C. DO NOT CHANGE NAUTICAL MILES PER POUND OF FUEL.

● FULL-THROTTLE CONDITIONS -
    A. INCREASE RPM 1.5%.
    B. DECREASE NAUTICAL MILES PER POUND OF FUEL
        BY ONE PERCENT.

3. FOR EACH 10° C. BELOW STANDARD DAY CONDITIONS,
APPLY CORRECTIONS IN REMARK 2 IN THE OPPOSITE
DIRECTION.

DATA AS OF: 1-1-57
BASED ON: FLIGHT TEST DATA, REPORT NO. NA55H-235

FUEL GRADE: EITHER 115/145 OR 100/130
FUEL DENSITY: 6.0 LB/GAL

T-28C-1-93-78B

Figure 11-89

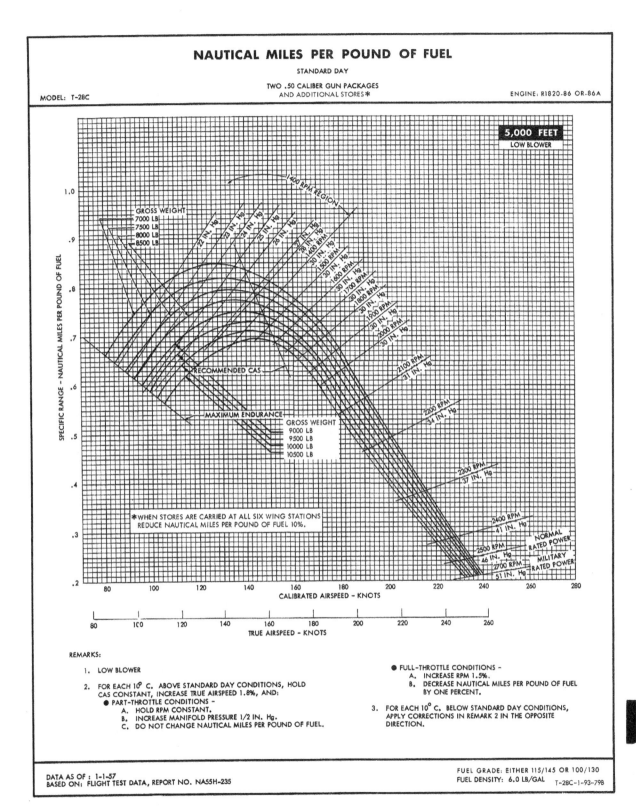

NAUTICAL MILES PER POUND OF FUEL

STANDARD DAY

TWO .50 CALIBER GUN PACKAGES
AND ADDITIONAL STORES *

MODEL: T-28C

ENGINE: R1820-86 OR-86A

REMARKS:

1. LOW BLOWER

2. FOR EACH 10° C. ABOVE STANDARD DAY CONDITIONS, HOLD
   CAS CONSTANT, INCREASE TRUE AIRSPEED 1.8%, AND:
   ● PART-THROTTLE CONDITIONS —
      A. HOLD RPM CONSTANT.
      B. INCREASE MANIFOLD PRESSURE 1/2 IN. Hg.
      C. DO NOT CHANGE NAUTICAL MILES PER POUND OF FUEL.

● FULL-THROTTLE CONDITIONS —
   A. INCREASE RPM 1.5%.
   B. DECREASE NAUTICAL MILES PER POUND OF FUEL
      BY ONE PERCENT.

3. FOR EACH 10° C. BELOW STANDARD DAY CONDITIONS,
   APPLY CORRECTIONS IN REMARK 2 IN THE OPPOSITE
   DIRECTION.

DATA AS OF : 1-1-57
BASED ON: FLIGHT TEST DATA, REPORT NO. NA55H-235

FUEL GRADE: EITHER 115/145 OR 100/130
FUEL DENSITY: 6.0 LB/GAL   T-28C-1-93-79B

Figure 11-90

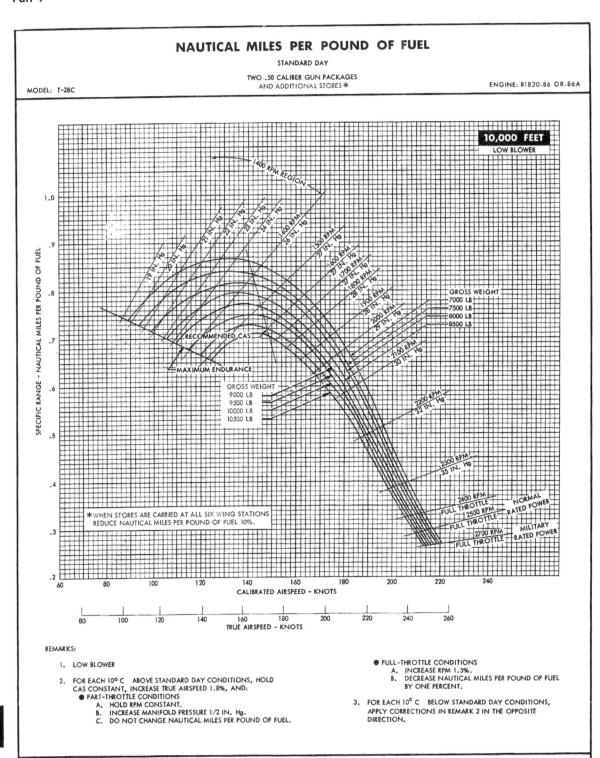

NAUTICAL MILES PER POUND OF FUEL

STANDARD DAY

TWO .50 CALIBER GUN PACKAGES
AND ADDITIONAL STORES *

MODEL: T-28C

ENGINE: R1820-86 OR-86A

REMARKS:

1. LOW BLOWER

2. FOR EACH 10° C ABOVE STANDARD DAY CONDITIONS, HOLD
   CAS CONSTANT, INCREASE TRUE AIRSPEED 1.8%, AND:
   ● PART-THROTTLE CONDITIONS
      A. HOLD RPM CONSTANT.
      B. INCREASE MANIFOLD PRESSURE 1/2 IN. Hg.
      C. DO NOT CHANGE NAUTICAL MILES PER POUND OF FUEL.

● FULL-THROTTLE CONDITIONS
   A. INCREASE RPM 1.5%.
   B. DECREASE NAUTICAL MILES PER POUND OF FUEL
      BY ONE PERCENT.

3. FOR EACH 10° C BELOW STANDARD DAY CONDITIONS,
   APPLY CORRECTIONS IN REMARK 2 IN THE OPPOSITE
   DIRECTION.

DATA AS OF: 1-1-57
BASED ON: FLIGHT TEST DATA, REPORT NO. NA55H-235

FUEL GRADE: EITHER 115/145 OR 100/130
FUEL DENSITY: 6.0 LB/GAL

T-28C-1-93-80B

Figure 11-91

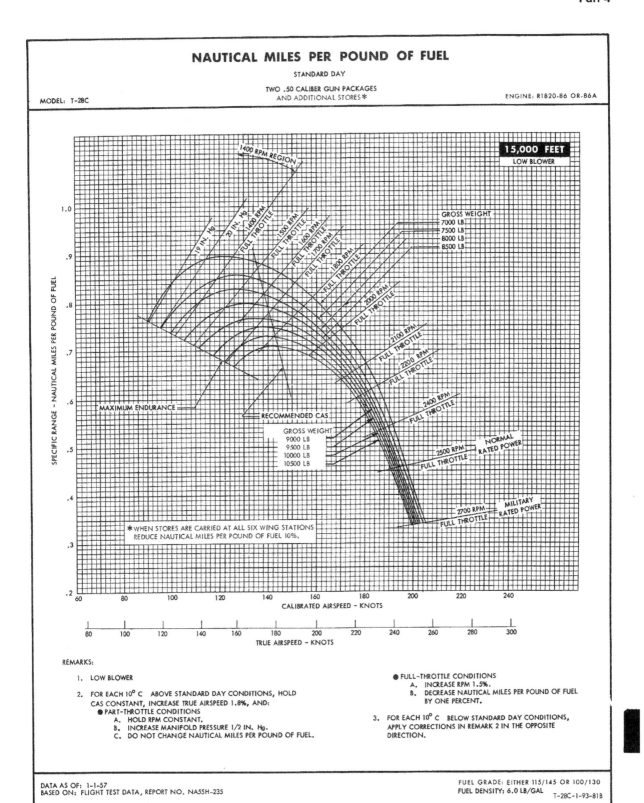

NAUTICAL MILES PER POUND OF FUEL

STANDARD DAY

TWO .50 CALIBER GUN PACKAGES
AND ADDITIONAL STORES *

MODEL: T-28C

ENGINE: R1820-86 OR-86A

15,000 FEET
LOW BLOWER

REMARKS:

1. LOW BLOWER

2. FOR EACH 10° C ABOVE STANDARD DAY CONDITIONS, HOLD
CAS CONSTANT, INCREASE TRUE AIRSPEED 1.8%, AND:
  ● PART-THROTTLE CONDITIONS
    A. HOLD RPM CONSTANT.
    B. INCREASE MANIFOLD PRESSURE 1/2 IN. Hg.
    C. DO NOT CHANGE NAUTICAL MILES PER POUND OF FUEL.

● FULL-THROTTLE CONDITIONS
    A. INCREASE RPM 1.5%.
    B. DECREASE NAUTICAL MILES PER POUND OF FUEL
       BY ONE PERCENT.

3. FOR EACH 10° C BELOW STANDARD DAY CONDITIONS,
APPLY CORRECTIONS IN REMARK 2 IN THE OPPOSITE
DIRECTION.

DATA AS OF: 1-1-57
BASED ON: FLIGHT TEST DATA, REPORT NO. NA55H-235

FUEL GRADE: EITHER 115/145 OR 100/130
FUEL DENSITY: 6.0 LB/GAL

T-28C-1-93-81B

Figure 11-92

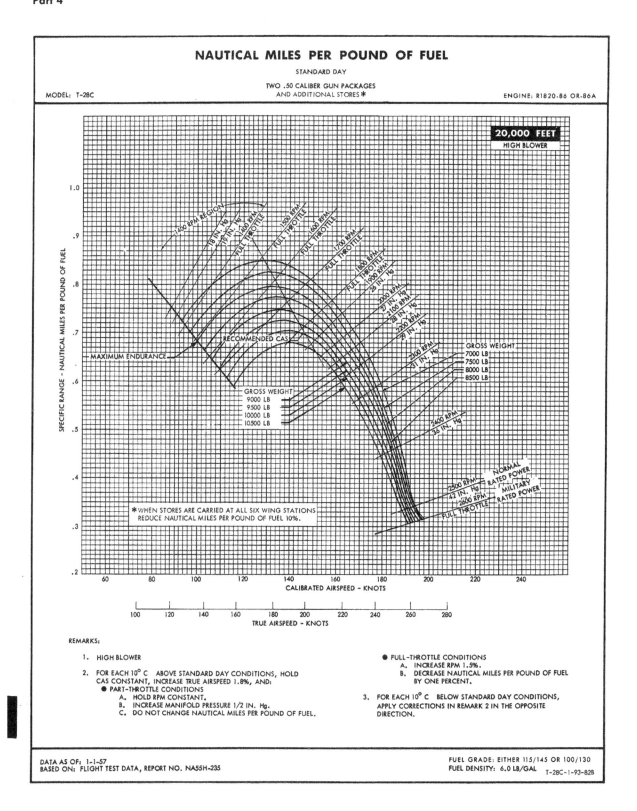

NAUTICAL MILES PER POUND OF FUEL

STANDARD DAY

TWO .50 CALIBER GUN PACKAGES
AND ADDITIONAL STORES ✱

MODEL: T-28C

ENGINE: R1820-86 OR-86A

20,000 FEET
HIGH BLOWER

✱ WHEN STORES ARE CARRIED AT ALL SIX WING STATIONS
REDUCE NAUTICAL MILES PER POUND OF FUEL 10%.

REMARKS:

1. HIGH BLOWER

2. FOR EACH 10° C ABOVE STANDARD DAY CONDITIONS, HOLD
   CAS CONSTANT, INCREASE TRUE AIRSPEED 1.8%, AND:
   ● PART-THROTTLE CONDITIONS
       A. HOLD RPM CONSTANT.
       B. INCREASE MANIFOLD PRESSURE 1/2 IN. Hg.
       C. DO NOT CHANGE NAUTICAL MILES PER POUND OF FUEL.

● FULL-THROTTLE CONDITIONS
    A. INCREASE RPM 1.5%.
    B. DECREASE NAUTICAL MILES PER POUND OF FUEL
       BY ONE PERCENT.

3. FOR EACH 10° C BELOW STANDARD DAY CONDITIONS,
   APPLY CORRECTIONS IN REMARK 2 IN THE OPPOSITE
   DIRECTION.

DATA AS OF: 1-1-57
BASED ON: FLIGHT TEST DATA, REPORT NO. NA55H-235

FUEL GRADE: EITHER 115/145 OR 100/130
FUEL DENSITY: 6.0 LB/GAL   T-28C-1-93-82B

Figure 11-93

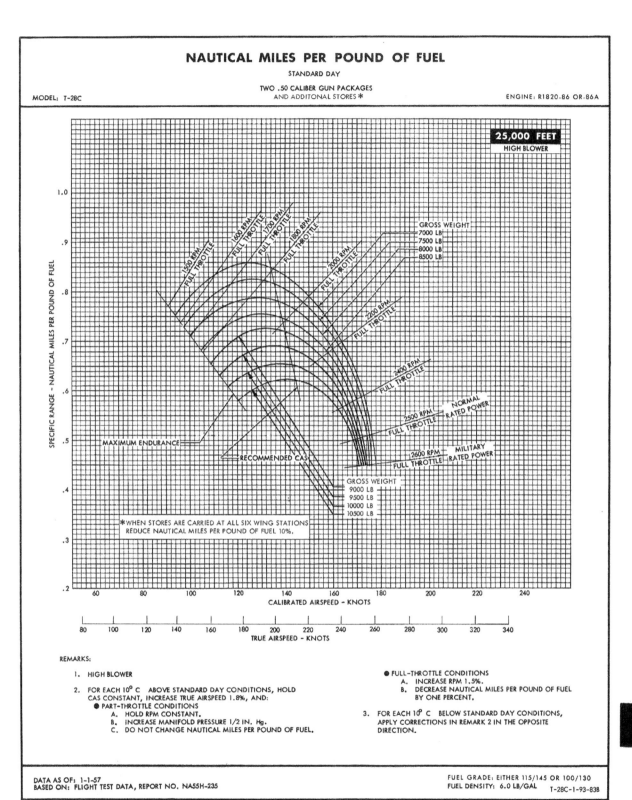

Figure 11-94

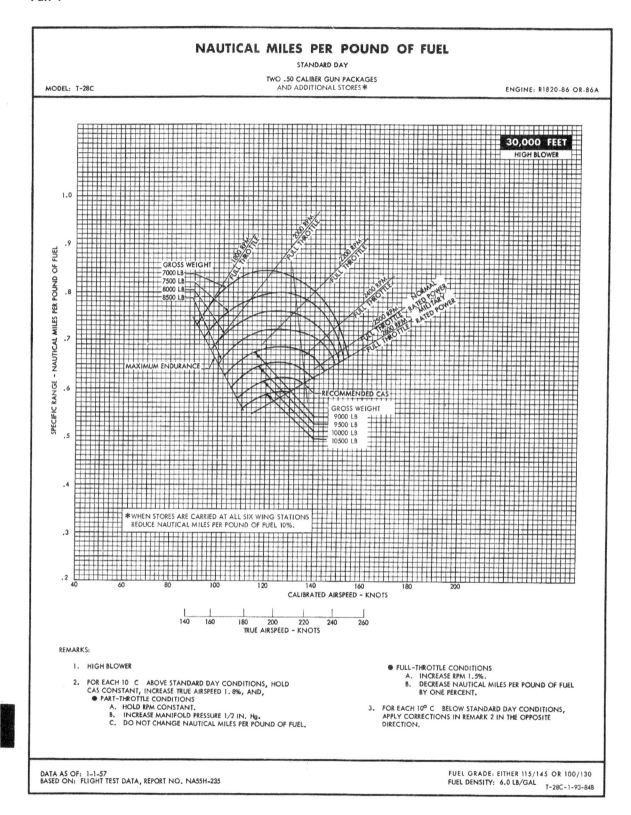

NAUTICAL MILES PER POUND OF FUEL

STANDARD DAY

TWO .50 CALIBER GUN PACKAGES
AND ADDITIONAL STORES*

MODEL: T-28C

ENGINE: R1820-86 OR-86A

30,000 FEET
HIGH BLOWER

REMARKS:

1. HIGH BLOWER

2. FOR EACH 10 C ABOVE STANDARD DAY CONDITIONS, HOLD
CAS CONSTANT, INCREASE TRUE AIRSPEED 1.8%, AND,
   ● PART-THROTTLE CONDITIONS
      A. HOLD RPM CONSTANT.
      B. INCREASE MANIFOLD PRESSURE 1/2 IN. Hg.
      C. DO NOT CHANGE NAUTICAL MILES PER POUND OF FUEL.

● FULL-THROTTLE CONDITIONS
   A. INCREASE RPM 1.5%.
   B. DECREASE NAUTICAL MILES PER POUND OF FUEL
      BY ONE PERCENT.

3. FOR EACH 10° C BELOW STANDARD DAY CONDITIONS,
   APPLY CORRECTIONS IN REMARK 2 IN THE OPPOSITE
   DIRECTION.

DATA AS OF: 1-1-57
BASED ON: FLIGHT TEST DATA, REPORT NO. NA55H-235

FUEL GRADE: EITHER 115/145 OR 100/130
FUEL DENSITY: 6.0 LB/GAL

T-28C-1-93-84B

Figure 11-95

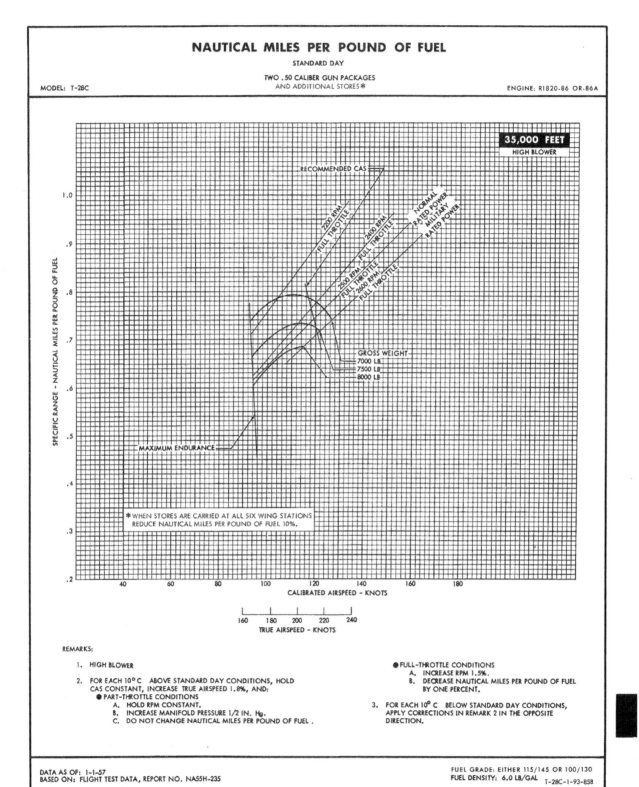

NAUTICAL MILES PER POUND OF FUEL

STANDARD DAY

TWO .50 CALIBER GUN PACKAGES
AND ADDITIONAL STORES *

MODEL: T-28C

ENGINE: R1820-86 OR-86A

REMARKS:

1. HIGH BLOWER

2. FOR EACH 10° C ABOVE STANDARD DAY CONDITIONS, HOLD
CAS CONSTANT, INCREASE TRUE AIRSPEED 1.8%, AND:
- PART-THROTTLE CONDITIONS
  A. HOLD RPM CONSTANT.
  B. INCREASE MANIFOLD PRESSURE 1/2 IN. Hg.
  C. DO NOT CHANGE NAUTICAL MILES PER POUND OF FUEL.

- FULL-THROTTLE CONDITIONS
  A. INCREASE RPM 1.5%.
  B. DECREASE NAUTICAL MILES PER POUND OF FUEL
  BY ONE PERCENT.

3. FOR EACH 10° C BELOW STANDARD DAY CONDITIONS,
APPLY CORRECTIONS IN REMARK 2 IN THE OPPOSITE
DIRECTION.

DATA AS OF: 1-1-57
BASED ON: FLIGHT TEST DATA, REPORT NO. NA55H-235

FUEL GRADE: EITHER 115/145 OR 100/130
FUEL DENSITY: 6.0 LB/GAL   T-28C-1-93-85B

Figure 11-96

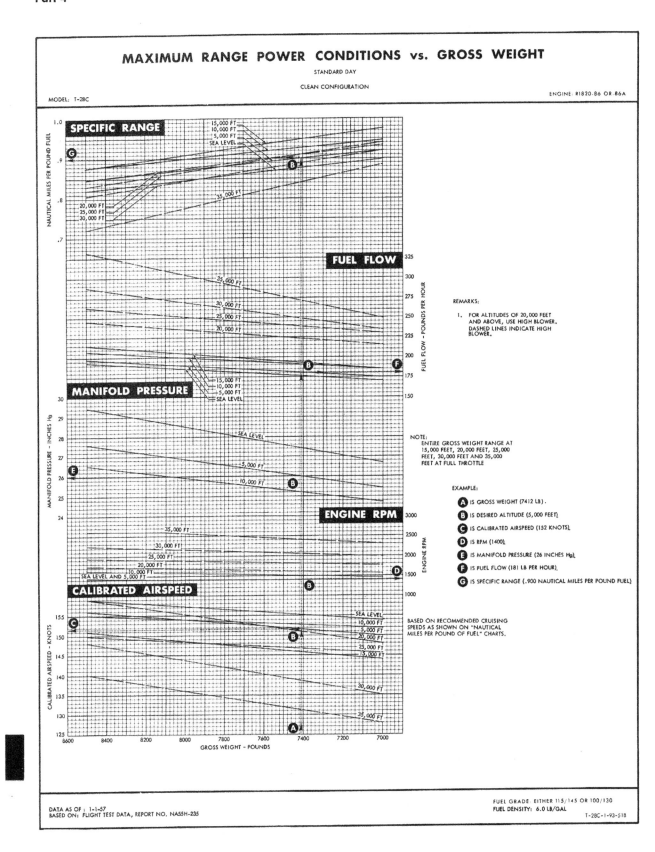

Figure 11-97

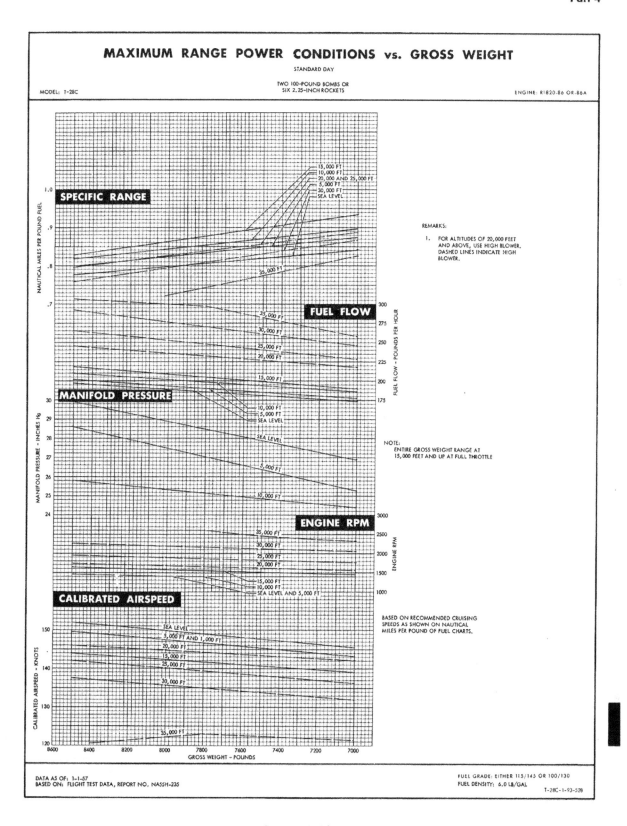

Figure 11-98

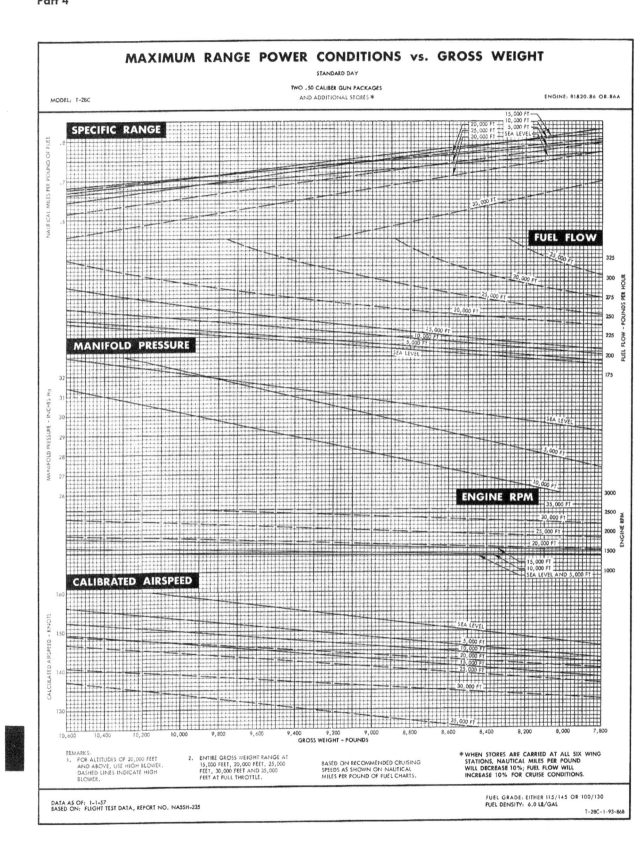

MAXIMUM RANGE POWER CONDITIONS vs. GROSS WEIGHT

STANDARD DAY

TWO .50 CALIBER GUN PACKAGES
AND ADDITIONAL STORES *

MODEL: T-28C

ENGINE: R1820.86 OR.86A

REMARKS:
1. FOR ALTITUDES OF 20,000 FEET AND ABOVE, USE HIGH BLOWER. DASHED LINES INDICATE HIGH BLOWER.

2. ENTIRE GROSS WEIGHT RANGE AT 15,000 FEET, 20,000 FEET, 25,000 FEET, 30,000 FEET AND 35,000 FEET AT FULL THROTTLE.

BASED ON RECOMMENDED CRUISING SPEEDS AS SHOWN ON NAUTICAL MILES PER POUND OF FUEL CHARTS.

*WHEN STORES ARE CARRIED AT ALL SIX WING STATIONS, NAUTICAL MILES PER POUND WILL DECREASE 10%; FUEL FLOW WILL INCREASE 10% FOR CRUISE CONDITIONS.

DATA AS OF: 1-1-57
BASED ON: FLIGHT TEST DATA, REPORT NO. NA55H-235

FUEL GRADE: EITHER 115/145 OR 100/130
FUEL DENSITY: 6.0 LB/GAL

T-28C-1-93-86B

Figure 11-99

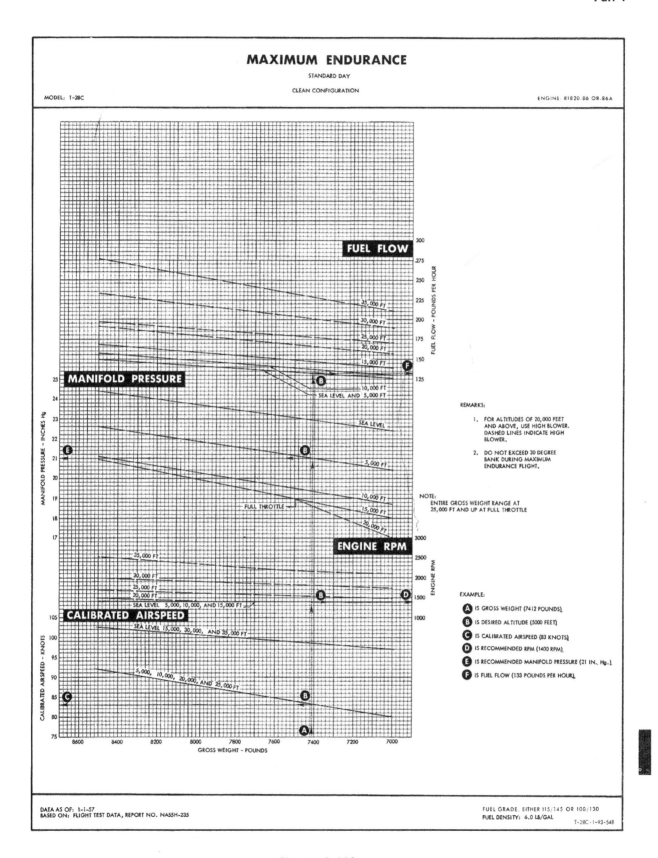

MAXIMUM ENDURANCE

STANDARD DAY

CLEAN CONFIGURATION

MODEL: T-28C

ENGINE: R1820-86 OR-86A

FUEL FLOW

MANIFOLD PRESSURE

ENGINE RPM

CALIBRATED AIRSPEED

REMARKS:

1. FOR ALTITUDES OF 20,000 FEET AND ABOVE, USE HIGH BLOWER. DASHED LINES INDICATE HIGH BLOWER.

2. DO NOT EXCEED 30 DEGREE BANK DURING MAXIMUM ENDURANCE FLIGHT.

NOTE:
ENTIRE GROSS WEIGHT RANGE AT 25,000 FT AND UP AT FULL THROTTLE

EXAMPLE:

Ⓐ IS GROSS WEIGHT (7412 POUNDS).

Ⓑ IS DESIRED ALTITUDE (5000 FEET).

Ⓒ IS CALIBRATED AIRSPEED (83 KNOTS).

Ⓓ IS RECOMMENDED RPM (1400 RPM).

Ⓔ IS RECOMMENDED MANIFOLD PRESSURE (21 IN., Hg.).

Ⓕ IS FUEL FLOW (133 POUNDS PER HOUR).

DATA AS OF: 1-1-57
BASED ON: FLIGHT TEST DATA, REPORT NO. NA55H-235

FUEL GRADE: EITHER 115/145 OR 100/130
FUEL DENSITY: 6.0 LB/GAL

T-28C-1-93-54B

Figure 11-100

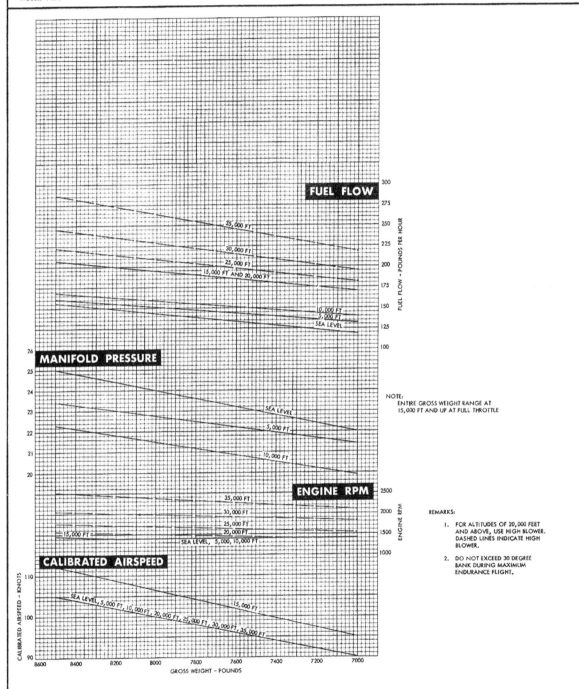

MAXIMUM ENDURANCE

STANDARD DAY

TWO 100-POUND BOMBS OR
SIX 2.25-INCH ROCKETS

MODEL: T-28C

ENGINE: R1820-86 OR-86A

FUEL FLOW

MANIFOLD PRESSURE

NOTE:
ENTIRE GROSS WEIGHT RANGE AT
15,000 FT AND UP AT FULL THROTTLE

ENGINE RPM

REMARKS:
1. FOR ALTITUDES OF 20,000 FEET AND ABOVE, USE HIGH BLOWER. DASHED LINES INDICATE HIGH BLOWER.

2. DO NOT EXCEED 30 DEGREE BANK DURING MAXIMUM ENDURANCE FLIGHT.

CALIBRATED AIRSPEED

DATA AS OF: 1-1-57
BASED ON: FLIGHT TEST DATA, REPORT NO. NA55H-235

FUEL GRADE: EITHER 115/145 OR 100/130
FUEL DENSITY: 6.0 LB/GAL

T-28C-1-93-55B

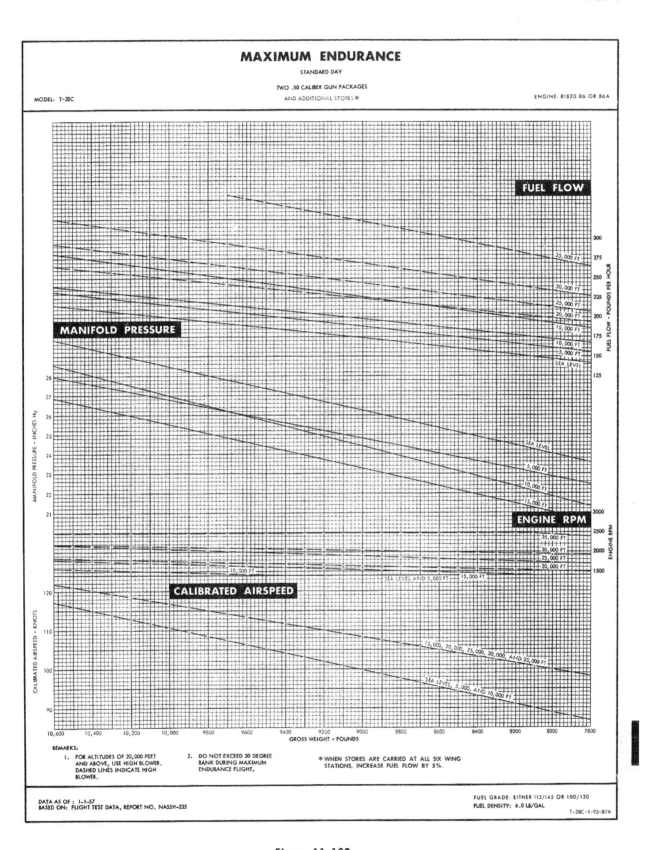

MAXIMUM ENDURANCE

STANDARD DAY

TWO .50 CALIBER GUN PACKAGES

AND ADDITIONAL STORES *

MODEL: T-28C

ENGINE: R1820-86 OR 86A

REMARKS:

1. FOR ALTITUDES OF 20,000 FEET AND ABOVE, USE HIGH BLOWER. DASHED LINES INDICATE HIGH BLOWER.

2. DO NOT EXCEED 30 DEGREE BANK DURING MAXIMUM ENDURANCE FLIGHT.

* WHEN STORES ARE CARRIED AT ALL SIX WING STATIONS, INCREASE FUEL FLOW BY 5%.

DATA AS OF : 1-1-57
BASED ON: FLIGHT TEST DATA, REPORT NO. NA55H-235

FUEL GRADE: EITHER 115/145 OR 100/130
FUEL DENSITY: 6.0 LB/GAL

T-28C-1-93-87A

Figure 11-102

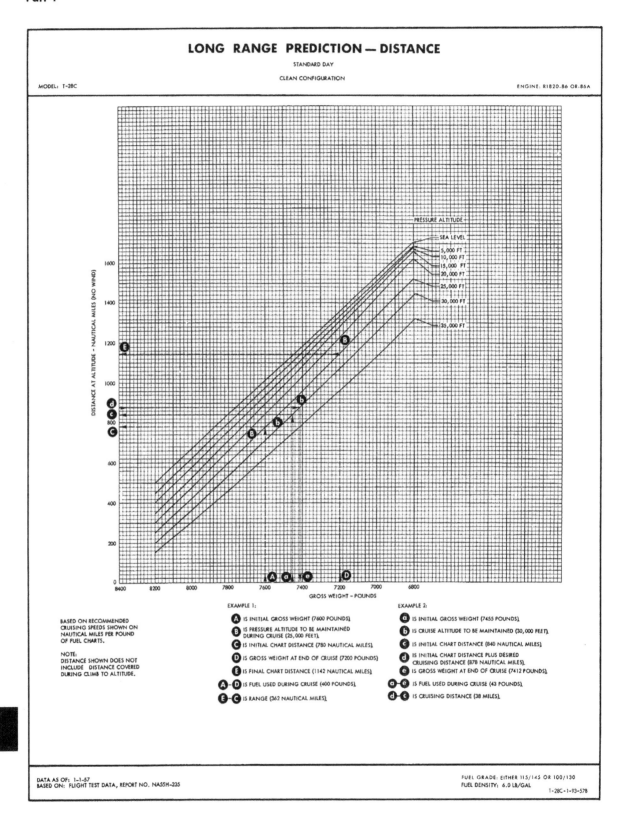

LONG RANGE PREDICTION — DISTANCE

STANDARD DAY

CLEAN CONFIGURATION

MODEL: T-28C

ENGINE: R1820-86 OR-86A

BASED ON RECOMMENDED
CRUISING SPEEDS SHOWN ON
NAUTICAL MILES PER POUND
OF FUEL CHARTS.

NOTE:
DISTANCE SHOWN DOES NOT
INCLUDE DISTANCE COVERED
DURING CLIMB TO ALTITUDE.

EXAMPLE 1:

(A) IS INITIAL GROSS WEIGHT (7600 POUNDS)

(B) IS PRESSURE ALTITUDE TO BE MAINTAINED
DURING CRUISE (25,000 FEET)

(C) IS INITIAL CHART DISTANCE (780 NAUTICAL MILES)

(D) IS GROSS WEIGHT AT END OF CRUISE (7200 POUNDS)

(E) IS FINAL CHART DISTANCE (1142 NAUTICAL MILES)

(A)-(D) IS FUEL USED DURING CRUISE (400 POUNDS)

(E)-(C) IS RANGE (362 NAUTICAL MILES)

EXAMPLE 2:

(a) IS INITIAL GROSS WEIGHT (7455 POUNDS)

(b) IS CRUISE ALTITUDE TO BE MAINTAINED (30,000 FEET)

(c) IS INITIAL CHART DISTANCE (840 NAUTICAL MILES)

(d) IS INITIAL CHART DISTANCE PLUS DESIRED
CRUISING DISTANCE (878 NAUTICAL MILES)

(e) IS GROSS WEIGHT AT END OF CRUISE (7412 POUNDS)

(a)-(e) IS FUEL USED DURING CRUISE (43 POUNDS)

(d)-(c) IS CRUISING DISTANCE (38 MILES)

DATA AS OF: 1-1-57
BASED ON: FLIGHT TEST DATA, REPORT NO. NA55H-235

FUEL GRADE: EITHER 115/145 OR 100/130
FUEL DENSITY: 6.0 LB/GAL

T-28C-1-93-57B

Figure 11-103

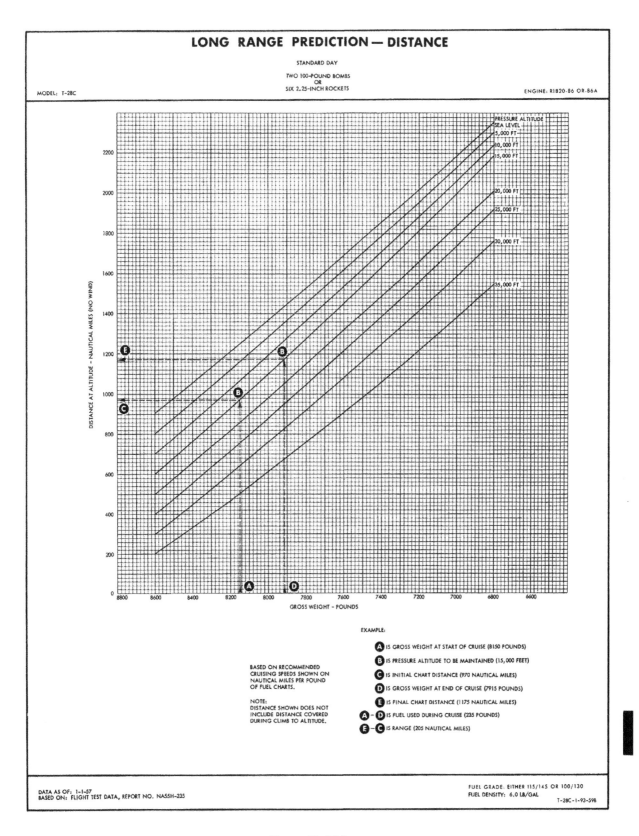

LONG RANGE PREDICTION — DISTANCE

STANDARD DAY

TWO 100-POUND BOMBS
OR
SIX 2.25-INCH ROCKETS

MODEL: T-28C

ENGINE: R1820-86 OR-86A

EXAMPLE:

A IS GROSS WEIGHT AT START OF CRUISE (8150 POUNDS)

B IS PRESSURE ALTITUDE TO BE MAINTAINED (15,000 FEET)

C IS INITIAL CHART DISTANCE (970 NAUTICAL MILES)

D IS GROSS WEIGHT AT END OF CRUISE (7915 POUNDS)

E IS FINAL CHART DISTANCE (1175 NAUTICAL MILES)

A – **D** IS FUEL USED DURING CRUISE (235 POUNDS)

E – **C** IS RANGE (205 NAUTICAL MILES)

BASED ON RECOMMENDED
CRUISING SPEEDS SHOWN ON
NAUTICAL MILES PER POUND
OF FUEL CHARTS.

NOTE:
DISTANCE SHOWN DOES NOT
INCLUDE DISTANCE COVERED
DURING CLIMB TO ALTITUDE.

DATA AS OF: 1-1-57
BASED ON: FLIGHT TEST DATA, REPORT NO. NA55H-235

FUEL GRADE: EITHER 115/145 OR 100/130
FUEL DENSITY: 6.0 LB/GAL

T-28C-1-93-598

Figure 11-104

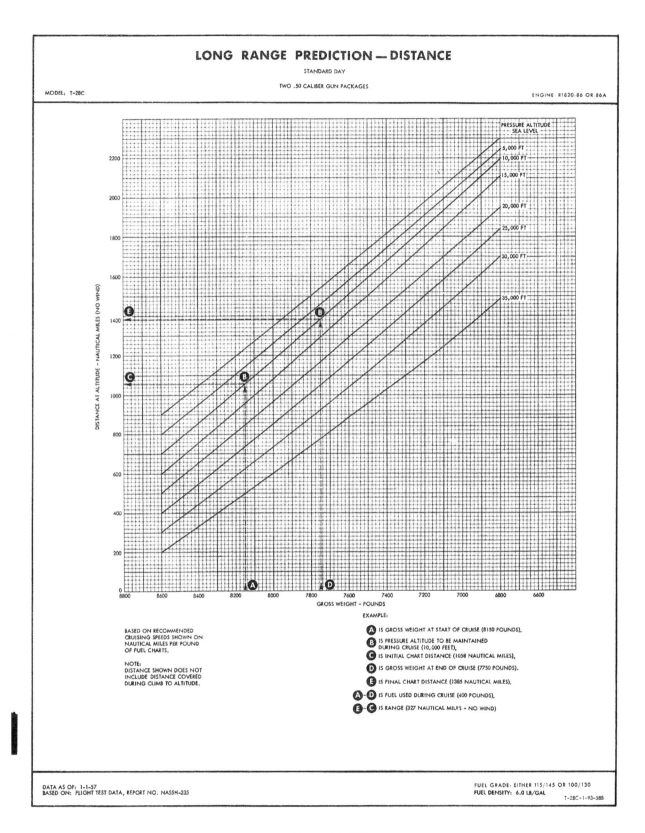

LONG RANGE PREDICTION — DISTANCE

STANDARD DAY

TWO .50 CALIBER GUN PACKAGES

MODEL: T-28C

ENGINE: R1820-86 OR -86A

EXAMPLE:

Ⓐ IS GROSS WEIGHT AT START OF CRUISE (8150 POUNDS).

Ⓑ IS PRESSURE ALTITUDE TO BE MAINTAINED DURING CRUISE (10,000 FEET).

Ⓒ IS INITIAL CHART DISTANCE (1058 NAUTICAL MILES).

Ⓓ IS GROSS WEIGHT AT END OF CRUISE (7750 POUNDS).

Ⓔ IS FINAL CHART DISTANCE (1385 NAUTICAL MILES).

Ⓐ-Ⓓ IS FUEL USED DURING CRUISE (400 POUNDS).

Ⓔ-Ⓒ IS RANGE (327 NAUTICAL MILES - NO WIND)

BASED ON RECOMMENDED CRUISING SPEEDS SHOWN ON NAUTICAL MILES PER POUND OF FUEL CHARTS.

NOTE:
DISTANCE SHOWN DOES NOT INCLUDE DISTANCE COVERED DURING CLIMB TO ALTITUDE.

DATA AS OF: 1-1-57
BASED ON: FLIGHT TEST DATA, REPORT NO. NA55H-235

FUEL GRADE: EITHER 115/145 OR 100/130
FUEL DENSITY: 6.0 LB/GAL

T-2BC-1-93-58B

Figure 11-105

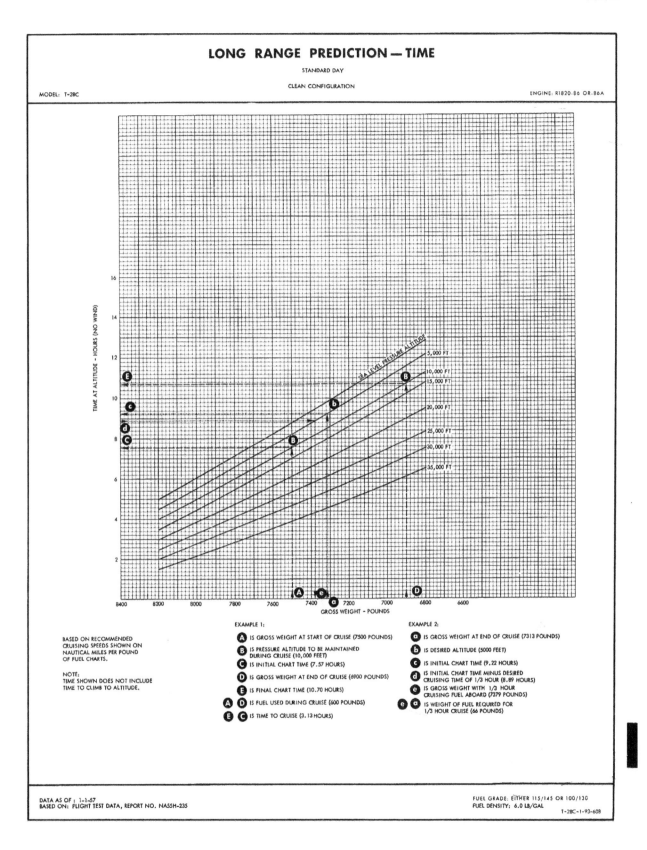

Figure 11-106

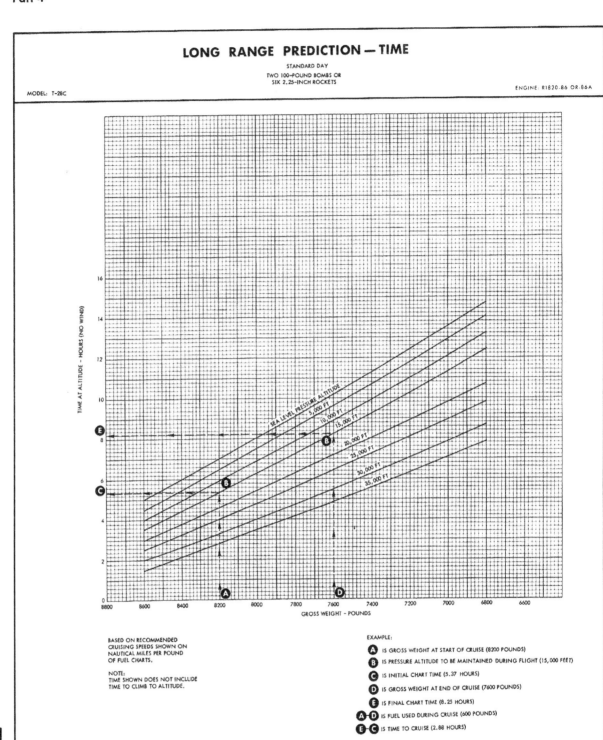

LONG RANGE PREDICTION — TIME

STANDARD DAY
TWO 100-POUND BOMBS OR
SIX 2.25-INCH ROCKETS

MODEL: T-28C

ENGINE: R1820-86 OR-86A

BASED ON RECOMMENDED
CRUISING SPEEDS SHOWN ON
NAUTICAL MILES PER POUND
OF FUEL CHARTS.

NOTE:
TIME SHOWN DOES NOT INCLUDE
TIME TO CLIMB TO ALTITUDE.

EXAMPLE:

A IS GROSS WEIGHT AT START OF CRUISE (8200 POUNDS)

B IS PRESSURE ALTITUDE TO BE MAINTAINED DURING FLIGHT (15,000 FEET)

C IS INITIAL CHART TIME (5.37 HOURS)

D IS GROSS WEIGHT AT END OF CRUISE (7600 POUNDS)

E IS FINAL CHART TIME (8.25 HOURS)

A-D IS FUEL USED DURING CRUISE (600 POUNDS)

E-C IS TIME TO CRUISE (2.88 HOURS)

DATA AS OF: 1-1-57
BASED ON: FLIGHT TEST DATA, REPORT NO. NA55H-235

FUEL GRADE: EITHER 115/145 OR 100/130
FUEL DENSITY: 6.0 LB/GAL

T-28C-1-93-62B

Figure 11-107

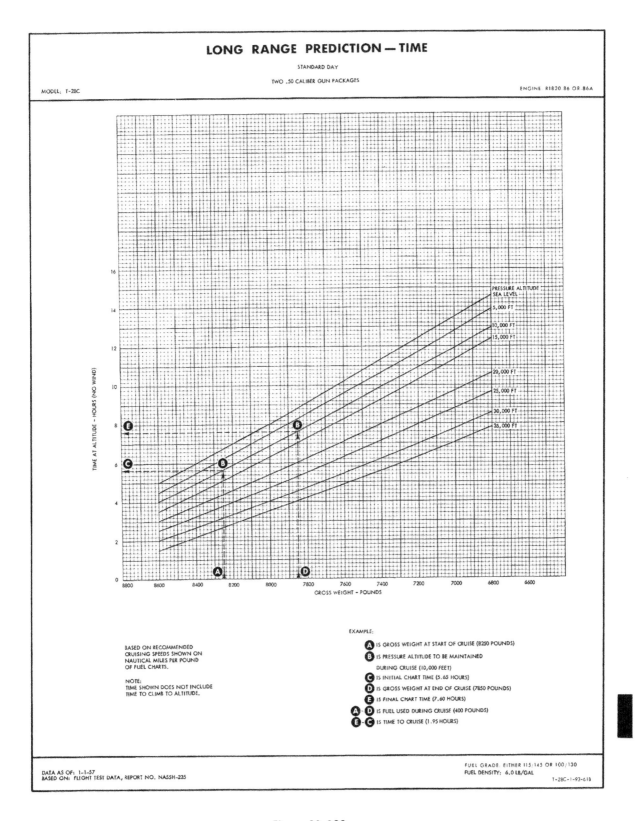

LONG RANGE PREDICTION — TIME

STANDARD DAY

TWO .50 CALIBER GUN PACKAGES

MODEL: T-28C

ENGINE: R1820-86 OR -86A

BASED ON RECOMMENDED
CRUISING SPEEDS SHOWN ON
NAUTICAL MILES PER POUND
OF FUEL CHARTS.

NOTE:
TIME SHOWN DOES NOT INCLUDE
TIME TO CLIMB TO ALTITUDE.

EXAMPLE:

Ⓐ IS GROSS WEIGHT AT START OF CRUISE (8250 POUNDS)
Ⓑ IS PRESSURE ALTITUDE TO BE MAINTAINED
    DURING CRUISE (10,000 FEET)
Ⓒ IS INITIAL CHART TIME (5.65 HOURS)
Ⓓ IS GROSS WEIGHT AT END OF CRUISE (7850 POUNDS)
Ⓔ IS FINAL CHART TIME (7.60 HOURS)
Ⓐ - Ⓓ IS FUEL USED DURING CRUISE (400 POUNDS)
Ⓔ - Ⓒ IS TIME TO CRUISE (1.95 HOURS)

DATA AS OF: 1-1-57
BASED ON: FLIGHT TEST DATA, REPORT NO. NA55H-235

FUEL GRADE: EITHER 115/145 OR 100/130
FUEL DENSITY: 6.0 LB/GAL

T-28C-1-93-61B

Figure 11-108

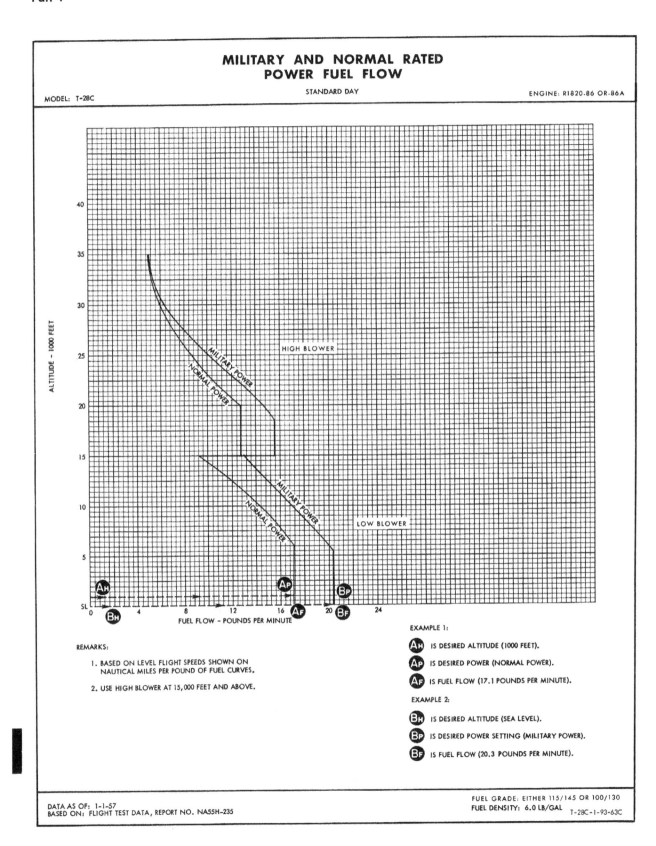

MILITARY AND NORMAL RATED POWER FUEL FLOW

STANDARD DAY

MODEL: T-28C

ENGINE: R1820-86 OR-86A

REMARKS:

1. BASED ON LEVEL FLIGHT SPEEDS SHOWN ON NAUTICAL MILES PER POUND OF FUEL CURVES.

2. USE HIGH BLOWER AT 15,000 FEET AND ABOVE.

EXAMPLE 1:

(AH) IS DESIRED ALTITUDE (1000 FEET).

(AP) IS DESIRED POWER (NORMAL POWER).

(AF) IS FUEL FLOW (17.1 POUNDS PER MINUTE).

EXAMPLE 2:

(BH) IS DESIRED ALTITUDE (SEA LEVEL).

(BP) IS DESIRED POWER SETTING (MILITARY POWER).

(BF) IS FUEL FLOW (20.3 POUNDS PER MINUTE).

DATA AS OF: 1-1-57
BASED ON: FLIGHT TEST DATA, REPORT NO. NA55H-235

FUEL GRADE: EITHER 115/145 OR 100/130
FUEL DENSITY: 6.0 LB/GAL

T-28C-1-93-63C

Figure 11-109

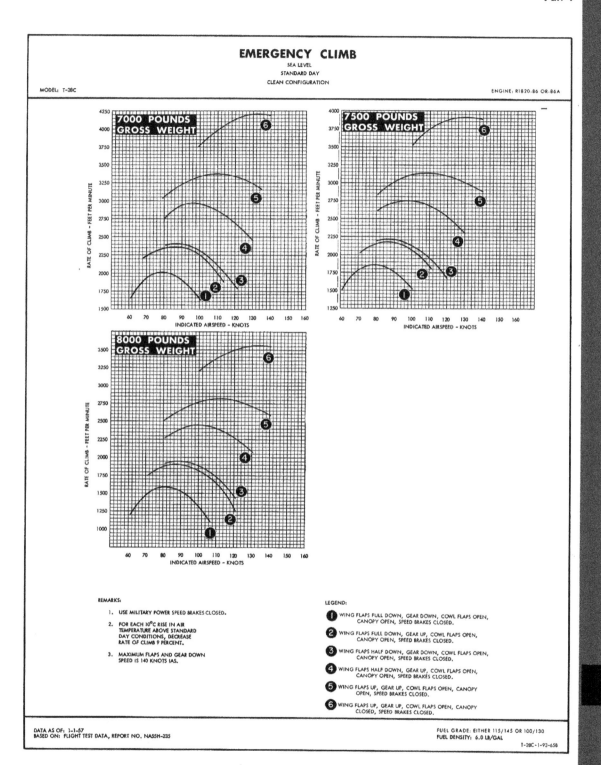

EMERGENCY CLIMB

SEA LEVEL
STANDARD DAY
CLEAN CONFIGURATION

MODEL: T-28C

ENGINE: R1820-86 OR-86A

7000 POUNDS GROSS WEIGHT

7500 POUNDS GROSS WEIGHT

8000 POUNDS GROSS WEIGHT

RATE OF CLIMB - FEET PER MINUTE

INDICATED AIRSPEED - KNOTS

REMARKS:

1. USE MILITARY POWER SPEED BRAKES CLOSED.

2. FOR EACH 10°C RISE IN AIR TEMPERATURE ABOVE STANDARD DAY CONDITIONS, DECREASE RATE OF CLIMB 9 PERCENT.

3. MAXIMUM FLAPS AND GEAR DOWN SPEED IS 140 KNOTS IAS.

LEGEND:

1 WING FLAPS FULL DOWN, GEAR DOWN, COWL FLAPS OPEN, CANOPY OPEN, SPEED BRAKES CLOSED.

2 WING FLAPS FULL DOWN, GEAR UP, COWL FLAPS OPEN, CANOPY OPEN, SPEED BRAKES CLOSED.

3 WING FLAPS HALF DOWN, GEAR DOWN, COWL FLAPS OPEN, CANOPY OPEN, SPEED BRAKES CLOSED.

4 WING FLAPS HALF DOWN, GEAR UP, COWL FLAPS OPEN, CANOPY OPEN, SPEED BRAKES CLOSED.

5 WING FLAPS UP, GEAR UP, COWL FLAPS OPEN, CANOPY OPEN, SPEED BRAKES CLOSED.

6 WING FLAPS UP, GEAR UP, COWL FLAPS OPEN, CANOPY CLOSED, SPEED BRAKES CLOSED.

DATA AS OF: 1-1-57
BASED ON: FLIGHT TEST DATA, REPORT NO. NA55H-235

FUEL GRADE: EITHER 115/145 OR 100/130
FUEL DENSITY: 6.0 LB/GAL

T-28C-1-93-658

Figure 11-110

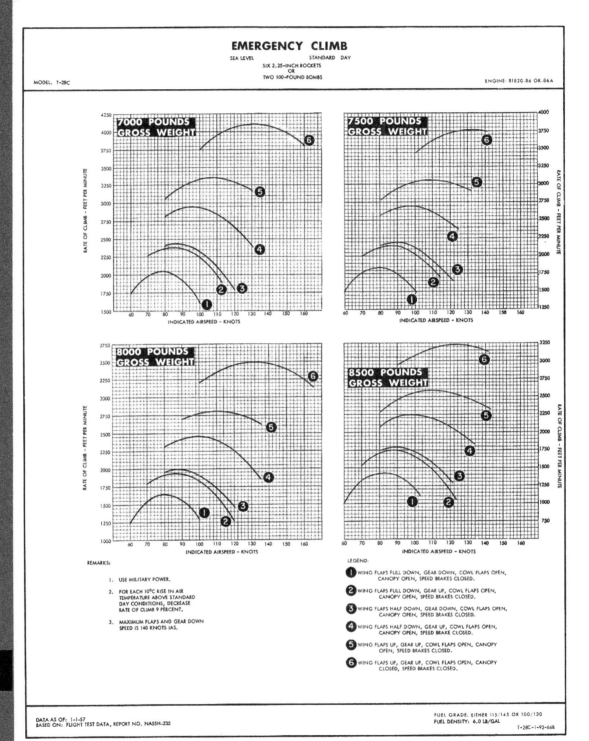

EMERGENCY CLIMB

Figure 11-111

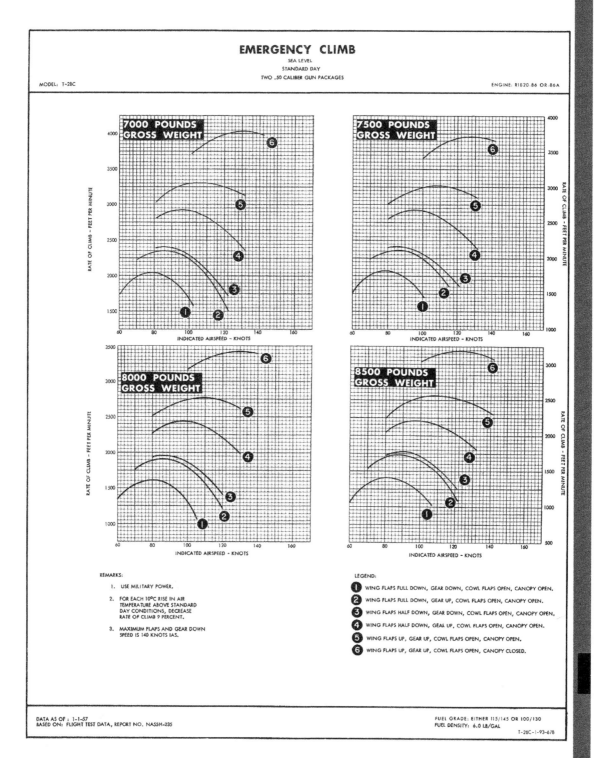

Figure 11-112

WARSHIPS DVD
SERIES

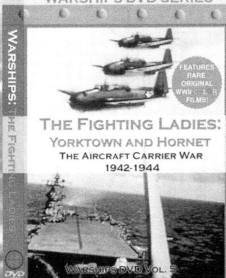

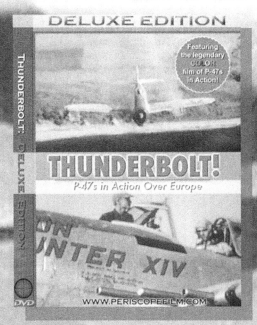
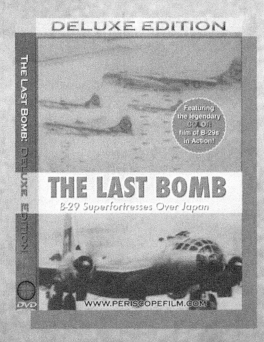
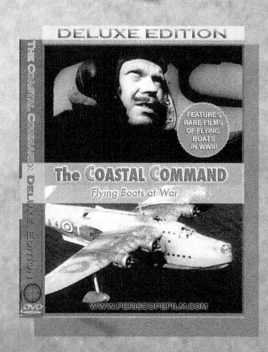

EPIC BATTLES
OF WWII

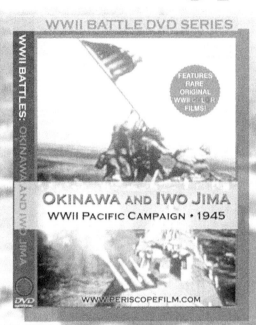
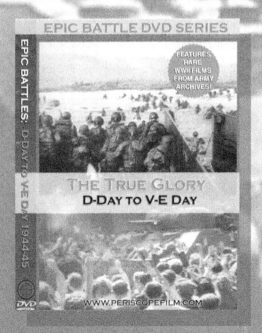

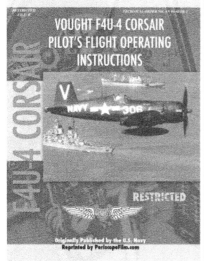
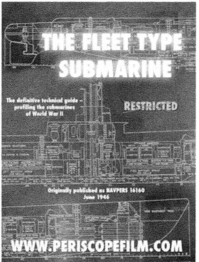

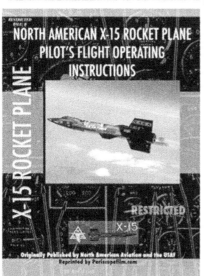

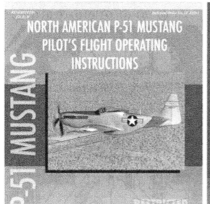

This manual is sold for historic research purposes only, as an entertainment. It is not intended to be used as part of an actual flight training program. No book can substitute for flight training by an authorized instructor. The licensing of pilots is overseen by organizations and authorities such as the FAA and CAA. Operating an aircraft without the proper license is a federal crime.

Lightning Source UK Ltd.
Milton Keynes UK
UKOW05f0954050916

282220UK00003B/14/P